CRITICAL ACCLAIM
FOR *TRAVELERS' TALES*

"The *Travelers' Tales* series is altogether remarkable."
—Jan Morris, author of *Journeys*, *Locations*, and *Hong Kong*

"For the thoughtful traveler, these books are an invaluable resource.
There's nothing like them on the market."
—Pico Iyer, author of *Video Night in Kathmandu*

"This is the stuff memories can be duplicated from."
—Karen Krebsbach, *Foreign Service Journal*

"I can't think of a better way to get comfortable with a destination than
by delving into *Travelers' Tales*…before reading a guidebook, before seeing a travel agent. The series helps visitors refine their interests and read-
ies them to communicate with the peoples they come in contact
with…."
—Paul Glassman, Society of American Travel Writers

"…*Travelers' Tales* is a valuable addition to any pre-departure reading list."
—Tony Wheeler, publisher, Lonely Planet Publications

"*Travelers' Tales* delivers something most guidebooks only promise: a real
sense of what a country is all about…."
—Steve Silk, *Hartford Courant*

"These anthologies seem destined to be a success…*Travelers' Tales* promises to be a useful and enlightening addition to the travel bookshelves.
By collecting and organizing such a wide range of literature, O'Reilly
and Habegger are providing a real service for those who enjoy reading
first-person accounts of a destination before seeing it for themselves."
—Bill Newlin, publisher, Moon Publications

"The *Travelers' Tales* series should become required reading for anyone
visiting a foreign country who wants to truly step off the tourist track
and experience another culture, another place, first hand."
—Nancy Paradis, *St. Petersburg Times*

"Like having been there, done it, seen it. If there's one thing traditional
guidebooks lack, it's the really juicy travel information, the personal
stories about back alleys and brief encounters. The *Travelers' Tales* series
fills this gap with an approach that's all anecdotes, no directions."
—Jim Gullo, *Diversion*

INDIA

TRAVELERS' TALES GUIDES

INDIA

Collected and Edited by

JAMES O'REILLY AND LARRY HABEGGER

TRAVELERS' TALES, INC.
SAN FRANCISCO, CALIFORNIA 94133

A million lotuses swaying on one stem,
World after coloured and ecstatic world
Climbs towards some far unseen epiphany.

—SRI AUROBINDO GHOSE

Table of Contents

                          ⋆ ⋆ ⋆

                       THE NEXT STEP

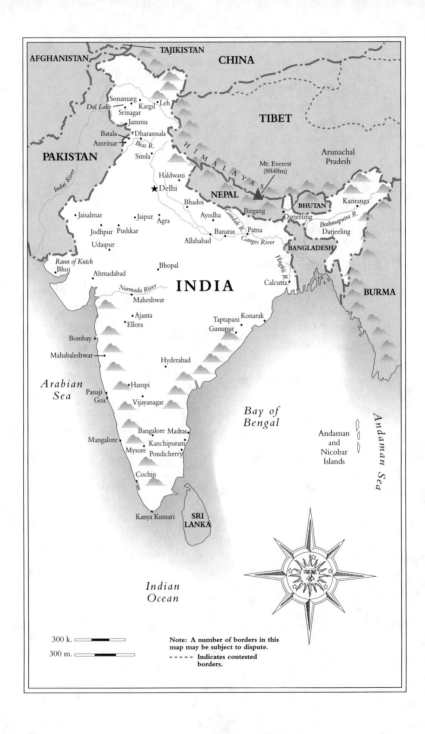

Preface

TRAVELERS' TALES

We are all outsiders when we travel. Whether we go abroad or roam about our own city or country, we often enter territory so unfamiliar that our frames of reference become inadequate. We need advice not just to avoid offense and danger, but to make our experiences richer, deeper, and more fun.

Traditionally, travel guides have answered the basic questions: what, when, where, how, and how much. A good guidebook is indispensable for all the practical matters that demand attention. More recently, many guidebooks have added bits of experiential insight to their standard fare, but something important is still missing: guidebooks don't really prepare *you*, the individual with feelings and fears, hopes and dreams, goals.

This kind of preparation is best achieved through travelers' tales, for we get our inner landmarks more from anecdote than information. Nothing can replace listening to the experience of others, to the war stories that come out after a few drinks, to the memories that linger and beguile. For millennia it's been this way: at watering holes and wayside inns, the experienced traveler tells those nearby what lies ahead on the ever-mysterious road. Stories stoke the imagination, inspire, frighten, and teach. In stories we see more clearly the urges that bring us to wander, whether it's hunger for change, adventure, self-knowledge, love, curiosity, sorrow, or even something as prosaic as a job assignment or two weeks off.

But travelers' accounts, while profuse, can be hard to track down. Many are simply doomed in a throwaway publishing world. And few of us have the time anyway to read more than one or two books, or the odd pearl found by chance in the Sunday travel section. Wanderers for years, we've often faced this issue. We've always told ourselves when we got home that we would prepare better for the next trip—read more, study more, talk to more people—but life always seems to interfere and we've rarely managed to do so to our satisfaction. That is one reason for this series. We needed a kind of experiential primer that guidebooks don't offer.

Another path that led us to *Travelers' Tales* has been seeing the enormous changes in travel and communications over the last two decades. It is no longer unusual to have ridden a pony across Mongolia, to have celebrated an auspicious birthday on Mt. Kilimanjaro, or honeymooned on the Loire. The one-world monoculture has risen with daunting swiftness, weaving a new cross-cultural rug: no longer is it surprising to encounter former headhunters watching *All-Star Wrestling* on their satellite feed, no longer is it shocking to find the last guy at the end of the earth wearing a Harvard t-shirt and asking if you know Michael Jordan. The global village exists in a rudimentary fashion, but it is real.

In 1980, Paul Fussell wrote in *Abroad: British Literary Traveling Between the Wars* a cranky but wonderful epitaph for travel as it was once known, in which he concluded that "we are all tourists now, and there is no escape." It has been projected by some analysts that by the year 2000, tourism will be the world's largest industry; others say it already is. In either case, this is a horrifying prospect—hordes of us hunting for places that have not been trod on by the rest of us!

Fussell's words have the painful ring of truth, but this is still our world, and it is worth seeing and will be worth seeing next year, or in 50 years, simply because it will always be worth meeting others who continue to see life in different terms than we do despite the best efforts of telecommunication and advertising talents. No amount of creeping homogeneity can quell the endless variation of humanity, and travel in the end is about people, not places. Places only provide different venues, as it were, for life, in which we are all pilgrims who need to talk to each other.

There are also many places around the world where intercultural friction and outright xenophobia are increasing. And the very fact that travel endangers cultures and pristine places more quickly than it used to calls for extraordinary care on the part of today's traveler, a keener sense of personal responsibility. The world is not our private zoo or theme park; we need to be better prepared before we go, so that we might become honored guests and not vilified intruders.

In *Travelers' Tales,* we collect useful and memorable anecdotes to produce the kind of sampler we've always wanted to read before setting out. These stories will show you some of the spectrum of experiences to be had or avoided in each country. The authors come from many walks of life: some are teachers, some are musicians, some are entrepreneurs, all are wanderers with a tale to tell. Their stories will help you to deepen and enrich your experience as a traveler. Where we've excerpted books, we urge you to go out and read the full work, because no selection can ever do an author justice.

Each *Travelers' Tales* is organized into five simple parts. In the first, we've chosen stories that reflect the ephemeral yet pervasive essence of a country. Part Two contains stories about places and activities that others have found worthwhile. In Part Three, we've chosen stories by people who have made a special connection between their lives and interests and the people and places they visited. Part Four shows some of the struggles and challenges facing a region and its people, and Part Five, "The Last Word," is just that, something of a grace note or harmonic to remind you of the book as a whole.

Our selection of stories in each *Travelers' Tales* is by no means comprehensive, but we are confident it will prime your pump. *Travelers' Tales* are not meant to replace other guides, but to accompany them. No longer will you have to go to dozens of sources to map the personal side of your journey. You'll be able to reach for *Travelers' Tales*, and truly prepare yourself before you go.

—JAMES O'REILLY AND LARRY HABEGGER

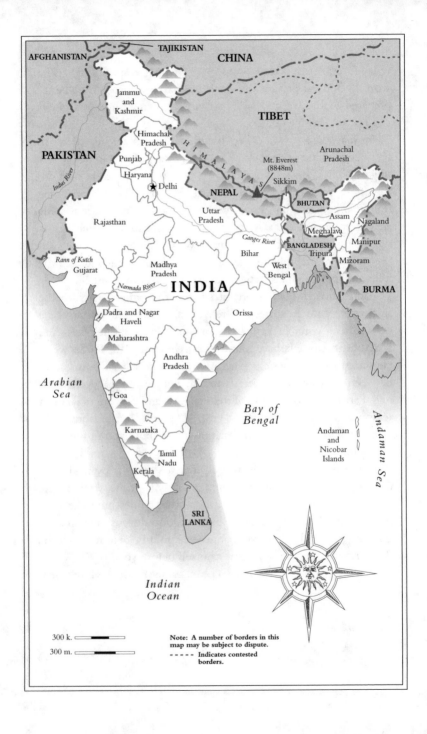

India: An Introduction

We confess a deep bias towards India, an attraction that goes back, for one of us, to teenage years spent reading Aurobindo and Tagore, meditating and doing hatha yoga, for the other, to time spent roaming India as a young man, a temporary *sadhu* from Minnesota.

India is everything human. It is all of our history: it is the past, it is the future. If it has been thought, experienced, or imagined, it has all happened before in India and you can be sure it is happening right now.

It is among the most difficult of places to travel, and the most rewarding. Some say India stands for "I'll Never Do It Again"; many more are drawn back time and again because India is the best show on earth, the best bazaar of human experiences that can be visited in a lifetime. It has been said that there are 330 million gods in India, and there are at least that many varieties of experience available, religious or otherwise.

Many go to India on the eternal pilgrimage, looking for enlightenment and answers, and India has plenty, from the genuine article to those devised by the cleverest touts and swindlers born. India will dissolve your ideas about what it is to be a human being, what it is to be compassionate, what it is to be spiritual or conscious. Its people give new meaning to perseverance, courage, ingenuity, and friendship. India's is a bewilderingly old culture, with myth and history so intertwined and layered that one knows immediately it cannot be known nor understood, only experienced.

Similarly, it is an exercise in futility to compile a single volume on India, where ten would not suffice. In *Travelers' Tales India,* we've admittedly only dipped our toes in, but one has to begin somewhere.

India, of course, is more than gods and swamis and ancient art, ashrams and temples and ruins too numerous to count, it is a vast expanse of jungle, desert, oasis, and the utterly peerless Himalayas, which tear open the hearts and minds of all pilgrims. India, an embarrassment of riches, is also home to elephants and tigers, leopards and rhinos, and maybe even the elusive *yeti* in the rhododendron forests of Sikkim.

It is also a country strained beyond belief with people and pollution, an incomprehensible bureaucratic labyrinth, and the calcification of caste structure, laws against it notwithstanding. It is home to the world's largest movie industry and some of the world's worst living conditions, a place where advanced technology and science coexist with crushing poverty and disease, where exquisite music and dance and the science of right action live side by side with political corruption and mob violence on a massive scale.

India's colonial relationship with Great Britain produced one of the most fascinating meldings of civilizations ever, and one of the bloodiest nation-birthings during the Partition of 1947. India is the world's largest democracy but one threatened by Hindu-Muslim religious conflict, an ever-tense border situation with Pakistan in Kashmir, trouble in Tamil Nadu state spilling over from civil conflicts in Sri Lanka, and numerous movements trying to break off autonomous pieces from the nation.

India—monsoon and marigold, dung and dust, colors and corpses, smoke and ash, snow and sand—is a cruel, unrelenting place of ineffable sweetness. Much like life itself. And, like life itself (if reincarnation be true) worth visiting repeatedly, in this turn of the wheel and the next.

PART ONE

ESSENCE OF INDIA

First Tango in Ladakh

Blindness can be a function of seeing.

SPRING CAME AND I FELT CLAUSTROPHOBIC, HEMMED IN BY THE city. Meanwhile, I had fallen in love with a whimsical and unpredictable ballerina. In fact, she was so unpredictable that by the end of June she had vanished in an ultimate pirouette. That was how I found myself embarking on a most extraordinary journey. Someone told me that she had gone to India, to the Himalayas, Kashmir, and Ladakh.

Ladakh. I tried to remember. Years ago I had seen some photographs of a fertile valley amid a fantastic wilderness of stone. The air was so thin that you could distinguish the texture of the rock, crevasses, and stratified folding, and beyond, towering above, the far snowcapped peaks of the mountains.

I had always been reticent about going to India. I felt that I needed to know more about it, that such a huge subcontinent should not be experienced haphazardly. Nevertheless, today I am off to India on an impulse.

Standing in the middle of New Delhi airport with my bag, I am suddenly aware of the folly of my venture. I do not know India; I have never been here before. How do I get to Kashmir, the

3

Himalayas, when I do not even know how to get out of this airport or where to end the night? I left New York so suddenly that I had no time to call anyone for advice or practical information. It must be around one o'clock in the morning, but judging from the hubbub in this vast hall, you would think it was the middle of the day. Footsteps, hurried yet slack, pass me on all sides. I attempt to stop them, but in vain; they are driven by their karma to urgent business from which, I fully realize, I am excluded. I feel utterly helpless. I have been told that there is no plane to Srinagar before three o'clock tomorrow afternoon. I am exhausted from lack of sleep and badly need a shower.

*H*ugues de Montalembert spent a dozen years wandering the world, often lingering in places to get a clear view of things; he shot documentary films for television, took photographs, wrote. This life came to an end when he was mugged in Manhattan by thugs who threw acid in his eyes, blinding him for life. After three months in the hospital and two years of rehabilitation, he wondered if his life would now be confined to a small apartment, a city block. The idea of travel terrified him, but in time he became an excellent traveler around Manhattan. Then, after one recent winter...

◆

—JO'R and LH

"Sir!" A hand is tapping my arm. "Sir! Can we help you?" Before I have time to answer, my passport, bag, and a fistful of money are whisked away. I am left standing alone. Everything happens so fast that I have no time to ask the people who they are or, for that matter, to count my money. Hardly have I arrived in India, land of Gandhi, birthplace of nonviolence, than I am stripped of my belongings; yet, I admit, without violence.

More than half an hour has gone by. I am considering going back to New York when all of a sudden my passport is thrust into my hand with my money stuck between the pages, changed into rupees. Somebody grabs hold of my wrist and pulls me along at such a speed that I have difficulty following. This is an abduction!

We are now outside on the sidewalk in the hot, turbulent Indian night. A taxi is hailed, my bag put in the back, a hotel name given.

"Auto-rickshaw, three-wheel taxi, sir. Very cheap, only thirty rupees to your hotel. Good-bye. God bless you, sir." I am flabbergasted. "Wait! How can I thank you? You have been fantastic! Let me give you something." No answer. I extend my hand and meet only hot air. "Who were they?" The rickshaw driver laughs. "Beggars, sir, beggars."

The small vehicle zigzags to avoid the potholes. Cramped between the roof and my bag, I endure endless bumps and vibrations. Like everyone else, my driver ensures our safety by honking all the way.

The Imperial Hotel is an old-fashioned building on Janpath with vast rooms. At six a.m., after a short but restful night, I start looking for the swimming pool. A very old man in a very clean loincloth and turban, with measured movements and a vaporous voice, leads me from the changing room to the pool.

My vision, which is just as real as yours, just as unique, enables me to describe here the whiteness of a turban, the shades of brown in the rock, and the expression of greed on a face. Believe me when I tell you that this visionary state overcomes me unawares. It is almost as if the generosity of the world surrenders itself to me if I wish. The swimming pool is deserted. I dive in. The water is still cold from the night before. I swim enthusiastically, tearing twenty hours of flight

> This "visionary state" the author describes allows him to see not in the usual sense but through mental images formed by feedback from those around him, his own memory, sensory stimuli including smell, touch, sound, and emotion, and some amount of light.
>
> ◆
>
> —JO'R and LH

from my muscles. Suddenly, something hits my forehead. For a fraction of a second, I think I am going to smash into the wall. I extend my hand and find no obstacle. I start swimming again, gently at first, but as I regain self-confidence, throwing myself into it once more, I am again forced to stop. A hard object actually brushes against me. This time I am faster, and in one fell swoop, as if catching a fly, I grab hold of…my cane! Yes, my cane, just as the old man's voice directs my attention from the edge of the pool, "This way, sir, this way!"

He had noticed how I guide myself by following my cane. Since it was obvious that I could not use it to swim with, he was running around the pool, pointing it in front of my nose to indicate the line I should follow. Rescued by beggars, led while swimming by a galloping old man—I am enchanted by such irrationality. I may not run into any serious difficulty in India after all.

That afternoon, the plane is postponed every hour, and I end up sleeping at the airport. Finally, we take off on time…the following day.

In the warm Srinagar afternoon, I jolt along in an old taxi sent by one of the houseboats on Dal Lake. At the lake we abandon the car for a kind of gondola called a *shikara*. Showing me to a wide seat covered with cushions, the driver tells me to stretch out and relax like a rajah.

The mountains on the north horizon, the lake, all are still. Only the birds move over the evening waters. The sound of hawks cawing is somehow sinister. It must be past five o'clock. The children are coming home from school. So much laughter. The boatman's hook hits the hull at regular intervals with a thud. Without seeing, I perceive all this beauty—the mountains, the lake, the floating islands, the sunset blurring softly—and it stabs me like a dagger. I plunge my hand into the water. It is warm, thick. Half a million human beings defecate into it daily.

The houseboat is built entirely of sandalwood and smells like a pencil sharpener. All around, the creaking of floorboards. It must come from the many gangways linking the houses to each other. A cup of tea is brought in silently. A gin and tonic would

be more appropriate. Life seems to flow here, more than anywhere else, in a sort of static frenzy or frantic stillness. A breeze
coming down from the glac-
iers makes the lake shiver.
How am I going to find her?

In the pale morning, I
board a *shikara* padded with
stuffed rags and shaded from
the sun by a plastic patchwork. We set off for the
palace of the maharajah of
Kashmir, which has now become the Oberoi Palace
Hotel. Built around 1925, it
stands in the middle of lawns
like a great white elephant
overlooking the lake.

Doormen welcome me
with pomp and circum-
stance. At the reception, I am
told that the young lady has
indeed been staying here but left two days ago.

> *D*al Lake, once a popu-
> lar place for travelers,
> sees few visitors now. The seeds
> of the conflict go back to the
> 1947 partition of India by the
> British, which created indepen-
> dent countries and cleaved the
> subcontinent into India, West
> Pakistan (now Pakistan) and East
> Pakistan (now Bangladesh). The
> borders of Kashmir were con-
> tested at the time and still are.
>
> ◆
>
> —JO'R and LH

I decide to review the situation over a cup of tea served on the
lawn. An acrid smell rising from the lake, carried over on the gentle breeze, mingles with the scent of Darjeeling tea and marmalade.

"Good morning, sir. Allow me to introduce myself. Here is my
card." He reads, slowly, over my shoulder, "Kemala, that is my
name, sir. Guide No. 1 for hunting. Underneath it is written,
Srinagar, Kashmir, India. Please keep it, sir. You are looking for one
lady. I know where she is."

I ask him to sit down. His voice sounds virile and wily. An old
fox, in fact, he smells of earth, leaves, and rain. He must be around
fifty years old. "This lady has gone to see a holy man. He is my
friend. I can take you there."

I have no illusions whatsoever. The old fox may well have in-
vented the whole story, but it does not matter. He says that there

is no road to the village and that it is two days' ride from Sonamarg. A car will take us to meet the horses. I suggest we leave tomorrow. We agree on a price, and, busy already, he stands up, touches me on the forehead, and walks away across the lawn.

Next day we drive for three hours. At the edge of a saffron field that has a sickly sweet smell, a boy is waiting for us with three ponies, one of which is laden with a tent, supplies, and kitchen utensils.

For several hours we ride up rocky paths that become progressively steeper. By evening we have reached a grassy plateau dotted with trees and shriveled bushes at the edge of a glacier. The sun has slipped behind the ridge, and the cold from this mass of ice at proximity penetrates our clothes. The boy, who has been trotting all the way alongside his horse, gathers some dead wood and builds a small fire. The water is soon singing in the kettle. Behind us, the fettered horses munch the hard, dry grass. My thigh muscles are stiff from the ride. Suddenly we are very far away, and instinctively we huddle together around the little fire. Kemala drinks his tea with long, noisy slurps. We eat a meal of rice and curry cooked over the embers. Kemala reminisces about hunting and women. He muddles up the furry animals with the pretty ladies. Wood fires, nights on high plateaus, incite fantasizing. Kemala guarantees that it will not rain tonight.

All is quiet. The silence is awesome. Lying in the grass, in this wide open space under the stars, cradled in the warmth of my sleeping bag, I drift off into the wisdom of uncertainty.

We leave before dawn and soon reach the other side of the plateau, now covered with a cedar forest. Birdsong echoes through the undergrowth. Followed by the boy, Kemala takes a shortcut too steep for me to attempt. I let go the reins and let the little horse follow the trail. The other two ponies are waiting for me ahead. We ride on for a while, until they leave me again for another shortcut. Once more their steps grow fainter. Then there is silence. I sink into a formidable mineral and botanical world. Sometimes the way is barred by a small torrent, which my pony crosses, meticulously putting down his feet, punctuating the difficult moments with an unforeseen movement of his withers to get us over the obstacle. Suddenly, a rumbling resonates up above, rolling down into the valley. And again—thunder!

All at once I realize that I must have been riding alone for more than half an hour. Where have the others gone? I bring the horse to a halt. A few raindrops fall on my face. Taking hold of the reins again, I urge the little horse forward. Having listened to me, he too is worried now. After a while, soaked through and freezing, I jump down by a tree trunk as big as a medieval tower and flatten myself against the bark while the horse leans against me. I am buried in this forest, these mountains, this India. There is no question about it, I am well and truly lost.

Suddenly Kemala emerges from the rain like a sad, vegetal Don Quixote. He dismounts agilely and comes and leans against my shoulder. His voice cracks like dry wood. He says that the rain has put the horses off the scent. He hands me a lighted cigarette. "Only small rain. Rainy season is finished." Without another word, we wait in silence.

A few hours later, under a clear sky, we reach our destination. A small, unruly, and boisterous crowd is standing outside the holy man's house. We walk through the groups of people, who step aside to let us through. An old woman greets us, laughing. Kemala thrusts a plastic bag into my hand. "Fruit, sir, no money." But the woman has already snatched the bag away from me and is leading us to a room at the back of the house.

The room is dark, windowless. The noisy crowd outside has suddenly ceased to exist. I can hear the woman placing the bag of fruit before the man; then he speaks. His voice is gentle but firm. Didn't Kemala say he was a hundred and thirty years old? I would have said he was a hundred years younger. Kemala launches into a long-winded monologue, interrupted by the short, precise questions of the saint, then turns to me with disapproval in his voice. "He can do nothing for your eyes."

"Tell him I know, not to worry. Ask him about the young lady."

The holy man laughs. He asks that I sit on the mat near him. The tips of our knees are touching. He has placed one of my hands, the right one, on his knee. Under the cotton, his skin feels surprisingly young and elastic. And yet, if one is to believe Kemala, he lives here on this mat without having slept or eaten for years. He seems to be enjoying our meeting. I am conscious of this by the smile in his voice, the way he puts his hand on mine, flat on his knee. He says, "Learn to live slowly—that way there will be no hazard in death." Kemala translates.

As I leave him, I almost feel as though I am abandoning him to his strange destiny, sitting there on his cushion in this dark room with a crowd at his door. Perhaps he has felt my compassion, for he grabs hold of my hand again just as I am getting up and says, "Surviving life is everything." Kemala translates. I find the idea hilarious, and we laugh heartily together.

Back in Srinagar, the receptionist at the Oberoi says that the young lady most likely went on to Leh, the capital of Ladakh.

In the early dim gray morning, I board the plane for Leh. We fly over the rock face of the Himalayas, the col, and then a fluffy mass of cloud suspended between the mountains like an eiderdown beneath which lies the valley of Ladakh. After a while I realize that we are going around in circles. The man on my right, who has introduced himself as Krishna, a dry-fruit merchant, says that the pilot cannot find the hole in the cloud.

Even a man with a hundred horses may need to ask another for a whip.

◆

—Ladakhi saying, quoted by Helena Norberg-Hodge in *Ancient Futures: Learning from Ladakh*

Suddenly the plane drops, leaving our stomachs in our mouths. The pilot found the hole. A few minutes later, we land.

A bit shattered, I disembark on the concrete runway amid the general excitement of guttural shouting and laughter. Beyond the runway, yet uncannily close, however, looms a formidable presence that reduces our little troop to a handful of ants. Krishna asks me where I am staying and recommends the Sankar Guest House.

As the taxi drives through the plain, Krishna does not say a word; he seems just as much in awe as I. We drive to Leh, through its main street swarming with animals and human beings.

The Sankar Guest House is a small squat building that stands on a hillock at the north end of town. Already the land here begins its ascent toward the surrounding monstrosity; its mass does not seem to grow out of the earth but to descend from the sky.

"*Jullay...Jullay...*" is the local greeting. Smiling voices, quiet and mischievous. My room is like a bare cell. There is absolutely nothing to disturb the mind. Outside my window, conversations linger on in the pure air. Immense, the void in the valley reverberates against all the rock, assailing us. The ephemeral tender green cultivation enhances the hardness of the rock. Naked children are jumping off a bridge into the icy water. Their cries pierce the air like raining pins. A sudden breeze enters the summer of my room. I strain to listen to the void outside. Suddenly I am filled with an intense desire, a mad, aimless desire to go out on the plain and climb up to the horizon. I start to laugh. A laughter provoked by the absurdity of my situation and by the altitude, which has gone to my head. The valley of Ladakh is situated thirteen thousand feet above sea level.

Next morning, Krishna and I walk to the little bank of Leh to change some money. The clerk recognizes me immediately as the "strange tourist" whose arrival was announced on the local radio.

In the street I can feel Krishna's plump body shaking with laughter. I listen to footsteps—small steps, dragging steps, bright skipping steps—thudding on the ground. "Listen," I say to Krishna. "Stop laughing. The girl I'm looking for is here. Help me find her." But how is he going to recognize her? I assure him that as soon as she sees me, she will stop dead in her tracks and stare at me in such a way that he will not be able to miss her.

Despite all the rupees that we lavish on the rapacious Kashmiris, the hotels yield no result. Krishna suggests the Dreamland Restaurant, where all the Westerners hang out. To get there we struggle through the market, an extraordinary mixture of smells, noises, and mud.

As we walk through the door, Krishna squeezes my arm: "There she is!" Heart pounding, I step forward, when he suddenly pulls me back. "Now there are three women staring at you!" He laughs. "You are a strange tourist, my friend."

In silence, we walk back up the road in the cool evening air. On the way we pass a peasant pushing his donkey along by kicking his behind, while his friend, laughing, is doing the same to him.

"Since you can't find your girl, why don't you come to Rizong with me to buy apricots from the Julichen nuns?" I agree.

Next day, in glorious light, the jeep speeds along the wide, muddy bank of the Indus. The river winds its way toward the Lamayuru pass, flowing by the ancient monastery of Alchi, then dips from the Himalayan heights into the Arabian Sea, bringing wealth and death, alluvial fertility and floods.

Suddenly Krishna starts cursing. "The road has been cut off! There has been a landslide." On our right a gentle breeze whistles through the tall trees; on our left a vigorous torrent gushes where the road has been destroyed. We hide the car in the bushes. We cross the fault and continue on foot. My bag is not meant for trekking. I keep shifting it from shoulder to shoulder, but after a while both shoulders hurt just as much. I try to relieve the pain by carrying it on my head, but the load only makes my foot stiff, forcing me to walk like a robot.

We fork left and cross the torrent through a shallow ford. The ice-cold water soothes my aching feet. The sun is now directly over us; it must be midday. Sitting on round boulders at the edge of the little river, we make a meal out of *chapatis* and cold chicken.

We resume our rugged walk along a steep path. I desperately keep shifting my bag, trying hard to avoid the question burning my lips: how much farther? We keep on climbing in undisturbed silence except for the cries of a few birds of prey. At last we hear voices. We have arrived at Rizong and the apricot orchards of the Julichen nuns.

It is a humble retreat. We pass under the arch that leads through the main building to an open courtyard that smells of apricots. The nuns greet us with much hilarity and gentle hissing, owing to their toothless mouths. They are all old, ageless, drier than their apricots drying in the sun. They invite us to drink rancid butter diluted in tea and offer us apricots. Afraid of catching dysentery, I stuff them into my pocket. The nuns chatter incessantly and regularly throw me a "*Jullay!*" I feel them to be extremely light, as light as the air around us. They are stoning the apricots before drying them on the terrace overlooking a tiny valley. Krishna describes them to me. They are dressed in rags, never bothering to mend or sew their torn skirts, bodices, or shawls. He says that he is going to do business with them but that it will take time; therefore, we will have to spend the night here.

In the evening, which goes on forever, two nuns who seem even older than the rest bring us an indefinable, frugal supper. We eat it in front of the stone hut that serves as the convent guest house. Rather than spend the night in that windowless hovel, I decide to find a relatively flat piece of ground where I can put down a mat. The only possible place, after getting rid of the stones, is the path that leads to the Rizong monastery. Despite Krishna's disapproval, something to do with the effect of the moon on the "already lunatic spirits," I spend a delightful night in my sleeping bag on the roof of the world. Between the infinite and myself, I can hear an imperceptible whistling—God whistling between his teeth, between the high, sharp ice peaks, in the night.

In an infernal racket, all the mountain demons tumble down on me at once. Sounds of iron banging on rock, gongs resounding, shrieks of laughter. Dust is getting into my nostrils, throat, and ears. I sit up with a bolt. "What the…?"

"*Jullay…Jullay…*" answer voices. They are not demons but a group of monks who have started at dawn to repair the track gullied by the rains. I roll up my sleeping bag and mat, then, helped by a young monk, go and wake up Krishna. In his stone box, he has not heard a thing and laughs when he sees me covered with dust.

As I wash in the little spring near the hostel, Krishna informs me that he had bought the nuns' harvest and is ready to go down. I point out that although he has found what he wanted, I still have not.

I do not go down to the plain with Krishna. I am beginning to enjoy this adventure. From beggars to a galloping old man, from Kemala to Krishna, I realize that if I am willing to be patient, something will always happen, somebody will appear, and even though I may get stuck, it will never be for long. The prodigious energy of this land and its people will push me onward as far and as long as I want.

At midday I accompany the road-worker monks back up to their monastery. The same young monk who helped me wake up Krishna takes a firm grip on my hand and, laughing all the while, asks me questions in Ladakhi that I do not understand. We have been walking for some time, and the path is very steep. My bag seems heavier than ever.

Suddenly, the characteristic hammering of little hooves on the ground. A mountain dweller and his donkey. Amid many *Jullays*, I try to explain that I want to rent the donkey. Everyone laughs, but no one understands. Finally the man begins to suspect a change in the course of his journey when I take hold of the donkey's halter, forcing the animal to take a *demi-volte*, placing its tail where its head had been a few seconds before. Next, I poise my bag on its withers, sit astride the tiny mount, and, pointing up ahead, cry "*Gompa!*"—which means "monastery"—as you would cry "Charge!" There is a moment's silence, then everybody bursts out laughing. The owner agrees to twenty rupees, but the donkey has not been consulted. With all the obstinacy of its breed, it refuses to budge an inch. The young monk tries to push the animal, then remembers a universal technique and grabs hold of its tail, twisting it violently. Suddenly it takes off with a bolt, to its own surprise.

Finally the ground levels out. We enter a little circus-shaped valley. "*Gompa*," says one of the monks, taking my hand and pointing it up. Between the peaks the great monastery of Rizong stands in all its majesty.

As we reach the top of the steps, the monks gather around me. Among them I notice the voices of very young boys, children, little novices, no doubt. They laugh and blurt out high-pitched interjections. Yet despite their constant energy, a sense of peace emanates from their brouhaha. They guide me to a terrace where I am presented to the *rimpoche*, the abbot of Rizong. He takes the fingers of my left hand; although I understand not a word of what he is saying, my fingers perceive that I am welcome. Beside him, a monk translates into somewhat tantric English. The *rimpoche* says: "Come under our roof and stay as long as you wish. The food is very bad. The people who come here from the West are usually sightseeing with their cameras. Not you. Why did you come to Ladakh?"

After a few days, the monks seem to have totally adopted me in a particular way and let me sleep on a high terrace: Lama Lampu, the translator, calls it the Terrace of Solitude.

In the morning, I hear sandals shuffling. "*Jullay! Jullay!*" It is Lama Lampu. He sits down. The cry of a bird of prey tears through the air, and way down in the valley, lost among the trees, I can hear water flowing. Lama Lampu touches my chest and laughs. He says that my insisting on sleeping in the open air leaves me vulnerable to all kinds of spirits who willingly enter into me. He says that my face is still dark from the night. We get up and go to breakfast on some miserable concoction.

Buzzing with activity, the kitchen is a square room with a high ceiling. In the middle a charcoal fire is

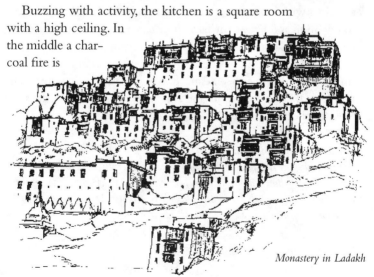

Monastery in Ladakh

kept burning all day long. The room is full of smoke; the vault, wall, shelves, all seem cooked; everything is black with soot except for the shiny brass and copper utensils. The smoke floats in the room without seeming to bother the monks, who melt into the monochrome background. Framed by the small openings pierced in the thick wall, the landscape seems all the brighter. We sit down by a window with our small wooden bowls.

Lama Lampu guides me everywhere, makes me touch everything, see everything. The great façade, with its classical, uncluttered, serene layout, hides an extraordinary labyrinth of corridors, passages, split levels, corners, and terraces jutting out under the sky. The original chaos, disorder of the soul, ferreting through thought. Unexpected passages, windows looking out onto walls, rooms apparently without purpose. But after a while, one realizes that all this imbroglio of architecture corresponds to well-determined functions, that there is reason in the madness. In the main sanctuary he stands on my left, his right arm around my waist, and takes my right hand, not only to direct me but to apply it to books centuries old, to the chair reserved for the Dalai Lama, to the multiple statues of the incarnations of Buddha. He spares me nothing. And, of course, according to the rules, we walk around the sanctuary clockwise. A sequence from the film *Some Like It Hot* springs to my mind and I close my hand over Lama Lampu's and draw him into a tango, keeping the beat with onomatopoeia. "*Ta-DUM, ta-DUM, tadada-DUM…*" There is no question that this is the first time a tango has ever been danced in a Himalayan monastery. The monks guffaw, and my behavior, which surprises even me, does not seem to shock them at all.

Before being blinded by muggers in New York City, Hugues de Montalembert was a painter, film maker, and writer. In his book, Eclipse, *which was translated from the French into four languages, he writes about his blinding and search for a cure. He still travels widely and writes regularly for French and U.S. publications. He lives in Paris.*

★

India shows what she wants to show, as if her secrets are guarded by a wall of infinite height. You try to climb the wall—you fall, you fetch a ladder—it is too short, but if you are patient a brick will loosen and then another. Once through, India embraces you, but that was something I had yet to learn.

When I arrived in Delhi it was my ladder that was too short. I wanted everything immediately. The monsoons had broken. Black, swollen rain clouds brought the usual rain, humidity and chaos. Roads were awash, taxis broke down, peacocks screamed. I perspired, worried, and developed prickly heat—and I had only been there a few days.

Inevitably I consulted a fortune-teller. "You are married, yes," he stated wisely.

"No," I replied.

"But you are having a companion, I think."

"Yes."

"You are most fortunate, sir. Soon you will be having another one. I am seeing many problems. But do not worry, sir," he added brightly. "They will only be getting worse."

—Mark Shand, *Travels on My Elephant*

DAVID YEADON

A Bath for Fifteen Million People

The world's largest gathering happens every
twelve years, and the next one is in 2001.
Mark your calendar.

THE ULTIMATE CLEANSING OF BODY AND SPIRIT! AT ALLAHABAD IN north central India one splash, paddle, and body-wash in the fast flowing Ganges—the holy mother of rivers—at the right moment of the right day "reaps the benefit of bathing on ten million solar eclipse days." It's an offer any self-respecting Hindu cannot possibly refuse. A whole lifetime of sin, debauch, and spiritual uncenteredness washed away in a few wet moments. A new beginning, a promise of eternal bliss, salvation, Nirvana!

"You should see the Kumbh Mela at Allahabad," I'd been advised by a friend in Kathmandu. "It's an incredible festival of cleansing. Fifteen million people—all coming to the Ganges once every twelve years. Incredible. You might just make it. It's worth a try!"

At first glance Allahabad is not a particularly prepossessing city. (Second glances don't help much either.) Nonetheless this dusty, hot place is a renowned center of learning, an intellectual nexus, for students from all over India. But much more important, it is the meeting place of the three most sacred rivers, the Ganges, the Yamuna, and the "invisible river," Saraswati.

From the distance the *Mela* looks like a vast military encampment: thousands of square white tents with four-sided pyramidal roofs lined up in endless rows fill the dusty flats around the Triveni Sangam, the confluence of the three rivers (you can actually see only two, but in India nothing is what it seems and everyone insists that it is the third, invisible river of Saraswati that endows this place with unique significance).

It's very hot. A white dust hangs in a cloud over the site, giving a haloed, mystic feeling. I've been walking for almost an hour now from the cordoned-off entrance to the Sangam. Actually, walking is not quite the word, more like half-carried, half-trampled by a thick mélange of humanity filling the hundred-foot-wide "corridors" between the tents and the fenced encampments of the *sadhus*, the gurus, the *sanyasins*, and the swamis. Each encampment

> ———— ✹ ————
>
> *G*ange Cha Yamune Chaiva
> Godavarai Saraswati
> Narmade Sindhu Kaveri
> Jale Asmin Sannidhim Kuru
>
> (O Holy Mother Ganges! O Yamuna! O Godavari! Saraswati! O Narmada! Sindhu! Kaveri! May you all be pleased to be manifest in these waters with which I shall purify myself!)
>
> *Prayer to the Seven Sacred Rivers recited by every devout Hindu at the time of taking his bath*
>
> ◆
>
> —Eric Newby,
> *Slowly Down the Ganges*

has its own ceremonial entrance made up of rickety scaffoldings and tied bamboo poles topped with painted symbols, logos, and depictions of Hindu deities. A vast supermarket of salvation specialists. Hundreds of them from all over India, each surrounded by his own faithful disciples and followers. The women in their bright saris feverishly cook and clean outside the square tents, while men, bearded, ascetic, and clad in *dhotis* or dark robes, gather in hunched groups around their chosen wise men to listen and debate and nod and sleep and listen again.

And the crowd churns on. Once in it's almost impossible to break free without the risk of being squashed to a sweaty pulp by a million shoeless and sandaled feet. I'm not even sure where we're going but I'm part of the flow, and there's nothing I can do to stop it.

"Are you understanding the significance, sir, of this event, sir?"

A young man in long white robes links his arm in mine and smiles brightly into my dust-smeared face.

I don't really feel like talking (I'm far too busy trying not to trip on the pebbly track), and I mumble something about having read an article in *The Times of India*.

The youth smiles sympathetically.

"Ah the *Times,* sir. That is a good paper. But I think it is possible that you don't understand everything, sir. It is a very long history."

"Yes," I mumble again. "Yes, I suppose it is." Everything in India has a long history.

"The spiritual tradition, sir, of *tirthayatra*, the bathing at sacred river crossings, can be traced back to the Vedic period of our history, sir, about 1500 B.C. There are quite a few important bathing places, sir, but here— the Triveni Sangam—is the most important. And the Kumbh Mela is the most famous holy festival—and this one"—he pauses for drama—"this one, today, is the most important for one hundred forty-four years due to the astral signs, sir, which are the same as when Jayanta dropped the liquid of the Amrit Kumbh, sir, on this very place."

He looked closely to see what impact this startling information

> *G*radually I was seduced by India itself. I have often been asked why, and I always find it very difficult to explain. I am not a poet, and so I can't pretend to be able to describe how or why I fell in love. It certainly had something to do with all those friends I made. In India, the problem is not making friends, it's retaining privacy. Friendship almost seems to assail you.
>
> ◆
>
> —Mark Tully, *The Defeat of a Congressman and Other Parables of Modern India*

had made on me. His eyes gleamed; he was obviously very excited and I felt it only fair to let him continue.

"The Amrit Kumbh. I haven't heard of that."

A great grin cleaved his hairless jaw. "Ah, sir. That is why everyone is here, sir. All these people. They say fifteen million. Maybe many more. How can one know, sir?"

That was one of the reasons I'd come. It was a substantial detour from my route to Rajasthan and the remote western regions of India. But I wanted to see what it was like to be among such an incomprehensibly large crowd of believers, all converging for the simple act of bathing in the Ganges. I wanted to feel the force, the power of such numbers. So many people all sharing the same purpose, all here at substantial cost and inconvenience and discomfort, all of one mind and spiritual intent—surely something miraculous would happen with all this centered energy. A river might stop flowing, apparitions might appear, the skies might turn black, and a god might descend....

My informant smiled again. "I am your friend, sir. I do not want money, sir. Just to be your friend."

I'd met many of these so-called "friends" throughout India but this one seemed to be less grabby than most. He hadn't even asked the ritual string of questions yet—country of origin, qualifications, profession, salary, wife, children, address—"in case I should ever be fortunate enough to visit your country"—and the old clincher, "I collect foreign coins, sir; if you happen to have any...."

"Sir, are you hearing me, sir?" My friend looked hurt. He had been talking.

"I'm sorry I missed that...."

"Yes, sir, it is very difficult. Too many people. Too much commotion, I think. But nevertheless I was saying to you about the Kumbh, sir. The Kumbh means a jar, sir, a thing for holding liquids. And according to my religion, sir, there was a time, many many many long times ago, when our gods were all very tired and weak and the great Brahma told them to make a special 'liquid of life' to help them become strong again, but they used the bad spirits to help them and the bad spirits wanted to keep the liquid in the Amrit Kumbh—in the special jar, sir."

I nodded, trying to focus on his words, still nervous about being pulped on the rough track.

"But then, sir, then Jayanta, a young god, sir, flew toward heaven with the jar and was chased by all the bad spirits, and as he flew he spilt drops of the special liquid at four places on earth—in India, sir. Now at each one of these places, in turn, they hold a festival of life, sir, every three years, a different place every three years, and on the twelfth year they come here, sir, for the *purna*, the most important Kumbh and, as I have told you, this one now, today, is the very special one because of the astrological signs, sir."

"That's quite a story."

"Yes, sir. It is a very famous story. All Indian people know about this. It is good for you to know this too, I think."

"Yes, it is. Thank you."

"You want to meet *sadhu*?"

"A wise man?"

"Yes. Very famous *sadhu*, sir. You can see his sign."

He pointed to one of a line of camp entrances, this one was painted a garish red, topped with a triangular pediment on which was painted numerous ferocious Hindu gods.

"Come, sir, we go and see *sadhu*."

Somehow he tugged me sideways out of the churning crowd and through the entrance. It felt wonderful just to pause on soft sandy ground and not have to move.

"Wait here, sir. I will find out where the *sadhu* is, sir."

A few yards away the crowd serpentined on, sheened in dust haze, down the long slope to the Ganges herself, gleaming soft silver in the sun. There were police everywhere and other more military types bristling with guns and grenades. Apparently previous *melas* here have produced outbursts of "cultural divisiveness" (a *Times* euphemism for outright revolution) in which scores lost their lives. Also fires, drownings (the Ganges is not always a tolerant mother), and anarchistic outbursts from students of the Allahabad universities. It was obvious in the amazing organization of this tent city of millions and the stern-faced wariness of the guards that the government was determined to make this particular one a model *mela*.

I could see the black superstructures of the pontoon bridges across the river, smothered in pilgrims. The smoke from thousands of cooking fires rose to mingle with the dust haze. I could smell the hot oil in which the *chapatis* and *papadums* and *samosas* and a dozen other varieties of deep-fried delights were being prepared and sold.

Near the entrance to the *sadhu's* compound, an old man in a large pink turban used a tamed canary to pick fortune cards at random from a line of little boxes set in the ground. A group of spectators stood solemnly and silently as he read the fortune text to a client, another equally old man who fingered a string of black beads and tugged nervously at his long gray beard. He didn't seem at all happy with the reading. The fortune-teller took his coins, shrugged, and gestured to the canary, which had nimbly hopped back into its cage and closed its own cage door. The crowd snickered, pleased it wasn't their fortune that had just been read. The old man painfully pulled himself to his feet, grumbled at the reader, and was swallowed up in the slithering crowd.

"He is over here, sir."

My friend had returned, bright-eyed and smiling again. We walked between the rows of tents toward the center of the compound where a large green canvas awning stretched over a low painted platform.

It was cool and dark under the awning. A score of men sat in a circle around a central dais. They all had long beards and were dressed in layers of crumpled cotton robes, black and gray. They shuffled around a bit to make room for us. I felt self-conscious in my jeans and checked shirt and pushed the bulging camera bag behind me. Cameras seemed out of place here, like laughter at a funeral. And it felt funereal. Everyone looked very glum except for the *sadhu* himself, a tiny, virtually naked man with spindly ribs and arms seemingly devoid of muscles. His matted black hair tumbled in sticky tresses over his shoulders. Offerings of rice and fruit and books and brass vases and painted pendants lay all around his feet, but he seemed oblivious of everything and everyone. His eyes were closed. His face was turned upward, his mouth curved in a half smile, and his hands rested limply in his lap.

It was very quiet.

"They say he has not spoken for six hours," my friend whispered.

"And they've been sitting here all this time?" There was something almost sculptural in this hunched bunch of devotees.

"I think so."

So we sat. And sat. And sat some more. My legs had gone numb but no one moved, so I tried not to fidget.

"What do you think they're waiting for?" I finally asked my friend.

"Something," he whispered mysteriously. Then he giggled softly. "Anything."

More sitting. Now my arms were numb too. I was hungry and hot and thirsty. And bored.

"I think I'm ready," I whispered. I'd never make a guru lover. A bit of meditation once in a while is all right, but I suffer from an overactive brain and an underdeveloped sense of patience.

"Yes. We'll try another one." Even my friend seemed perplexed by all the silence.

"They usually talk more," he explained as we rejoined the throng. "He was one of the silent ones."

As the heat and dust rose together and the crowds grew thicker, silence became

> *I*ndians still hear the call of the hermitage, and still they obey. Every year thousands upon thousands of them renounce the world to look for something greater. Spiritual values are besieged by secularism and Western materialism, but even the crassest and most cynical Bombay businessman feels the pull of the forest. The most august title a man can hope to bear, today as much as in epic times, is not "maharajah" but "maharishi."
>
> ◆
>
> —Jonah Blank, *Arrow of the Blue-Skinned God: Retracing the Ramayana through India*

hard to find. This was a strange affair—part carnival, part religious revival, part showcase for the nation's cream-of-the-crop gurus. A high-hype commercialized religious romp—or something else?

My Kathmandu friend had lent me one of his religious books, a delightful nineteenth-century account of an English Victorian woman's wanderings with a swami in the Himalayan foothills. I sat with my new friend in the shade of an empty canvas tent as the crowds milled by and read a few fragments of Sister Nivedita's (her Indian name, given her by the swami) truth-seeking experiences:

> So beautiful have been the days of this year. I have seen a love that would be one with the humblest and most igno- rant, seeing the world for a moment through his eyes. I have laughed at the colossal caprice of genius; I have warmed myself by heroic fires and have been present at the awakening of a holy child…My companions and I played with God and knew it…The scales fell from our eyes and we saw that all indeed are one and we are condemned no more. We worship neither pain nor pleasure. We seek through either to come to that which transcends them both…Only in India is the religious life perfectly conscious and fully developed.

I looked up. Among the crowds were the occasional Western faces, the faces of seekers, coming to the *mela* to find answers to all mysteries, coming to find comfort, coming to "play with God," coming to experience the "perfectly conscious religious life."

Singing, chanting, dancing, and discordant sitar sounds ex- ploded from a score of pavilions. Babies rolled in the sand while sari-clad mothers washed and polished huge copper rice cauldrons at the water taps; ancient hermit-like men displayed themselves in the most contorted positions in little tents with hand-painted signs nailed to bamboo posts. "Guru Ashanti has sat in this same posi- tion without moving for eight years." "Rastan Jastafari eats only wild seeds and drinks one glass of goat's milk every eight days to the honor of Shiva." A fairground of fakirs! There were men with necklaces of cobras and pythons; a troupe of dancing monkeys playing brass cymbals; more fortune-tellers with their little trained birds; peanut vendors; *samosa* stands, reeking of boiling oil; groups of gurus huddled together deep in gossip ("So what's new in the enlightenment business, Sam?" "How's your new ashram going, Jack?" "Harry, can I borrow your cave up on Annapurna for a couple of years?").

There were special compounds for Tamils, for Tibetan refugees, for Nepalese pilgrims from the high Dolpo region of the Himalayas, for ascetic members of the Jain religion, and a hundred other far more obscure sects.

Sometime in the middle of the afternoon a scuffle occurred near the river. A bronzed Swedish cameraman had just had his expensive video camera smashed into bits of twisted metal and broken computer chips by a crowd of irate Bengali tribesmen. Generally everyone seemed to tolerate cameras and tape recorders but this unfortunate individual had broken some taboo of propriety and now stood towering head and shoulders above his antagonists, gazing at his ruined machine in disbelief. The police arrived, then the army, and together they formed a flying wedge to rescue him, while shouting, cursing, and spitting roared all around them.

"You have to be very careful," my friend whispered. "You never know what can happen here."

A few minutes later there was another commotion on the far bank. Thousands of *dhoti*-clad bathers were running around, shouting and pointing at the fast-flowing river. Loudspeakers were urging calm and I could see another phalanx of police and soldiers scurrying down the dusty slope to the water where they stood hopelessly gazing at the water. Stories spread like a brush fire through the tent city. Someone had been lost in the river. An old woman, a young child, a famous *sadhu*—someone—had stepped beyond the cordoned-off section of shallow water into the main flow of the current, eddied with whorls and churning froth. He, or she, had been caught in the undertow and had vanished. People strained to spot the body. But mother Ganges swirled on, India's eternal stream of life and death, filled with the ashes of cremated bodies, bestowing fertility on the flat lands, rampaging over them in furious floods, swirling and whirling its way from the glaciers of the high Himalayas to the silty estuaries of the Indian Ocean. Omnipresent, indifferent, endless.

My friend had to leave (suitably rewarded with rupees and two rain-stained copies of *Newsweek* "to improve my English"). I sat on a bluff overlooking the merger of the two rivers. The sun sank, an enormous orange globe squashing into the horizon, purpling the dust haze, gilding the bodies of the bathers.

The moon rose, big, fat, and silver in a Maxfield Parish evening sky. There were thousands of people by the river now. The bathing increased but everything seemed to be in slow motion. I watched one old man, almost naked, progress through the careful rituals of washing. He was hardly visible through the throng and yet he acted as if he were the only person there by the river, unaware of everything but the slow steady rhythms of his cleansing. After washing every part of his body he began to clean his small brass pitcher, slowly rubbing it with sand, polishing the battered metal with a flattened twig, buffing its rough surface with a wet cloth, until it

The *Laws of Manu,* the ancient text spelling out all rules for Hindu existence, speaks of four types of holy man. There is the *brahmacharya* (one who has taken a vow of celibacy), the *bhikku* (wandering mendicant), the *vanaprastha* (forest hermit renouncing worldly things), and the *grahastha* (simple householder). The householder, Manu says, is the highest of all. By his honest trade and industry he keeps all the others alive. Without him, society could not exist.

◆

—Jonah Blank, *Arrow of the Blue-Skinned God: Retracing the Ramayana through India*

gleamed in the moonlight. Then he disappeared and other bodies took his place by the river.

I sensed timelessness and began to feel the power of this strange gathering. Each person performed the rituals in his or her own way and yet from a distance there seemed to be a mystical unity among all of them, all these souls as one soul, cleansing, reviving, touching eternity in the flow of the wide black river, linking with the infinity, becoming part of the whole of which we are all a part.

I made my way slowly to the river and knelt down. For a moment there was no me left in me. The river, the people, the movements, the night breeze, the moon, life, death, all became as one continuum. A smooth, seamless totality. An experience beyond experience. A knowingness beyond knowledge.

I washed my face and arms and let the water fall back to the flowing river where it was carried away into the night.

David Yeadon has written and illustrated sixteen travel books, including New York: The Best Places, Backroad Journeys of Southern Europe, *and most recently,* Lost Worlds: Exploring the World's Remote Places. *He lives with his wife, Anne, in Mohegan Lake, New York. This story was excerpted from* The Back of Beyond: Travels to the Wild Places of the Earth.

✦

Saying that Indians are a gentle, dreamy, fatalistic people, detached from the world only describes the effect, not the cause. "Strange" is the word, for spontaneously, in their very physical substance, without the least "thought" or even "faith," Indians plunge their roots deep into other worlds; they do not exclusively belong here. And in them, these other worlds rise constantly to the surface—*at the least touch the veil is rent,* remarks Sri Aurobindo. This physical world, which for us is so real and absolute and unique, seems to them but one way of living among many others; in short, a small, chaotic, agitated, and rather painful frontier on the margin of immense continents which lie behind unexplored.

—Satprem, *Sri Aurobindo or The Adventure of Consciousness*

Monument of Love

*The heartstrings are sometimes
anchored by place.*

NOT ALL ARRANGED MATCHES ARE EMPTY OR LOVELESS. SOME bloom into blissful harmonious romances, some blaze and smolder as lifelong seductions. After all, the *Kama Sutra* is an Indian text.

The Taj Mahal, the very symbol of India in Western eyes, is the world's greatest monument to love. It was built by a heart-broken Mughal emperor at the death of his adored wife. In the courtly gardens of the Taj, I met an old man who might well be Shah Jahan reincarnate.

His hair was snowy white, his mouth had not a single tooth, and his dark walnut skin was creased like crinkly wax paper. He wore a long black formal frock coat in the heat of the afternoon, leaned on a weathered teak walking stick, and gazed at the world through thick glasses with smart cherry-red frames. His name was Mr. Krishnan. If he had not actually existed, he would have been dreamed up by Gabriel García Márquez.

"I have come here at least once a week for seventy years," he told me. "My wife and I used to sit by that fountain in the shade. Sometimes she would cook a basket of *samosas*, and we would spend the hours feeding them to each other. She was always at her loveliest in the light reflected off the walls of the Taj."

The light *is* different here, just as to painters the light in Venice is unlike light anywhere else. Perhaps the walls of the mausoleum reflect not only light but love.

"When my wife died," Mr. Krishnan went on, "I began coming to the garden each and every day, I felt closer to her here even than in our home, because this was where we shared our happiest moments. For nearly two decades I walked about the hedges each afternoon, by myself but not quite by myself. When I sit by the fountain and shut my eyes, I can still taste the *samosas.*"

Their two children have long since moved away, to Delhi and to Chandigarh, but Mr. Krishnan could never bring himself to abandon Agra. He has left the city only three times in his life, and on each occasion he felt unbearable pangs of loneliness that did not subside until he sat in the gardens of the Taj once again. In recent years the government had begun charging an entrance fee for the monument. It is two rupees—less than a dime—but Mr. Krishnan cannot afford such a daily extravagance on his civil service pension. Now he visits only on Fridays, when admission is free. "All the other days of the week," he said, "I spend eagerly looking forward to Friday."

The Taj is always overrun with tourists, and on Fridays even more so. Most of the gawkers are Indian, but there are also Germans, Brits, French, Americans, Japanese, and Aussies by the busload. Mr. Krishnan does not mind. He does not even seem to notice.

Mr. Krishnan has no favorite time of day to see the Taj. He has been here countless mornings, when the sunlight bounces off the white marble—marble inlaid with semiprecious stones and then sanded smooth as fresh butter—with such brilliance it hurts your eyes. He has been here countless evenings, when the sun turns into a blazing red comet, paints the mausoleum yellow, then orange, then pink, then deep purple before dropping from the sky to make room for the moon. He has been here countless nights, when the crowds have all gone and the site is silent, when the air is so crisp and clean you don't even notice the swarms of mosquitoes from the mud flats of the Yamuna River below, when all you can do is stand spellbound by the contrast of the pure, man-made whiteness of the alabaster minarets against the deep and infinite blackness of the heavens.

Mr. Krishnan has seen the Taj at all hours and from all angles. One of the custodians is a friend of his, and once let him climb up to the gilded dome at midnight. He has explored the structure from top to bottom. Many times

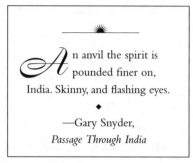

An anvil the spirit is
pounded finer on,
India. Skinny, and flashing eyes.

♦

—Gary Snyder,
Passage Through India

he has descended to the tomb far beneath the exquisitely tiled floor, its dead air hot, humid, and thick with the trapped sweat of centuries. Although a Hindu himself, he always speaks the name of the Islamic holy place with hushed reverence. God is love, he says, and this is most certainly a temple of love.

"Shah Jahan did not plan to be buried here," said Mr. Krishnan. "The Taj was meant to be a mausoleum only for Mumtaz, his dear lady. Do you know what the name 'Mumtaz' means? It means 'excellent,' and she was indeed the most excellent of women. As for his own tomb, the Shah intended to build an exact replica of the Taj, but all in black marble instead of white. A perfect mirror image, for the wife is a perfect reflection of the husband."

Beneath a tree to our left, a family of Sikhs had spread out a blanket for a picnic. The father was happily lifting his baby daughter up above his head with one hand, bouncing her in the air to make her laugh. The mother was unpacking a small case of food: curries in metal pails, breads wrapped in tin foil—and a basket filled with delicate brown *samosas*.

"Why was the black Taj never built?" I asked.

"A sad thing," Mr. Krishnan replied. "The emperor Jahan was deposed by his wicked son Aurangzeb. He was imprisoned over there," the old man pointed up the river to Agra Fort. "For years he would sit in his cell, unable to do anything except stare out of the tower window at the city he once ruled. But I like to believe that every day when he stared downriver at the Taj, he was cheered by the sight of his dear wife's resting place."

Mr. Krishnan's gaze strayed to the marble dome, and he was silent for a solid minute.

"But one good thing arose from this tragic situation," he said. "Because Shah Jahan could not build a separate tomb for himself, he was buried here in the Taj alongside his lady love. Whenever I think of them, side by side for all eternity, I cannot help but feel happy."

The afternoon was waning, and Mr. Krishnan had to go home to take his heart medication. After we'd shaken hands and started to walk away, he turned around and called out to me:

"May God bless you with happiness—may you get married very soon!"

Jonah Blank has worked as a newspaper editor and foreign correspondent in Japan, Sri Lanka, Sudan, the Philippines, Burma, Thailand, and India. He was educated at Yale and Harvard and lives in Cambridge, Massachusetts. This selection was taken from his book, Arrow of the Blue-Skinned God: Retracing the Ramayana through India.

★

From a distance it looks like all the photographs you have ever seen; floating in space, heat waves diffusing its focus. It is not until you pass through the Jilo Khana, the red sandstone gateway, that you really see it: the central tomb of Begum Mumtaz-i-Mahal, white marble, soaring brilliant in the midday sun. You run your fingertips over the traceries and arabesques formed by semi-precious stones inlaid in the marble. It is then that you understand your massive failure of imagination. You take a very deep breath, shade your eyes and peer up at one of the towers, glaring white against a blue sky, and you know what you had not known before: that 350 years ago, before settlers hardly had a foothold in the New World, at this place on earth men had the ability to create such astonishing beauty. It is a triumph of what can be, and a reminder of a past only dimly understood.

—Shirley Streshinsky, "Interlude in India"

JERROLD STEWARD

* * *

Chai! Chai! Chai!

Drink a cup of chai *and imbibe
the essence of India.*

"CHAI GARAM. CHAI GARAM."

A deep, disembodied voice echoes from the railway platform, calling to the train's sleepy passenger. Roused from a miserable attempt at sleep, the weary traveler quickly withdraws a single rupee from his wallet and eagerly thrusts it through the bars of the compartment's open window. Soon he holds a red clay cup, brimming with steaming liquid. Like a parched wanderer in the desert, he brings it to his lips. Bliss.

Loved by some, hated by others, *chai*—the Indian tea consumed by the masses as well as the maharajahs—is one of the constants on the subcontinent.

If you're like most Westerners, when you think of tea you probably picture an elegant porcelain pot with some exquisitely aromatic Assam or Darjeeling leaves steeping inside. Nearby stand milk and sugar, ready to serve if called upon. A decidedly British sort of arrangement. To no great surprise, considering the long years of the Raj, this setup can be found all over India, but only in first class waiting rooms, Western-style restaurants, and starred hotels. If this is what you want, be sure to order "tray tea." Alas, it won't always be available.

On the other hand, maybe you're visualizing something a bit more utilitarian. But the tea bag has failed to penetrate very deeply into Indian culture.

Okay, you're wondering: what is *chai*? What are its magical ingredients? What special alchemy produces it? Pull up a chair in one of my favorite *chai* stands and watch the *chai-wallah* at work.

Squatting by a brazier of glowing coals, the maestro reaches for his favorite pot, a much-dented, fire-blackened thing made out of the cheapest metals possible. Deftly he knocks out the remains of the last batch of *chai*, wipes out the pot with a dirty rag, and sets it on the brazier. He adds several cups of water (better not to ask its source) and two ladles of whole milk.

As the mixture begins to heat, the *chai-wallah* reaches for a large red tin of Brook Bond Red Label, the best CTC tea money can buy. (CTC tea is the name given to what's left of the tea after the finest leaves have been sold for export. The letters stand for the Crush-Tear-Cool process that these remains are subjected to.) Into the pot go several generous pinches.

Now a critical step. Out comes another tin, this one full of coarse crystals of partially refined sugar. In goes a spoonful. And another. And another. And another. You lose count. The mind boggles.

With effortless grace, the maestro reaches for a *bidi*, a cigarette hand-rolled in a leaf of tobacco or the cheaper *saal*. Now it is time to wait and have a smoke. There's no hurrying this last, all-important stage: the cooking.

Minutes pass. At last the *bidi* has burned down, and the *chai* is ready to be served. A serious young boy in stained pajamas steps forward: the sorcerer's apprentice. He deferentially hands his master a mismatched cup and saucer. With practiced showmanship, the *wallah* flourishes a strainer and pours the tea.

Following the example of your fellow patrons, you pour the piping hot *chai* into the saucer and take a sip. A feeling of sublime well-being spreads slowly through body and soul.

Strange to say, *chai* is not for everybody. There are those, in fact, who think that it is the absolute nadir of tea preparation on our small planet—particularly poignant, no doubt, in a land so blessed with fine tea. For me and those I hold dear, however, *chai* is the very best essence of travel in India.

In the old days, before bottled water became ubiquitous in India, *chai* was one of the few "safe" things to drink, and it still is today. (In theory, the boiling kills off all the bad stuff, and you just try to ignore the cup's dubious hygiene.) What surprises many Westerners is how refreshing a hot cup of *chai* can be, even on the most sweltering of Indian days.

In the middle of the afternoon, when you've been out roaming the dusty streets for hours in search of the perfect Kashmiri shawl or the quintessential sandalwood box, a cup of *chai* can revive body and spirit in an almost mystical way. Sit on a simple wooden bench beneath the shade of a giant banyan tree. Taking a soothing sip, relax, and watch the world go by. A pair of bullocks, their horns painted blue and green, pull a cart heavily laden with scraps of cardboard. An ash-covered *sadhu* strides along, a trident grasped firmly in one hand. A scooter flies past, its four passengers hanging on nonchalantly. Spotting a captive audience, a boy demands to shine your shoes. He's joined by a young woman pointing to the infant slung across her arm and crying, "Baby, *Sahib!*"

The best *chai* stands, of course, are something more than a place to sit and relax. Like any good coffeehouse in the Western world, a *chai* stand is a social center. Newspapers are read, politics debated. Friendly patrons, observing that you are a foreigner, may draw you into conversation, inquiring into the country of your origin, the nature of your journey, the frequency of your sex life. Give them an enigmatic smile and continue sipping.

If you're hungry, even the most modest of *chai* stands offer some bits of food. Tall glass jars full of biscuits and crackers stand on the counter. A nearby plastic bowl holds a few bananas, a papaya, some oranges. Freed from the nagging of the surgeon general, you might be attracted by the large selection of cigarettes and *bidis*, sold individually or by the pack.

Some *chai* stands are more like full-blown restaurants, offering many kinds of Indian snacks: *samosas, pakoras, aloo tikki, chole batura.* And who can ignore the sweets? *Landus, jalebis, halwa, ras gullah, gulab jamun*…all sweet enough to make your teeth ache and your blood sugar levels drop to around your ankles.

My favorites are the milk sweets, and one of my all-time favorite places to eat them is in Mussoorie, the apex of Raj hill stations. Situated at the Library Bazaar end of Mall Road, Maha Laxshmi's offers to the casual passerby an alluring selection of sweets and snacks. From dawn until well into the evening, a steady stream of patrons fills the place. Others simply walk up to one of the streetside counters for take-away. During the Dewali festival of lights, the lines stretch down the block.

My favorite time to drink *chai* there is in the late afternoon after a long walk in the countryside. Finding an empty bench at one of the inside tables, I flag down one of the child waiters and order some *burfi* (unappetizingly pronounced "barfi") and a cup of *chai*. In no time, the boy returns with the tea and two shiny little rectangles on a metal plate.

> *M*any varieties of cardamom, with its exotic green-and-purple-petaled flowers and its aromatic seed-pod, flourish wild on the coastal hills of western India. But the original cardamom was first cultivated in south India for aromatic, culinary, and medicinal purposes.
>
> The pharmacological value of the cardamom is to be found in the seed, which is of particular assistance against urine retention and stomach disorders…In India it is common practice to offer aromatic cardamoms at the end of a meal, as digestives and for freshening the breath. But they are also used in cooking, not just for flavoring savory dishes like curries, but also in Indian sweets, which often combine cardamoms with rose water and thickened milk.
>
> ◆
>
> —Naveen Patnaik, *The Garden of Life: An Introduction to the Healing Plants of India*

Often covered with a thin foil of edible silver, *burfi* is made with ground cardamom, almond, or pistachio, milk, and sugar syrup. It is the perfect accompaniment to a good cup of *chai*.

And speaking of cardamom, some of India's more upscale *chai* stands like to infuse their brew with it or other indigenous spices. Ginger, cloves, cinnamon, nutmeg, and black pepper are all common choices. The cardamom, some say, is best when chewed fresh by the *chai wallah*, then spit into the pot. I've never witnessed this myself, but wisdom might dictate keeping a close eye on the maestro while he is brewing your tea.

One of the best ways to enjoy a cup of *chai* is in the privacy of one's room. Even India's budget hotels usually come equipped with a buzzer above or beside the bed. Like a maharajah of old, you can lie back and ring for a servant. In a few minutes "the boy" will knock loudly on your door. This fellow might be a man of eighty years old or a youth of only ten, but if he's fetching

Cardamom seeds

chai, he's still "the boy." In minutes he will return with a piping hot glass, lingering on his way out long enough to let you understand that some modest gratuity is desired. Treat him well, and he will work wonders for you at all hours of the day and night.

One final tip. If you have an aversion to milk and sugar, you can always risk the *chai-wallah's* wrath, not to mention the derision of your fellow patrons, and try ordering your *chai* without milk and/or sugar. "*Chini bina chai*" should produce the sugarless variety. "*Dudh bina chai*" will have the offending dairy left out. If you want decaf tea, lowfat milk, or Sweet-and-Low instead of sugar, you will be better off staying at home.

Jerrold Steward worked in the computer field for fifteen years before turning to writing murder mysteries and traveling in Asia. He is also a painter and photographer (of little renown, by his own estimate) and lives in Berkeley, California.

✳

In India, conversation often seemed to go round in circles. In Chittaurgarh (City of Valour, said my map) the man at the guest house knocked on my door and said, "Sir. Good evening but your country of origin is what please?"

"You've already written it down five times on five different bits of paper," I said.

"What is the fine name of your father?"

"You've written that five times as well."

"In the morning," he said, "you are wishing for a breakfast mealing?"

"Yes, that would be very nice. You have porridge?" I inquired hopefully.

"Porridge—yes."

"How much your porridge?" I asked, surprised.

"Porridge three rupee only."

"Okay. One bowl porridge in the morning please."

"Porridge? No, no porridge."

"But you just said porridge—yes."

"No. Omelette, *chapati*."

"Do you have yoghurt—*dahi*?"

"*Dahi*. Yes."

"Okay, I'll have *dahi* then."

"You want omelette?"

"No, just *dahi*."

"No problem omelette."

"No, just *dahi*."

"Just *dahi*?"

"Yes, just *dahi*."

In the morning I was presented with a bowl of porridge.

—Josie Dew, *The Wind in My Wheels: Travel Tales from the Saddle*

WILLIAM DALRYMPLE

A Sufi Spring

New Delhi reveals its layers through a
scholar's eyes—and the want ads.

THE WINTER RAINS ARRIVED PROMPTLY AT THE END OF JANUARY.
During the last week of the month Olivia and I had gone to stay
outside Delhi, in a fort just over the Rajasthani border. The day
before our return, as we looked out over the battlements, we saw
a succession of thick black clouds driving slowly over the sand flats
and camel grass. By the end of the afternoon the clouds had thickened into solid curtain walls of charcoal cumulus. They blotted out
the sun and cast a dark shadow over the land.

The next day we returned to Delhi to find that the storm had
broken. The clouds were scudding low over the rooftops; it was
pouring with rain and the streets were flooded. In the Old City,
Muslim women were dragging their *chadors* like wet black crows.
Gusts of rain lashed down the narrow alleys; rickshaws sluiced
through the water, more like boats than bicycles. It was no day to
be out, but I had an appointment to keep. I had arranged to see
Dr. Yunus Jaffery, a historian and an archetypal Old Delhi-*wallah*.
His ancestors had been Persian tutors at the Red Fort; today Dr.
Jaffery pursued exactly the same career in Zakir Hussain College
on the margins of Old Delhi. His rooms were in the original col-

39

lege, the Ghazi-ud-Din Medresse, a seventeenth-century Mughal
building just outside the Ajmeri Gate.

Balvinder Singh [the driver] dropped me outside during a brief
pause in the rain. A low Mughal gateway led on into a wet and
glistening flagstone courtyard; it was deserted but for a solitary
pupil running late towards his class. The flagstones were slippery
and so hollowed-out by three centuries of passing feet that along
some of the walkways the puddles had coalesced into shallow
canals. The courtyard was bounded by a range of cloisters two stories high. Classrooms filled the ground-floor rooms. On the first
floor, leading off a covered balcony, were the chambers of the fellows and scholars. The arcades were broken on three sides by
vaulted gateways, and on the fourth, the principal axis, by a red
sandstone mosque. Before the mosque, filling both sides of the
cloister garth, was a garden of healing herbs and shrubs.

I climbed a narrow staircase leading to the first floor balcony.
Outside the scholars' rooms sat a line of bearded old men busily
correcting specimens of Arabic calligraphy. Dr. Jaffery's room was
the last on the corridor.

The door opened to reveal a gaunt, clean-shaven man. He wore
white Mughal pyjamas whose trouser-bottoms, wide and slightly
flared, were cut in the style once favoured by eighteenth-century
Delhi gallants. On his head he sported a thin white mosque-cap.
Heavy black glasses perched on the bridge of his nose, but the effect was not severe. Something in Dr. Jaffery's big bare feet and the
awkward way he held himself gave the impression of a slightly
shambolic, absent-minded individual: "*Asalam alekum*," he said.
"Welcome." Then looking behind me, he added: "Ah! The
rains…Spring has arrived."

Dr. Jaffery's domed room was small and square and dark.
Lightning from the storm had cut off the electricity and the cell
was illuminated by a bronze dish filled with flickering candles.
The shadows from the candlelight darted back and forth across
the shallow whitewashed dome. Persian books were stacked in
disordered piles; in the corner glistened a big brass samovar in-
cised with Islamic decoration. The scene of the Sufi scholar in his

room was straight out of a detail from the *Anvar-i Suhayli*—or indeed any of the illuminated Mughal manuscript books—and I said this to Dr. Jaffery. "My nieces also tell me I live in the Mughal age," he replied. "But they—I think—mean it as a criticism. You would like tea?"

Dr. Jaffery blew on the coals at the bottom of his samovar, then placed two cupfuls of buffalo milk in the top of the urn. Soon the milk was bubbling above the flame. While he fiddled with his samovar, Dr. Jaffery told me about his work.

For the previous three years he had been busy transcribing the forgotten and unpublished portions of the *Shah Jehan Nama*, the court chronicle of Shah Jehan. He had converted the often illegible manuscript into clear Persian typescript; this had then been translated into English by a team of Persian scholars in America. The manuscript, originally compiled by Shah Jehan's fawning court historian Inayat Khan, told the story of the apex of Mughal power, the golden age when most of India, all of Pakistan and great chunks of Afghanistan were ruled from the Red Fort in Delhi. It was an age of unparalleled prosperity: the empire was at peace and trade was flourishing. The reconquest of the Mughals' original homeland—trans-Oxianan Central Asia—seemed imminent. In the ateliers of the palace the artists Govardhan, Bichitr, and Abul Hasan were illuminating the finest of the great Mughal manuscript books; in Agra, the gleaming white dome of the Taj Mahal was being raised on its plinth above the River Jumna.

The book which contained the fruits of Dr. Jaffery's labours was about to be published. Now Dr. Jaffery was beginning to transcribe a forgotten text about Shah Jehan's childhood. The manuscript had just been discovered in the uncatalogued recesses of the British Museum; it was exciting work, said the doctor, but difficult: the manuscript was badly damaged and as he had not the money to go to London he was having to work from a smudged xerox copy. The new transcription absorbed his waking hours; but, despite the difficulties, he said he was making slow progress.

"As the great Sa'di once put it: 'The Arab horse speeds fast, but although the camel plods slowly, it goes both by day and night.'"

As we chatted about Shah Jehan, Dr. Jaffery brought out a plate of rich Iranian sweets from an arched recess; he handed them to me and asked: "Would you not like to learn classical Persian?"

"I would love to," I answered. "But at the moment I'm having enough difficulty trying to master Hindustani."

"You are sure?" asked Dr. Jaffery, breaking one of the sweets in two. "Learning Persian would give you access to some great treasures. I would not charge you for lessons. I am half a dervish: money means nothing to me. All I ask is that you work hard."

Dr. Jaffery said that very few people in New Delhi now wanted to study classical Persian, the language which, like French in Imperial Russia, had for centuries been the first tongue of every educated Delhi-*wallah*. "No one has any interest in the classics today," he said. "If they read at all, they read trash from America. They have no idea what they are missing. The jackal thinks he has feasted on the buffalo when in fact he has just eaten the eyes, entrails, and testicles rejected by the lion."

> *H*industani refers to the combination of Hindi and Urdu, which are almost the same language when spoken, but they have separate scripts and some differences in vocabulary. Urdu is associated with Muslims, Hindi with Hindus, and about half the population of India understands the two languages.
>
> ◆
>
> —JO'R and LH

I said, "That must upset you."

"It makes no difference," replied Dr. Jaffery. "This generation does not have the soul to appreciate the wisdom of Ferdowsi or Jalaludin Rumi. As Sa'di said: 'If a diamond falls in the dirt it is still a diamond, yet even if dust ascends all the way to heaven it remains without value.'"

I loved the way Dr. Jaffery spoke in parables; for all his eccentricities, like some ancient sage his conversation was dotted with pearls of real wisdom. After the banalities of life with Balvinder

Singh and Mrs. Puri [the author's landlady], Dr. Jaffery's words were profound and reassuring. As he told little aphorisms from Rumi or the anecdotes of Ferdowsi's *Shah Nama*—the Mughal Emperors' favourite storybook—his gentle voice soothed away the irritations of modern Delhi. But overlaying the gentle wisdom there always lay a thin patina of bitterness.

"Today Old Delhi is nothing but a dustbin," he said, sipping at his tea. "Those who can, have houses outside the walled city. Only the poor man who has no shelter comes to live here. Today there are no longer any educated men in the old city. I am a stranger in my own home." He shook his head. "All the learning, all the manners have gone. Everything is so crude now. I have told you I am half a dervish. My own ways are not polished. But compared to most people in this city…"

"What do you mean?"

"Here everyone has forgotten the old courtesies. For example…in the old days a man of my standing would never have gone to the shops; everything would be sent to his house: grain, chillies, cotton, cloth. Once every six months the shopkeeper would come and pay his regards. He would not dare ask for money; instead it would be up to the gentleman to raise the matter and to give payment when he deemed suitable. If ever he did go to the bazaar he would expect the shopkeepers to stand up when he entered….

"All these things have gone now. People see the educated man living in poverty and realize that learning is useless; they decide it is better to remain ignorant. To the sick man sweet water tastes bitter in the mouth."

"But don't your pupils get good jobs? And doesn't their success encourage others?"

"No. They are all Muslims. There is no future for them in modern India. Most become *gundas* or smugglers."

"Is learning Persian a good training for smuggling?"

"No, although some of them become very successful at this business. One of my pupils was Nazir. Now he is a big gambler, the Chief of the Prostitutes. But before he was one of my best pupils…."

To have had an Indian childhood is to have been initiated very young into horror as well as miracle. I had only to look out of the car window to see the fingerless lepers in the streets, the poor huddled under patchwork blankets in midwinter, the old women hardly able to walk dragging pails of water or working on building sites in blinding sun. My grandmother's shaved and colonnaded garden was full of snakes that the snake man caught and threw, hissing, into a gunnysack; a Russell's viper I saw one morning glittering at the bottom of the garden well killed two cows and a child. One night when my parents had gone to a party I lay in their bed and listened to a howling that sounded like the misery of all India rising to the night sky. Next morning I saw a thin, brown, rabid dog being strapped to the back of a bicycle, its mouth a mop of blood and foam. Its terrible face appeared in my dreams for years.

◆

—Andrew Harvey, *Hidden Journey: A Spiritual Awakening*

At that moment, the cry of the *muezzin* outside broke the evening calm. Dr. Jaffery rustled around the room, picking up books and looking behind cushions for his mosque cap before remembering that he was already wearing it. Muttering apologies he slipped on his sandals and stumbled out. "Can you wait for five minutes?" he asked. "I must go and say my evening prayers."

From the balcony I watched the stream of figures in white pyjamas rushing through the pelting rain to the shelter of the mosque. Through the cloudburst I could see the old men laying out their prayer carpets under the arches, then, on a signal from the *mullah*, a line of bottoms rose and fell in time to the distant cries of "*Allah hu Akbar!*"

Five minutes later, when Dr. Jaffery returned, he again put a cupful of milk on the samovar and we talked a little about his home life.

"The death of my oldest brother in 1978 was the most important event in my life," he said. "From my boyhood,

I always wanted to live in a secluded place, to live like a Sufi. But since my brother's death it has been my duty to care for my two nieces. I cannot now become a full dervish; or at least not until my nieces are educated and married. Until then their well-being must be my first concern."

"And after that?"

"Afterwards I want to go on *haj,* to visit Mecca. Then I will retire to some ruined mosque, repair it, and busy myself with my studies."

"But if you wish to retire can't you find some other member of your family to look after your nieces for you?"

"My elder brothers were killed at Partition," said Jaffery. "My elder sister is also a victim of those times. To this day she still hears the voices of guns. You may be sitting with her one evening, quite peacefully, when suddenly she will stand up and say: 'Listen! Guns! They are coming from that side!'

"In fact it was only by a miracle that my sister and I survived at all: we took shelter with our youngest brother in the Jama Masjid area. Had we been at the house of my parents we would have shared the fate of the rest of the family..." Dr. Jaffery broke off.

"Go on," I said.

"My parents lived in an area that had always been traditionally Hindu. During Partition they went into hiding, and for a fortnight their good Hindu friends brought them food and water. But one day they were betrayed; a mob came in the night and burned the house down. We learned later that the traitor was a neighbour of my father's. My father had helped him financially. This was how the man repaid him...." Dr. Jaffery shook his head. "In this city," he said, "culture and civilization have always been very thin dresses. It does not take much for that dress to be torn off and for what lies beneath to be revealed."

William Dalrymple is the author of In Xanadu *and* City of Djinns: A Year in Delhi, *from which this story is excerpted. He was born in Scotland and now divides his time between London and Edinburgh. He is married to the artist Olivia Fraser.*

★

I did not go to India in search of my soul, but just to be a foreign correspondent. But somehow from the beginning, I understood in India, as
never before, that virtue lies in rushing toward each day with its joys and
adventures, and even its pain, and that the only real sin is demeaning God's
gift of each day by turning away.

　　　　　　　　　—A. M. Rosenthal, "India's Gift: The Discovery of Each Day,"
　　　　　　　　　　　　　　　　　　　　　　　　　　　　　The New York Times

PALLAVA BAGLA

Predator

The Lady or the Tiger:
must we choose?

SHIVA'S FATHER HAS BEEN KILLED. MAULED BEYOND RECOGNITION, they tell me. With Shiva just turning ten, there is only despair ahead, for him, for his illiterate mother. I drive through the huge, broad-leaved forest with incredibly mixed feelings, painfully aware of the small-built ten-year-old crouching beside me. The fading summer evening settles light and eternal around us. The jeep bumps past a rough, tall, green bamboo haze, and I stop. My long-accustomed eyes have spotted a golden-yellow blur, and as I begin to stare into the bamboo clump, I know I have sighted a tiger.

Shiva sees it too, he is scared now. The child believes that he has caught up with his father's murderer. As the tiger emerges into full view, I can feel Shiva's elbow, poking me, urging me on. I know the child's fear and would be glad to allay it, but the accused feline holds me by an unseen force. Silent, huge, and so very elegant, so much in possession of himself. He moves slowly towards the jeep and I can see the muscles rippling under the gorgeous garb of black and golden-yellow. But it is those slightly slanting, beautiful eyes that keep me frozen. For want of any apt words to describe them, I can only call them "tiger-eyes."

The eyes of a killer? Shiva's eyes are only unbelieving. Scared, as he stares at me. Wondering, as he waits for me to lift my gun and slay this wicked man-eater who preens himself so shamelessly before us. I cannot take my eyes off the tiger. There are many years behind me, years of loving the wilderness, its wild children and the wild code of natural justice, its inexplicable, selfless generosity. Against all that I try—I really try hard—to hate this "man-eater," to stuff all my hatred into my hand, my mind, and my gun. I fail, and it is Shiva who begins to hate me, hard and strong.

Through this fog of my preoccupation, the bamboo haze swings back into focus. I see the tiger's back, receding into the slowly descending half-light. Has he sensed animosity? I wish—with a desperation alien to me—to communicate to him my harmless obeisance. I want him to know that to me he is a man-eater I cannot hate, a killer I cannot hunt, however much I try. And that I am grateful for this inadequacy in me, humbly grateful.

Perceiving my mood, or so I hope, my tiger reappears. Very, very close to the jeep. Gently and with colossal dignity. Shiva starts and clutches me. Holding the child, I watch the tiger's face. Each detail is so clear. I can even see the whiskers moving. There is a scar on his nose, an old wound? I will never know. It is not a haughty face, but it emanates strength, discipline, self-possession. All eight feet of him speak of wiry energy. And there are those eyes again, gold flecks dancing. Just then he blinks and turns away.

That blink is like the end of a chapter. He—they call him Sher Khan in the village—does not come back this time. The sound of the engine revving up under my unwilling hands is strange, enveloped as we are in the varied sounds of a jungle settling in for the night. I drive away, leaving my heart and soul behind.

Sher Khan is finally hunted down, by a man more competent, less philosophical than I am. As Shiva rejoices, Sher Khan becomes for me a grave symbol. He symbolizes the disturbed food chain, upset environmental balances, and the superficial concerns of wildlifers. I lose count of the number of times that I try to explain to Shiva the "law of diminishing returns." My theorizing is branded as urban rubbish, but I know—in my heart—that Sher

Khan's, or his clan's, man-eating "malady" has no cure in the muzzle of a gun. How many Sher Khans would you kill after all?

I know the facts, I have always known them. But, like a time-worn secret, my knowledge is useless. Only human killers are allowed the luxury called psychotherapy. Sher Khan is one of a large group of terrorized tigers. Terrorized by lethal, tiger-bone, tiger-blood, and tiger-skin poachers. Cold, unfeeling hunters who stalk the jungle by night. With weapons. Kill, cut, remove, disappear. And the tigers? Hunted, haunted, running scared. Pitiful ode to the king of the jungle. What of those "tiger-eaters" then? Why are they so free, so efficient, so confident?

There are epitaphs, yes. To Sher Khan and the likes of him, memories of tiger-filled forests are "heartening," say the well informed. To me, they must only be ignored if I must keep that old wound from smarting. There have been changes. Poachers do not wait for nightfall anymore. It is blatant, open, nothing to be clandestine about. Operations are more slick, sophisticated. Nobody need know anything.

What of the likes of Sher Khan then? The tigers that dwell in the wondrous, broad-leaved jungles of majestic teak and *saal*, the tigers that roam the bamboo fringes and the tigers that kill villagers and forest guards. If only they knew the kind of media attention they attract. That might even be an antidote to their problems. Or should one steer clear of sarcasm as Project Tiger celebrates its entry into adulthood?

Pallava Bagla was trained as a botanist but works as an editor and photographer. His first love is the wilderness, and he spent much of the past three years touring India's national parks and wildlife sanctuaries. He lives in Delhi.

✳

Tigers have always been poached. Villagers poison them to protect themselves or their livestock, and some skin smuggling has continued despite an international ban on the trade. But compared to the twin menaces of expanding population and dwindling habitat, poaching has been a relatively minor threat to the tiger's survival. Now that has changed. If allowed to continue at its current pace, poaching will swiftly undo whatever good Project Tiger [an Indian government conservation project] has managed to do over the past two decades.

The immediate crisis was caused by the peculiar demands of Chinese medicine. For hundreds, perhaps thousands, of years, tiger bones and other tiger by-products have played an important part in Chinese healing. The catalogue of physical ills which tiger bones and the elixirs brewed from them are supposed to cure includes rheumatism, convulsions, scabies, boils, dysentery, ulcers, typhoid, malaria, even prolapse of the anus. Tiger remedies are also said to alleviate fright, nervousness, and possession by devils. Ground tiger bone scattered on the roof is believed to bar demons and end nightmares for those who sleep beneath it. A "miraculous medicine" made from tiger bone and sold in Vietnam and elsewhere promises "six lovemakings a night to give birth to four sons."

The demands for these products is enormous, not only in China and Taiwan, but in South Korea and in Chinese communities throughout Southeast Asia and some Western communities as well. A single brewery in Taiwan imports two thousand kilograms of tiger bones a year—perhaps one hundred fifty tigers' worth—from which it brews one hundred thousand bottles of tiger-bone wine.

—Geoffrey Ward with Diane Ward, *Tiger-Wallahs: Encounters with the Men Who Tried to Save the Greatest of the Great Cats*

RORY NUGENT

The Calcutta Fowl Market

"Know thy poultry," said the sage.

IN THIS CITY WHERE STREET SIGNS ARE AS RARE AS TREES, I NEED some information. I've been wandering about Calcutta for a day and a half looking for a pink-headed duck, but the only people who will talk to me are shop owners and hucksters trying to sell me something. Then, by chance, I happen upon the Calcutta Tourist Office.

Inside, a kettle boils atop a stove, and the smell of Darjeeling tea scents the air. Three men in *dhotis* shuffle behind brooms, whisking them in a tired rhythm. The officials behind the reception desk appear preoccupied as they thumb through stacks of paper. As I touch a guidebook, a large man lifts his gaze to my face. His drooping jowls and double chin bury the knot of his tie.

Pink-headed duck

"Do you need help?" he asks in an indifferent voice.

"I sure do."

51

He nods, reaches into his coat pocket, and hands me a business card. His name is printed in Hindi and English, but appears impossible to pronounce. I decide to call him "Sir."

He motions for me to sit as I unfold a city map, the best one I could find. Yesterday, while searching bookstores, I discovered that maps of Calcutta are surprisingly inaccurate, missing streets, out of scale, and improperly oriented. Locals joke that the maps are a strategic ploy engineered by the army to confuse invading Pakistani generals.

"Ah, here we are," the official says, puncturing the map, obliterating lower Park Street with the tip of his pencil.

He proceeds to point out the usual tourist attractions, which are all clearly marked: the Botanical Gardens, Howrah Bridge, Victoria Memorial, Calcutta Museum, and other places that hold little appeal for me. Finally he asks where I want to go.

"Well, Sir, I'm trying to find the fowl market."

He swallows hard and tugs a jacket button.

I repeat my request. He looks even more surprised. Shaking his head disapprovingly, he grabs a legal pad.

Calcutta's lively performing-arts scene inspires the rest of the country. Its museum collections range from the whimsical to world-class. There's always time for another opinion and tumbler of coffee. Marching bands squawk through labyrinthine New Market on yet another Bengali holiday. There's so much activity and public living that the city, except in traffic jams, seems to be in fast forward. Wander the streets and talk with the people: Calcutta is a safe and friendly city. Cautious tourists shouldn't skip Calcutta because of horror stories. Stay put in the comfortable, less-crowded "downtown" (around Park St.) until you're ready to explore further. A sense of unity, a common language, and the intense cultural life anchor Bengalis—grumbling but not exploding—to the city. If you let it, Calcutta will burrow its way into your heart, too.

—Mary Orr, "India Sketches"

"Name," he demands, narrowing his jet-black eyes.

"Excuse me?"

"Name and passport." He's breathing heavily now. I hand over the document.

"Why do *you* want to go *there*?" he asks. "The market is not—umm, how shall I say—it is not very clean."

I have to smile. Calcutta is anything and everything but clean. Built atop a swamp the Mogul emperor Aurangzeb gladly rented to the English in the seventeenth century, it may be the dirtiest metropolis on earth. Several feet of backfill have not been enough to bury all the muck on which Britain floated its empire.

The 1991 census lists the city population at ten million, but an official at the West Bengal Welfare Department laughs at that figure, considering it absurdly low. For every person living in a building, at least two people live on the streets. If he's right, Calcutta qualifies as the most populous city in the world.

The official finished jotting down information from my passport and resumes his warning. "What I meant to say is that the fowl market is not a safe place. I cannot recommend it."

I say nothing, which makes him nervous and even more suspicious. As I soon learn, people sitting behind state desks interpret reticence as disagreement.

"You must answer me. Why do you want to go to the fowl market?" he says loudly, glancing about the room to make sure his colleagues are watching. If I'm arrested, he wants the others to know that he tried to discourage me.

"I'm looking for the pink-headed duck, Sir...a very rare bird."

He scribbles something and begins tapping his head with the pencil. "Who? Do you have an address?"

I explain that the pink-headed duck has no address, at least not a permanent one. Though half a dozen or so appeared each year in the Calcutta fowl market when Victoria ruled as empress, the bird hasn't been sighted for 50 years. And Calcutta, hub of the Raj, once the center of the pink duck trade, is the logical place to begin my search. I hope I'll find an old-timer in the fowl market who is familiar with the duck and can point me in the right direction.

The official covers his face with his meaty hands, muttering something I can't understand. I imagine him imploring Vishnu, the Hindu god of preservation, for protection. To calm him, I pull out a 1979 edition of Salim Ali's *The Book of Indian Birds*. The author is well known throughout India, and the book is published by the Bombay Natural History Society, keeper of all records concerning the pink-headed duck. I try to pass it to him, but he jerks his hand away and purses his lips. On page nineteen is a color illustration of the pink-headed duck. Pointing to it, I explain that the pink-headed duck is one of India's greatest treasures, a spectacularly plumed bird, and the rarest, most elusive duck in the world. This intrigues him, and he scrutinizes the plate. The bird's Hindi name is *gulab-sir*, but ornithologists refer to it as *Rhodonessa caryophyllacea*. The last confirmed sighting was in 1935 by a sportsman hunting in the Darbhanga area of Bihar. Unfortunately, he recognized the prize only after wresting it from the mouth of his retriever. Every attempt to breed the duck in captivity failed; in fact, within days of being caged, the birds appeared listless and refused food, defying the intentions of their captors. Without their freedom, pink-headed ducks, it seems, would rather be dead.

I explain that most naturalists believe the pink-headed duck is extinct, but my theory is that it's actually in hiding, having learned, for good reasons, to remain scarce. Although most of its natural habitat around Calcutta has been destroyed, there are still some isolated pockets of undisturbed marshland in the Bengal plain and suitable nesting spots in remote northeast India.

The official remains silent but no longer appears alarmed. I keep up my chatter, hoping that he, too, will appreciate the magic of this beautiful bird. The words tumble from my mouth. At last my fantasy takes shape for him and elicits a laugh.

"You're putting me on, aren't you?"

"No more that I do myself, Sir."

He returns to the map and traces an outline of the game-fowl market, which he refers to now as the easiest place to buy a bird in Calcutta. Handing the map back to me, he grins and says, "At first, I thought you were a drug addict or a smuggler."

"Heaven forbid!"

"Good luck," he says, pushing back his chair and rising. He's taller and fatter than I suspected. He hands me another business card. "Call me if you find it."

With ice a luxury, and refrigeration a symbol of wealth, Calcutta is a city of noxious odors. The fowl market is aptly named: I smelled it long before sighting it. I wander along its perimeter, surveying the countless small shops and street vendors hawking birds. Most of the birds are tied at the feet and dangle upside down, suspended from door frames, street posts, or the hands of children; pigeons are cooped ten to a cage; geese, throttled by short lengths of twine, are muted with rubber bands.

I'm uncertain where to begin my search until I spot a parked van and join the queue leading to it. Inside the vehicle an unmuffled generator jiggers loudly; a young man wearing a grease-stained *lungi* is haunched over a copy machine, tweaking knobs and feeding it documents. His

*O*nce I arrived in an Indian town exhausted after a long train ride. I found a cheap, nondescript place to stay, slept soundly for twelve hours, woke up, showered, and went exploring. Hours later, when it was time to head back, I couldn't remember the name of the hotel or where it was!

After months of staying in inns named after Lakshmi, Durga, and all the Indian gods, guest houses named Rose and Daffodil and every flower in a bouquet, and hotels named to reassure the wary traveler—Honest, Friendly, Clean Hotel—I simply blanked out.

That experience led to a simple new routine: each time I sign in at a new hotel, I take their business card and slip it into my pocket. It comes in handy when I ask for directions, especially if the name is written in more than one language. And, if I like the place, I tuck the card into my journal or pack to recommend to someone else.

◆

—Thalia Zepatos, *A Journey of One's Own: Uncommon Advice for the Independent Woman Traveler*

two associates lean out a window, conducting business under the sloppy red letters advertising "The Copy Shop."

Hastily I compose a poster of sorts, ripping a color plate from the book and taping the picture of the duck over the caption "LOST! Pink-Headed Duck." In smaller print is the name of my hotel and a request for any information about the bird. The blasting radio and noisy generator render speech useless, so I flash my order for 25 copies with my fingers. Acting like an anxious parent looking for a runaway child, I hastily post them around the district.

During my first couple of days in the fowl market, I feel dispirited and out of place. People on the street seem to keep their distance. Perhaps I do look odd: I'm the only Westerner walking the area, and because of my height, pale complexion, and baldness, I look a bit like a walking floor lamp, a Gyro Gearloose invention ambling the darker streets of Calcutta.

I develop a routine, awakening before dawn to meet the boats floating down the Hooghly River. Usually they are filled with fresh produce and laborers from the north. I inspect each cargo, hoping to find my duck, constantly showing skippers and crews a picture of the missing bird. By the time the sun slices through the haze coughed up by millions of cook fires, I head away from the river to a teahouse in the center of the fowl market.

Gradually I become more comfortable, and the workers of the district begin to accept me. Inquisitiveness replaces suspicion once they've decided that I'm not a policeman. A cardinal rule of the neighborhood is to avoid the police. "They mean trouble," one vendor informs me, "and who needs more of that?"

On the fourth day, everything changes: I'm invited to share a meal, street hawkers start greeting me as the Duck Man, and a few even seek me out before slaughtering their ducks. Soon captains of river boats are inviting me aboard, insisting on taking me for complimentary rides. On a Tuesday I cross the Hooghly sixteen times.

One day toward the end of the week, I finish my waterfront inspections early. The teahouse won't be open for another hour, so I walk downstream to a bathing *ghat* next to the flower market. Nearby, in the shadow of Howrah Bridge, four men stand in water up to their waists. Each is praying in a loud voice while splashing himself.

I strip and dive into the supposedly cleansing water of the Hooghly, a branch of the Ganges and a sacred channel flowing to the home of the gods. For a Hindu, the holiest way to leave this world is to have one's ashes scattered on the Ganges. I swim out toward the middle of the channel, diving for the bottom about fifty yards from shore. As I surface, something bumps the back of my head. Thinking it a stick, I thrust my hand out to fend it off. To my horror, my fingers sink into the spongy remains of a bloated, partially burned corpse. Seconds later my feet are on dry land.

Firewood is scarce in Calcutta because all of it must be transported from the dwindling forests to the north. The price is high everywhere but highest at the funeral *ghats*. Since the average family in Calcutta earns barely enough to subsist on, the bereaved can seldom afford enough wood to cremate an entire body. When the fires diminish, the remains are simply heaved into the river to be carried out to sea, beyond the beaches of Janput, nearly forty miles away.

Shaken, I rest for several minutes on the stone ramp, staring at my hand. An old man sitting nearby is watching me intently, so I wave and greet him in the traditional fashion, bowing with my hands outstretched, palms together. Ashes are smeared over much of his nearly naked body. He's wearing boxer shorts, and a bell hangs from his neck. Pulling on his beard, he shouts to me: "What did you say? Can you speak English? Your Bengali is awful….Come here and sit by me."

We spend the next several minutes talking about Albany, New York, where he worked as a cook in the early 1960s. He tells me his pigeon pie was famous, the best in the Empire State.

"The governor, that Rockyman, ate my pigeons all the time," he says, picking at his toes.

Upon hearing that Nelson Rockefeller is dead, he muses, "Hmmm…must have missed my cooking."

The old man has been watching me for days and wants to know what I'm doing in the district, which he refers to as his "kingdom."

I produce the illustration of the pink-headed duck and explain my search. As I talk, he nods in a knowing way, waiting for me to finish before holding out his hand and introducing himself: "Call me Babba, for I am without enemies."

Babba takes the picture of the duck and stares at it for some time. Then he starts to ring the bell around his neck and presses the picture to his forehead.

"Yes," he confides, leaning on my shoulder, ringing the bell louder. "Yes, I know this bird. I know where one lives."

"Let's go!" I exclaim, jumping to my feet. My enthusiasm is not contagious. He motions with his grimy hands for me to sit. Complaining that he's old and infirm, he tells me to calm myself. I continue to beg for directions until finally it occurs to me that money might be able to cure his painful condition. Yes, he will lead me for a price, assuring me that fifty rupees is the proper balm for his aching body. Babba, friend for life, is able to spot a meal ticket a hundred yards away.

I follow him as he hobbles along the narrow streets. People are selling goods and services of all types. "Sahib need girl? Yank. Yank. Feel good. Suck…Ah! Sahib want boy?" But my thoughts are fixated on the pink-headed duck with its cotton-candy feathers and electric-pink bill; not even the alluring smell of opium persuades me to tarry.

The streets deteriorate into alleys awash in green piss as we distance ourselves from the Hooghly and head ever deeper into one of the poorer, tougher parts of town. The decrepit, two-story tenements have dun-colored façades and stockyard odors. Water drips from hand pumps at every other corner. There are no cars and

> *I*ndians defecate everywhere. They defecate, mostly, beside the railway tracks. But they also defecate on the beaches; they defecate on the hills; they defecate on the river banks; they defecate on the streets; they never look for cover.
>
> ◆
>
> —V. S. Naipaul,
> *An Area of Darkness*

only a few pedal rickshaws, which, like the pedestrians, follow the English tradition of keeping the curb to the left. Groups of men squat near doorways. Whenever I get close, they stop talking and hurriedly fling shawls over items at their feet. Their scowls tell me to keep moving.

"Black market," Babba explains. "Do you need cigarettes? Ivory? Silver?"

Along the curb, rising like giant termite hills are mounds of trash encircled by human scavengers. Babba explains that recycling is the only legal industry in the area. For the trash pickers, still considered untouchable by many Brahmins, all bits of creation have value, anything can be reborn. Most garbage collection is a family affair, with children stalking the city, returning in the evening to their hovels with burlap bags of discarded treasures. Parents cull the heaps of trash, rearranging them into smaller piles. Cardboard is sold to one broker, tin to another; one buyer even specializes in pull rings from soda cans, paying a penny for every three gross.

"What's the name of this neighborhood?" I ask.

"Heaven's Gate."

At last my guide stops and waves his arthritic hand toward a small shop. "There, inside that place, you will find your duck," Babba declares as he turns to leave.

I grab his arm and remind him of his promise to show me the pink-headed duck. Steering him back on course, I make a mental note never again to pay in advance for guide services.

Four holy cows, painted with indigo and wearing garlands of marigolds, laze in front of the shop. Flies swarm in tight circles around a row of plucked chickens suspended in the open window. We walk inside slowly, allowing our eyes to adjust to the dimness. The pungent odors of the street mingle with the dank air of the shop. A cleaver lies on a blood-splattered newspaper near the pile of chicken heads oozing at one end of a butcher block. The dirt floor is littered with feathers and entrails.

An obese man emerges from the shadows. With each step, his body shakes, especially his gelatinous face, the color and texture of meat aspic. He talks hurriedly to Babba, far too fast for me to understand. Occasionally he stares at me, running his eyes over my body as if he's sizing up a flank of lamb. I retreat several paces, making sure Babba is between us.

Babba thanks the butcher and moves closer to me, saying, "Follow him to the back yard."

"You first."

We walk down a corridor too narrow for the fat man, who has to turn sideways to squeeze through. The light fades with every step, and shortly we're in total blackness. Alarmed, I pull out my flashlight and lag behind, ready to bolt. My apprehension is somewhat dispelled when I hear a muffled but unmistakable "quack." Ten steps farther on, we enter a shrouded courtyard. Stacks of bamboo cages rise up the walls; most of them are empty, but some contain chickens, none of which are moving. Feathers of all kinds cling to the wooden latticework. An industrial drum full of inky water sits in a corner by the entrance.

The butcher shuffles to the other end of the courtyard and grunts for me to follow. I stay put, shining the beam of my flashlight toward him. So far I've seen no ducks, only chickens.

"The ducks are on the other side," Babba informs me.

I focus the light on a cage the butcher is pointing to. He thrusts his fist inside as if punching someone. A "quack," loud and clear, draws me nearer. He pulls the bird out, attempting a smile as he speaks. "He says it's yours for nineteen rupees…a good price." Babba interprets.

I close in to identify the duck, steadying the light on its rust-colored bill. What? Yes, a rust bill and a dull brown neck. It's not a pink-headed duck but rather a common red-crested pochard, annual winter visitor to India.

"Please, don't tell him," Babba advises. "Just buy it and we can leave without trouble."

Babba grabs the duck and I hand over the money. Dejected, the two of us leave the shop. Babba doesn't want the pochard; he became a vegetarian long ago. Its wings have been clipped, so we can't release it. I give it to a family living on the street, and we walk back to the river along one of the city's larger avenues. The return trip takes half the time the original trek down the side streets, but as Babba explains, "You get your money's worth the other way."

At the bathing *ghat,* I decide to bid Babba farewell. This doesn't sit well with him.

"How can you leave me? How can you be so cruel? Are we not friends? Look at my legs, my hands…I will cook for you. Pigeon pie. Duck stew…."

"Enough," I shout and lead him into a teahouse.

Over sweet cakes, we agree that he will become my tutor, giving me language lessons for half of every day. He will also act as my guide, with the understanding that when I want to be alone, he will disappear. In return I'll pay him the fifteen dollars a day he has asked for.

This arrangement works well. Occasionally problems arise, but Babba is always quick to explain that I'm at fault. My morning routine stays the same, while the time I previously spent prowling the museums and libraries is given over to Hindi lessons. Babba uses the street as our classroom. We roam Calcutta together, Babba pointing something out and then stating its name in both Hindi and Bengali; a half block away, he tests me on the word or phrase. When I fail, he theatrically asks anyone nearby to help teach me. During the course of a normal afternoon we share pots of tea with four or five different people, all volunteer tutors.

One day, unbeknown to me, Babba tells the workers at the game-fowl market that I will pay a handsome fee for a pink-headed duck. This sends the cogs of local commerce into high gear. A day later, my thirteenth in Calcutta, while standing on the left bank of the Hooghly, I spot one of the riverboat captains sprinting toward me. He's carrying a bamboo cage containing three wildly pink ducks. Fortunately for the birds, the paint is latex and easily washes out.

Only hours later another pink bird is laid at my feet. Fluorescent overspray dapples the sandals of the eager seller, Amrik, a young man who usually peddles screwdrivers and wrenches near the bus stop. What attracts me to Amrik, besides his winning smile, is his capacity for lying. He swears that he has just scooped the bird from the river, insisting that the coloring of all Indian birds comes off when touched by foreigners.

"It's your white skin crying for color," he tells me, gently stroking the bird.

When I point out that he's holding not a duck but a red turtle-dove, he quickly corrects me: "It may look like a *biki* [dove] now, but it was a duck."

My eyebrows arch in disbelief; Babba turns away, wheezing, trying unsuccessfully to swallow his laughter. Amrik is undeterred. "It is true," he continues. "You see, when a pink duck leaves the water, it changes into a *biki*. If it was raining, it would still be a duck, but it is not raining today. That, my American friend, is why it looks like a *biki*. Don't you understand?"

For a small price I buy the distressed bird from him. As I sit in the back of the teahouse, swabbing the *biki* first with kerosene and then with soap and water, I decide to leave Calcutta. Originally I had planned to spend only five or six days in this city, and now I can foresee what will happen to me if Amrik brags of his sale, telling his pals that the American will buy any pink bird.

At first, Babba is angered by this news, but noting my reaction, he starts chastising himself for being inadequate. "I know why you leave. Because I am miserable, I make you miserable. Because I am poor, I make you feel poor. Because my bones ache, you suffer....Yes, you must go. Who wants to watch me die?"

He drones on and on as I try to think of a satisfactory way to part. I summon the owner of the tea shop, and after twenty minutes of haggling, we stand and shake hands. I've just leased the shop for the night in Babba's name. Like the mythical phoenix, Babba rises from the ashes of misery, becoming a new man. He will be the host of a party.

"There is much to do and little time," he says, excusing himself from the table. "I must invite everyone and keep an eye on the kitchen."

I leave for my hotel as Babba begins to harangue the shop attendants, ordering them to clean the place. It's a thirty-minute walk to the Rest Happy Lodge, my residence for the past week. I chose it for its name, cheap price (six dollars a night), and pleasant staff. It's the perfect antidote to the Fairlawn Hotel, where I spent my first nights in the company of impolite Westerners, burly Australians, and Japanese shutter-clickers. Where the Fairlawn aspires to recreate the atmosphere of the Raj (the employees dress in silly get-ups and call the guests Sahib or Memsab), the Rest Happy, not listed in any brochure, doesn't pretend to be more than it is: a quiet place run by a sleepy family.

Packing is no great chore for me; I'm content to wear the same outfit for days on end. If I need something new or fresh, I buy it. But when it comes to camping and camera supplies, experience has taught me to arrive in a foreign country fully equipped. My gear fills two bags and weighs nearly fifteen kilos. Cameras and film count for most of the weight, and the remainder is survival or medical equipment. I've also brought a variety of presents to give away at opportune moments: a gross of "New York, New York" pencils, a dozen wrist watches with built-in AM radios, plenty of 3-D pins of Godzilla, and a hundred disposable lighters printed with the image of Michael Jackson.

Two hours later there's a sharp knock at my door. Babba has sent some of his friends to escort me to the party. What a pleasant surprise, I think, until one of them tells me to hurry: the dining and music can't start until I arrive. Music?…I didn't hire musicians.

The teahouse is packed; the entire neighborhood seems to be here. Babba is king tonight, and he breaks away from his court to greet me. To my relief he reports that the musicians and the special items he has added to the menu cost less than twenty dollars.

"What's a party without music, Searcher of the Duck?" he asks.

All along I've assumed Babba to be celibate, a man dedicating the last part of his life to god. But as the night rolls on, his true self is revealed. Instead of walking, he starts sashaying; his hands rove and his skinny legs straddle anything warm and round. When I ask him about this, he stands on a chair to shout, "I love sex."

Luckily, only three people brought painted birds to the party. Without much argument, they agree to clean off the birds before joining the festivities. Although many Hindus are disdainful of liquor and drugs, this crowd, the citizens of the fowl market, swig from flasks and light pipes filled with various substances. Off in a corner, near the musicians, people dance, using their eyes and hands to interpret the lively *ragas*. The party is a success and continues, I'm sure, long after I've left. A little after midnight, as I make my exit, Babba stops the music to make a toast. His words follow me all the way to the hotel.

"To the gods, to us, to the pink-headed duck!"

Rory Nugent has sailed the Atlantic by himself numerous times and looked for dinosaurs in the Congo. He was born in New York, graduated from Williams College and now lives in New Bedford, Massachusetts. In The New Yorker, *George S. Trow said of him: "If the world ended, I'd want to be with my friend Rory because he would find a way for it not to end—up to a point, that is. He'd gravitate to the small part that wasn't going to end, because of some obscure hitch: a colonial contract that was still in force, perhaps." This story was excerpted from his book* The Search for the Pink-Headed Duck: A Journey into the Himalayas and Down the Brahmaputra.

★

Calcutta was born in 1690, nearly a century after that historic launching of the East India Company in London. Job Charnock landed in the village of Sutanati at the mouth of the Hooghly, and pitched his tents to found a city called Calcutta and sow the seeds of the mightiest empire the world has ever known.

In 1756, the new *nawab,* Siraj-ud-daula, ascended the throne in Murshidabad at the age of twenty-five. He looked around his mini-empire and decided that the British down south in a strange place called Calcutta were getting too big for their boots. So he embarked on an impulsive attempt to enrich himself quickly by grabbing all those masses of golden coins that the foreigners were rumored to have stuffed in their vaults.

The *nawab* decimated the British. Governor Roger Drake fled down the Hooghly in ignominious defeat. Anyone who could, did likewise. The conquering forces of Siraj-ud-daula imprisoned 146 English captives in an eighteen-cubic-foot underground cell with one window, when the temperature outside was over 100°F. Next morning, on June 20, 1756, when the door to the prison was opened by the warders, there were only twenty-three people still alive. One hundred and twenty three men and women had died overnight, in an episode that would be forever immortalized as the "Black Hole of Calcutta." At least this is the received version of the incident in British history books. Local historians dispute the veracity of the tale.

Six months after the tragedy, Robert Clive returned from Madras with an armada of ships, soldiers, and munitions to wreak the most monumental revenge in recent military history. He recaptured Calcutta in one short night and went on to defeat both Siraj-ud-daula and the French army captain Dupleix—who had sided with the Muslim ruler in the earlier battle.

It was in Calcutta that India was humiliated as she had never been before.

At about the same time, George Washington was unshackling his country from the British yoke…When His Britannic Majesty had lost both his head and his North American dominions, India was to provide a soothing solace.

—Sasthi Brata, *India: Labyrinths in the Lotusland*

MADHUR JAFFREY

✦ ✦ ✦

Food for Body and Spirit

*The author tells us just how big
the taste bud spectrum is.*

AS A CHILD GROWING UP IN DELHI, NOTHING EXCITED ME MORE than an announcement by my middle uncle that he had asked the *khomcha-wallah* over for our Saturday tea. That was akin to telling a Western child that he could have a whole sweet or candy shop for an entire afternoon.

A *khomcha-wallah*, as it happened, had nothing sweet to offer. His normal habitat was the street, usually busy thoroughfares. Here he wandered eternally, or so it seemed to me, a basket balanced on his sturdy head, a cane stool tucked into the crook of his free arm. Whenever the crowd seemed promising, he set his stool down, lowered his basket to rest on it, and then began hawking his wares.

The basket was a mini-shop, containing a category of foods unknown in the West—hot, sour, and savory snacks known through much of North India as *chaat*. The food was half-prepared and many permutations—of ingredients, seasonings, sauces, and dressings—were possible. If one asked, say, for *dahi baras*, the *khomcha-wallah* would take split pea patties (they had already been fried and softened in warm water, which also got rid of their oiliness) and put them on a "plate" of large, semi-dried leaves. Then he took some plain yogurt, beaten to a creamy consistency, and spread it over the top. Over the yogurt went the salt and one or more of the yellow, red and black spice mixtures that sat in the wide bowls. Those who wanted a mild, cumin-black pepper-dried mango flavor got only the black mixture. Those who said gleefully like I did, "Make it very hot," also got the yellow and red mixtures, filled with several varieties of chilies. If we had an extra craving for a sweet-and-sour taste, we could ask for a tamarind chutney. A wooden spoon would disappear into the depths of a brown sauce, as thick as melted chocolate. It would emerge only to drop a dark, satiny swirl over our *dahi baras*. As we ate them, the *dahi baras* would melt in our mouths with the minimum of resistance, the hot spices would bring tears to our eyes, the yogurt would cool us down and the tamarind would perk up our taste buds as nothing else could. This, to us, was heaven.

From childhood onwards, an Indian is exposed to more combinations of flavors and seasonings than perhaps anyone else in the world. Our cuisine is based on this variety, which, in flavors, encompasses hot-and-sour, hot-and-nutty, sweet-and-hot, bitter-and-hot, bitter-and-sour and sweet-and-salty; in seasonings, it stretches from the freshness and sweetness of highly aromatic curry leaves to the dark pungency of the resin, asafetida, whose earthy aroma tends to startle Westerners just as much as the smell of a strong, ripe cheese does Indians.

Our spice shelves often contain more than thirty seasonings. The Indian genius lies not only in squeezing several flavors out of the same spice by roasting it, grinding it or popping it whole into hot oil (a technique known as *baghar*), but in combining seasonings—curry leaves with popped mustard seeds, ground roasted cumin seeds with mint, ginger and garlic with green chilies—to create a vast spectrum of tastes. It is this total mastery over seasonings that makes Indian foods quite unique.

When I was growing up in India and there was plenty of help around, most kitchens (and I speak here only of affluent homes), aside from having cooks and bearers, also had a *masalchi*, an underling to whose lot fell the tedious task of grinding, on a heavy stone, twice a day, all the spices the cook deemed necessary. The *masalchi* would arrange little hills of yellows, browns and greens on a metal plate, sometimes single seasonings such as turmeric, fresh coriander, and ginger, sometimes mixtures of, say, cloves, cinnamon, nutmeg, mace, and black pepper, all ground in one lot for a specific dish. Once this chore was done, it was the job of the expert—either the housewife or the head cook—to combine different spices for different dishes—ground spices with whole ones, roasted spices with fresh herbs—and to cook them to just the necessary degree. My mother, when asked to comment on a dish (cooked in a house other than her own, needless to say), might venture the opinion, "Well, it was all right, I suppose, but the spices did taste a bit raw." For maximum effect, the spices needed to be not only expertly blended but expertly cooked as well.

As sold in the West, curry powder contains powdered cumin, coriander, cardamom, fenugreek, and turmeric. Traditionally Bengalis have preferred not to use a ready-ground spice mix such as curry powder. Instead they combine different spices for each dish to enhance the unique flavor of the ingredients. Also, if you use curry powder, all your curry dishes, whether chicken curry, beef curry, or potato curry, will taste alike.

◆

—Bharti Kirchner, *The Healthy Cuisine of India: Recipes from the Bengal Region*

If the choice of seasoning gives one kind of variety to Indian foods, regional traditions give it quite another. India is a large country. Its size came home to me for the first time when I was still in school. But it was not in the classroom. Our official school atlases (India was still a British colony then) had the British Isles on one page, India on another. To a child, they looked just about the same size. Then, one day an older cousin brought home an "underground" book distributed secretly by Indian freedom fighters. There was much excitement as we poured over its illicit pages. One of the pages showed an outline of India and, fitted neatly inside it, as in a jigsaw puzzle, was not just the British Isles, but all of Europe except for Russia. We were very impressed.

The country is vast, and, rather like Europe, it is not homogeneous. Before independence, it consisted of about six hundred semi-independent kingdoms ruled over by Hindu maharajahs and Muslim *nawabs* under British supervision, as well as large tracts of land ruled directly by the British, land that the British had divided, as and when they acquired it, into governable provinces. There were about fifteen major languages spoken across the land, as well as 1,652 minor languages and dialects, and the people belonged to at least five major faiths.

With independence, the princely kingdoms were "coaxed" into merging with India. When the Indian government began the task of dividing this huge land into states, it wisely followed the line of least resistance and divided the country up on a linguistic basis. Each area with a major language and culture was given its own state. The idea of forcing a common language on the country has been shelved time and time again. The people are just not amenable to being herded into a melting pot. They are proud of their separate cultures. Many have traditions (as well as poetry and literature) that go back a thousand years, and they are not about to give them up. This is true of foods as well, which are as different from one state to the next as, say, French food is from that of its neighbors, Italy and Spain.

India is, in that sense, very similar to Europe, with each state rather like each European nation, having not only its own language, culture, and foods, but its own history, its own unique geography, and its own set of dominant religions. There are, of course features that link all the states. We do, after all, have one central government. The entire country was influenced by Muslim rule, which began in earnest around the eleventh century, and later, by British colonization. And, where foods are concerned, the whole country has in common the total command over spices and seasonings.

But these foods are quite different from state to state. It is a pity that most of the Indian restaurants scattered across the world do not reflect our richly varied cuisine. They could have been the perfect showcase. One can hardly blame them, though. India has had no long tradition of fine public dining such as exists in France or Japan. Upper-class Hindus, who rarely crossed the "seven seas" for fear of losing caste and whose meals had to be cooked and served by freshly bathed Brahmins, could scarcely be expected to dine in public places where the food had been prepared and touched by God knows who. Even in my family, where we were quite liberal, I never took a sip from my sister's glass or a bite from her apple. At least not without my mother's disapproval. Any food eaten by someone else was considered "unclean" or *jhoota*.

With such taboos, fine restaurants did not get going until after Indian independence in 1947. It just so happened that the first few were owned and run by Punjabis. The food they served was vaguely Punjabi, vaguely North Indian "royal." The menu stuck. Restaurant after restaurant copied it. Home-style foods were never served, as it was felt, quite rightly I suppose, that no Indian would want to go out and pay for something that he could get in his own house. Regional foods were never served, because no one wanted to risk altering a successful formula.

While Indian restaurant food can be quite good, it is a world unto itself. India hides its real food—and the best of its food—in millions of private homes, rich and poor, scattered across its provinces. In the temperate state of Kashmir, tucked into the highest mountains of the world, I have eaten a wonderful dish of dried turnip rings cooked with sun-dried tomatoes. Snow covers much of the land in the winter so, come autumn, everything that can be dried is festooned around rafters, ceilings and roofs. The local tea, a green tea similar to some Chinese teas, is served sprinkled with almonds and cinnamon, ingredients which are known to warm the body. In tropical Tamil Nadu, where the needs of the body are quite the opposite, I have dined on superb crabs poached in a tart tamarind broth. Tamarind is cooling. Much of the South uses its temperature very cleverly to take care of some of the culinary details. Many staple dishes here require fermentation. No yeasts are used, as the mean temperature of about 80°F (25°C) does the work quite effortlessly. *Idlis*, small savory rice cakes, made faintly sour by an overnight fermentation, are served up for millions of southern breakfasts. They rely almost entirely on the weather to change a batter of ground rice and split peas into a light froth which only requires a quick steaming to become a deliciously light, highly nutritious and very digestible breakfast dish.

The South does a great deal of its cooking over steam, as a result of which every single home is equipped with large and small steaming pots. The North, where I come from, does not do any steaming at all, though it does use a technique learned from Muslim rulers known as "doing a dum." For this, half-cooked rice and meat dishes, usually liberally sprinkled with aromatic flavorings such as attars, saffron, *garam masala*, and browned onions, are put into a pot and the lid clamped shut with a seal of dough. The pot is then placed over a thin layer of smoldering ashes. A few embers are placed on the lid as well. The dish "bakes" thus, slowly and gently. When the lid is removed, the foods are not only cooked through, but quite impregnated with haunting aromas.

Even within states, some foods are common to most of the

> The pulp of the tamarind fruit, an important source of vitamin C, is a popular ingredient in the curries and preserves of South India, a region known for its punishingly hot summers. Valued as an antidote to heat stroke, tamarind pods are often preserved in salt and sold by weight so that they can be mixed with molasses and water to provide a sherbet which is both cheap and capable of lowering body temperatures. Mixed with salted water the pulp makes a laxative so gentle it is even administered to children suffering from stomach disorders.
>
> ◆
>
> —Naveen Patnaik, *The Garden of Life: An Introduction to the Healing Plants of India*

people while others are cooked only by special communities. In Tamil Nadu, for example, I have been served foods preceded by remarks such as "this is a typical Iyer Brahmin dish," or "only we Chettiyars [a trading community] make this." The Muslim Mopals of Kerala serve stunning rice pilafs, as most Muslims do throughout India. Pilafs, after all, came to us from the Middle East. Even the Indian word for pilaf, *pullao*, is a corruption of the Persian *polo*. But, as with everything in India, the Keralites have modified the pilaf to suit their own tastes and conditions. On this coastal strip, the most favored pilaf is studded with fresh Arabian Sea prawns, subtly flavored with coconut milk!

All Indian food is served with either rice or bread or both, following each other in succession. In the North, it is whole-wheat breads, such as *chapatis* and *parathas*, that are commonly eaten, and in the South it is plain rice. The traditional Indian bread used to be flat, baked on cast-iron griddles rather like tortillas. The Muslims introduced ovens where sour dough and plain breads—such as *naans* and *shirmals*—could be baked. Those with natural yeast managed to rise almost an inch. The Europeans (Dutch, French, Portuguese and English) outdid the Muslims, coming in with fat, yeasty loaves. The first Indian to set his eyes on one must have been left quite stunned. The Indians called this new bread *dubble roti*, or "the double bread," and happily used it to mop up good juices of many spicy stews. No foreign food was discarded. It was just made Indian. I remember that one of our favorite treats as children was to come home from school, kick off our restricting shoes and socks and pad in our loose Indian sandals to the pantry, where an obliging oven kept the leftovers from our parents' lunch warm for our after-school snacks. Sometimes there were *chapatis*, into which we would roll up some *sookhe aloo*, dry, well-spiced potatoes, and then gobble them up. At other times we would slice off about two inches from an end of a crusty *dubble roti*. The soft, fluffy part of the slice would be dug out and discarded—usually fed to the parrots in the garden. The hollow that resulted was filled with meat *koma* or whatever dish happened to be in the oven. A little mango pickle was sprinkled over the top. We then carried this treasure over to the study. Homework suddenly became almost bearable. Of course when my mother yelled out, wanting to know who had cut off both ends of both loaves of bread, we just giggled hysterically and buried our heads in our books.

The meat served in most Indian homes is generally fresh goat meat. The English referred to it as "mutton" and that is what Indians speaking English call it to this day. I refer to it as "lamb," simply because, in the recipes, Western lamb is the nearest equivalent to our goat and because phrases like "leg of goat" sound somewhat less than felicitous. If the English could get away with "mutton," I could get away with "lamb."

At most Indian meals, aside from the meat, vegetables, split peas, and rice or bread that are served, there are invariably relishes, yogurt dishes, pickles, and chutneys. They round off the full cycle of flavors and textures, adding bite, pungency, and often vital vitamins and minerals as well. They also perk up the appetite, which tends to get sluggish in the hot weather (though, I must add, I have never suffered from this alleged sluggishness).

We eat with our hands—with the right hand, specifically, the left being used to pick up glasses of water or to serve ourselves more food. Finicky Northerners use just the very tips of their fingers, while Southerners, rather impatient with Northern pretensions, think of the whole hand as an implement—rather like a spoon—and use any part of it if they deem suitable.

Around the world, food is eaten to fill stomachs and to keep bodies strong and healthy. In India, there is, frequently, a shift in emphasis. We, like everyone else, eat to survive, but we also eat to keep our bodies finely tuned, physically and spiritually.

The physical fine-tuning is achieved by a series of weekly fasts to "cleanse the system," and by careful selection of the seasoning used in daily meals. According to the ancient Indian system of Ayurvedic medicine, all spices and herbs have been assigned medical properties. Turmeric, for example, is an antiseptic, both internal and external. Perhaps that is why it is always applied to fish before it is fried. Asafetida is a digestive which combats flatulence. Hence it is always put into pots of dried beans and split peas.

Garlic is good for circulatory ailments, coriander and tamarind for constipation, cloves for toning up the heart, and black pepper for giving energy to new mothers. Indians, however subliminally, are aware of this as they cook. I remember arriving in the city of Lucknow recently with the most depressing cough and cold. My octogenarian aunt, whom I was visiting, had already noticed that I had my tea without milk and sugar, my toast without butter, and that I declined offers of clotted cream (*malai*) that the city residents are very partial to. "No wonder you are sick," my aunt declared. "But I will fix you up." At that, she disappeared, returning with a special tea, made with fresh ginger, black peppercorns, cloves, holy basil leaves (*tulsi*), and a little sugar. I do not know if it was my aunt's gentle ministrations or the tea, but I did start to feel much better.

Fine-tuning the spirit is quite another matter which appeared, at first, very puzzling to me. Millions of Hindus are vegetarian. Three thousand years ago however, our forbears were meat eaters. They even ate beef. Somewhere, as the B.C.s were changing to the A.D.s, the cult, if one can call it that, of vegetarianism began to take hold—and grow. It might have been influenced by Buddhism and Jainism, two very successful movements that preached *ahimsa* or the "non-hurting of life." Around this time, the cow also became sacred and its meat taboo. But Hindu vegetarianism today seemed, as I examined it, to have less to do with the hurting of animals than with advancing the individual spirit along its upward path. I discovered that on holy days and on days of partial fasts, it was considered acceptable for vegetarians to eat tubers, *moong dal*, and rice. Aubergines and tomatoes were not acceptable. Neither was brandy. I did not have much hope for brandy but I did want to know just how it was decided that one vegetarian product was better than another.

Answers were either unavailable or were of the "my mother and grandmother did it" variety. Finally a friend, the author of a book on Hinduism, offered the explanation which I paraphrase here: In Hinduism, our earthly journey from birth to death is divided into four parts. At first we are students and our duty is to study the scriptures, arts, and sciences. Then we are householders and our duty is to raise and look after our families. But throughout our journey on earth, our souls are seeking union with the Universal Soul, God. To achieve this, starting with the third stage, *vanaprastha* (literally, "retiring to the forest"), we must move away from worldly things and from all "negative forces" in order to allow our "soul force" to rise upwards. By the fourth stage, which few achieve, we should be totally detached ascetics.

All things (my friend continued) have their own magnetic force: some are negative, some positive. This applies to everything we eat. The only foods that Hindus should eat on days of partial fasts—and during their later life—are the positive ones.

But how does one know which foods are "positive" and which "negative?" For most Indians, tradition suffices. Patterns laid down by ancestors are followed without questioning. Those who, like myself, question endlessly, can resort to a "test," devised, I was told by my friend, by a Swami Poornananda. If a certain seed, a

*O*n one level of explanation, cow protection, beef avoidance, and the large number of useless cattle can all be safely attributed to religious zeal. Hinduism is the dominant religion of India, and cattle worship and cattle protection lie at the very heart of Hinduism. Few Westerners realize, for example, that one of the reasons for the saintly reputation and mass appeal of Mohandas Gandhi is that he was an ardent believer in the Hindu doctrine of cow protection. In Gandhi's words: "The central fact of Hinduism is cow protection.... Cow protection is the gift of Hinduism to the world.... Hinduism will live as long as there are Hindus to protect the cow."

♦

—Marvin Harris, *The Sacred Cow and the Abominable Pig: Riddles of Food and Culture*

rudraksha, were to be suspended by a thread over a given food, it would begin to swing clockwise if the food was "positive," counterclockwise if the food was "negative."

Could we do the test, I wanted to know. We set up a time and place. All kinds of food, from salt to nuts, were laid out on a large table at some distance from each other. The *rudraksha* did, indeed, swing in circles, sometimes wildly, sometimes gently, confirming, as I later found out, the detailed calibrations of the Swami. Onions were very "negative." The seed seemed to show active anger as it swung. Ginger was as "positive" as onions were "negative." Salt was on the "negative" list, as were garlic cloves, sugar, aubergines, tomatoes, and red chilies. On the "positive" list were honey, *ghee*, *toovar dal*, *moong dal*, limes, almonds, apples, rice, turmeric, ginger, and green chilies. Potatoes were neutral. They seemed to mesmerize the seed to a standstill.

You may make of this what you will. I know that Indian foods from all its different regions will thrill your palates. They may, if you play your cards right, even uplift your soul.

Madhur Jaffrey is an author and actress who grew up in Delhi and lives in New York. She is known for her books on Indian cuisine, and has appeared in films, on stage, in television and radio plays. This story is excerpted from her book, A Taste of India.

★

Here are some rules for street dining in India. Following them, I never got sick:

Eat the food when it is freshly prepared. It may take you a while to figure out which food is fresh and which isn't. When people crowd around a certain cart or fill the tables at open restaurants, you know that the time is right.

Make sure the cooks look clean and neat, and that the stall or cart is well-organized. A swept dirt floor is superior to a messy marble one.

Pots or plates should be covered. Choose places that serve on disposable leaves and terra-cotta bowls. Notice if diners include families and women.

Go to places near the market and where there are the most people and commercial activity. Find out what streets or parts of the city specialize in certain dishes and eat them there; you can ask the doorman at your hotel.

Drink only bottled water, boiled tea or bottled soda. Some fruit drinks or yogurt drinks such as *lassi* may have unbottled water or ice mixed into them.

—Patricia Unterman, "Culinary Nirvana in the Streets of India,"
San Francisco Chronicle

PETER AIKEN

The Boxer from Calcutta

An unemployed stenographer and former prize-fighter
provides a simple lesson in footwork.

WE DECIDED TO BREAK THE FLIGHT UP BETWEEN BANGKOK AND Nepal by stopping in Calcutta. Leslie, a photographer I was traveling with, was reluctant. She would rather have the mountain views of Darjeeling.

"We'll see enough mountains in Nepal. This city is a human phenomenon," I told her. "It will be fascinating."

"But nobody goes to Calcutta," she said. "It's just another over-crowded city."

The bus from Calcutta Airport dodged some of the boniest white cows on earth. Their hides draped loosely over skeletal haunches, they nosed against the dry earth for edibles. Women in saris squatted by the roadside arranging cow dung into patties to be sundried for fuel.

We checked into a hostel in the city center that was recommended as being clean, inexpensive, and a good place to get information.

In the hallway, I asked a fellow traveler what he was doing in the city. I said, "What's there to see?"

"In the park, there's a man selling peanuts to feed the rats that are all around him and on the way to the bridge is a tree with no leaves full of vultures. It's near the cemetery."

He gave directions and we found what he said was true. Leslie had had enough and retired to our room. I continued to Howrah Bridge.

I stopped to photograph a street scene with beggars sitting on the sidewalk. A man in white walked up to me and said, without introduction, "I am tired of tourists taking pictures of only the nasty things here. When I go to another country, I try to keep memories of the good things."

He was just the man I was looking for. I was about to ask him where the good things were when he turned on his heels and was gone.

I walked on to the bridge and soon reached the bank of the Hooghly River.

Teeming would be the word—there were thousands of people in sight going about their business; holy men on the banks exercising, foot porters pulling huge baled carts, women with thin crying babies holding up out-stretched palms for alms, Sikhs with turbaned heads. No tourists in sight.

When I lined up a picture of the bridge, someone cried out, "CIA!" I was confused but took the shot. A policeman walked up behind me and asked what I was doing.

I told him.

"Bridges," he said, "are vital military targets in India and it is forbidden to photograph them."

I apologized and left quickly, wondering how it was possible the enemy didn't have accurate information on this ancient bridge traversed by millions.

I was stopped once more on my return. While photographing a conference of large black ravens on the riverbank, a stocky Indian dressed in western clothes approached me and I put away the camera. The ravens had looked harmless enough.

"Good afternoon, sir," he said.

I was relieved but wary.

"Good afternoon," I replied.

"Do you know anyone in need of a good stenographer, sir?"

"No, I don't believe I do. I'm a visitor here."

"Sir, you look trustworthy," he said and came closer. "I am in trouble. I am a true Christian like yourself, sir, but I am an Indian with a Christian name and these Indians here don't give us a chance. They call us turncoats and we can't find work."

Rather than tell him I was a Buddhist and completely confuse the issue, I kept quiet. I wanted to hear the whole story.

"Sir, please read this," he said and handed me a worn, typed letter. On it was written this:

St. Xavier's School
4 Ludlow Castle Road
Delhi 6

Dear Mr. Manly,

You may be offering a post to Mr. Lawrence Mitchell. I have known him since a boy and he is a good man. But he will probably tell you that he has been in jail for ten years. This is because of genuine misfortune. He was traveling in a train with a man who tried to attack him and throw away his Bible—in self defense he struck him. He is a trained boxer—he hit too hard in the solar plexus, so the man died instantly. The magistrate should have given a verdict of accidental death but gave one of manslaughter. Mitchell is not a bad man but was overtaken by catastrophe. So I hope this will not spoil his record. He deserves a chance to make good.

Yours Sincerely,
Father Luke

"Sir, why are you copying this down?"

"If I find someone who needs a stenographer, I'll be able to show this to him."

"But I need assistance now. I have a job waiting for me in Delhi."

He took out another letter postmarked Delhi.

"I don't have enough for the train fare. I waited six days on the road and no one would give me a lift."

"They noticed you were Christian?"

He pretended not to hear.

"Can you help me sir? I would like to catch the 4 p.m."

I gave him some rupees and wished him luck.

That evening over a platter of *tandoori* chicken, Leslie told me of the silk she had bought at bargain prices.

"The only thing I bought today," I said, "was a man's ticket to Delhi."

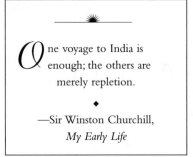

*O*ne voyage to India is enough; the others are merely repletion.

◆

—Sir Winston Churchill,
My Early Life

"Was he a stocky man looking for work?"

"As a stenographer."

"But he was going to Varanasi," she protested.

"Either there are a lot of unemployed stenographers in this city or you just got the cheaper fare," I said.

"All of the half-starved people and we give to him. He was one of the healthiest men I saw all day."

"He was a boxer, remember?"

Peter Aiken is an author and photographer who has traveled the world in search of the perfect bridge. He lives in Nantucket, Massachusetts.

✳

I was standing on a street corner. A few pedicab drivers were lounging under an awning, awaiting customers who seemed unlikely to come. After a few minutes, one of them detached himself from the group and came up to me.

"Tell me, sir," he asked, "do you think violence is inherent in the heart of man, or is it learned?" I said I thought it was probably inherent, that it had to be unlearned. The other drivers came over. We had a seminar. It lasted an hour, under the hot sun.

—Jon Carroll, "Phantom India Stays in the Mind,"
San Francisco Chronicle

JAN HAAG

✦ ✦ ✦

A Wedding in Mahabaleshwar

An uninvited guest enters the foreign world
of a Muslim wedding and is
treated like family.

IN THE LATE AFTERNOON OF A HOT FEBRUARY DAY, I WAS SITTING
in a restaurant in Mahabaleshwar with a man from Pakistan. I met
him on the bus from Poona when a whole crowded busload
missed death by one propitiously placed, *huge* boulder, which
stopped us from plunging over a cliff when the bus lost its brakes.
Having become friends, the Pakistani man and I had successfully
gone guesthouse hunting together and were now having supper.
He was waiting to have his meat, and I was waiting to have my
vegetables as we sat on an open veranda high above the street.
Below us, the terraces of the Raj's once famous "hill station" descended step by step down the mountain. It was the time of year
when many Indians take their vacations; the town was full. I was
looking up the street, which was crammed, as all Indian streets are,
with people walking and sitting and living and being.

Suddenly the crowd erupted. People, who had been walking or
standing in the middle of the street, scattered back. A band of men,
leaping and hunched, straightening up and doubling over, singing,
and playing drums, beating on pots and pans, indeed, pounding on
anything that would make noise, came whirling and dancing
along. As they moved down the street they circled around a pranc-

ing white horse. Astride the horse sat a man, hung like a Maypole with maybe a hundred ribbons on which were strung white flowers. The ribbons flowed down from his head and cascaded over the horse like streams from a fountain. The blossoms looked like stephanotis: little, waxy-white, trumpet-shaped flowers with their maws facing downward. At points along the ribbons, the white flowers were interspersed with small crimson roses. The horse lifted its hooves high; the man sat perfectly still. His companions drummed, cried out, leapt, laughed, and sang.

"What is it?" I asked my companion.

"A wedding," he said, "a Muslim wedding."

"Is that the groom?"

"And his friends."

"And the bride?"

"She's at home. Would you like to go?"

"Go?"

"To the wedding?"

"Do you know them?"

"They would be delighted to have you."

I giggled. I couldn't imagine dropping in on the wedding of someone neither he nor I knew. Nonetheless, I had been wandering the subcontinent long enough to shed some of my American "cool," and had even began to develop some of the friendly nosiness and ravenous curiosity of an Indian. I watched as the beautifully flowered young man came by. His head was bowed under a crown, and the ribbons of stephanotis were so dense around his face that I couldn't see through them. "Yes, let's go," I said. But still unable to shake the Western ideas of decorum, I couldn't help adding, "If we may."

My Pakistani friend then assured me he couldn't go, but that I must.

"Why can't you go?"

"It wouldn't be proper."

I never did get quite clear on his reasoning. It might have been that he was unmarried, and, therefore, mustn't go to a wedding; or that he, a Pakistani, was in India somewhat illegally, and, therefore, mustn't be seen at anything so public as a wedding; or that it was unseemly for a strange man to go to a wedding, but not for a strange woman; or that he, as a Muslim, mustn't look upon a woman who was a bride. I never did quite understand his explanation, but my curiosity pulled me to see more of the ceremony that included this enchanting "knight" on the white horse: a flower bedecked version of the dreams of all Western maidens. I fancied that, above the scent of the street, the spice and dung odor of all Indian streets, I could even smell the flowers. I had never seen any-thing—anyone—so beautiful. In his long white satin tunic and his tight white satin pants on the white horse with the white flowers, he was a veritable vision of loveliness.

But we needn't, my friend assured me, hurry. The groom, he said, would ride all over town with his friends dancing and singing and drumming before the wedding began.

Then, though I wasn't aware of it at the time, my Pakistani friend must have excused himself or spoken to a waiter to find out where the wedding was, for when we had finished our meal, he directed me, without hesitation, down an immensely long flight of steps. Ancient and uneven, they flowed from the terrace we had been on to the level below between mud-walled and stone buildings. Along with my tiny orange backpack and my shawl over my shoulder, I carried in my hands a small newspaper-wrapped parcel of black raspberries I had bought when we had strolled, at sunset, out to the famous waterfalls through the strawberry fields.

As we turned the corner from the step at the bottom into a wide dusty street, I saw a great crowd milling about. A hundred feet down the road was a large area covered with awnings attached to poles and to the surrounding buildings. Beneath the shelter at the end nearest to us was an empty platform, and on another platform, opposite the street side, were chairs. However, I couldn't see the far end of the covered area because one wall of a small building hid the view. On the street side, there were many rows of chairs, some sheltered by the awning but many out in the street itself.

My Pakistani friend was skittish. He didn't want to go beyond the foot of the steps. He said I must just walk over, that they would be delighted to see me, meet me. I was embarrassed, reluctant, shy. Nonetheless, my friend left me there, and I, as unobtrusively as I could, sidled forward. Someone greeted me, offered me a chair. I smiled, and, as my form of politeness demanded, declined. He insisted. I tried to take the least desirable chair in the back row closest to the street where I could barely see into the ceremonial area. My new acquaintance insisted I sit in the first row, an honored guest. He selected my chair, made sure I sat. Our exchange took place in bits of English, and I don't know what other language. The Indian tourists in Mahabaleshwar, I had already found, spoke more English than those who lived there.

As I gazed around, I saw I was the only seated guest. Most of the other members of the large crowd, which was composed almost entirely of men, were still milling around, talking. Once again I had to wonder if they, or my Pakistani friend, had mistaken me, a lone traveler who wore, unlike my saried Indian sisters, a plain long nunish gown and a closely shaved head—I wondered if they had mistaken me for a man. But not so. Leaving my red shawl on my chair, I got up again to do I knew not what. At that moment, a young man came pushing through the crowd, and, though he spoke no English, still, with a brilliant, welcoming smile and delightful enthusiasm, he managed to convey to me that he was the bride's brother. He wanted to take me to meet the bride.

Flushed and flustered, I didn't know if I should leave my shawl. Should I take my backpack? I still held the small newspaper-wrapped package of fruit. I wasn't sure I did want to meet the bride. What would I say to her? I wasn't dressed for a wedding; I wasn't even invited. Though I guess I had been. Just now.

The brother chatted and chatted, and I understood not a word, as he led me away from the crowd down dark streets, into a tangle of alleyways, from which I knew I would never find my way out again. The houses were barely taller than my head. They were made of mud walls and some had stone foundations. The path was rough. There were no lights. It was very dark. If there was to be a moon, it hadn't risen yet. The crowd of people had been left behind. There were maybe one or two people I sensed more than saw, walking softly in the dark, hurrying in through a doorway, drawing water from a well. Surely not guests at a wedding. But I had made a vow long ago, on my very first taxi ride, that "I Would Never Never Never Be Afraid of Dying in a Road Accident in India"; now I amended the wording to include of "being a wedding guest" either. Besides, the young man was so solicitous, taking my hand occasionally to lead me over fallen rocks or away from a crumbling wall. It seemed that we walked for an eternity, but it couldn't have been far because we were still among the buildings of a town, and Mahabaleshwar is not very large. There were no lights in any of the buildings or houses, no fires. People cook outdoors on the dusty streets, but, as I recall, we passed no cooking fires either. Dinner is at twilight. It was now night.

At last we came to a rather wide cleared space. Across from it was a house, very low, certainly no more than six feet high, if that. From it, glimmered flickering light. The young man led me forward. We had to step up and over the threshold, and then stoop to avoid hitting our heads against the ceiling. The hallways and the rooms were tightly packed with women who, for the most part, seemed to be about my age, a very few were younger. Everyone was standing. Some of the women moved about, in and out of the warren of mud-walled rooms that seemed to extend in every direction. It was as if I had entered into some sacred rite in a cave beneath the earth. The whole interior of this extensive home was lighted solely by the golden light of oil lamps and flickering candles, perhaps one to a room. The atmosphere, thickened and dimmed by the drifting smoke from incense, was magical. I felt as if I were nodding in on a ritual of a time long past. And it was quiet.

Some of the women were murmuring to each other, but no one spoke very loudly. No one seemed surprised to see me, which was surprising in itself, as Indians are usually uninhibitedly curious. The young man urged me forward. Turning me toward the right, he led me into a small room whose earthen walls were partly covered by elaborately carved wood. Between the carvings hung glittering pictures, sparkling with glass or mica, or was it gold? A young woman sat engulfed in a high-backed chair. It was covered with layers of embroidered clothes and woven carpets and seemed to be the only chair in the house. Older women were gathered around the seated girl, doing things to her and for her. Immediately, I sensed she must be the bride—but she was dressed so plainly. I couldn't see her face because she kept it lowered, but I perceived she was very very young.

The young man introduced us. It was his sister, he indicated, and she was the bride. She said a few words, but spoke no English, and I did not speak her language. Her face, her hands and her arms were painted red with henna. When I took the hand she timidly held out, it felt rough, as if it were covered with dried mud. She looked up. There were tears in her eyes, and moisture darkened the henna on her cheeks. I smiled at her. I bowed. I did not know what else to do. It was as if all that crush of women, all older, and, who knows, perhaps wiser, had organized to create an image, an icon. They were busy painting it, dressing it and putting it forth for the wedding night. They were in no hurry.

I wanted to give her something. It seemed appropriate to give her a present. I only had the small newspaper-wrapped package of raspberries. I put it in her hands, but, in the flickering light of the smoke-filled room, it did not look as if she smiled. I did not know what

*I*n many parts of India, the night before a wedding is known as the Night of Henna, when the bride's palms and soles of her feet are decorated in elaborate floral and fertility designs with a paste made from the powdered leaves of the henna plant. The paste is also used in some regions to stain a bridegroom's palms because the deep red color left on the skin when the dried paste is washed off is the color that symbolizes the deep love between a husband and wife.

♦

—Naveen Patnaik, *The Garden of Life: An Introduction to the Healing Plants of India*

else to do. I was no longer frightened, but I was terribly puzzled. Should I be happy for the bride? I had wished her well when I handed her the fruit. I folded my hands in *Namaste*. I knelt, touched my lips to one of her hands. Then bowed my way out of her presence.

The young man had stepped outside by now. I had the feeling he was not supposed to be in here among the women, that he had only entered for my benefit. As I moved about a little among the women, trying discreetly to satisfy my curiosity, glancing in a room here and there, they touched me. Some smiled, some said words I did not understand, and soon, though it was like wandering about in an exotic temple sensing strange moods, peering at mysterious tableaux, inhaling the scents of, I think, henna, a sharp, pine-like scent, and sandalwood, I lost heart and retreated.

Ducking, I stepped back out across the threshold, away from the glittering array of saried women, from the golden candlelight, from the hieratic ritual and display into the darkness of the night again. The stars were out. I thanked my companion, *Namaste*, and he led me—it was hardly any distance at all—back to the wide place in the road where the crowd still milled about. The young man showed me to my seat again, and left me, sweetly smiling, enthusiastic still. He had been very kind to me.

I sat. I stood and lurked about. I sat again. Several people attempted conversation with me, but there was surprisingly little English spoken, which made me surer still that these were townspeople who lived here on top of the Deccan plateau. Not far away, I knew, stood the fort near which Shivaji had used his "tiger claws."

A long time later the ceremony began.

On the empty platform to my right was a standing microphone, and someone had now placed a few chairs on the bare boards, the edges of which were decorated with flowers, swags and garlands of red and white flowers. Here the speeches began—many and long. Straight across from me was the raised platform with both folding and household chairs, all filled with men. I assumed these were the dignitaries, the honored guests, perhaps the fathers and brothers and grandfathers. The area to my left remained open. There were no chairs there, no platform, just the odd small structure I could not see around. Beyond its further wall, right over to the dignitaries' platform, an area of bare dirt remained unoccupied. Sometime later, when I glanced that way, I was amazed to see a whole line of women, seated on the ground in front of the small building. They were the women, it was my guess, who had been in that house with the bride. Though I recognized none of them, still they had an aura of incense and candlelight about them. The bride's entourage. But I did not see the bride.

I never saw the bride.

The ceremony went on and on and on. Men spoke, men in turbans. People often glanced at me and smiled. I was treated with great respect and kindness. I believe I was even greeted from the platform. Perhaps I was a talisman of good luck. In India, I knew, the guest is God.

At last, the groom, still in white and partly draped with flowers, entered and came directly to the microphone to speak. He was beautiful, incredibly beautiful, veiled with the small white flowers, and, I now saw, crowned with white roses. Here and there his costume was accented with tiny crimson buds, like drops of blood on a field of snow. He looked across the room as he spoke. I followed his gaze, but all I saw was the line of older women seated on the ground under the dazzling fluorescent lights, their somber saris, shot through with metallic threads, glowed like a bed of coals—and still no bride. I thought perhaps it was because I could not see beyond the wall of the small mud and rock building that formed the corner with the street. The ceremony went on and on.

Later, when the ceremony was over, I stepped out into

"*I*n India," concludes the *Mirza Nama* [*The Book of the Perfect Gentleman*, 1650], a gentleman "should not expect intelligence and good behaviour from those who put big turbans on their heads."

◆

—William Dalrymple, *City of Djinns: A Year in Delhi*

the large empty space in the middle of the ceremonial ground and looked beyond the little building. The awnings covered the space to the wall of the building behind, but there was no evidence that anyone was there, or had been there. There was nothing there.

No bride.

The festivities gathered momentum. There was much talking and laughing and eating, but I was too tired and too shy to join in. I drifted away, not quite knowing whom to thank or part with, and trudged back up the long flight of steps to where I had first seen the groom on the street above. There again I met my Pakistani friend. Accidentally? Waiting for me? I do not know. He asked me if I had enjoyed the wedding.

"Oh yes." But it had been hours and hours long and I was very tired.

As he walked me to the guesthouse in which we had both taken rooms, I asked him about not seeing the bride. I said I thought it was strange to have a wedding to which the bride didn't come. He said she had been there; he said she had been in that little house to the left, the one behind where the women sat cross-legged on the ground. She had been, he assured me, dressed like the groom, with a crown of roses and cascades of flowers. I wanted to ask how he knew, but I thought it might be a bit rude to challenge his statement. I could only assume that he knew what a bride wore to a Muslim wedding, and where she would be.

He then assured me that I could see the bride the next day. At nine o'clock in the morning, she would come again to the area where the wedding had taken place to meet the groom's family and go home with them. She had gone home to her own family after the ceremony, he said, but would go home with the groom's family tomorrow.

"Wouldn't it be strange," I asked, "For a stranger to come and watch?"

"Not at all."

I got up before nine o'clock and found my way back down the main street, down the stairway to the wide dirt area below, and waited. I waited until nine-thirty, and then until ten, knowing that Indian time is far more flexible than American time. Then I waited until ten-thirty, but the street remained wide and dusty and all but deserted. The awnings had been removed from the square where the ceremony took place. It grew warmer and warmer. The merciless Indian sun rose higher.

I prowled around and looked into the little building where my Pakistani friend said the bride would have been. I had assumed I would see a back door through which the bride had entered, but inside the walls were solid. There was nothing in it, nothing at all, no windows, no doors. Four mud walls and a stone floor. The whole structure, thick walls and all, was only about six feet square.

But then again, I had had my back turned when the saried women had come to sit on the ground. I had not noticed their entrance. Could the bride, too, have entered when I wasn't looking? Perhaps. And yet, how odd. Odd that the ceremony had been so *uninterrupted* by her, the bride's, arrival. I remembered the tears of the red-daubed girl, I thought of the beauty of the flower-bedecked groom. And I wondered.

The sad young bride never came that morning. Whether my timing was off, or theirs, I do not know. Or perhaps she had come earlier—or had she declined to come at all?

I met my Pakistani friend and he escorted me to the edge of town to begin my walk to Wai, a temple town on the Krishna River.

The bride never came, I told him, but he could not tell me why. He had known so much, why not the ending?

Namaste.

We parted.

Though I never learned what happened to the bride, I had learned, and am still reminded once in a while, that no Westerner should ever attempt to pronounce "Mahabaleshwar" until they have closely listened to an Indian say it. Closely. Maybe a hundred times. I have listened. But I still pronounce it so that no Indian ever understands where I have been. The name appears to have five syllables. They say it, as closely as I can tell, as if it were one.

Jan Haag, travel writer, novelist, poet, and former executive with the American Film Institute in Hollywood, began her solo traveling late in life, discovering that white hair and a slim pocketbook were great assets for adventure, safety, fearlessness, and fun. She lives in Northern California.

★

As the sun grew more fierce, our complexions darkened and Olivia's freckles sprang into prominence. I thought them beautiful, but they clearly alarmed Mr. Singh who was not used to my wife's Celtic colouring. One morning, while driving through the Old City, he turned quite suddenly into the Meena Bazaar near the Jama Masjid. Without any explanation, he jumped out and approached one of the Ayurvedic healers who for centuries have sat on the roadside here, surrounded by the ingredients of their trade: live iguanas whose fried juices are said to cure impotence; ginseng for philtres used to spread or extinguish the fires of love; tree bark to ward off a woman's menopause; the bringraj herb from the high Himalayas said to conquer baldness or thicken the beard of the most effete Sikh.

As I sat in the hot taxi I could see Balvinder Singh haggling with one of the healers. Eventually Balvinder handed over a pocketful of change and the healer gave him a small pot of white powder. On returning to the car, to my surprise Balvinder solemnly handed the pot to me.

"For Madam," he said earnestly.

"Thank you," I said. "But what is it?"

"Medicine," said Balvinder. "To cure Mrs. William."

"Of what?"

"Her face," said Balvinder, drumming his fingers on his cheekbones. "This powder will cure Madam's pox." He pointed to the sky: "Indian sun. Very bad for Britisher ladies."

I looked baffled; my friend looked embarrassed.

"*Sahib,*" he whispered, "this powder will make Mrs. William's skin white again."

—William Dalrymple, *City of Djinns: A Year in Delhi*

ANDREW HARVEY

* * *

God and Chocolate

The Lord indeed works in mysterious ways.

IN INDIA THE MIRACULOUS IS COMMONPLACE, SO WHEN I WAS told at six by my favorite aunt, B, who lived in the apartment upstairs, that a saint was going to visit her that afternoon—a woman who had died and come back to life again—I was curious, not skeptical.

I am not sure what I expected to see when I entered B's bedroom, but it was not two old women lying on the bed laughing and eating chocolates. I had imagined saints would always be in trance; I had not imagined one would sprawl on a bed, enormous in her white cotton sari, looking very much like any other worn and plump old Indian woman.

"Come onto the bed," B said, "and lie down between us."

I climbed up onto the bed gingerly.

The saint gave me a vast toothless smile and produced from the folds of her sari a chocolate, which she opened and held out to me.

"Oh," she sighed, "I am *too* fond of chocolates." She smelled of biscuits and incense and played with my ears.

"What big ears you have. This is good. The Buddha had big ears. I, too, have big ears."

She lifted a strand of dank white hair and showed me her ears. They were huge and ugly.

"Shantih knows everything there is to know," B said. "Her name means peace; she has seen God. She sees God all the time. Ma is a great saint and thousands worship her and she has done many miracles."

"Have you really done miracles?" I asked.

"They come through me like water through a pipe. But the water is not mine."

"Where does the water come from?"

She yawned slightly, pointing upward.

"Have you really died and come back to life, and did you see God?"

B laughed, got off the bed, and went into the bathroom to have a bath.

"You want to know?" Shantih asked.

"Yes," I said, feeling frightened.

She stroked my cheek dreamily with one of her fingers and said, "God is gentle, gentle as my finger.

"About seventy years ago," she went on, "I was another person, a woman, living in a North Indian village, married with several children. I got ill and died. When I died, a Light came to me, and in it I saw my Lord Krishna. This is what will happen to you, too, when you die. A Light will come and you will see whoever you believe in. If you believe in Krishna, you will see him; if you are a Christian, you will see Christ. From this light Krishna spoke to me. 'You have loved me in your life,' he said, 'and I love you and will give you liberation. But you must go down to the earth and tell them what you have experienced so humans can lose their fear of death and love me more.' I did not want to come down here again; I wanted to be there with him in the Light; but gods are strong, you know, and you have to do what they tell you. So I came back."

She said all this as if she were describing the train schedule to Agra or giving shopping instructions to the *ayah*.

She said, "Go and close the curtains. I will show you something."

I did as I was told.

Shantih leaned over, wheezing a little, and switched on the light by the bed. The swirling red and gold dragons on the lampshade that had been dull a moment before flared into life.

She clapped her hands.

"In everything and everyone the Light is shining. It is not like this light. It is softer. It is everywhere."

"Is it in me?"

"It is in you and all around you and in everyone and around everyone and everything. Without it nothing could exist. It is God."

"Do you see this light?"

"Yes," she laughed. "I see this Light always. You, too, can see it. It is simple. God is simple; we are complicated."

She turned the lamp off. I opened the curtains, and sun flooded the room. I turned to Shantih. She was seated on the bed in meditation, immense and calm, a half-unwrapped chocolate on her lap.

Andrew Harvey is the author of A Journey to Ladakh, Burning Houses, The Web, *and* Hidden Journey: A Spiritual Awakening, *from which this story is excerpted. He was the youngest fellow ever elected to Oxford, and has written several books of poetry and works of translation.*

✦

Gentle George Herbert had also spoken for me, near sixteen hundred years after Thomas Didymus:

> Love bade me welcome: yet my soul drew back,
> Guiltie of dust and sinne.

And so, unwilling to surrender all that was required of me, my far too logical and sceptical mind became my shield and my defence. I could no more ignore religion and deny my instinct for the numinous than a child could abandon its comforter or the earth defy the natural law regulating its passage round the sun. But I had long since ceased to hope that one day, with Herbert, I might sit and eat with the true and certain believers in a kingdom of heaven. And India, above all the places I knew across the earth, had helped me to come to terms with this, had taught me no longer to strain and fret against my inadequacy; for India was, above anywhere else, the land where every distinction of faith, every equivocation, every contradiction, every doubt, every reticence was commonplace, often glorified and always accepted as if any variant at all was the natural condition of man. For that reason alone, I could have surrendered myself to the spirit of this country without any ifs or buts. There were, in fact, many reasons why such a submission was possible: for all its manifold and obvious darknesses, India had cast a spell over me, as much as any land could that was not my own. Kneeling there at the shrine [Basilica of San Thomé, Madras] I wondered when and even whether I would see the subcontinent again. Once, the prospect of my end would have alarmed and tormented me, but I had since come to accept it calmly and with curiosity, almost disinterestedly, as though it were an abstraction, something quite detached from me, stripped of its old power to hurt and terrify. I believed India had played a big part in teaching me how to accept that as well.

—Geoffrey Moorhouse, *OM: An Indian Pilgrimage*

SALMAN RUSHDIE

Hobson-Jobson

The Raj is long dead, but its
linguistic heritage endures.

THE BRITISH EMPIRE, MANY *PUNDITS* NOW AGREE, DESCENDED like a *juggernaut* upon the *barbicans* of the East, in search of *loot*. The *moguls* of the Raj went in *palanquins*, smoking *cheroots*, to sip *toddy* or *sherbet* on the *verandahs* of the *gymkhana* club, while the *mem-sahibs* fretted about the *thugs* in *bandannas* and *dungarees* who roamed the night like *pariahs*, plotting *ghoulish* deeds.

All the italicized words in the above paragraph can be found, with their Eastern family trees, in *Hobson-Jobson*, the legendary dictionary of British India, on whose reissue Routledge are to be congratulated. These thousand-odd pages bear eloquent testimony to the unparalleled intermingling that took place between English and the languages of India, and while some of the Indian loanwords will be familiar—*pukka, curry, cummerbund*—others should surprise many modern readers.

Did you know, for example, that the word *tank* has Gujarati and Marathi origins? Or that *cash* was originally the Sanskrit karsha, "a weight of silver or gold equal to one–four hundredth of a *Tula?*" Or that a *shampoo* was a massage, nothing to do with the hair at all, deriving from the imperative form—*champo!*—of the Hindi verb *champna*, "to knead and press the muscles with the view of relieving fatigue, etc.?" Every column of this book contains revelations like these, written up in a pleasingly idiosyncratic, not to say cranky, style. The authors, Henry Yule and A. C. Burnell, are not averse to ticking off an untrustworthy source, witness their entry under *muddle,* meaning a double, or secretary, or interpreter: "This word is only known to us from the clever—perhaps too clever—little book quoted below… probably a misapprehension of *budlee*."

The chief interest of *Hobson-Jobson,* though, lies not so much in its etymologies for words still in use, but in the richness of what one must call the Anglo-Indian language whose memorial it is, that language which was in regular use just forty years ago and which is now as dead as a dodo. In Anglo-Indian a *jam* was a Gujarati chief, a *sneaker* was "a large cup (or small basin) with a saucer and cover," a *guinea-pig* was a midshipman on an Indian-bound boat, an *owl* was a disease, *Macheen* was not a spelling mistake but a name, abbreviated from "Maha-Cheen," for "great China." Even a commonplace word like *cheese* was transformed. The Hindi *chiz,* meaning a thing, gave the

---

The fifteen main Indian languages are:

Hindi	Kashmiri	Sanskrit
Assamese	Malayalam	Sindhi
Bengali	Marathi	Tamil
Gujarati	Oriya	Telugu
Kannada	Punjabi	Urdu

Most of the languages have their own script, and these are used along with English. In some states, such as Gujarat, you'll hardly see a word of English whereas in Himachal Pradesh virtually everything is in English. For a sample of different scripts, look at a Rs5 or larger banknote where thirteen languages are represented. From the top they are: Assamese, Bengali, Gujarati, Kannada, Kashmiri, Malayalam, Hindi (Devanagari), Oriya, Punjabi, Rajasthani, Tamil, Telugu, and Urdu.

◆

—Hugh Finlay, et al., *India – a travel survival kit*

English word a new, slangy sense of "anything good, first-rate in quality, genuine, pleasant, or advantageous," as, we are told, in the phrase, "these *cheroots* are the real cheese."

Some of the distortions of Indian words—"perhaps vulgar lips"—have moved a long way from their sources. It takes an effort of the will to see, in the Anglo-Indian *snow-rupee,* meaning "authority," the Telugu word *tsanauvu.* The dictionary's own title, chosen, we are told, to help it sell, is of this type. It originates in the cries of *Ya Hasan! Ya Hussain!* uttered by Shia Muslims during the Muharram processions. I don't quite see how the colonial British managed to hear this as *Hobson! Jobson!,* but this is clearly a failure of imagination on my part.

It's more than a century since this volume's first publication, and in 1886 it was actually possible for Yule and Burnell (whom it's tempting to rename Hobson and Jobson) to make puns which conflated Hindi with, of all things, Latin. The Anglo-Indian word

I got into conversation with Mr. Bhajan Lal, the *Pradhan* (headman) of the village.... Thanks to our twice weekly lessons, Olivia and I had now become confident enough in Hindi for the practice of it to become enjoyable rather than tiresome—if only because people were so surprised to hear any non-Indian speak even the most stumbling version of it. Mr. Lal was no exception.

LAL: *Sahib!* You are speaking Hindi!

WD: A little.

LAL: Oh, *sahib!* Truly this is day among days! What is your good name, *sahib?*

WD: (confident now; a phrase I knew) My name is William.

LAL: Oh thank you Mr. Will-Yums *Sahib.* Where are you learning this beautiful Hindi?

WD: In Delhi. A *munshi* comes to our house...

LAL: In Delhi! Heaven be praised....

◆

—William Dalrymple, *City of Djinns: A Year in Delhi*

poggle, a madman, comes from the Hindi pagal, and so we're offered the following "macaronic adage which we fear the non-Indian will fail to appreciate: *pagal et pecunia jaldé separantur.*" ("A fool and his money are soon parted.")

British India had absorbed enough of Indian ways to call their Masonic lodges *jadoogurs* after the Hindi for a place of sorcery, to cry *kubberdaur (khabardaar)* when they meant "look out," and to *puckerow* an Indian ("catch him") before they started to *samjao* him—literally, to make him understand something, but, idiomatically, to beat him up.

Strange, then, to find certain well-known words missing. No *kaffir,* no *gully,* not even a *wog,* although there is a *wug,* a Baloch or Sindhi word meaning either loot or a herd of camels. (*Hobson-Jobson* can be wonderfully imprecise at times.) I thought, too, that a modern appendix might usefully be commissioned, to include the many English words which have taken on, in independent India, new "Hinglish" meanings. In India today, the prisoner in the dock is the *undertrial;* a boss is often an *incharge;* and, in a sinister euphemism, those who perish at the hands of law enforcement officers are held to have died in a "police *encounter.*"

To spend a few days with *Hobson-Jobson* is, almost, to regret the passing of the intimate connection that made this linguistic *kedgeree* possible. But then one remembers what sort of connection it was, and is moved to remark—as Rhett Butler once said to Scarlett O'Hara—"Frankly, my dear, I don't give a small copper coin weighing one tolah, eight mashas, and seven surkhs, being the fortieth part of a rupee." Or, to put it more concisely, a *dam.*

Salman Rushdie was born in Bombay in 1947 and was awarded the
Booker Prize in 1981 for his novel, Midnight's Children. *His novel* The
Satanic Verses *earned him a death sentence from the late Ayatollah*
Khomeini for allegedly profaning Islam. Today he lives and writes in hiding.
This story was taken from his book of essays, Imaginary Homelands:
Essays & Criticisms, 1981–1991.

★

In India, English is widely spoken but with its own unique vocabulary. "Number two" is not second place, but illegal. Indian politicians don't fly—they "air-dash." A woman is not sexually harassed—she is "eve-teased." A "jackal's wedding" is not a canine nuptial but an occasion when it rains while the sun shines.

To help travelers unravel the mysteries of subcontinental English, Nigel B. Hankin, seventy-three, a retired British embassy attaché, shares the knowledge he has accumulated during more than four decades in India. The title of his glossary, *Hanklyn-Janklin*, is a tribute to *Hobson-Jobson*, a similar lexicon assembled in the nineteenth century. It is also an allusion to the local penchant for echo words: in India one may throw a party-warty, drink a cup of *chai-wai* (tea), read a *kitab-witab* (book)—or suffer from Delhi belly. Hankin includes definitions of commonly used Indian words, especially those that have entered the parlance of the country's English-language newspapers, and in the process illuminates such hurly-burly aspects of Indian life as *gherao*, the act of surrounding that takes place during a common form of protest in which workers encircle an office to prevent a manager from leaving. Or a *darshan*—the term means glimpse and is applicable to sightings of both deities and politicians. Crammed with twelve hundred entries, this "Indophile Disneyland," as the fortnightly *India Today* calls it, is refreshingly free of colonial condescension.

—Emily Mitchell, "Traveler's Unraveler," *Time*

Caretakers of the Dead

*India has trouble caring for the living,
but it perhaps reveals more of itself
in how it cares for the dead.*

LAWS CAN BE MADE AND UNMADE WITH A STROKE OF A FOUNTAIN pen, but attitudes must be crafted with time and unflagging will. In India the greatest barrier to class integration may well be the attitude of the Untouchables themselves. The poorest and least-educated members of society, *Harijans* are often the most conservative as well. At election time they may vote to shake the tree in hopes of dislodging choicer fruit, but most would never consider chopping the tree down. They may use government programs to get more out of the caste system, but they have little desire to abolish the system entirely. For most of them, caste is a fact of life not even worth thinking about. Something that always has been, something that always will be.

The lowest, most contemptible wretch in all India is the charnel man. Thieves, whores, and garbage pickers look down their noses at him. The only person as detested is the tanner of leather, who cuts up dead cows and sells their hides for tainted money. But almost all Hindus are cremated when they die, and somebody has to do the burning.

When I walked up to the Harishchandra Ghat in Varanasi, Suraj

Chaudhri had long since set the morning's corpses in a row. He and his fellow *doams* were now working on a middle-aged man, making sure the limbs were properly arranged for incineration. The other bodies had been brought here on a stretcher of green bamboo borne by close kin. Each had been lovingly wrapped in white cloth, then swathed in gaudy silk brocade laced with threads of spun gold, then lashed to the palanquin with rough twine and covered with orange garlands. Now each was alone. Each band of mourners, with flutes and drums and women singing through their tears, had gone home. The only people left on the *ghat* were a few midday idlers, the charnel men, and the cadavers themselves.

Suraj Chaudhri was sawing away at the bamboo poles, cutting them down to the same size as the body they carried. It makes the fire neater. As a *doam*—the Untouchable clan responsible for burning corpses—Suraj works from four a.m. until midnight every single day. There is no time for a holiday. What could he do, ask people to stop dying merely because he wanted a rest?

It is his job, it is his life, it is him. There is no point in searching for any other way. When I ask what he thinks about caste, Suraj shakes his head. He does not think at all. He never asks why he is a *Harijan*, any more than he asks why his hair is black and his eyes brown.

His place in the universe, Suraj knows, is to burn bodies. That is why he was put on the earth. It is an important task, a necessary task, a task vital to the survival of society. He fully supports the caste system, although technically he is not even a part of it. How (he asks) could he feel otherwise? The system was instituted by God Himself—who is Suraj Chaudhri to challenge fate?

By working hard and living an honest life, Suraj hopes to scale the rungs of caste and one day reach Nirvana. It is not an impossible dream. The Ramayana provides him inspiration. He cannot read and has no television or radio, but he knows the stories well. When Rama was ferried across the Ganges, he embraced the low-born boatman as a friend. The episode gives Suraj comfort, for it shows that even a *Harijan* can be loved by God.

A goat ambles over to the row of corpses and starts nibbling on one of the flowery garlands. Eventually an idler gently chases the animal away.

It is not only Suraj's father and grandfather who were charnel men. Every member of his family, those still living and those dead for centuries, has worked the Burning Ghats of Varanasi. It binds them together, makes them one. A harmonious home, Suraj says, is the greatest blessing any man can have.

A boy of six or seven, Suraj's son, is hopping among the cadavers. Here he straightens an arm, there he tucks in a brocade shroud, proudly helping out as best he can. One day father and son will work side by side, one day the son will take the father's place, one day the son may even burn the father on his own bier. Today the boy is whistling cheerfully as he picks his way through the corpses.

I ask Suraj if he is happy with his life.

Happy, not happy, he says the question has no meaning. A man's life is his life, nothing more, nothing less.

An old woman is burning on the pyre Suraj has built. She lies on top of four cross-stacked logs, with smaller sticks piled tidily on her chest. The fire melts the air, blurring all the scenery behind it, like the jet flow from an airplane. Downwind, the stench of fleshy corruption is almost intolerable. Much of the woman's skin is charred, some of it flaking off, and a bright white bone is all that is left of her leg. But the flames have not yet reached the head. Eyes shut, lips slightly parted, moisture just beginning to bead on the forehead—she could as easily be basking on a beach. When her scanty hair finally catches fire, her lips twitch without losing their serenity. The woman greets oblivion with an involuntary smile.

And do thy duty, even if it be humble, rather than another's, even if it be great. To die in one's duty is life: to live another's is death.

◆

—*Bhagavad Gita* 3-35, quoted by Geoffrey Moorhouse in *OM: An Indian Pilgrimage*

There is no way to know anything about the woman's life. Perhaps she had been born a Brahmin, perhaps a Shudra. Perhaps she had been the wife of a fisherman, perhaps a cabinet minister in her own right. She entered the world nothing more than a body, left it a body and nothing more. In the end, fire burns away all class, all caste, all wealth, all luck, all social distinction, all human inequity.

Death is the only leveler, for there is none in life.

Jonah Blank also contributed "Monument of Love" to Part I. Both of these selections were taken from his book, Arrow of the Blue-Skinned God: Retracing the Ramayana through India.

✳

I regard untouchability as the greatest blot on Hinduism. This idea was not brought home to me by my bitter experiences during the South African struggle. It is not due to the fact that I was once an agnostic. It is equally wrong to think that I have taken my views from my study of Christian religious literature. These views date as far back as the time when I was neither enamored of, nor was aquainted with, the Bible or the followers of the Bible.

I was hardly yet twelve when this idea had dawned on me. A scavenger named Uka, an Untouchable, used to attend our house for cleaning latrines. Often I would ask my mother why it was wrong to touch him. If I accidentally touched Uka, I was asked to perform the ablutions, and though I naturally obeyed, it was not without smilingly protesting that untouchability was not sanctioned by religion, that it was impossible that it should be so. I was a very dutiful and obedient child and so far as it was consistent with respect for parents, I often had tussled with them on this matter. I told my mother that she was entirely wrong in considering physical contact with Uka as sinful.

—Mahatma Gandhi, Speech at the Depressed Classes Conference, Ahmedabad, 1921

My Delhi Home

Family is where the heart is.

IN MY INDIAN NEIGHBORHOOD, PESKY LITTLE THREE-WHEELED auto rickshaws, old bicycles, 1950s-style Ambassadors—the matronly car of India's bureaucracy—sputtering motorcycles carrying entire families, and the middle class's favorite auto, the zippy Maruti, yip and bellow in a perpetual traffic jam. Along with pedestrians, tourists, beggars, cobras in baskets, fortune tellers, crows, touts, ear cleaners, shoe shiners, peddlers, and dogs, they scrabble for every atom of free space.

The York Hotel rests one story above this show, but it does not attempt to remove itself from the bustle below. It is a wise decision, for nothing in India is isolated from life's mayhem, and its mystery.

Many years ago my reservations at another hotel were muddled, and I found myself needing a place to stay. Having learned that there is often wisdom behind India's cosmic or comic—I have never decided which—design with its mission of unerringly scrambling careful plans into chaos, I accepted my mishap good-naturedly and ended up at the York.

The match with the hotel has been blessed. Staying there has drawn me to the street, where much of Indian life, from hawking to bathing to peeing, unfolds and has included me in the neighborhood's pulse, which in spite of the street frenzy, is slow, stretched out to encompass the living and dying of endless generations. And most of all, it has ceased being just the hotel in which I stay during my frequent trips to India and become, instead, my Indian home.

On its two-story perch above Connaught Circle, New Delhi's heart, the York boasts cherry-red carpets, massive gray granite tubs inviting long soaks until you find it takes an hour to fill them, and bulky furniture with faux wood veneer. Its best rooms face away from the street and have no windows. But I always know the time of day by the sounds of traffic leaking in, despite of the rooms' resolute backs to downtown. In the cool gray Delhi mornings, noises are soft, like prayers. By ten o'clock they have become as fierce as Indian summers. Mid-evenings they subside into the hush of the dark.

The York has all the middle class comforts—television, telephone, and air conditioning, but something usually breaks down. Part of the rhythm of life there is to phone in the complaint several times, listen to promises to send a repairman up "in five or ten minutes," the Indian euphemism meaning any time between now and eternity, and finally watch with admiration as our hero arrives, jiggles wires, and shakes ailing instruments, coaxing them back to life with string and a prayer.

In this country where many branches of families live together, staying at the York is like being an arm of one of India's extended families. You learn to accommodate each other's bad moods and foibles. The bearers know to get a move on when dealing with this impatient American, and I try to ignore the blatant hints for *baksheesh*, especially from the beady-eyed bathroom cleaner who eternally stations himself outside my door panting to be tipped for unrequested and unwanted services.

But all is forgiven when I return from California and instead of inquiring when did I arrive, someone asks in gentle accusation, "Madam, where have you been?" hinting that the York has felt an emptiness that only I can fill.

Every morning the *dobie-wallah*, or laundry man, bicycles in to collect laundry. I have long since stopped asking that my clothes return un-ironed. This nation with its exquisitely silken sari-swathed women does not appreciate the natural look.

He delivers my garments, crisply pressed and fresh-smelling, the same evening except when the monsoons pelt Delhi. During the rainy season it takes several days to dry pieces. Those times even the hotel's towels come back soggy.

But I don't mind. I savor the idea of my things being dried in old-fashioned sunshine (laundry draped over fences and lawns is a common Delhi sight) and enjoy the novelty of my cushioned life's bow to nature.

The York is on the outer circle of Connaught Place, a series of neat concentric circles laid out by the British, no doubt to impose a sense of order on the pandemonium of India. Today the white paint of its stately pillars has sunk deep within the wood into a patina of timelessness, and the once glistening marbled walkways dulled by a half century of grime. Connaught Place wears the look of India, always crumbling away, but never changing.

On the York's block are a tiny mosque atop a Muslim food stand, two tailors who ply their trade with antiquated sewing machines, and Rajinder's, a shop supplying car seat-covers and radios. Men from Rajinder's work on the sidewalk, snipping and hammering and never cleaning up after themselves, but in this crowded country

> *I*n Delhi there seem to be more people who shine and repair shoes than people who actually wear them. When a weasely-looking man tapped me on the shoulder to tell me that my shoes were stained, I chased him away: Connaught Circus con men know more tricks than you can imagine, and one of their favorites is to daub ketchup (or worse) on your shoes and then clean it up for a fee.
>
> ◆
>
> —Jonah Blank, *Arrow of the Blue-Skinned God: Retracing the Ramayana through India*

where any empty space is fair game for colonization, no one complains.

Across the street businesses such as Bhandari Homeopathic Stores, Alankar Shirtswala, and Moonlight Tailors and Drapers occupy molecules of storefronts. Most have been owned by the same family for generations and in India's ancient linkage of lifetimes will be passed on to the sons of the current owners.

But many do not have even slivers of shops and exist only from the uncertain gifts of the street. I met nine-year-old Sanjoy several years ago when we chatted while I waited for a bookstore to open. "Madam," he purred in the prim Indian English that seemed at odds with his merry hazel eyes, "if only I had a shoeshine box to make my way in the world."

My American respect for initiative promptly gifted him with 100 rupees.

Of course, Sanjoy never bought his box; but since I had already fallen in love with his snappy repartee and mop of sandy curls, we became friends. Later, his pal Deepak, less clever but gentler than Sanjoy, peered at me with brown soulful eyes and also crept into my heart.

The boys live in a peculiar world, half adult and half child. They spend their days conning tourists, handing over half of their earnings to policemen in order not to be hassled, and playing. Bequeathed by generations of their families, their inheritance is the street, their dreams dependent on the discards of others.

I bring them presents with each visit. The kids whoop with delight. I feel pangs of guilt that I cannot do more.

Sanjoy and Deepak are a cut above the beggars who work the area. One filthy family often turns up in the next block. The granny has honed one mean sales pitch. Having discovered you can get almost anything by hounding your quarry into submission, she follows me for blocks moaning, *"Chapati! Chapati!"* ("Bread! Bread!") until I cave in with a few rupees.

At the corner weaving in and out of cars waiting for the light to change are a beautiful young woman with luminous eyes and a thick plait of black hair falling down her back and a man who looks you in the eye with alert intelligence. Both are as clean as you can be if your home is the street. Her lower body is paralyzed. She drags it along behind her as she pulls herself with her hands into the road soliciting motorists. He has no legs at all.

I often bring them food from Nirula's, the fast food restaurant in the next block. Although I am curious about these two attractive, intelligent people, I have learned from the helplessness that my involvement with Sanjoy and Deepak often stirs up, to keep my distance. I have begun to understand why most of my Indian friends steer clear of the poor. The more you enter their lives, the more you feel powerless to fill their enormous needs.

Sprinkled throughout the neighborhood are the large, old-fashioned restaurants that were formerly Delhi's most glamorous eating places. The York itself has such an establishment, a cavernous place manned by elderly, gentle waiters with sloping shoulders.

As do most Connaught cafes, the York restaurant probably spans at least half a century. My friend Vijay remembers eating there forty years ago during excursions from his home in the state of Rajasthan. In Vijay's boyhood eyes, the York was the epitome of sophistication.

Today, though, with the advent of private clubs and five-star hotels for the elite, the York and other Connaught Place eateries are merely bastions of basic Indian cuisine and sweet but unpolished service. They cater to large families and the lower echelon of businessmen. I retire to them when I want to be alone. Losing my procession of touts and beggars at their doors, I become the fly on the wall, eavesdropping on the buzz of the politics of the B JP [Bharatiya Janata Party], the Hindu-revivalist party, at the Embassy; or the humdrum of business-speak at the Volga; or the jabber of mom and pop and babies at the York.

But it is to Nirula's that I go when I long for a bit of Americana. Years ago Papa Nirula sent a son to Cornell to study restaurant management and has been raking in the profits ever since. Nirula's was a pioneer in take-out food and salad bars.

During my frequent Nirula fixes, I met Kasim, one of the hosts. The soft-spoken, middle-aged Kasim traveled the hefty journey from his home in Old Delhi by motorcycle six days a week to work ten-hour days. He arrived at work early and stayed until the last diner dribbled out, often at midnight. Always sensitive to his customers, he knew my routine after only a couple of visits. I had only to walk through the door for a fresh orange juice and pot of tea to appear at my favorite table, which had been saved, even though Nirula's has no reservations, because Kasim knew it was my breakfast hour.

Over the years Kasim's story unfolded. He had worked in an Arab country, saved a nest egg of thousands of dollars, and spent almost every bit of it throwing his brother a lavish wedding—not a strange deed in India, where the family is sanctified almost as much as the gods.

Still, Kasim often regretted his extravagance as he struggled on his meager Nirula's salary. He was forced to dip into his small remaining savings to send his younger children to private schools and the eldest son to university.

Three years ago I returned to India, expecting Kasim's big smile of welcome, only to find that he had been fired. The waiters said that the owner had chosen him as the scapegoat for an innocent misunderstanding.

In India jobs are hoarded

Most of my childhood was lived in a house on Alipur Road in Old Delhi. The Turkish and Moghul tombs nearby and the abandoned British residences even then starting to crumble taught me that history was a game decay always won. My first paintings were of tombs and my first poems drenched with the easy pathos of vanished grandeur. When I first visited London at seven, I saw in my mind's eye cows grazing around Nelson's column as they graze around Kutb Minar. My *ayah* used to sing an old Hindi song:

"All things pass away except God

O my God show me your face before I die."

♦

—Andrew Harvey, *Hidden Journey: A Spiritual Awakening*

like the rare treasure they are. Kasim has been unable to find another one.

His son has dropped out of university; his younger kids no longer go to private schools.

The last time I saw him he had landed a one-night waiter's job and talked about it throughout the summer, the one claim to productivity this once proud man could chalk up.

Not long ago I tried to avoid the pain caused by the Kasims and Sanjoys by staying in a hotel far away from Connaught Place.

My trip was peaceful, painless—and vapid. The York had made me grow too accustomed to real life. The visitor's shield I had thought would protect me from the Connaught Place dramas had long ago fallen away, probably becoming a part of the neighborhood's abundant garbage, waiting to be recycled by another traveler who wanted to take pictures, have a few safe adventures, and return safely to her native land.

I wish her well, but I don't envy her. Like it or not, the York and environs have become part of who I am. Through India's strange alchemy, my secure, strong, American self has been vanquished by a fragile world perpetually teetering on the verge of collapse and sorrow. It is a world I worry about, suffer with, and miss when I am away from it.

Maybe that's what having a home is all about.

Cheryl Bentley spent time in El Salvador during its civil war, taught school in the Iranian desert, served in the Peace Corps in Thailand, and birded around the world. She lives in San Francisco and says she never steps on ants.

★

How do you cope with poverty? That must be the question I have been asked the most frequently by visitors to India over the many years I have lived there. I often reply, "I don't have to. The poor do." It's certainly true. I live a very comfortable life in Delhi, while the taxi drivers just across the road have to sleep in the open during the hot summer. I have a three-bedroom flat. The taxi stand is their home. I am surrounded by India's poverty, but I don't suffer it. I also know there is very little I can do about the poor and that no one has yet found an answer to their problems. The crocodile tears that have been shed over India's poor would flood the Ganges; that's why I don't feel any need to add my drop to them. Graham Greene once wrote, "Pity is cruel, pity destroys." I agree that we must not pity the poor. I believe, however, that we can respect them.

—Mark Tully, *The Defeat of a Congressmen and Other Parables of Modern India*

PART TWO

SOME THINGS TO DO

JAMES O'REILLY AND LARRY HABEGGER

* * *

Merle Haggard and the Ambassador

A drive in the south offers countless rewards.

COLONEL WAKEFIELD WORE A FAINT SMILE. "ANYONE WANT TO SEE a leopard?" We nodded, cold but still eager after hours of bouncing around the forest in a jeep. The Colonel shone his flashlight on a sign at the entrance to Nagarhole National Park. Indeed there was a leopard on it, a very nice leopard, a painted wood leopard. Not exactly what we had in mind, but it gave us a good laugh as we headed back to the lodge.

Nagarhole is a little-visited game preserve in the south of India in Karnataka state, two hours southwest of the fabled city of Mysore. It is home to a stunning array of beast and bird, from leopard, elephant, gaur, and yellowhorn to tiger, fish owl, peacock, and kingfisher. You can watch the charge of a bull elephant from an elevated hide, from a jeep, from a coracle on the water at dawn, or ride elephant-back into the bush at sunset.

The lure of leopards and tigers drew us here, but it is just one small attraction of the south of India, that vast stretch of the subcontinent from Bombay to Goa to Cochin to Madras. The south is ignored by many first-time visitors to India for two simple reasons: the Taj Mahal and the Himalayas, both of which are in the north. But the south offers an Indian experience sometimes lost in the obligatory pilgrimages to Agra or Varanasi: the India of villages loved by Gandhi, the spectacular unspoiled beaches of Goa and Kerala and Karnataka states, the wild subtropical national forests, the exquisite temples of Kanchipuram and Mahabalipuram outside Madras, the cool hill stations of Ooti and Coonoor.

While tourism amenities in the south lag behind those of the north, Bombay is indisputably India's most international city, and home to the world's largest film industry. We began our trip through the south here, in this busy city where people move in a kaleidoscopic mix, from rich Japanese teenagers to the slum children of *Salaam, Bombay*, from spice merchants outside the Victoria Terminus to a Middle Eastern shiek who brings a strongbox of money to a turbaned Sikh cashier to pay his hotel bill. Black and yellow taxis rush through streets lined with garish movie billboards that make American advertisers seem timid. The famous Gateway of India, where George V landed in 1911, stands as a stately and somewhat incongruous reminder of the Raj on the waterfront where foreigners arrived at the turn of the century, and where boats now come and go from Elephanta Island, site of stonecut caves dating back to 450 A.D.

We boarded the boat in a mad scramble of women in exquisite saris and made the six-mile crossing accompanied by a middle-aged woman who was a full-time guide and a part-time schoolteacher. She grew up in the Punjab and was ten years old at the time of Partition in 1947. She spoke freely of the bloodshed it brought and the scars it left on her, and she held a deep bitterness for those who talked of India's "peaceful" transition to independence.

Elephanta resembled a slumbering beast in the morning haze. We climbed her back to the caves, temples devoted to Shiva with powerful sculptures. The most remarkable is Trimurti, the three-headed Shiva, representing the unity of God in the form of Brahma, Vishnu, and Shiva. The only likeness of its kind in India, it seemed to emanate an energy so palpable that its image stayed with us for days.

Back in Bombay, we visited the house where Gandhi lived during his stays in the city. It has been turned into a wonderful, modest museum, whose scale, particularly the rough handmade scenes from his life, might have pleased Gandhi himself.

Probably the best place to get a feel for Bombay is Victoria Terminus, a fabulous place to visit even if you have no train to catch. Built in 1888, it was the first train station in India, and is covered with elaborate carved griffins and other beasts whose eyes have watched hundreds of millions of passengers over the years. Beggars and merchants and passengers swarm by in a boggling stream: unending dark eyes, flashing smiles and grimaces, betel juice–stained fangs, silk ties on businessmen, a thalidomide card player. A man with no legs sells toys. A crowd gathers around a wallet seller who chants the virtues of his plastic product arrayed by color. Intricate henna "tattoos" adorn the hands of beautiful women, auspicious signs for special occasions.

This is a place where the mundane becomes eternal, where the visitor has to come to grips with beggars and the meaning of life. What should you do? Does giving encourage? Is it a duty, as the Muslims say? Can you pretend to be Christ? Every time you are approached is unique: you give out of pity, guilt, sometimes love, duty, exasperation, disgust, haste. You finger the wad of rupees in your pocket, wondering about your destiny. Then a filthy beggar boy, whom you've just rejected, smiles at you and melts into the crowd, blessing you in your selfishness. Patterns of thought and belief crumple.

We made our way southeast to Bangalore, India's fifth largest city and home of Kingfisher Beer. It is a favorite place for many Indians because of its temperate climate, booming economy, and many city parks. "Government Work is God's Work" is carved into the stone of a state building, recalling James Cameron's uniquely Indian image:

> ten thousand civil servants drift homeward on a river
> of bicycles, brooding on the Lord Krishna
> and the cost of living.

Looking for a way to Nagarhole National Park, we hooked up

*B*eing a Night Rat Killer in Bombay may not seem like a desirable job. The city is overrun with millions of gray-black bandicoots, the largest and hungriest species of rat in the world, that its people seem resigned to sharing their homes and streets with them.

The method of extermination is to shine a flashlight in the rat's face, then belt it with a long bamboo stick. But the city is so broke that often it cannot afford batteries for the flashlight.

Still, when Bombay announced openings for seventy new rat catchers, more than forty thousand people applied, half of them university graduates.

India has the highest number of university graduates in the world: more than one million earn degrees annually. A college education is seen as a way of changing class and caste status. "You try to get a cleaner job," said Ashish Nandy, a sociologist. "But this rat race for rat catchers' jobs makes a mockery of that."

◆

—Tim McGirk, "Night Owl? Bombay Needs Rat Killers," *The London Independent*

with a guide named Bhaskar and a Merle Haggard-loving driver named Bennie, who was newly wed and looking for a better-paying job.

We left Bangalore in a frenzy of traffic which from the back seat of our redoubtable Indian-made Ambassador resembled a Buster Keaton comedy. Vehicles crossed, passed, merged, and separated with no apparent order—auto rickshaws, bullock carts, pushcarts, mopeds, and horsecarts, cars, trucks, buses, and bicycles, women and children and hordes of men, all dove into the chaos with reckless abandon under the implacable gaze of wandering cows. It's a miracle that more people don't get hurt or killed, even though India already has one of the highest mortality rates in the world.

We headed southwest toward Mysore, Bhaskar always laughing when we nearly ran somebody over. We saw a sign with an arrow pointing right around roadworks, exhorting us to "Keep Left." This brought Bennie and Bhaskar to tears. Over the next few days they would break out laughing, shouting "Keep left! Keep left!" and we would hear Bennie muttering it to himself when we were stymied in traffic. It became a standing joke in the car, the very embodiment of Indian bureaucracy.

Bennie had a deep curiosity about everything, which showed in his energetic questioning of us from the driver's seat, at meal breaks in roadside cafes and over whiskey in our rooms at night. Sadly, we were not able to satisfy his longing to know more about country-western music, as he already knew far more than we did.

An Ambassador

At every opportunity Bennie gave us keen insights into driving defensively. "Horn Please!" is written on the rear of all trucks, and Bennie happily obliged, taking us to the edge of doom every few minutes. But we had to admit he was an excellent driver, passing cows at high speed with millimeters to spare, always aware of what was on the road, always vigilant. After one particularly close shave, an anguished herder shouted after us, "You have steering, my bulls have no steering!"

We rolled through village after village. The landscape was dotted with strange granite formations, and Bhaskar pointed out the caves where a climactic scene from *A Passage to India* was filmed. (The real caves from E. M. Forster's novel of the same name are in the Barabar Hills near Patna in Bihar.) The road ran through fields of rice and flowering sugarcane with its lavender, feather-like blossoms that took their color only in groups and only in the proper light.

The sun went down in reds and oranges as we passed the ruins of the fortress of Tipu Sultan, the Tiger of Mysore. We were surprised to find a connection with our own history here—in 1770, Tipu Sultan showed his solidarity with revolutionaries in a far off land who were also trying to throw off the yoke of British imperialism by being among the first to send an ambassador to America.

But in Mysore, with its old colonial bungalows, one knows with deep certainty that the Raj is gone forever, a hiccup in the vastness of Indian history. There we stayed in a nearly empty *nawab's* palace (the Lalith Mahal) and drank sweet coffee and listened to live sitar and tabla at dinner before venturing forth to visit the Maharajah's palace, whose Sunday evening illumination of 120,000 bulbs was quite a spectacle. The next day we visited the temple of Sri Chamundeswari high above the city, where golden eagles soared and black-garbed pilgrims with painted faces piled out of buses and lined up to pay homage to Parvati, who killed the demon king Maheshasura in a ten-day battle. The pilgrims were mostly men, but there was a smattering of girls and old women (menstruating women are not allowed because many of the deities are bachelors and wouldn't be able to resist them, according to Bhaskar).

From Mysore, we rattled farther south, past fields of rice, sunflowers, and cotton sprinkled with brilliant white egrets and ibises. Bullock carts with impossibly huge loads of hay lumbered along and everywhere

---

I had somehow expected there to be a soundtrack to my first trip to India. I would explore the country to the muted sounds of Ravi Shankar, the plaintive sitar playing in the background as I stood looking up at the Taj Mahal. It had never occurred to me that classical Indian music was to India as classical Western music was to America, enjoyed by a few but ignored by the many. This is not to say that music is not an important part of Indian life. Perhaps nowhere in the world is music more a constant than in India. The ever present strains of Indian movie music dominate the urban Indian experience. The constant, high-volume blasting of the latest show tunes quickly becomes an almost unnoticed part of the background noise in the cities.

◆

—Jim Keener, "The Sound of Music, Indian Style"

village India revealed itself. We encountered a cow traffic jam which brought us to a halt and generated much discussion between Bhaskar and Bennie about how best to get through it, which finally proved to be just waiting until the cows moved. Every village seemed to have its own irrigation reservoir, and the land was cultivated from horizon to horizon until suddenly we reached the forest that marked the border of Nagarhole National Park.

The fragility of such sanctuaries was never so clear. Villages and fields run right up to the park boundaries, exerting enormous pressure on the wilderness. How long these islands of natural habitat for India's wildlife can survive is up to strong management and a commitment to conservation by the state and national governments. There are no easy answers and no real consensus on the best way to preserve these areas and take care of human needs.

In the early evening we arrived at the government-subsidized Kabini River Lodge, where we met Colonel John Wakefield, a veteran of World War II in Singapore and Burma, and the Punjab during India's bloody Partition. Over dinner he told us he was from Bihar state, near Bodh Gaya, home of the Buddha. "The Lord Buddha and I saw the light," he said, glasses perched on his head. "He saw enlightenment and I saw the light of day." He chuckled, sneezed, and his glasses fell onto his nose. After he left military service in 1954 he worked as a safari guide leading tiger hunts until 1970. Shortly thereafter he did an about-face and became a conservationist, and has been working in Nagarhole since 1978. The Lodge, he told us, was once a maharajah's tiger hunting retreat where Lord Mountbatten was a guest. At that time, the story goes, tigers were so plentiful they could be shot from the verandah.

At dawn we paddled onto the lake in a coracle made from buffalo hide, a circular vessel that looked as though it would offer little buoyancy but rode easily on the surface with four of us in it. The sun worked to burn off the mists rising from the water and the boatman paddled us toward the far, forested shore. As we approached he spotted four grazing elephants and paddled in figure eights to draw us silently closer. We watched them for a long time while myriad colorful birds flitted across the water. Eagles soared above; a white-breasted kingfisher flashed its iridescent blue back as it dove for a meal.

We floated for hours in deep tranquility, listening to the birds, watching for big game, and letting wild India surround us. A deep roar resonated from far back in the bush and we were sure we'd heard a tiger. "Elephant," the boatman whispered, shaking his head.

We pulled the coracle out of the water at an elephant camp, where two *mahouts*—elephant handlers—were bathing their charges in the lake. Their communication with the animals was remarkable—a few clucks and the elephant lifted a foot to be scrubbed, another guttural word and he lowered his head. The Colonel told us the Indian elephant is more intelligent than his cousins in Africa, capable of remembering 160 commands to the African's very few. Almost all trained elephants are Indian. Both species have some fourteen hundred muscles in their trunks, which keep busy stuffing six hundred pounds of food into their mouths every day.

> The Indians have a proverb, "Listen to the elephant, rain is coming."
>
> ◆
>
> —Mark Shand,
> *Travels on My Elephant*

By midmorning the heat was on, and we spent most of the day relaxing, watching the kingfishers skim over the lake, napping in the cool of our high-ceilinged rooms. In the evening we rode into the bush on elephant back, a slow, lurching trip that offered a completely different perspective of the forest. Spiders as big as our hands hung in webs at eye level and we had to duck as we passed; a huge tusker poked his head out of the bush, gave us a look, and crashed off through the underbrush. We saw no big cats but got a good laugh out of the flatulent lead elephant, who emitted powerful clouds from his backside, which our trailing elephants dutifully carried us through.

We wore sweaters on our game drive that night, this time

prepared for the forest chill. A group of Indian tourists who'd arrived that afternoon were in shirt sleeves, however, and we had to laugh at the Colonel's knowing smile and the unspoken initiation to the ways of his forest. We should have advised them, but we would have spoiled his fun. We saw lots of spotted deer, gaur, and elephants, but no leopards or tigers. It's not that they aren't out there, just that spotting these big cats requires a little luck. The Colonel told us the actress Goldie Hawn had spent two nights there some years ago, and saw four tigers—the luck of the stars, perhaps.

We'd been carrying a bottle of scotch with us since we'd landed in Bombay, and when we said good-bye we presented it to the Colonel, knowing he was a drinking man. He tucked it under his arm like an Oxford don would a precious tome, smiled, and said simply, "This is hard to get here."

We headed for Madras, India's fourth largest city and gateway to the south, to visit the famous temple sites of Kanchipuram and Mahabalipuram. Both are an easy day trip from Madras through a flat, green landscape covered with miles of rice fields dotted with spindly ice fruit trees that look like coconut palms after a hurricane. Kanchipuram is one of India's seven sacred cities and one of its most spectacular temple sites, whose huge, ornate towers (*gopurams*) can be seen from miles away.

In the main temple we were greeted by a tiny man who proceeded to become our self-appointed guide. It helped little to ignore him, since he followed us around anyway, exhorting us to worship the sacred bull, the sacred mango tree (said to be thirty-five hundred years old and still bearing fruit), the sacred this or that. He bowed deeply to everything we looked at, even worshipping our camera when it flashed.

It was quite funny but also illuminated an essence of India—religious devotion, self-effacement, and resourcefulness. There isn't enough to go around here, and the little man in his *dhoti* accompanied us for karma, company, goodwill, and a few rupees.

Indeed, there is no resourcefulness like that in India, where

people find a million ingenious ways to make a living—a pup-
peteer at a Bangalore market, drawing children with his marionette
on a pole and then selling penny candies to the parents; men with
portable merry-go-rounds for tots; peanut sellers carrying portable
braziers and wrapping the oily peanuts in yesterday's newspapers
along the Bombay promenade at sunset; a man selling rubber
bands on the street in Madras; even the hustlers who sell trinkets
in the cities and at tourist sites, offering ten items for the price of
one because a sale is a sale and there is no welfare plan.

Other livelihoods driven by caste seem degrading until you understand that the alternative would be worse: women and children
all over the south breaking rocks with hammers to make gravel;
groundskeepers cutting lawns with scissors.

Our trip ended at the beach in Madras. Fishing boats made
from beams lashed together set out onto the Bay of Bengal as the
sun set behind us, beyond the subcontinent. We made our way
among groups of men repairing nets along the long stretch of sand,
watching our step (the beach is "dirty," we'd been warned, and indeed it was, punctuated by steaming piles of human shit), exchanging smiles and occasional conversation with fishermen. A
man wiping his behind in the surf rolled his *lungi* back to his knees
and leapt up as we passed, saying "How are you, what is your
name?" without missing a beat. Rather than shake his proffered
hand we tented ours in the traditional Hindu greeting, said,
"*Namaste*" ("I bow to the divine in you"), and continued our stroll,
knowing we'd experienced an India as ageless and fascinating as
the one we'd imagined.

James O'Reilly and Larry Habegger are the editors of the Travelers' Tales
*series. They also write "World Travel Watch," a column that appears in
newspapers throughout the United States.*

★

Caring for the daily needs of a Hindu god is similar to coping with a bed-
ridden invalid. At midday the god is given a hot bath and annointed with
saffron powder. Sandal paste is applied to the statue's breast and feet. It is

clothed in clean garments and decked with jewels and garlands of flowers. When the god is ready, the curtain is reopened so that the god can be seen by the devotees. Next comes lunch, specially prepared by Brahmin cooks in the temple kitchens. Baskets of food are placed before the god. Finally the statue is offered quids of betel nut and its mouth is washed with water.

—Peter Holt, *In Clive's Footsteps*

PETER SHELTON

The *Dharma* of Heli-Skiing

The author learns ascension-through-falling
in the Indian Himalayas.

Once there was a holy man named Narada, whose great learning impressed even the gods, even Vishnu who sleeps on a bed of cobras above
the dark lake of infinity and whose dream is the universe as we know it.

One day Vishnu came to Narada and offered him a single wish;
Narada answered that he would like to understand the Maya, the illusion of the world as dreamed by Vishnu. "Very well," said the god. "Let's
go for a walk."

So Vishnu and Narada began a trek that would take them across the
whole of Hindustan: through the teeming streets of Calcutta, along the
banks of the holy Ganges, into the stifling forests that belonged to the
Bengal tiger, and out across the plains of Uttar Pradesh, which grew hotter and hotter until the grass disappeared and their feet trod the burning
desert of Rajasthan.

In the desert, Vishnu beckoned Narada to him. "My son, I'm thirsty.
There is an oasis around this dune. Please go and fetch me some water."
So Narada went. He found the oasis, where springwater greened the
fields of a small village. Seeking permission to draw from the well, he
knocked on the door of the first hut. A young woman answered, and the
moment Narada's eyes met hers he forgot his mission, forgot everything
from before.

Narada stayed and married the beautiful young woman. They had

The Dharma *of Heli-Skiing*   129

two children. He was very happy, coaxing grain from the soil, working
beside his loving wife, watching his children grow.

   Twelve years went by, and one day an unusually dark storm rolled in
from the north. Thunder boomed, and rain came down in sheets. Narada
tried to gather his family in his arms, but the flood hit too quickly and
plunged them into an inky swirl that separated them all. In a frenzy, he
dove and thrashed and cried the names of his wife and children, but in
the dark, swirling water he could grasp nothing. Exhausted, heartsick, he
gave in to the raging current, and the water took him, too.

   Narada awoke face down in the sand under a blinding hot sun. He
heard a voice: "My son, where is the drink you promised me? It's been
half an hour."

   Narada looked into Vishnu's face. After a moment, the god said,
"Now do you understand the power of my Maya?"

                                                          —Hindu legend

NONE OF IT—NEITHER THE IRONY NOR THE ECSTASY—WOULD BE
possible without the helicopter. This raging machine clatters and
roars over a vast Himalayan wilderness like something out of
Apocalypse Now minus the Wagner, and when Boris Hangartner,
the pilot for Himachal Helicopter Skiing, eases it in for a landing,
floating it down like an iron dragonfly onto the lawn of the Manali
Resorts Hotel, he invariably has an audience. This isn't one of
those twelve-passenger Bells, which perform so well in the lower
altitudes of British Columbia. Here in the Indian state of Himachal
Pradesh, where the elevations of the landing zones range from
7,000 to more than 17,000 feet, helicopters need to be smaller and
more powerful. Hence ours is a five-seater French Aerospatiale
Lama, which is tiny but it is also so potent that it holds the helicopter altitude record of 40,820 feet.

   Each day peasants in drab wool shawls and pillbox hats called
topis gather along the hotel wall to watch Boris's takeoffs and landings. They giggle and stare unabashed at the skiers inside, each
dressed in fluorescent Gore-Tex suits and big, stiff, plastic boots.
They point off toward the peaks with some concern, as if the skiers
may not know about the evil spirits that wait up there.

What is the helicopter doing here, they wonder, leased for $1,500 an hour in a land where rice in the priciest bazaar goes for three cents a kilo? This time, it was here to deliver me and eleven other pleasure seekers to places of sublime stillness and altitude from which we would descend in a state of charmed albeit capitalist-contrived nirvana. The helicopter was our magic carpet, a tool giddily suited to one of the most expensive and addictive pastimes of the late twentieth century: heli-skiing.

It is astonishing, really, the delicacy of the thing. Time and again, Boris brought the beast in for a landing just inches from our crouching forms, the basket on the copter's port skid lined up perfectly with our stacked skis for loading. Then there was the time our guide, Pablo (a.k.a. Paul Berntsen), dropped his radio somewhere in the middle of a run. Boris flew him up the tracks, nosing the Lama along the steep snowfield at walking speed. Finally, Pablo saw the radio; he jumped out, retrieved it, and scrambled back aboard the helicopter à la James Bond, while Boris, who dared not touch down, juggled gravity, wind, and the helicopter's awesome torquing power just a few feet off the ground.

Even at 15,000 feet, the Lama has the muscle to climb 1,500 vertical feet per minute. Not long after the dramatic radio retrieval, Chris Noble, the photographer in the group, spotted a delicate pinnacle across the valley cresting at about 14,000 feet with the hulking, glacier-hung summit of the sacred Deo Tibba in the background. "Great picture," he said. "Can you ski it?"

"Sure," said Pablo, and in a blink we were there. Boris let us off on a 14,000-foot knife-edge ridge just back from a perfect, thirty-five-degree slope, a white dune unmarred by even a single rolling snowball. Then the Lama lifted and dove back to the valley floor for the second half of our party.

Minutes later we were all together on the untracked snow. We had our skis on and pointed down the hill, and we watched as a golden patch of sunlight rolled our way. When it lit the snow at our feet, Chris gave the signal and we pushed off down the face, snow from one skier flying in the goggles of the skier behind him. Our skis were like a school of dolphins riding the bow wave of

*A*cute Mountain Sickness occurs at high altitude and can be fatal. The lack of oxygen at high altitudes affects most people to some extent. Take it easy at first, increase your liquid intake and eat well. Even with acclimatisation you may still have trouble adjusting—headaches, nausea, dizziness, a dry cough, insomnia, breathlessness and loss of appetite are all signs to heed. If you reach a high altitude by trekking, acclimatisation takes place gradually and you are less likely to be affected than if you fly straight there.

Mild altitude problems will generally abate after a day or so but if the symptoms persist or become worse the only treatment is to descend—even five hundred metres can help. Breathlessness, a dry, irritating cough (which may progress to the production of pink, frothy sputum), severe headache, loss of appetite, nausea, and sometimes vomiting are all danger signs.

◆

—Hugh Finlay, et al.,
India − a travel survival kit

gravity, leaping above the surface and then plunging into foam, again and again.

Down at the bottom, 3,000 feet and some 300 such turns later, Chris Olson, one of the founding partners of Himachal Helicopter Skiing, lay back in the snow and smiled. "If you didn't know you were in India," he asked, "where would you think you were?"

India doesn't exactly come to mind when heli-skiers daydream. More likely it's British Columbia, where the sport began, up there in the Cariboos, the Bugaboos, and the Monashees. Or perhaps heli-skiers dream of New Zealand's Harris Mountains. Or even Utah's Wasatch Range. But India? "It's true," said Olson one night over a plate of spicy *tandoori* chicken. "People think there isn't skiing in India, that it's impossibly far away and unbearably poor."

India is far away, and it is poor. But India does have the Himalayas, the world's highest mountains, an almost incomprehensibly huge line of peaks. As the Rockies dwarf the Appalachians and the Alps dwarf the Rockies, so the Himalayas, in both verticality and snowy surface, dwarf every other range on the planet. That's why we came here: to ski the highest and longest runs in the heli-skiing pantheon and to do it first, before the rest of the money-to-burn crowd caught on.

Heli-skiing is an addiction that can be satisfied only by long runs on endless slopes, a kind of tilted alpha-wave biofeedback on a grand canvas. But even after days of carving symmetrical, wavy lines on the snow, it is still never enough. The more you do it, the more you crave it. And the doctors and bankers and corporate farmers who can afford to feed their heli-skiing habit have started running out of new mountains to ski. In British Columbia, despite the big ranges, most of the runs have already been named and tracked by well-heeled junkies. In the United States, liability laws and public-lands policy have meant that most heli-skiing takes place in daily operations run out of established ski areas. In Europe, wilderness regulations prohibit heli-skiing in most of the Alps, save a few high points in Italy. For the moment, that leaves only New Zealand, where weather and snow conditions are chancy at best, and the Caucasus, where a couple of maverick outfitters fly old Soviet military helicopters from bases in the nation of Georgia.

And, obviously, it leaves India. Himachal Helicopter Skiing is not the first to fly in the Himalayas. That distinction belongs to Switzerland's Sylvain Saudan, the self-proclaimed Skier of the Impossible, who launched his Himalaya Heliski operation in 1987 in Kashmir. Saudan pioneered extreme skiing in the 1960s and 1970s; he fell in love with the Himalayas after he'd jump-turned for six straight hours down the 23,396-foot Nun-Kun in central Kashmir in 1977, the first time anyone had skied a 7,000-meter peak from the summit.

For the first three years of Saudan's heli-skiing operation all went well, despite perennial border tensions with Pakistan. Since 1990, however, the U.S. government has issued travel advisories for Srinagar, capital of the state of Jammu and Kashmir, where separatist violence has sporadically erupted. But Saudan keeps skiing (with a military attaché ever present), thanks to a growing, largely

European clientele that's both hungry for virgin snow and tolerant of Third World adventure.

Himachal Pradesh, where we went heli-skiing, is a benignly peaceful state. Still, that didn't save Chris Noble, his wife, Marjie, and me from a bomb scare in New York before our Air India 747 even left the ground. "It's not a good sign," Chris dead-panned, "when you look out the window and you're sur-rounded by Desert Storm vehicles." Who were the ter-rorists? Tamil separatists? Sikh militants? Kashmiri Muslim extremists? When we were finally allowed back on board, the pilot told us only, "The delay is because of se-curity of the aircraft."

Our second plane, which took us from New Delhi to Kulu, was a silver, twin-en-gine prop job that bore a striking resemblance to the one that crashed deep in the Himalayas in the 1937 Ronald Colman film *Lost Horizon*. Reality blurred in a fog of jet lag, culture shock, and free airport tea.

"Goodmorningsir." The flight attendant had shouted above the engine noise. "Teacoffeesir? Pleasesir?" She wore a turquoise-blue sari and a red *tika*, or "third eye," on her forehead. A section of

In 1947 the British had conveniently forgotten to complete the separation of India and Pakistan all the way across the Himalaya to the Chinese border. In 1984 Indian troops suddenly occupied the forty-seven-mile Siachen Glacier, the longest in the Himalaya, in a region Pakistan had always administered.... The highest war in history was being fought at altitudes up to 20,500 feet. The situation was virtually unknown to the outside world because photographers and jour-nalists were banned from the war zone by both sides.... After returning from the high camp, I wrote, "Men might as well shoot at each other on the moon as stand here on the pristine heights of the earth, gasping for breath with weapons in hand."

♦

—Galen Rowell, *Galen Rowell's Vision: The Art of Adventure Photography*

her soft, brown midriff showed through the swirls of silk even though, out the window, snow powdered the mountain ridges.

"Teacoffeesir?" she asked again in that lilting English left over from the days of the Raj. She moved ahead to other members of our ski party: to Willi, the Austrian ski-edge manufacturer, and Rainer, the chain-smoking surgeon from Germany; then on to Jean-Eric and Albert, French heli-skiing buddies who work in Bangkok and Hong Kong. Then she moved to Karen, the Montana horsewoman, and Wendy, the bond trader from Salt Lake City.

None of us knew what to expect in the Kulu Valley, a place whose ancient name, Kulantapith, means "the end of the habitable world." What it looked like when we landed was a kind of paradise. Deep March snow blanketed the mountainsides above us, while down in the valley it was spring. Green barley and new wheat sprouted in farm terraces, which marched like green honeycombs up the hillsides. Pink plum and white apple blossoms painted the bottom-land. The Beas River, India's fifth largest waterway (and reportedly loaded with the formidable, salmon-like mahseer) gurgled glacier-blue through white granite bedrock.

On the hour-long taxi ride from Kulu up to our hotel in Manali, we braked for children herding sheep and dove time and again to the road's left shoulder at the approach of a *Tata,* one of India's ubiquitous spangled orange buses. Sharp-featured, dark-skinned men stared as our string of ski-laden taxis rolled past. Women in finely woven shawls flashed shy, veilless smiles.

We passed low, smoky huts belonging to round-faced Tibetans who had fled their homeland in 1959 along with the Dalai Lama, who now lives just to the west in Dharamsala. We saw the squatters' camps of Nepalese migrant workers and the finer two-story houses belonging to local Hindus.

Our driver, Iqbal Sharma, told us that the town of Manali was a rich place for two reasons: "Because of the apples and because of the road." The apples were a gift of the British, brought here about a hundred years ago when the viceroys made their summer capital at Simla, a hill station a couple of hours to the south. The road, however, is not the bounty of imperialism. It's the result of a brief border dispute with China. In 1962, Chinese troops moved into a portion of Ladakh (a cultural and geographic extension of Tibet claimed by India), dealt the Indians a stinging defeat, and then claimed only a tiny section of the territory, apparently satisfied simply to humiliate their neighbors. Soon afterward, the Indian military carved this road to create a secure land route into the Himalayan border area. The road follows ancient trade routes, and though potholed and one-laned, it has meant increased, year-round access to the city.

After checking into our hotel—a new glass and cut rock affair with a sign in each marbled bathroom that read HOT WATER TIMING: MORNING 6:30 A.M. TO 10:30 A.M. EVENING 6:30 P.M. TO 10:30 P.M.—we strolled through the nearby hot-springs village of Vashisht with Murli, a coach of the Indian national ski team. Murli told us that the Indian ski championships were held at the head of this canyon, outside the village of Solang, where cleared field and halting poma lift constitute one of the two "ski areas" in India. In fact, more than a few Manali children have taken to the sport. They build their own skis out of wooden planks, nailing old band-saw blades on for edges. Twine lashed over their standard winter footwear, rubber galoshes, suffices for bindings. And they top their gear off with tree-branch poles.

The only snow we saw in Vashisht was in remnant piles from a big storm the week before. The real snow, the stuff we had come to ski, was out of sight, up over the nearest forested hills, which narrowed the valley down to a neck-craning slit. Late afternoon sunlight beamed in through firs and cedars, illuminating handsome wooden houses on the hillsides with animals housed on the ground floor, people above. These houses had slate-covered roofs at exactly the same pitch as those of chalets at similar elevations in alpine countries; they also had wraparound balconies with ornately carved railings over which were draped brilliant red scarves, blue trousers, and pink bedspreads and towels.

At the hot spring, tiny, pantless children splashed on the stone slab where steaming water poured from inside the mountain. The laughter of men and boys echoed from behind the carved stone walls of temple baths. Murli chatted with an old woman who formed cow dung into patties with her hands; later the dried patties would be burned as fuel. She grinned a near-toothless grin and greeted us, as everyone did, with the all-purpose *namaste.*

The next morning at breakfast we met Olson's Australian partner, Roddy Mackenzie, the strapping son of a wealthy Melbourne farmer. His great-grandfather had lived in India in the days of the Raj, and Roddy seemed a bit of a throwback himself, brusque and occasionally condescending. On the morning we met him, he was mumbling his impatience in Hindi to the white-jacketed waiters who were slowly serving up hotcakes and *lassi,* a creamy yogurt and banana drink. He, more than anyone else at the table, should have known better. "If you could put a price on patience," he told me in a more reflective moment, "India would be the richest nation on earth."

As a boy Roddy had accompanied his father to Nepal on a commercial trek. He remembered keeping a bunch of Nepalese kids enthralled for an hour outside his tent lighting matches. Then, in his late teens, an aborted adventure with a school chum had led him to Manali. They had planned to hike into Ladakh to "scrounge around in some caves" described by a distant relative in a diary kept during a three-year trek in the Himalayas. They'd ended up in Manali. "And I've been coming back ever since," he said in his quiet, yet somehow agitated, Aussie drawl.

On this first day, Roddy would not be skiing with us (neither would head guide Nick Craddock) but Olson would. Outwardly, Chris is Roddy's opposite: the son of a Michigan investment manager, he's a laid back, skinny, twenty-eight-year-old rock climber with a toothy grin. He got involved in the heli-skiing venture when a friend introduced him to Roddy, who in turn convinced him to put up $75,000 to have a helicopter dismantled and shipped from Switzerland for the first season in 1990. Since then, business has been sketchy at best: the Persian Gulf War, the recession, and Western preconceptions about skiing in India have all but conspired to keep business at a trickle. But Olson remains optimistic. "Just wait until you see where we're going," he said as we pushed back our chairs to dress.

Our first heli-ski drop would be Bant Rua, a mile-wide meadow draped from a ridge at 13,000 feet, 2,000 feet above timberline. Once out of the valley, the landscape turned pure white, and the mountainsides rose steadily toward the fluted spires and blocky summits of the area's highest peaks, around 20,000 feet in elevation. A high-pressure haze muted the day's snowy contrasts, but it also seemed to magnify the already impressive verticality. This was the Himalayas of the picture books.

The Bant Rau landing site was about as high as the highest heli-ski landings in Colorado, which are the highest in North America. And still we were just on the fringe of the really big stuff, which loomed ever higher all around. We skied Bant Rau, leaving hundreds of easy, regular turns in the snow. Then it was back into the helicopter for the next run, called Son of E. P., one bowl away from its namesake, Excellent Powder. This time we started from just below 14,000 feet. Rainer, the chain-smoker, went chalky white with the exertion and had to "voluntarily" cut back on his skiing. His condition was not unusual, since ancient Hindu traders had often felt dizzy and weak when crossing nearby Rohtang Pass. Back then they blamed their malaise on evil spirits, and called Rohtang the Pass of Death. For several of our next runs, we looked down on Rohtang's 13,000-foot saddle from far above.

Pablo, our guide, took things easy at first, biting off small chunks of each immense, naked slope. He'd ski twenty turns and stop, then thirty turns, then forty. Only once that first day did he lose himself, proving that guides too are susceptible to the sway of heli-skiing bliss. It was on a particularly fine pitch, a true north face running away from the sun and sparkling with big recrystalized surface flakes. The snow was knee-deep and bouncy, like angel food cake, and Pablo just didn't want to (or couldn't) stop himself. Down he went, forty turns, fifty turns, seventy. I tried to keep up while a small war raged within. Should I listen to the mantra of accumulating joy that gave me a sense of ascension-through-falling? Or to the lactic acid that was screaming its overweening presence into my thighs? They say nirvana is a blowing out, like the snuffing of a candle. By the time we finally stopped, I could have blown out a village of candles.

At the end of the day, Jim Bay, a Himachal guide from British Columbia, brought his group in last to the helicopter pickup. He stopped a thousand feet above us, atop a roll so steep that he couldn't see the middle third of it. Pablo radioed up, saying, "That's a nice little poke." In Colorado, I thought, that would be the biggest poke of my life. Jim led Albert and Jean-Eric into the throat of the couloir. He skied it with a liquid ease, surfing the forty-five-degree crux through the rocks without once upsetting his wool *topi,* which perched on his head like a book in a finishing-school balancing exam.

> Who put the seed in man saying, Let this thread of life be spun?
>
> ◆
>
> —*Atharva-Veda* (ca. 1000 B.C.)

That night, waiting for dinner with a golden Punjabi lager in his hand, Albert said, "It is fantastic. Ze best terrain I have ever seen." Everyone agreed, though the comments were oddly reserved—either because of fatigue or because of an unspoken superstition that it was too good, that it couldn't last.

Over the next two days we skied with Roddy—and with Murli when there was an extra seat—and after each run we flew higher, until we were sliding down as much as 6,000 vertical feet per run. One of the longest runs ended in the terraces of Sethen Village, a little Buddhist enclave that had been abandoned for the winter. The place seemed stuck in time. We kicked off our skis and wandered around, whispering for no good reason. Faded prayer flags flapped atop tall poles and wooden hoes and picks rested in the rafters of mud-chinked log houses.

A few days before our arrival, Boris had flown the Lama up to Deo Tibba and touched down on the summit—just for a second, just to see if he could do it. Boris knew it was a sacred mountain, but he also knew that just about every feature on Himalayan landscape has its deity and its story. From the slopes above Sethen Village, for instance, we'd been able to see Hanuman Tibba, across the valley to the northwest, which was named for the monkey god, Hanuman, who led an army of monkeys to rescue Prince Rama's wife, Sita, in one of India's most cherished Sanskrit epics, the *Ramayana.* Roddy pointed to another peak with a necklace of cliffs near the top. "It seems this god took a shine to a beautiful girl and miraculously impregnated her, and she had sixteen snakes for babies, which she kept in an earthenware jar," he said. "Someone who wasn't supposed to opened the jar, it flew apart into the landscape, and the snakes became mountains. That one there still has the jar's ring around its neck."

Over the past few days, we'd noticed that many of our landing sites were marked with stone cairns, some of them taller than a man could reach. They'd been erected by villagers who climb up each October during festival season, scrambling onto one another's shoulders to add one more rock to the cairn's top in homage to the god of that particular ridge or meadow. We skied in virgin, silent snow, but everywhere around us the land hummed with spirits.

After three days of glorious, uninterrupted skiing, it rained— then rained some more. The helicopter couldn't fly, so we drove to the bazaar. Some of the Tibetans in Manali have become merchants; a few have become prosperous by selling woven fabrics, silver jewelry, bells, and telescoping horns. They now live in fine houses. Still, the majority of local Buddhists live in mud-floor shacks along the road. River boulders are painted with LONG LIVE H. H. THE DALAI LAMA and CHINA INVATES TIBET 1959 and so on. But local Hindus aren't particularly sympathetic. One man told me, "If they want to retake Tibet, why don't they go do it?"

At the bazaar, examples of the disparity between rich and poor were everywhere. Thanks to the road leading up the valley, Manali has become a kind of Indian Niagara Falls, a honeymoon mecca for the nation's middle class. They come in the summer to escape the oppressive heat of the plains, and they come in winter, too, especially February, which is the month Indian astrologers favor for weddings. There are more than a hundred hotels in town, with still more in the valley's evergreen forests. After we'd walked around the bazaar for a while, staring at the wares, I watched from under my umbrella as a taxi pulled to a stop in front of one of the town's finest hotels. The street was a river of snowmelt, garbage, and excrement, and as the taxi's door opened, a dainty foot shod in a white linen pump swung out and stepped up to its ankle in muck.

There was more rain the next day, Thursday, and we tried not to mope. It seemed now that even the memory of that exquisite skiing was slipping away, like Narada's family, down the swollen Beas River. We ate in glum silence. As usual at the hotel, the food was delicious: lentils, saffron rice, startling red carrots, *chapatis,* and a chewy goat cheese cooked with garlic and spinach. We played *caroms* in front of the fire. We watched television. A cricket match yawned along on one channel. "No real power in that shot," droned the announcer. "It just seemed to stagger its way through for Andrew Jones's fourth boundary." On another channel was a repeat of the serialized program *Ramayana,* first aired in 1988. Indians were so hooked on the original weekly episodes (all seventy-eight of them) that riots broke out in Uttar Pradesh when the show ended. But of course the dialogue was incomprehensible to us.

We wanted to be coursing down those endless, womanly slopes in the high country. We had been adjusting to the altitude, feeling stronger with each day. We had hoped to fly to 16,000 feet before the week was out. And we had accumulated less than half of the 100,000 feet of helicopter lift that Helicopter Skiing had guaranteed. On Thursday afternoon, some of the Euros began getting antsy about catching their plane out of the valley on Saturday. They had a point; if it kept raining no one would fly out of Kulu. A car trip to Delhi would take two days. Who knew? Friday might be a ski day. Heli-skiers are, out of necessity, gamblers.

Rainer, however, couldn't wait. He hired a car and left the valley Thursday afternoon. A few of us went the other direction, back up to Vashisht, this time with the intent to slip into the hot baths. But the water was unusually low and, perhaps because of the rain, had turned an uninviting brown. We splashed water on a scowling stone god and retreated to the temple courtyard. Rain polished the already slick stone floor. Children collected the shoes of worshipers and bathers at the gate, and bare feet shuffled across the stones, polishing, polishing.

Friday dawned as wet and dreary as the previous days. Chris and Roddy were empathic but not apologetic; those skiers in our group who'd bought the guaranteed 100,000 feet of vertical would be issued a partial refund. Before we left, Jean-Eric and Albert signed up for another Himachal week the next winter, a Himalayan hunger in their eyes already. They knew they had just scratched the surface.

For twelve hours, crammed with our baggage in an armada of taxis, we bumped down the road to Punjab. Over that time we stopped for three flat tires. We stopped to buy puffed rice from a roadside ascetic, rice that our driver insisted we touch to our *tikas* in order to bless our travels. We wondered aloud about India and quizzed one another for confirmation of the skiing, trying to hold on to the immensity and beauty of it all. We wondered if maybe we had dreamed it, or if we might, in fact, be the illusion.

Peter Shelton began skiing in 1956 at the age of seven and since has skied most of the world's mountain ranges. He taught skiing for eight years and was director of the ski school at Telluride in Colorado. He's a four-time winner of the Harold Hirsch Award for excellence in writing about skiing, and he's the author of four books on the sport, most recently Ski the Rockies *from Graphic Arts Center Publishing in Portland, Oregon. His two teenage daughters are avid snow boarders.*

✳

In nearby Faizabad I played confessor to an embittered rickshaw-*wallah*. In hopes of a bigger tip, he'd been complaining about how tired his legs became at the end of a day. I surprised him by offering to switch places: I'd do the pedaling and he'd sit in the passenger seat, on condition that he truly played the part of a passenger by telling me all his life troubles.

"You will find it so difficult," he laughed. "Rickshaw-man's job is hard work." But we traded seats nonetheless.

It was hard work, hard both to propel the lumbering vehicle forward and to control its unwieldy momentum. I gained a new appreciation for the legions of skinny boys and grizzled grandfathers who pump the pedals fourteen hours a day.

The rickshaw-*wallah* had hulking shoulders and brawny legs as thick as logs. The gray hair growing out of his ears was so thick I wondered how he was able to hear. He said that he generally enjoyed his job because it had kept him fit and healthy for nearly fifty years, that he earned enough money to keep his family fed, and that his wife had proved herself by giving him three sons. But still he was not happy, he said, because of his brother.

"He went off to America," the beefy man said, "to Boston, USA. So many years ago. Asked me to come and join him, but I have seen American television on videotapes—"Dallas", you know it? I want to see America, but there every man is sleeping with the other man's wife. I love my wife, I do not want to be sleeping with the other women, and so I cannot go."

Like a good rickshaw-*wallah* I did not correct him, did not argue, just nodded my head and kept on pedaling.

"Now, ten years later," he went on, "my brother is so rich. He has about, oh, a hundred million dollars. And now when he comes to India, my brother will not visit me. He will not even talk to me, because I am a poor man. He thinks I will be asking him for money. But I do not want his money, just my brother."

Abandonment of one's family is, to Indians, an abomination.

—Jonah Blank, *Arrow of the Blue-Skinned God: Retracing the Ramayana through India*

ALEXANDER FRATER

✦ ✦ ✦

Greeting the Monsoon

The annual monsoon defines India as
no other natural event does.

A LINE OF SPECTATORS HAD FORMED BEHIND THE KOVALAM
beach road. They were dressed with surprising formality, many of
the men wearing ties and the women fine saris which streamed
and snapped in the wind. Their excitement was shared and sharply
focused, like that of a committee preparing to greet a celebrated
spiritual leader, or a victorious general who would come riding up
the beach on an elephant; all they lacked was welcoming garlands
of marigolds. As I joined them they greeted me with smiles, a late
guest arriving at their function. The sky was black, the sea was
white. Foaming like champagne it surged over the road to within
a few feet of where we stood. Blown spume stung our faces. It was
not hard to imagine why medieval Arabs thought winds came
from the ocean floor, surging upwards and making the surface waters boil as they burst into the atmosphere.

We stood rocking in the blast, clinging to each other amid
scenes of great merriment. A tall, pale-skinned man next to me
shouted, "Sir, where are you from?"

"England!" I yelled.

The information became a small diminishing chord as, snatched
and abbreviated by the elements, it was passed on to his neighbors.

"And what brings you here?"

"This!"

"Sir, us also. We are holiday-makers! I myself am from Delhi. This lady beside me is from Bangalore and we too have come to see the show!" He laughed. "I have seen it many times but always I come back for more!"

The Bangalore woman cried, "Yesterday there were dragonflies in our hotel garden. They are a sign. We knew monsoon was coming soon!" She beamed at me. "It gives me true sense of wonder!"

More holiday-makers were joining the line. The imbroglio of inky clouds swirling overhead contained nimbostratus, cumulonimbus, and Lord knows what else, all driven by updraughts, downdraughts, and vertical wind shear. Thunder boomed. Lightning went zapping into the sea, the leader stroke of one strike passing the ascending return stroke of the last so that the whole roaring edifice seemed supported on pillars of fire. Then, beyond the cumuliform anvils and soaring castellanus turrets, we saw a broad, ragged ban of luminous indigo heading slowly inshore. Lesser clouds suspended beneath it like flapping curtains reached right down to the sea.

"The rains!" everyone sang.

The wind struck us with a force that made our line bend and waver. Everyone shrieked and grabbed at each other. The woman on my right had a plump round face and dark eyes. Her streaming pink sari left her smooth brown tummy bare. We held hands much more tightly than was necessary and, for a fleeting moment, I understood why Indians traditionally regard the monsoon as a period of torrid sexuality.

The deluge began.

Alexander Frater was born on a South Pacific island and now lives in London and works as chief travel correspondent for the Observer. *He's written for* The New Yorker *and* Punch, *and is the author of three books. This story was excerpted from his book* Chasing the Monsoon.

★

One aspect of wearing a sari has remained constant through time: the tucked-in pleats. Sanskrit literature from the Vedic period insists that the pleats are absolutely necessary for a woman to be truly a woman. These pleats must be tucked in at the waist, front or back, so that the presiding deity, Vayu, the wind god, can whisk away any evil influence that may strike the woman in two important regions, the stomach and the reproductive organs.

The brilliant colors of the sari are also partly ruled by custom: colors are held to represent moods. Yellow, green, and red are festive and auspicious colors which stand for fertility. Red, which also evokes passion, is a bridal color in some parts of the country and a part of rituals associated with pregnancy. Pale cream is soothing in the summer and also symbolizes bridal purity.

A married Hindu woman will not wear a completely white sari, as it is only for widows: life without a husband is life without color. Black alone is thought to bring misfortune and must be mixed with another color. Blue evokes the thirst-quenching, life-giving force of the monsoon and visions of the beautiful boy-God, Krishna.

> —Annapurna Weber, "The Evolution of the Indian Sari,"
> *India Currents*

WILLIAM DALRYMPLE

The Other Raj

Centuries before the British arrived in India,
the Portuguese were in Goa.

IN THE NARROW COBBLED LANES OF FONTAINHAS—A SMALL BIT
of Portugal washed up on the shores of the Indian Ocean, where
old spinsters in flowery dresses sit on their verandahs reading the
evening papers—I finally found Perceval Narona, the Goan historian. He was sitting in a taverna drinking a glass of red Goan wine.
He was in an expansive mood.

"We were ruled from Portugal for 451 years and 23 days!" he
said in an accent heavy with southern European vowels. "The result of this is that we are completely different from other Indians—
completely different, I say! We Goans have a different mentality, a
different language, a different culture. Although we are now under
Indian occupation, I feel awkward when I cross the old border into
India….Suddenly everything changes: the food, the landscape, the
buildings, the people, the way of life…."

What Narona said was quite true: the minute you arrive in Goa,
you become aware that the place feels very different from anywhere else in India. But it takes a little time to work out exactly
why. Partly, you realize, it is the relative absence of people. Most
Indian scenes—even remote rural landscapes—always seem to be
packed with hundreds of men, women, and children, all shoving,

146

pushing, chatting, poking, giggling, begging, laughing, defecating, tripping over each other, and getting in the way. Much of the sub-continent feels like a vast, well-stuffed sardine can.

But—as the empty lanes of Fontainhas indicate—Goa is differ-ent. The red-roofed houses are spaced father apart; crowds are a rarity. From this flows a certain prosperity. There is no hunger in Goa, no beggars, little poverty, and, as a result, virtually no crime. It is a radical contrast to most of the rest of India.

Goa is marked out from its surroundings by its striking religious tolerance. While the rest of India becomes sporadically caught up in the waves of Hindu-Muslim hatred ripping outward from the ghettos of the labyrinthine cities of the north, Goa remains a rare haven of peace, sense, and proportion. The driver who took me to the state capital of Panaji on my first day discreetly crossed himself each time we passed a church. It was only later that I discovered that far from being a Roman Catholic, he wasn't even a Christian: He was a Hindu. I asked why he bothered to cross himself. His reply: "It is good to show respect to all gods."

But undoubtedly the biggest distinction between Goa and the rest of the subcontinent (just as Perceval Narona had indicated) is the Mediterranean *douceur* that hangs—palpably, almost visibly— over the state, the result of nearly half a millennium of Portuguese colonial rule. The Portuguese had been in Goa for two and a half centuries before the British conquered a single inch of Indian soil; they were still there in 1961, fourteen years after the British had gone home again.

The Portuguese first visited Goa in the last days of the Middle Ages, when in 1498 Vasco da Gama discovered the sea route to the Indies. Only twelve years later, Alfonso de Albuquerque, "the Caesar of the East," arrived off the coast of Goa with a vast fleet of war barks. He massacred the Muslim defenders of the local fort, then carved out for himself a small crescent-shaped enclave cling-ing to the western seaboard of the Indian subcontinent.

The conquistador chose his kingdom well. Goa is an area of great natural abundance, and the state is envied throughout India for its rich red soils and fertile paddy fields, its excellent mangoes, and its cool sea breezes. The state has always considered itself a place apart: a cultured Mediterranean island, quite distinct from the rest of India. As the Goans will quickly tell you, they eat bread, not *chapatis*; they drink in tavernas, not tea shops; a great many of them are Roman Catholic, not Hindu; and their musicians play guitars and sing *fados*. None of them, they will tell you, can stand sitars or *ragas*.

The history—some four hundred fifty years of intermingling and intermarriage—has forged uniquely close bonds between the Portuguese and the Goans, many of whom still talk about "those Indians" and "crossing the border to India," while happily describing their last visit to their cousins in the Algarve as if they had been revisiting some much-loved childhood home.

Moreover, as I quickly discovered on my first day in Goa, the state is still full of rather grand Indo-Portuguese donas who are liable to burst into tears if you remind them that since the "liberation" of Goa in 1961, they now owe allegiance not to Lisbon but to New Delhi.

"Liberation?" said Dona Georgina Figueiredo when I went to see her in her eighteenth-century ancestral mansion near Lutolim. "Did you say *liberation*? Botheration, more like!"

Dona Georgina clapped, and her barefoot servant came running down the passage from the kitchen: "Francis, bring Mr. Dalrymple a glass of chilled mango juice. *I* will have a cup of tea."

The servant padded off down the bare wooden floorboards. As he went, his mistress clasped her hands and raised her eyes to heaven: "Now where was I? Ah, yes. Now understand this, young man: when the Indians came to Goa in 1961, it was one hundred percent an invasion. From what were they supposed to be liberating us? Not the Portuguese, because the Portuguese never oppressed us. Let me tell you exactly what it was the Indians were freeing us from. They were kindly liberating us from peace and security."

Dona Georgina had fearsome beady black eyes, and her hair was arranged with a tight quiff. She wore a flowery Portuguese blouse bought in Lisbon, offset by a severe black skirt. She nodded her head vigorously.

"In fact, since 1961 we've had two invasions. First it was the Indians. They plundered Goa: cut down our forests and took away our woods. Their politicians created havoc. Then after that it was the turn of the hippies. Disgusting. That's what those people were. Disgusting. All that nudity. *And* sexual acts: on the beach, on the roads—even in *Panaji!* Of course, it was because of the *drugs* that their behavior was like it was. Disgusting people. Drugs and I-don't-know-what-else."

The history of Goa is written most eloquently in the portraits of the viceroys that line the great colonial museum in the state's ancient capital, Old Goa.

Typical of early Portuguese viceroys is Pedro da Alem Castro. He is a vast bull of a man with great mutton-chop whiskers. He wears knee-length leather boots that terminate in a pair of finely turned golden spurs; his plate-metal doublet is bursting to contain his beef-cake physique. Around him are others of his ilk: big men with puritanical hanging-judge eyes and thick growths of facial hair; each is pictured holding a long steel rapier.

Then, sometime late in the eighteenth century, an air of moral ambiguity suddenly sets in. Fernando Martins Mascarenhas was the governor of Goa only two decades

The state of Goa is known throughout the world for its beautiful beaches and inexpensive beer—and for the first time in my travels in India, I felt hostility. The people staring at me all had scowls on their faces and foreign passports in their pockets. They were Europeans who had found their beach paradise and were obviously reluctant to share it with anyone.

The few people who *would* speak to me had two things in common—they were in India because it was cheap and they disliked Indians. "They never stop staring," said one man. I suggested this might be due to the fact he was naked and half of his head was shaved. He didn't respond.

◆

—Willie Weir, "Cycling India: Letters from the Road"

after Castro had returned to Portugal, but he could have been from another millennium. Mascarenhas is a foppish dandy in silk stockings; a fluffy lace ruff brushes his chin. He is pictured leaning on a stick, his lips pursed and his tunic half-unbuttoned, as if on his way into a brothel. Just as in contemporary North India a couple of generations in the heat of the Indian plains turned the Moguls from hardy central Asian warlords into pale princes in petticoats, so by the end of the eighteenth century the fanatical Portuguese conquistadors had become effeminate fops in bows and laces.

This transition completely changed the course of Goa's history. In its earliest incarnation, Old Goa was a grim fortress city, the headquarters of a string of fifty heavily armed forts stretching the length of the Indian littoral. From it, a vast fleet of Portuguese war barks enforced their monopoly of the spice trade. The Portuguese decreed that every ship in Asia would have to carry a Portuguese permit and call in at the Portuguese forts to pay customs duties. Any boat traveling without a permit, or which had neglected to pay its customs duties, was immediately confiscated.

The arrogance and the sheer audacity of the conquistadors was astonishing, but while the Portuguese remained strong, they were able to back up their decrees with force. By 1600, Old Goa, rich from its limitless customs duties, had grown from nothing to a metropolis of seventy-five thousand people: It was larger than contemporary Madrid and very nearly as populous as Lisbon. The mangrove swamps were cleared, and in their place rose vast viceregal palaces, elegant town houses, austere monasteries, and towering Baroque cathedrals.

But with this easy wealth came a softening of the hard edges. The second generation of Portuguese colonists were not the men their fathers had been. The fops and dandies lost interest in war and concentrated instead on their harems. Old Goa became more famous for its whores and brothels than for its cathedrals. According to the records of the Goan Royal Hospital, by the first quarter of the seventeenth century at least five hundred Portuguese a year were dying from syphilis and "the effects of profligacy." The ecclesiastical authorities condemned not only the concubinage (which was practiced on a vast scale) but also the sexual "laxity" of the married women who "drugged their husbands, the better to enjoy their lovers."

As quickly as Old Goa had sprung up, it went into decline. The Portuguese monopoly of the Indian spice trade lasted less than a century. By the 1590s the first Dutch galleons were defying the Portuguese monopoly; by 1638 the Portuguese had lost control of the sea lanes, and Goa itself was being blockaded by Dutch warships. Overnight, the city became a forgotten backwater. By 1700, according to a Scottish sea captain, it was a "place of small Trade and most of its Riches ly in the Hands of indolent Country Gentlemen, who loiter away their days in Ease, Luxury, and Pride."

The best view of the old metropolis can be had from the Chapel of Our Lady of the Mount. To get there, you must leave your taxi and climb a half-mile-long flight of steps. What was once a fashionable evening walk for the Goan gentry is now a deserted forest path frequented only by babbler birds, peacocks, and monkeys. Scarlet, flamboyant trees corkscrew out of the cobbles. Bushes block the magnificent gateways into now collapsed convents and lost aristocratic palaces. The architrave of a perfect Renaissance arch is rotted to the texture of old peach stone. Roots spiral over corniches, tubers grip the armorial shields of long-forgotten Goan families. As you near the chapel, its façade now half-submerged under a web of vines and creepers, there is no sound but for the eerie creek of old timber and the rustle of palms.

The panorama from the chapel's front step is astonishing. The odd spire, a vault, a cupola, a broken pediment can be seen poking out of the forest canopy. Other than the churches, the entire Renaissance city has disappeared: palaces, shops, theaters, circuses, tavernas, houses. Everything has been submerged by the jungle, and only the energetic rearguard action of the Roman Catholic Church has managed to save the larger monasteries and cathedrals.

The most magnificent of these is Bom Jesus, the church that now houses the remains of Goa's great saint, the sixteenth-century Jesuit missionary Saint Francis Xavier. (At least what remains of his remains. In 1554, one Portuguese lady was so overcome with devotional fervor that she bit off the little toe of the saint's left foot and tried to smuggle her relic out of the church in her mouth. Part of the right hand was sent to Rome in 1615, and the remainder of the hand wound up with the Japanese Jesuits four years later.)

To modern tastes, Saint Francis seems to have been rather a brute—when he visited Goa, he was so shocked by the lingering pagan practices performed by the colony's converted Hindus that he successfully petitioned for the import of the dreaded Inquisition from Europe—but strangely, this does not stop Goans of all faiths from revering his memory four hundred years later. The reputed healing powers of the saint are today particularly sought after by the very "pagan" Hindus he sought to prosecute. Outside Bom Jesus stand the usual lines of postcard and trinket sellers that you can find around any of the great churches of Europe. But among the men selling effigies of the Virgin and pictures of the Pope, if you look carefully you will see one Hindu gentleman squatting on the pavement selling wax models of legs, arms, heads and ribs. When I first came across him, I asked him what the models were for.

"To put on the tomb of Saint Francis," replied the man. "If you have a broken leg, you put one of these wax legs on Mr. Xavier's tomb. If you have a headache, then you put one wax head, and so on."

"How does that help?" I asked.

"This model will remind the saint to cure your problem," replied the fetish salesman. "The pain will be finished in a jiffy, double quick, no problem."

After the fall of Old Goa, the Portuguese did not leave. Despite the collapse of their trading system and the end of their days as a world-class sea power, the Portuguese still clung to their precious Indian colony for three long centuries, adjusting their way of life to the new realities and moving their capital from the rotting grandeur of Old Goa to the less pretentious town of nearby Panaji.

Panaji is still the capital, and despite the recent changes brought about by the new Indian authorities—the rickshaws and the *pan* sellers, the garish new Hindu temples and the ugly high-rises—the

town still remains quite unlike any other in India. It is
distinguished by its red tile
roofs and its ornate Art
Nouveau balconies, its large
stuccoed town houses and
small but elegant piazzas.

The most beautiful area
remains the old quarter now
known as Fontainhas. It is a
little bit of Iberia in India: its
haphazard, narrow, cobbled
lanes could be anywhere in
Spain or Portugal, and it is
the last place in Goa where
Portuguese is still spoken as
the first language.

The great town houses
and palaces have all gone
now: the mansion of the
Count of Menem, the last of
the great Panaji aristocratic
town houses, was destroyed
in 1986 to make way for a
new six-story block of flats.
Nevertheless, in many of the
more humble houses of Fontainhas live the last impover-
ished survivors of the old
Indo-Portuguese Goan aristocracy. Wandering through
the old quarter of an evening,
you come across scenes impossible to imagine anywhere
else in India. Violinists practice in front of open win-

*G*oans remain proud about
their own language, Kon-
kani. Whatever you do, don't call it
a dialect. They see it as a distinct
and separate language, well over a
thousand years old, and once subject to ferocious persecution by
their Portuguese overlords.

"It is a perfect language for poetry," I was informed by a man
who ran a newsstand in Margao.
"We have many literary prizes for
Konkani and many fine writers
like Bakibab Borkav, R. V. Pandit,
Nagesh Karmali—and of course,
Manohar Sardesai. But it is a
struggle. The Indian government
does not encourage its use so," he
laughed, "we use it even more."

He showed me a piece of yellowed paper with a finely inscribed print in Konkani.
He translated:

Into the realm unknown to man
Into the heart unfound on earth
Into the eternity unread in life

"I keep this," he said, and patted
the pocket next to his heart.

♦

—David Yeadon, *The Back of
Beyond: Travels to the Wild Places
of the Earth*

dows; caged birds sit chirping on the windowsills; old boys in pressed linen trousers and homburgs spill out of the tavernas. With walking sticks in their hands, they make their way unsteadily across the cobbles of the *piazzas* and past the lines of black battered Volkswagen Beetles slowly rusting themselves into oblivion....

Meanwhile, only five miles away on the beach at Anjuna, a very different evening ritual is taking place. Instead of the rusting Volkswagens, a line of Enfield Bullet motorbikes is parked beneath the palm trees: the weekly hippie flea market is packing up; the German holy man is returning his stock of Hindu charms to his bag under the next palm tree; the Mexican bootlegger is putting his remaining cans of imported lager back into his knapsack. Only the French hippie who sells old Joni Mitchell cassettes remains in station, sitting cross-legged on a drape, humming "Blue" to herself as she watches the sun go down.

On the dunes by the shore, a bonfire is roaring; what appear to be members of a topless six-per-side female football team—an odd sight anywhere in the world but an astonishing one in India—are kicking a ball around. To one side, another group of bangled back-packers—all bombed out of their minds—are cheering them on while passing a ten-inch joint from hand to hand.

In the sixties, Anjuna was the goal of every self-respecting hip-pie in Asia. From Hampstead and Berlin, from the barricades of Paris to the opium dens of San Francisco, streams of bangled and tie-dyed teenagers crossed Asia to reach this beach and make love—to the horror of the Goans—on the breakers. Whole nomad communities formed around the beaches: Anjuna, Chapora, Colva, and Calangute, previously backwaters barely known even to the sophisticates in Panaji, became mantras on the lips of hipsters across Europe and the United States. The Stones were always about to appear to give a free concert at Anjuna; the Beatles were always on the next flight.

But they never came. The sixties turned into the long hangover of the seventies, and the hangover into the Decade of Greed. Most of the hippies either died of overdoses or went home. The young who come today are mostly students, generally a pretty affluent bunch who in due course will go home, cut off their ponytails, and become investment bankers. But a few of the genuine die-hard flower children of 1967 remain. Some have become very rich—it doesn't take much imagination to work out what trade their fortunes have come from—but most of the stayers-on are good-natured old freaks who grow their own, flop around in flared denim, hold forth on world harmony, and get by by selling chocolate brownies and Indian waistcoats to the backpackers.

It's an amusing little colony—an unlikely, fossilized relic of Haight-Ashbury—but its presence in Goa has had sad side effects. The young Goan bucks envy and admire the free-loving life of the neo-hippies and, in attempting to keep up, have jettisoned much of their own culture. There is a growing heroine problem in Panaji and, increasingly, a rejection of the straitlaced Catholic ways of old Portuguese Goa.

This came home most clearly on my last day in the state, when I went to see Dona Rosa, an old Indo-Portuguese widow, in her beautiful house in Lutolim. To get there from Panaji I passed along a lagoon edged in coconut groves, breadfruit trees, and flowering hibiscus. The village revolved around the large white Baroque church. In front of it stood a small piazza; to one side was the school, to the other side the taverna, the Good Shepherd Bar. In it, appropriately enough, you could see the priest sitting at a table in a white cassock, reading the daily paper.

Near the church stood the beautiful ancestral mansion of Mario Miranda, one of India's most distinguished artists. The house was built in 1690 and centers on an arcaded courtyard. Around it, flagstone floors give onto the principal rooms: the library, the ballroom (now Mario's own gallery), and the dining room with its wonderful collection of carved Indo-Portuguese furniture.

Casa Dona Rosa is more modest. With its carved rosewood four-posters and wickerwork divans, it resembles nothing so much as an enlarged doll's house. Dona Rosa herself is a small lady in Iberian widow's weeds. Her hair is tied up in a bun, and a holy medal hangs around her neck. She lives alone, with only her two servants for company; every day, twice a day, the household meets to say the rosary in front of Dona Rosa's ancient *oratorio*. The cup-board-like object opens up like a tabernacle to reveal its ranks of devotional images, crucifixes, icons, and flickering candles.

"The new generation don't understand our values," Dona Rosa told me as she showed me around the house. "They want flashy new flats. They don't like these old houses."

"Why?" I asked.

"My nieces in Mapusa complain about the intermittent electricity here. I was fifty before we had a single lightbulb in the house! Now my only worry is who is going to look after this place when I die."

Dona Rosa led me out onto her long verandah.

"It was the Indians that did it," she said. "When they invaded in 1961. Them and the hippies. Between them they destroyed the values of the younger generation…drugs and all."

Dona Rosa paused and sighed. "It was never like that when the Portuguese were here," she said. "Has anyone told you how wonderful it was in those days? When Goa was still ruled from Lisbon…?"

William Dalrymple also contributed "A Sufi Spring" to Part I, "Breaking the Fast" to Part III, and "Beyond Turkman Gate" to Part IV.

★

Generally speaking, the early Europeans in India were quite ignorant of Hinduism. One of the first parties of Portuguese soldiery in the early sixteenth century in Goa sat through a religious rite in the Hindu temple of Kali (the dark goddess) under the mistaken impression that it was the shrine of a local Black Madonna.

—Bruce Palling, *India: A Literary Companion*

G. BRUCE KNECHT

Through Rajasthan by Rail

*A first-time visitor discovers the palaces
and landscapes of northwest India.*

WHILE I WAS A VISITING FELLOW AT OXFORD UNIVERSITY, I ASKED
several of the India experts who are connected to the university to
help design the perfect trip for the first-time visitor to India. All of
them offered the same basic advice: first, I had to pick a single region; given India's vast dimensions, the two-week trip I envisioned
was too short to see anything more. Second, I should travel by rail;
the roads are among the world's most dangerous, but the trains, a
legacy of British rule, are safe and generally reliable. Finally, I
should be careful about timing; many regions are unbearably hot
in the summer, and many are pervasively wet during monsoons.

I eventually decided on Rajasthan, an arid state in northwest-
ern India where wealthy maharajahs once erected sprawling
fortresses and extravagant palaces. The four cities I especially
wanted to see—Jodhpur, Jaisalmer, Udaipur, and Jaipur—are readily reached by train, and since November to February is the best
period to visit, the region suited my December timetable. Not
only did my advisers endorse my plan but one of them, an Oxford
graduate and a journalist who had spent several months living in
India, agreed to join me.

Thanks to the Indian government's desire to increase tourist revenues, foreigners are given special treatment by the Indian railways. We were therefore not particularly alarmed when, having flown to New Delhi, we found a thick mass of humanity at the city's train station. Some people were waiting in long ticket lines; some were selling things, everything from oranges to shoes; and many others, some of them children, were begging. We went to the International Tourist Bureau, on the second floor, to buy fifteen-day first-class Indrail passes. Their cost would turn out to be greater than the individual fares for the journeys we would take, but since the passes would allow us to avoid the ticket-buying lines, they were a worthwhile investment.

When we returned to the station a few hours later, our names were posted and our compartment had, as we'd requested, just two berths. Although the chamber's condition was not consistent with most Westerners' idea of first class, dirty floors and grimy windows are hardly surprising in a country where the per capita income is less than a dollar a day. The train departed on time, and after a couple of hours talking with a group of rum-drinking army officers, we fell asleep to the train's steady rumble.

Food and drink were generally available on first-class trains, and the next day began when the conductor rapped on our door to deliver omelets and a thermos of sweetened coffee, along with the news that we would soon arrive in Jodhpur. We could see nothing but barren desert from our window, but as we rolled into the city, the Rajasthan my advisers had described was very much in evidence. Leaving the station, we were swallowed up by maze-like streets as we instinctively headed for the Mehrangarh Fort, the fifteenth-century fortress that Rudyard Kipling described as the creation of "angels, fairies and giants." As cows and colorfully dressed children wandered across the foreground, I tried to take photographs that framed the red sandstone fort between the narrow, shop-lined streets. Even as I stood in place, my lens was filled with kaleidoscope movement. I took so many pictures that I worried I had not brought enough film.

The legacies of the maharajahs are central to Rajasthan's appeal. The former rulers devoted much of their wealth to building projects, and although Indira Gandhi's socialist-leaning government limited their lucrative property rights and officially nullified their royal status in the early 1970s, the forts and palaces remain. Indeed, they have become valuable tourist assets as the royal families' diminished economic circumstances have led many of them to turn their palaces into hotels.

In Jodhpur, the Umaid Bhawan Palace, which took some three thousand workers sixteen years to build and which looks more like an American statehouse than a home, now incorporates both a palace and a one hundred-room hotel. Though the conditions of India's trains may disappoint the discriminating traveler, its top hotels are world-class. My friend and I strolled through the Umaid Bhawan's marble-clad halls and two rotundas with this-can't-really-be-here amazement. Eventually finding ourselves on a porch with a sweeping view of extensive formal gardens, we sat down to enjoy cocktails, one of the great sunsets of all time, and a leisurely dinner.

Our next stop was Jaisalmer, a remote desert city not far from the border with Pakistan. Here, too, a family of maharajahs built a sprawling hilltop fortress. With ninety-nine huge cone-shaped bastions, the golden-yellow sandstone stronghold is strikingly beautiful in spite of a gruesome history: an eight-year siege by a sultan of Delhi ended in 1295 with the defenders' defeat and the mass suicide of the city's women and children. Wandering through the stone-paved streets inside the fort, we visited a richly decorated Jain temple and saw how the fortress's modern-day occupants live. They are, by just about any standard, poor, but the only beggars were children who seemed to be more interested in social interaction than rupees. The feeling of having to stay on guard, which had caused us to keep a constant hold on our wallets in Delhi, was absent here.

One of the costs of India's exoticism (and sometimes unsanitary kitchens) is that its food can be too much for Western stomachs. Drinking bottled water is mandatory, and only recommended restaurants should be patronized. But even those precautions are sometimes insufficient or hard to follow: one morning in Jaisalmer after we ate at a simple restaurant that we happened upon, my friend woke up with stomach pain so great that he did not leave our hotel for the next two days.

While he recuperated, I set out on a two-day desert camel trek with two Britons and several local guides. Camel riding was a new experience for me, and although the desert is beautiful in its barrenness, it must be said that camels are not among the world's most attractive modes of transportation. Mine lowered himself to his knees and then sat on his haunches to receive me, but when he rose, by first unfolding and extending his hind legs, I thought I would fall right over the top of him. When he began walking, I was surprised by his attentiveness to the reins, but also astonished by the uncomfortableness of the saddle, which was fashioned out of several wool blankets. We spent the night in a small valley formed by sand dunes. The air turned cold as soon as the sun set and, shortly after the guides served a simple meal of *dahl* and *chapatis*, we retired.

Lying between the blankets that had been our saddles, we could

---

*D*ining at Indian restaurants outside the country does not prepare you for the experience of eating in India. No cuisine could be more exotic or particular to place, intricately reflecting a multi-layered culture defined by religion, history, and ritual.

Standing in the middle of an Indian marketplace, surrounded by swirling crowds of people, animals, bicycles, fume-belching motorized rickshaws and cow-drawn carts, all impossibly squeezing in and out of the narrowest alleyways, you marvel at how life can be lived at this density. Absolutely every human activity goes on in the streets, and that is where the best food in India is to be found, cooked on carts, or in cubby holes in buildings and alleyways.

◆

—Patricia Unterman, "Culinary Nirvana in the Streets of India," *San Francisco Chronicle*

see the profiles of our camels against a sky filled, astonishingly, with shooting stars.

When I returned to Jaisalmer, my friend was almost fully recovered. We left the next day for Udaipur. Along the way the desert turned into rolling hills and eventually rugged mountains; before we reached Udaipur, we passed through lush fields where teams of buffalo worked primitive-looking waterwheels to irrigate black soil. Udaipur itself, sometimes called the Venice of the East, is a romantic city full of temples, palaces, and art galleries. It is dominated by the largest palace complex in Rajasthan. With more than a thousand rooms, the City Palace now houses a museum and two hotels, including the Shivniwas Palace, where we stayed. The Shivniwas overlooks Lake Pichola and yet another hotel, the one that may be India's best known: the Lake Palace, an idyllic white-marble edifice that, because it occupies the entirety of a small island, appears to float. Udaipur was our favorite city, and so we

I climbed to a mountain lookout point and came upon an ancient Rajasthani man sitting alone singing. I sat beside him on a ledge, with just a tiny rail separating us from miles of flat, hard clay and scraggly growth below.

The old man sang in Hindi and played a hand-hewn instrument, his strong, work-hardened fingers moving nimbly across the fingerboard. When he finished, he looked at me and smiled. I gestured for another, and he gladly obliged. From reading about Indian folk music as part of my trip preparation, I guessed he sang of the desert earth, of the yellow mustard flowers, of the full colors of the crops as they grew. He put the instrument in my lap and showed me where to press my fingers on the horsehair strings and how to hold the high-arched bow. With his brown, lined face, he cheered me on and sang until dusk came and it was time for me to go.

◆

—Jo Yohay, "Solo Adventure: Six Weeks in India, the Hard Way—Alone," *Travel & Leisure*

spent three days there: we rode bicycles (they cost five rupees a piece, or about sixteen cents, a day), took a boat tour of Lake Pichola, went to the Lake Palace Hotel for dinner, and relaxed around the marble swimming pool at our hotel.

The City Palace and the Lake Palace both belong to the maharana of Mewar. (He is a *maharana,* or "light of the Hindus," rather than a maharajah because his ancestors not only ruled the province but also played an important spiritual role during their fourteen hundred-year reign.) The maharana was not the first among his peers to go into the hotel trade, but he is unique in that he has expanded his business beyond his own palaces and because he manages seven of his eight hotels himself. He commands great respect in Udaipur, partly because of his ancestry but also because of the extent to which he contributes to the local economy: his various enterprises employ more than a thousand people and support many times that number.

Curious as to how his family had transformed itself from royalty into hoteliers, I arranged to see the fifty-year-old maharana in his open-air office off the City Palace's innermost courtyard. Tall and bespectacled, the maharana dresses in the traditional *achkan* and has a thick white beard, which he carefully parts at the center of his chin. As we drank cups of tea, his familial pride and an aristocratic sense of duty were palpable, but his practical-mindedness seemed to leave him devoid of arrogance. "Respect is not automatic," he said. "And it does not come about because of what your ancestors did a thousand years ago. If we didn't know how to adapt, we would not have survived."

The last city on our itinerary was Jaipur, a place of broad avenues and bustling commerce. Many of its houses are painted pink, a tradition that began in honor of the 1876 visit of the Prince of Wales, later King Edward VII. Here the City Palace, the home of the current maharajah, contains two enormous silver urns that one of his ancestors filled with Ganges water to take on his six-month journey to witness Edward's coronation. Since some of Jaipur's most interesting sites were too far from the center for us to visit on foot, we hired a taxi to take us to the Amber Palace, which was the center of power in seventeenth-century Jaipur, and the Tiger Fort, built by the maharajah in 1734. By sunset we had returned to our temporary home, the Jai Mahal Palace Hotel, formerly a maharajah's residence. The weather was warm and clear, as it had been throughout the trip, and, sitting on the closely cropped lawn, we watched kites and birds dance across the darkening sky.

From Jaipur we could either return directly to New Delhi or make a one-day stop in Agra, the home of the Taj Mahal. Although Agra is in the state of Uttar Pradesh and our original plan was limited to four cities in Rajasthan, we decided that we would like to see the Indian equivalent of the Eiffel Tower. We began, however, to think that we had made a mistake when the conductor rapped on the door to say that three armed guards would be traveling with us "for your protection." Since the rifle-toting guards were obviously drunk, safer we did not feel. In early evening, when we arrived in Agra's darkened station, our supposed protectors disappeared, and we found ourselves surrounded by taxi and rickshaw drivers, all of them aggressively demanding our patronage.

The next morning we visited the Taj. Perhaps because I had been told repeatedly how disappointed I would be, I was not. On the contrary, I was awed by its serene beauty. Agra was as ugly as Udaipur was beautiful, but the Taj is still more captivating than the many photographic images of it would suggest.

When we left the Taj Mahal, we got another dose of Agra irritation: even with our Indrail passes, which had until then readily secured seats on every train we wanted to take, there was no room for us on the express train to New Delhi. Since my flight to London was departing that evening, we had to hire a car. The drive, all four hours of it, was terrifying. The highway we traveled operated according to the law of the jungle: big trucks had the right of way over small ones, small trucks over cars, and bicycles—well, it is better not to ride a bicycle. We saw the results of several head-on collisions, and had a few near misses of our own. In one we were forced off the road by an oncoming truck. In another we spun out of control as we sought to avoid a horse-drawn wagon that had no lights. The car stopped only a couple of feet from one of the horses.

In the end we made it back to the airport without phsycial injury. As we began reminiscing about our adventures, I realized that India had not so much differed from my expectations as exceeded them. The lows—namely, the extent of poverty and the seeming lack of respect for human life—were worse that I had expected. But the highs—the natural and man-made beauty— were far greater than I had ever imagined.

Before G. Bruce Knecht became a New York-based staff writer for the Wall Street Journal *in 1994, he wrote for a variety of publications from London. This article originally appeared in* The Atlantic Monthly.

★

I mailed books home from a post office on the outskirts of Jaipur. At the post office I discovered that I had to find a tailor to sew the books inside a cloth bag since they do not use boxes. Mission completed, I thought, back at the post office within an hour—having found a tailor who sewed the books inside a cotton bag. Then I discovered, after a pidgin-English, pidgin-Hindi exchange, that I needed my name imbedded on hot wax at the seams so that it would be obvious (for insurance purposes) if the bag had been opened. Sensing my exasperation, the clerk pointed to his head, smiled, motioned me to his seat in the chair at the window and went out- side to find some wax. Fortunately, the first customer at the window spoke English. He wanted three stamps which cost a total of one rupee. His smallest coin was a two rupee piece. I gave him the stamps and he left the two rupee piece on the table even though I had no change. My next customer spoke no English. He also wanted three stamps and didn't seem to have the right change. I gave him the stamps at no charge since I had an extra rupee from the first customer.

Then the postal clerk was back with a foil-wrapped piece of choco- late with the name Heller embossed on it. He gave it to me and pointed to a general store where I bought a red candle. The store owner dripped the wax along the seams of the bag and, as it turned out, onto the covers of the books. I have red sealing wax on my book jackets as a memento of the day I worked in the Jaipur post office.

—Carol Levy, "Vagabond in India"

MADHUR JAFFREY

✦ ✦ ✦

Stairway to Heaven

Fortunate Indians end their earthly journey on the
burning ghats *of the holy city of Banaras,*
but the city itself is full of life.

THE SUN'S RAYS HAD BARELY BEGUN TO LIGHTEN THE BLUE–BLACK
sky when our boat was nudged away from the banks of the Ganges
River in Banaras. As we moved upstream from Dasashwamedh
Ghat, the spot where the Ten Horse Sacrifice was performed in
pre-Christian times, I watched the visage of this ancient city, un-
blinkingly facing East, as it first appeared in dim relief and then,
bathed by the flattering amber light of dawn, burst into an ethereal glow.

Banaras, one of the holiest destinations for Hindu pilgrims, sits
high on a bluff, its skyline an uneven row of steeples, domes,
minarets and ramparts. This city has breathed without pause for
more than three thousand years. It is variously called Varanasi (its
ancient and recently resurrected name), Kashi (the traditional
name still used affectionately by the pious), and Banaras (its name
over the past few centuries, and the one most Indians use). The
city is believed to be the earthly home of Lord Shiva, the Creator
and Destroyer, and according to the scriptures it sits in the very
epicenter of spiritual India. Devotees who pray at its many shrines
believe that a dip in the holy waters of the Ganges here washes
away the sins of a myriad of lifetimes, and that Shiva whispers a

sacred mantra in the ear of those who die here, ensuring *moksha*—instant union with the Universal Soul and freedom from the painful cycle of rebirth and death.

Below the temples, palaces and monasteries, where once a curving earthen bluff stretched for several miles, a giant amphitheater of buff-colored stone steps comes all the way down to the water's edge. These are the much-photographed *ghats* (literally, "banks") built mainly from the 1700s onward by the pious rich. Their severe lines are softened by mushroom-shaped umbrellas, octagonal pavilions, pillared shrines, palace balconies, and, above all, by the masses of pilgrims from all over India who congregate here daily in ever-changing formations to bathe, to pray, and to cremate their dead.

The mighty Ganges River, it is believed, fell from heaven with torrential force. As it headed toward earth, Shiva caught it in his locks, tamed it, then let it proceed on its journey. The waterfront at Banaras was as sacred three thousand years ago as it is today. "If you bottle Ganges water, it will stay clear and pure forever,"

Banaras ghats

my boatman says. "The same cannot be said of our Banaras tap water."

As I travel upstream and then down, passing one *ghat* after another, the drama before me seems both medieval and eternal. It starts before dawn and plays itself out, impervious to the hundreds of photographers who come here to "capture" it. Women stand waist-deep in water, fully clothed, some with their heads covered by bright saris. They offer marigolds, roses, and water lilies to the rising sun, asking it for a share of its glory and wisdom in return. Then, filling little brass pots with the holy water, they climb the *ghat* steps, their bodies demurely covered yet revealed by their clinging saris. Soon they will change, discreetly, right there on the steps, and perhaps carry the Ganges water up to a temple to pour over a deity. Or they might take the water home. I once saw a lady, in a chauffeur-driven car, carefully balancing a very full pot on her knee. It could have been intended for someone sick—a few drops can work wonders—or for use in the kitchen. Several Banarasi ladies informed me that tea made with anything but Ganges water tastes quite horrible. And the Maharajah of Banaras says that his palace uses only Ganges water for cooking and drinking. (He quietly added that the water was collected farther upstream. Much, much farther. From another town!)

The men at the river are often more athletic than the women. Wearing skimpy loincloths, they wrestle, dive, swim, and contort their bodies into advanced yoga positions—yoga being another path to spiritual revelation.

> The city fascinated me and repelled me, like Yoga, like India. It was no good pretending the repulsion did not exist: Benaras is an incarnation of the Hindu mind, full of shocks and surprises. You cannot view her through the eyes of the flesh, or if you do you will want to shut them. Her real life burns in the Unconscious.
>
> ◆
>
> —F. Yeats Brown, *Bengal Lancer*, quoted by Peter Yapp in *The Travellers' Dictionary of Quotations*

Some brush their teeth with bitter twigs, then push two fingers vigorously down their gullets in quick succession, both acts part of their daily ablutions. Some, old and frail, stand quietly in the water, praying and chanting. All the while temple bells ring and the deep sound of conch shells reverberates over the river.

Each *ghat* has its own character. One is used mainly by South Indians, another by Bengalis. One *ghat* is for fishermen, one for laundrymen. But the real show-stoppers for tourists are the two *ghats* used for cremations.

Most cremation grounds in India are walled, and built on the outskirts of cities because of pollution. But Banaras is Shiva's city. In his capacity as Destroyer, Shiva reigns over the cremation grounds. One of the most hallowed spots on the river is Manikarnika Ghat, so named because Shiva's wife, Parvati, is thought to have dropped a jeweled earring here. It is believed that the world was created here, and here, one day, it will be destroyed. Death does not pollute here, it liberates. So bodies are cremated out in the open for all to see.

Biers, traditionally made of green bamboo, are deftly maneu- vered through the narrow lanes of the inner city where carriers chant "God's name is the Truth, speak Truth, Truth is." When a body enters Manikarnika Ghat it is in the kingdom of the Dom Rajas. Though they are untouchable by caste, the Doms have a monopoly: they control the prices of funeral wood, of shroud cloths and of the aromatic chips and resins that are scattered over the pyre. Even the eternal flame, without which no pyre may be lit, is for sale, priced according to the purse of the deceased.

Once the cremation has been completed, little children from the Dom's household sift through the ashes, scooping up the odd piece of gold or jewelry. Then the remains are consigned to the river. If a family cannot afford enough firewood, partially burned corpses are slipped into the water.

One time, a corpse like this, just barely singed, attached itself to the stern of our boat. For the next two hours it stayed with us, ris- ing and falling with the waves, moving when we did and stopping whenever we paused to go ashore. All this time the boatman, his boy assistant, and my guide, as well as the hundreds of people bathing and praying in the river an arm's length away, paid it no attention whatsoever.

It occurred to me then that the corpse was just one of millions that had used this waterway. Indeed, the Ganges has carried the ashes of almost every ancestor of mine, including my mother and father. (My parents were cremated privately in Delhi, and their ashes scattered in the Ganges at a more northern point.) If the sight of the open cremations here was so unsettling for me, a Hindu, what effect could they have on Westerners, who keep the business of death so totally separated from the business of life? Is Banaras, then, only for the strong-stomached traveler? Yet all around me, almost crowding out the pilgrims, were the boats of tourists— German, French, English, American. Was it just ghoulish fascination, or was something else happening here?

Actually, the concentrated spectacle of life and death on the *ghats,* so openly displayed, is almost cathartic. A traveler's

As I watched, as in a silently moving play, the skin grew black and cracked, the tongue protruded and a leg fell off where it had burned through at the knee joint; the fingers curled. I could smell the disintegrating flesh and ashes blew into my face, so I moved away, rather full of awe and a feeling of submissiveness that the living could so matter-of-factly yet with respect, handle the dead. And I thought how frail we are, how easily we die, how minute is the line existing between light and utter darkness, and how meaningless is the body once life had departed from it. And I thought with shame of my own country and how frightened and revolted we are by death and wished we could all come, one by one, to stand learning beside the burning *ghats.*

—Karen Eberhardt, "Banaras: Holy City"

exultation at the vision of a golden dawn quickly turns to agitation at the sight of the cremations. This is generally followed by an uneasy calm, when a thoughtful visitor is apt to begin searching for answers and meanings.

The waterfront is, in some ways, just the face of the city. To understand its heart, soul, and muscle, one must look elsewhere. Such a task might take a lifetime—or several lifetimes, as Hindus say. Banaras, throughout its long history, has taken pride in catering to those who wish to try. Ever since it was founded, the city has been a center of learning, drawing some of the worthiest national and international scholars—art historians, grammarians, theologians, philosophers. Today much of the scholarship is attached to two major centers: the Banaras Hindu University, set in thirteen hundred leafy acres and containing one of India's best museums, the Bjarat Kala Bhawan, and the Sanskrit University, which is housed, amusingly enough, in a grand Gothic extravaganza.

But a more ancient method of teaching and learning doggedly survives. This is the system of gurus—individual teachers and spiritual guides. "The great gurus," a young Banarasi lady once told me with conviction, "will even sacrifice their own liberation at death, coming back for as many lifetimes as needed to guide their pupils to salvation." Pupils, as many as a guru wishes, learn at his feet whatever and whenever he wishes to teach. There are gurus who can explain the intricacies of the scriptures, gurus for yoga, for music (sitarist Ravi Shankar and Bismillah Khan, India's greatest *shehnai* player, are both from Banaras), for weaving, and for fortune-telling.

Banaras also has some eminent minds who can turn into short-term gurus. When it became known that I would be writing about the city, suggestions poured in about the "knowledgeable ones" I should see: Priya Devi, the Sanskrit scholar who lives simply in a monastery by the water; Supakar, who runs the weavers' center; Ram Shankar Tripathi, head priest of Banaras's important Vishwanath Temple, who is a scholar, spiritual leader, university man, and (this was added for my particular benefit) a very good cook, and Professor Anand Krishna of Banaras Hindu University, aristocrat, art historian, Banaras incarnate.

I began to see Banaras anew through the eyes of the "knowledgeable ones." I learned that waves of Aryans from the Ural Mountains and the Caucasus had swept into India through the northwest passes in ancient times, settling first in the Indus Valley and then in the Gangetic plains. They probably reached Banaras about thirty-five hundred years ago. Professor Anand Krishna theorizes that the Dom Rajas at the cremation grounds might well have been the local rulers at the time, until they were conquered by the Aryans, enslaved, and given the menial tasks they have today.

Banaras sat on two major trade routes, the Ganges River and what is now the Grand Trunk Road. By 1000 B.C. the city was a thriving commercial center, where millionaires did business with sacks of gold, and bazaars offered emeralds, ivories, peacocks, and gossamer-fine fabrics. In its wooded site dotted with sacred ponds, lakes, and wells, Banaras was also called the Forest of Bliss. All manner of sages and philosophers were drawn here to set up retreats and ashrams, where they passed on their learning to their pupils. It was here, to the Deer Park named Sarnath, that Buddha came after his enlightenment—to preach his first sermon, make his first converts and start his new religion. By the twelfth century, both Hinduism and Buddhism flourished here, along with spiritualism and commerce.

It was at this stage that armies of Muslims came charging in from the same northwest passes the Aryans had used, destroying all the temples of "unbelievers" in their path. Under the com-

> To an outsider and, indeed, to most Hindus, the city may appear as a disordered, crowded jungle of temples. But to those Hindus whose vision is recorded in the mahatmyas of Kashi—those who see the city as a mandala—these temples are all part of an ordered whole, a structured universe with its own divine functionaries and its own constellations of deities. And their vision is embodied in the sacred geography of the city.
>
> ◆
>
> —Diana L. Eck,
> *Banaras: City of Light*

mand of their general, Qutub-ud-din Aibak, they proudly hacked down about one thousand temples in Banaras, using fourteen hundred camels to haul away their loot. The beautiful Sarnath complex, with its monasteries, pavilions, *stupas*, and exquisite statuary—here, a gently smiling Buddha draped in the sheerest of fabrics; there, a pillar from the third century B.C. topped with four magnificent lions—lay scattered in the dust. Buddhism in India never recovered from the attacks; Hinduism proved more resilient.

Muslim rulers kept a firm grip on India until the early eighteenth century. When they happened to be tolerant—or busy elsewhere—some Hindu temples were allowed to be rebuilt, but generally with a lower profile. Then a hard-liner would arrive, and with him another onslaught of destruction. The greatest indignity was reserved for the most sacred temples—they were razed, and then mosques were built on their rubble, sometimes (as in the Gyanvapi Mosque) using an old, very Hindu wall for support. There were many conversions as well, and today a good quarter of the city is Muslim; religious disharmony remains a constant threat. One of Banaras's greatest sages and poets, Kabir, a Muslim, arose in the fifteenth century to cry out that there was only one God for all mankind, whether we called Him Allah or Rama. Kabir is still read in every Indian school, but his message is largely ignored.

The next rulers in Banaras were the British. They set up an English system of education (it was they who built the Gothic university), considered the view from the Ganges quite grand (especially when a slight haze filtered out its more undesirable aspects), but thought the Hindu temples lacked both age and grandeur. They dismissed the "idols" as primitive, if not lewd. Many of the British showed their disrespect by tramping through holy precincts with their shoes on. Hoping that Christianity would save Banaras, they set up missions, but Banarasis refused to budge. Little did the British know that years later, in fair return, Banaras would be exporting its own Vedantic philosophers and Ravi Shankars to capture the minds and hearts of the West.

In the end, the British and the Indians seemed to live together in peace. When the Prince of Wales visited here in 1876 the

Maharajah of Banaras lit up the sky with welcoming fireworks, then floated thousands of small, glittering oil lamps in the Ganges River. "It seemed as though a starry sky were passing between banks of gold," wrote an almost delirious correspondent of the London *Times*.

While Banaras is ancient, scarcely a single whole building here is more than four hundred years old. The greatness of the city's temples—there are more than eight hundred of them, and hundreds of shrines and pilgrimage sites—has more to do with their perceived sacredness than their architecture. Almost every major god of the Indian pantheon has a temple. There is the blood-colored temple for Durga, the warrior god who rides a tiger and brandishes a sword. Large bands of monkeys have settled here, so children enjoy the visits as much as adults. Youngsters have even more fun at the Tulsi Manas Temple, dedicated to Rama, where scenes from the *Ramayana* are enacted by three-dimensional mechanical figures.

The temple dedicated to Hanuman, the monkey god who frees people from troubles is good to visit on Tuesday, Hanuman's day of worship. The Bharat Mata Temple has a large, informative relief map of Mother India as its central icon, thus offering pilgrims a sound lesson in geography as well as a chance for a quick prayer. There are shrines for Ganesha, the elephant-headed god, and for Lolarka, the sun god.

Shiva as Nataraja (dancing)

But the primary god in the city is Shiva. Of the more than five hundred temples dedicated to him, the most sacred is the gold-steepled Temple of Vishwanath, considered to be the spiritual heart of Banaras. No non-Hindu is permitted to enter its silver portals. The temple was built, destroyed, and rebuilt several times, and the present edifice dates to the eighteenth century. But its lingam, the phallic stone symbol of Shiva, is of great antiquity, having been saved during one attack by a fast-thinking priest who flung it down the Well of Wisdom in the yard.

This temple can only be reached on foot, through lanes so narrow that two people often rub shoulders as they pass. The best approach, used by the pilgrims for centuries, is the medieval Vishwanath Gulley. Only dappled sunlight enters here, filtered through the cloth awnings of the shops on either side. In the stores you can buy cooling attar of *khus* (similar to sandalwood) for the summer, or warming attar of musk for chilly January days. There are also betel leaves, specially treated here with a secret formula so they turn pale white. And what pilgrim can resist a rosary? Each god seems to have a preference in beads: Lakshmi, the goddess of wealth, likes dried lotus seeds; Saraswati, the goddess of learning, is inclined toward rock crystal.

Then there are the clay and lacquer images of the gods. It is said in Banaras that each week has seven days and nine religious festivals, and new images must be bought for each festival. Would you like a painting on ivory? "Very little ivory comes from Kenya nowadays," a shopkeeper complains, "so our great craftsmen are learning to do the same delicate carvings in sandalwood." Would you care for a sandalwood Ganesha? Perhaps you are saving your money for a choice piece of Banarasi fabric?

Ah, the fabric! No Indian bride worth her salt considers her trousseau complete without at least one Banarasi sari, at least one "splendid web" of silk and gold. It is said that the cloth chosen for Buddha's shroud almost twenty-five years ago was a length of Banarasi cotton. It was soft and malleable and yet so tightly woven that oil would not pass through it.

Today, much of the dyeing and weaving is done by families of Muslims, converted over the centuries from Buddhism and Hinduism. To buy a sari the old-fashioned, traditional way, we head toward one of the weavers' districts. It is almost dusk. Skeins of freshly dyed silk—peacock blues, rust reds, lichen greens, and silvery mauves—hang to dry on clotheslines. Behind every open doorway is a loom, set in a pit with one, perhaps two, naked bulbs suspended over it. Work will continue into the night.

We come to a doorway where a board says "Kassim's Silk Emporium." Shoes are left outside. After navigating through several anterooms and courtyards where relatives lounge, we come to one of the main showrooms. The floor is covered with mattresses and sheets. There is no furniture, just steel cupboards against the walls and a few pillows to lean against. A ceiling fan whirs noisily. We are welcomed in.

Social preliminaries, a part of business here, are carried out with leisurely formality. A thin gentleman with a hennaed beard offers us sweet, milky tea flavored with cardamom, and *thandai,* a local milk drink enriched with ground nuts, and cannabis, should we desire it. Betel leaves are consumed as we listen to gentle laments about the passing of better times when customers knew how to appreciate the finer points of fabrics. "Now they just look, lay down their money, grab their packets and leave."

Then the steel cupboards open and out come *gyasars,* thick brocades for the Buddhist trade covered with dragons and other Chinese symbols, and *jamevars,* the newest rage, silks woven with the paisley designs of Kashmiri shawls. There are *tanchois* to finger, satiny brocades with an enameling of subdued colors, organzas made with mixtures of cotton and silk, and Dacca *jamdanis,* fluffs of the sheerest cotton bordered with gold. For those with fat wallets, there are the wondrous "tissues," the dazzling stuff of dreams. As sheer and airy as clouds but with a fine weight to them, they have silk threads for the warp and gold of the weft—pure gold. There is only one man left in Banaras who can make this thread, but it is hoped that this dying art can be kept alive.

A private music recital, a fixture of Banarasi nightlife, is as leisurely an affair as the selling of fabric. In these, the aristocratic Banarasis are shown at their decadent best. The wealthy patrons of the recitals insist that concerts in large halls are a waste of time: "After all, how can the musician and audience interact?" Guests arrive, men in loose *kurtas* and pajamas, women in flowering *tanchois* and *jamdanis*. Everyone takes a seat on the carpeted floor. *Thandai* and betel leaves are passed around. A discussion starts on the finer points of miniature painting, on how to choose a perfect *langra* mango (a local specialty), or on the efforts being made to clean up the Ganges.

Then the musician arrives with his party, an assorted group of accompanists and pupils. If he is of the stature of a Bismillah Khan, the men might rise to touch his feet, then scamper around catering to his every whim. Would he like a betel leaf, tobacco, a whiskey-soda? The musicians settle down on an area of the carpet covered with a mattress and sheets and the recital begins. It will go on until the wee hours, perhaps until dawn breaks, with the audience crying *"vah, vah!"* in appreciation of every beautiful phrase.

Banarasis like to joke that their city has too much of four things: widows, sacred bulls, steps, and ascetics. It is true that widows, cast out by the often-cruel Hindu society, come here in droves. Wearing widow's white, sometimes with heads shaven, they congregate by the river to pray and sing, and live out their lives in ashrams set up by charitable organizations. I visited one such retreat, Mumukshu Bhavan, a hostel for those who are "bound for *moksha*" (liberation). Widows are welcome here, as are those who wish to spend their time in quiet contemplation and those who are dying.

Unlike the crowded, jostling, littered city around it, the hostel, to my surprise, was a quiet, clean haven. Its many spacious, whitewashed buildings are separated by well-swept walkways, gardens, and courtyards. I saw daily tasks being performed in a businesslike way: a 110-year-old widow being helped with her tea; a man half her age cutting vegetables and laying them on a mat to dry; a rani who had fled an unhappy marriage preparing to sing hymns. Up on a second floor an old man, once the head of a history department, was translating the works of the South Indian sage Shankaracharya. He looked up at me as I passed.

"I have some mantras I chant. They are of great help to me. Would you like to have them?" He added softly, "The spiritual vibrations in Banaras are a hundredfold greater than anywhere else in the world. If I die here, I will surely gain *moksha*."

Banaras: a city for the dying and a city for the living; confusing, maddening, and enlightening. In many ways, the most Indian of Indian cities.

Madhur Jaffrey also contributed "Food for Body and Spirit" to Part One.

✳

OM. This eternal word is all; what was, what is and what shall be, and what is beyond eternity. All is OM.... It is beyond the senses and it is the end of evolution. It is nonduality and love. He goes with self to the supreme Self who knows this, who knows this.

—*Mandukya Upanishad*

Sanskrit for OM

JOHN WARD ANDERSON

Worshipping the Wicket

If there is a national religion
in India, it's cricket.

IT STARTED AS AN ORDINARY MATCH, BUT AS THE HOURS DRIFTED by, it evolved into a uniquely Indian affair that showed why Calcutta's Eden Gardens is considered one of the great cricket stadiums and home to the world's most passionate fans.

First came the Wave—120,000 Indians leaping to their feet, raising their arms to the heavens and shouting in unison. Then came the showers of firecrackers, bottle rockets, and flares in the stands and on the field in the middle of the game—or more precisely, throughout the entire game. Finally, when India thrashed the West Indies by 102 runs to capture its first major international cricket tournament at home, tens of thousands of euphoric spectators—chanting "In-dya! In-dya!"—rolled up newspapers, set them ablaze and held them torchlike above their heads. Sheets of fire floated about the stadium and orange flames flickered in the stands.

"You will not find a crowd like this anywhere in the world. They're really fanatic," West Indies captain Richie Richardson said after the match, which culminated the thirteen-match game, five-country Hero Cup tournament. "Indians worship cricket, and their cricketers are like gods to them."

"The cult of cricket and Eden Gardens go hand-in-glove," said Krish Mackerthuj, president of the United Cricket Board of South Africa, which lost to India in the semifinals.

"If you had a stadium for 200,000 or 500,000, for a match like this, it would be full, and that wouldn't happen anywhere else in the world," he said. "And all the burning paper at the end—it's shocking, and at first you're a bit harsh, but later you realize people have different ways of sending the message they're happy their team won."

For many Indians, cricket is the finest legacy of the British Raj. In recent years, the game has supplanted field hockey as India's national pastime. On weekends, parks and vacant lots are crammed with cricket matches. City alleys from Bombay to Delhi teem with children playing cricket between the passing cars and motorbikes. In rural villages, boys pound stakes into the middle of fields or commandeer dusty roads and transform them into instant cricket grounds.

The sport, one of the few India competes in at a world-class level, has become an intense source of national pride and a rallying point for the country, which comes to a virtual standstill on big game days. Matches with Pakistan—most of which have been canceled in recent years for security reasons—are a sort of surrogate for the war no one wants, similar to the way U.S.-Soviet basketball games were once perceived as tests of superpower prowess.

India's cricket madness began in the early 1880s, when the country's British rulers needed cricket teams to play against and suited up Indian squads, according to Narrottam Puri, one of India's top sports authorities and cricket commentators. Indian traders were the first to play the game because it helped them develop British business contacts. "Once they were seen playing with the rulers, their whole stock in society rose up." Puri said, and gradually the sport became a sort of social equalizer.

Sociologist Ashis Nandy, who has written a book on cricket, said, "It's an Indian game that was mistakenly brought by the British. It's an unpredictable game where the variables are so many, where there are negotiations with fate, and we are playing not with an opponent but with our own destiny. That clicks with the Indian self-conscience, the South Asian way of looking at the world and our own fate."

John Ward Anderson is a staff writer for The Washington Post.

★

I was the Charlie Brown of my Little League baseball team. The only time I got on base was when "walked" or "hit-by-a-pitch."

In India, baseball does not exist, but its historical predecessor, cricket, reigns supreme. Boys of all ages can be seen playing in school yards, fields, street corners, and back alleys.

In the late afternoon, as I pedaled through a village, I noticed a large group of boys practicing their national sport. They waved me over and one boy yelled, "Do you play?" Before I had a chance to reply, I had a fat cricket bat in my hands and stood in front of the wickets. The tallest boy said, "I throw slow," and prepared with a short run to pitch or "bowl" the ball.

Having observed others playing, I knew to position the bat down by my feet as if I were preparing to hit a golf ball, but the laughter around me confirmed my stance was still unconventional.

The boy tossed the ball and it bounced right. I swung and missed. Over twenty years had passed and my fortune hadn't changed. The boy announced, "fast now," and smiled. Hadn't I borne enough humiliation? I set down the bat, but a small voice said, "C'mon Willie. Don't think Charlie Brown—think Ken Griffey, Jr."

I picked up the bat and dug in. The boy took a long running start and hurled the ball with all his fifteen-year-old might. It bounced and I swung wildly, connecting with a loud "thwack." The ball sailed over the head of the pitcher, over the heads of the boys out in the field, and disappeared behind some large boulders.

Suddenly I was surrounded by cheering boys, jumping up and down and patting me on the back, several of whom were shouting, "Six, six."

I had just enough knowledge of cricket to know what that meant. It had taken thirty-two years and a journey halfway around the world—but I had hit a home run.

> —Willie Weir, "Cycling India: Letters from the Road"

JAN HAAG

A Vision of Vijayanagar

A chance encounter with another traveler
leads to an other-worldly discovery.

I STEPPED OFF THE BUS IN THE MORNING AT HAMPI BAZAAR, A place so bewilderingly strange to Western eyes that I could hardly believe I was seeing it. There was a double row of broken columns, the equivalent of several blocks long. Though now roofless, you'd call it an arcade if you saw it in Italy or at a California mission. The columns were huge. They stood maybe as much as five or six feet apart, and, in places, two or three ancient steps still led up to a floor paved with granite slabs, straw, merchandise and people. It was such a jumble that it took me a few minutes of taking a step and staring, taking another step and staring, to realize that these were people's homes and people's stores. The merchandise—sandals here and pots there, basins, soap, cups, mats, cosmetics, food, fabrics, saris, a thousand item—formed the walls between the columns. Often the merchandise also formed a barrier between the front and back of the stalls. There may have been two families to a stall. Maybe more. There were multitudes crowded between the huge broken columns, sitting about in the streets, walking up and down, staring at the occasional foreigner, no doubt hoping they would buy something; but mostly the vast milling crowd was just living, friendly, curious, and welcoming.

It was as shocking as if one were to find the Athenians serving tea and having babies among the pillars of the Parthenon, or the farmers of Colorado storing their harvest and selling tortillas out of the cliff dwelling of Mesa Verde. What Westerners might think of as the homeless were, it seemed, putting an ancient monument to the pragmatic test of usefulness. But these people weren't homeless. This was obviously their home, and their delight. One long line of the arcade stretched in front of me as I walked into Hampi, and a shorter line stood to my right, columns, habitations, people, and straw. It was a bit, I guessed, like the stables at Bethlehem two thousand years ago.

The young Israeli woman I had met just after I visited the Ajanta caves, who had originally said, "Go to Hampi, go to Vijayanagar," had told me to look for a certain tea shop. I found it: a woman with a pot on a tiny dung fire and two stools by a column. I had sweet *chai*. But my adviser must have spoken a little Hindi or Kannada, for the proprietress, though very friendly, spoke no English. We smiled at each other again and again as I drank my tea. My eyes, looking over the rim of my tiny tea cup, wandered around like two barn-yard chickens, struck by the amount of life and dust, activity and a feeling of concealed exuberance the "town" or camp-out seemed to contain beneath its rustic tatters.

When I left the tea stool, it was a bit of a walk up a hill before I came to more ruins. Already the morning sun was searing hot, so on top of the hill I stopped to find something else to drink. In a shop made of palm fronds and sticks, I had a lesson from a little old man wrapped round by a colorful skirt—a *lungi*—on how to drink coconut milk straight from the pod. What a blessed alternative it became, from then on, to the always questionable water. After I had sucked up the sweet clear liquid through a straw, the seller, with a huge machete, hacked off a chip, then chopped the whole thing in two so I could scoop out the milky meat. I stood on the hill looking off to where the ruins were reported to be, savoring the coconut, mostly seeing nothing at all but dust and scrubby bushes.

Then I walked on. After a while, instead of dust, I was walking on a domed surface like a great lava flow, shiny and bald and immense. In my sandals, I skimmed over the dome of black rock and, as I did so, I caught a glimpse of the river. Along the river, strewn about on the landscape, were huge boulders of shiny black rock. They were so immense I couldn't really believe they were there. It was as if Brahma himself had spilled a bag of black marbles as big as automobiles, as houses, at random, along the river where no trees, no grass, no weeds grew. It was a landscape so desolate, so cataclysmic that I knew even five hundred years ago it couldn't have been that much different. Why had the Telugu princes, Harihara and Bukka, founded the capitol of what was to become the largest Hindu Empire in Indian history—here?

My young Israeli adviser had understated it when she said, "There's nothing like it."

I had asked: "What is it?"

"A river, ruins, rocks."

"Different than here?" We both had just been to see the river, ruins, rocks of Ajanta. I could not conceive of anything more spectacular.

"It's unique." She didn't say much else, except to urge me to go, and, "I slept out by the rocks."

"Safe? Where do you leave your stuff when you sleep out?"

"By a rock."

To step *into* Hampi, the modern name of the remains of the bazaar of Vijayanagar, was a little like traveling in space only to find Mars had long since been colonized, civilized to the point of wonders beyond belief, then abandoned and squatted-in by man's modern cousins. To *step out* from Hampi was like arriving on the moon, unreal landscape in every direction, perhaps early mappings for 3001. Still skidding across the immense black dome, I soon came upon the King's Balance where plaques told me it had originally been a scale on which the king sat on one side and his loyal subjects filled the other side with gold. It was a structure somewhat like a guillotine, or a Tori gate, with no visible weighing pans to sit in. Beyond it stood the Vittala Temple, like a three-dimensional mandala, like a vision, an illusion, or a mirage in the dust and haze of India.

I had never before seen filigree in stone. The temple, for the most part, was a vast, wall-less building, crowded with clusters of columns, maybe three, maybe five to a cluster. Each cluster was crowned with a capital of intricate stone work so delicate that I, who have tatted lace with silk thread, thought my work quite crude by comparison. Carved into and around the columns were gods and goddesses, demons, elephants, horses, beasts both mythical and real, peacocks, parrots, and plants which flowered with eternal blossoms. The ceiling was coffered and crisscrossed with yet more stone carved lace. The stone itself was a soft gold color, perhaps flecked with mica, as it shimmered in the sun. I stood in a gossamer golden temple made of stone, awestruck.

Someone near me said, though not to me, "Slap the stone." And they did. The columns began to sing. It appeared the columns were tuned like organ pipes. Music could be played upon them. I slapped with the light upward

---

*T*he ancient Hindus chose their temple sites with great care and they sometimes spent years looking for a place with the right power and energy. They would search for an area where cattle liked to graze. In a big pasture the cows always had a favourite place. Likewise, dogs were considered to be a good sign. If dogs were found wandering among the cattle, then the site was perfect. But any sign of a cat in the field, and the site was abandoned. According to the ancients, dogs and cows attracted positive energies, whereas cats were definitely negative. The priests tethered the cows and left them there for forty-one days. Then they slaughtered the cows and checked their internal organs. If any of the beasts showed signs of disease then the priests looked for another place. If the cattle were all healthy, the construction of the temple went ahead.

◆

—Peter Holt, *In Clive's Footsteps*

motion I had just seen. A deep rich tone rang in the columned court, evoking even with my light touch, harmonics from its neighbors. Was it middle C? I do not know. I hit again, another column, a higher tone. In and out among the multifaceted columns, I wandered round and round, testing their pitches, dazzled by their beauty. What wizard musician had designed them? What Stradivarius had built them? Who had gone and left them standing there, dust-blown in the blazing sun, beside the river of huge black stones?

I went down to the Purandara Dasara Mandapa that stood partly in the river where a little grass grew, clumps of weeds along the shore, a scrubby tree or two, and a dozen kids at least, young and lean and dark, yelling, jumping up and down, and diving into the water. They careened into the black river from the bits left of the ancient stone bridge as well. What is a *mandapa*? A temple it seems. It was black, carved, perhaps from the indigenous stone, and very dark inside where the sunlight didn't reach and the kids didn't go.

It was there in the cooling shadows someone surprised me: "Did you like the stone chariot?" in English, sing-song and lilting, as Indian speech is.

"What stone chariot?"

"By the Vittala Temple. The wheels are twice as high as you are."

I had been so intrigued with the Vittala Temple I had missed the stone chariot.

Stone chariot

I returned to gaze upon its amazing wheels. Made of stone, indeed, they could not have weighed less than a ton each, and yet, with a touch of the finger, they could be set in motion to revolve! Each spoke of each wheel was carved as delicately as a spoon's handle, its filigreed body carved, too, of golden stone. It sat there in the sun, the most ornamented cart I had ever seen, modeled on the wooden chariots used to carry images of the gods in festival processions, gigantic, and at least four hundred years old. How could I comprehend such elaboration and abandonment?

There were very few people about. The little map I had torn from the guidebook indicated it was about a nine kilometer walk around the road that now circled what was left of Vijayanagar, a city, it said, that had once covered thirty-three square kilometers. An easy walk. I set off down a country road, soft beige-colored dust whose edges merged with the land. With the major ruins at my back, I began to walk through weedy land dotted with short trees. On my right cultivated fields began, and after not too far, on my left, appeared another bazaar, like a skeleton of Hampi. It had the huge double rows of columns, long paved walkways, broken and weed-grown steps, and not a soul around. Here, if one paused to hear the slight sound of the wind playing about the columns, one could dream the marketplace that was: the silks and spices that must have been for sale, the jewels glinting in the sun, the exotic fruits and vegetables, the people from as far as Rome, Venice, Tibetans with their tasseled umbrellas. I could imagine the rugs that must have been for sale in

Vijayanagar had an almost Aztec thirst for blood sacrifice. Each of the sheep cut up for shanks in the bazaar was butchered on the steps of the temple, its blood and wooly head offered up to a sticky red idol. On one festival day the king personally presided over the ritual slaughter of 250 buffaloes and 4,500 nanny-goats. But the metropolis's citizenry had a romantic streak as well. Abdur-Razzaq, a Muslim diplomat, observed: "Roses are sold everywhere. These people coud not live without roses, and they look upon them as quite as necessary as food."

—Jonah Blank, *Arrow of the Blue-Skinned God: Retracing the Ramayana through India*

1509. I closed my eyes and saw in technicolor the merchants, the saried women, the opulence, the wandering goats, the cows, heard the noise, smelt the smell of India. But in fact there was no scent here in Vijayanagar. I opened my eyes again to the short trees, the weeds, and the columns—some of which were there and some that had vanished.

The dusty road made a gentle curve and I was surrounded on both sides by banana orchards, a banana plantation as might be seen in Hawaii, I thought, having never seen one. And a road leading, no doubt, to a house, a regular house, where the plantation owner lived, not like the squatters at Hampi.

I walked on and on, seeing scattered ruins here and there: a suggestion of a wall, a mound that had perhaps been a building. A sugar cane field on my right. I went through a vast crumbling gate and the road turned into desert, wide fields of nothingness. In the hot sun I was in bliss. I love the desert and the nothingness of blowing sand. I felt like Jesus on his trek—they say he came to India, you know—as if I had come on some meaningful mission to save humanity, humanity perhaps in the form of my own soul. I chanted Hari Krishna, and other *bhajans* I had learned at an ashram, to the peopleless landscape.

There was no one on the road. Not another tourist, not a single person, not one cultivator of the land. I was alone beneath the ruined wall that followed my path on the crest of the hill to my right and the desert extending out to what I could not make out on my left. In its day, they say, Vijayanagar had seven concentric lines of fortifications around a half million people—where I now walked in solitude.

The rocks. There were no more of the building-sized black rocks to be seen. Why choose, I wondered, to build something as exquisite as the Vittala Temple among the uninviting rocks? Fortifications? Very likely.

My little map said their were more ruins ahead, so I walked on, across a vast barren stretch of rocky ground.

There were, read the map, other ruins out there to my left, but they were too far away to see. To my right the hill rose. I walked on and on through the heat and dust. For me it was like heaven. I could worry about hunger and I could worry about thirst, the basics of life which I had hardly ever given a thought to. Had I been foolish to try a full circumnavigation? Nobody else seemed to have chosen my route.

Then to my right the hills tapered down, and the same barren rocky ground stretched itself on all sides, and emerging from it, I could see, on the left, a long way off the dusty road, buildings the same color as the land.

I left the road to cut across the intervening sand. I had to put my sandals on again, for the stones beneath the sand, some far bigger than marbles, hurt my feet. I had not seen any of the black rocks since leaving the river. Why were the huge black rocks only along the river? I would never know.

What had looked like a village from a distance turned out to be the King's Palace, the Lotus Mahal, the Hall of Victory, Dasara Platform, and Hazarama Temple. Even rinsed of their facings, rinsed right down to the same dirt across which I trod, they still had an elegance to them, with their fine straight walls. A winged roof still sheltered one tower, but the three-story-high stairway leading up to it was exposed to the elements. For the rest, you could wander in and out of the doorways and, in most of the buildings, in and out through the walls. The buildings had fallen to ruin—the Lotus Mahal, the Dasara Platform, the Khanavami-Dibba, the Zenana Enclosure—they had such beautiful names. And the most beautiful building of all, with its long row of curved stone walls, like enormous cylinders set side by side, was the elephant stables. Each of its domes roofed a huge round room where, presumably, each elephant had had a kingdom to itself. I ran my hands along the walls, murmured words to hear them echoed by the domes, stood enthralled. Elephants.

There were a few people here, like me, walking in and out of the ruins. All of us were silent in the deserted grandeur, gazing at the unfaced buildings, marveling at the colossal remnants of what had been the capital of an empire, a city surpassing Rome. It was like seeing a monarch in his undergarments. Embroidered though they were with a few remaining arches, the pomp and glory were missing, the robes, the crowns, the jewels were gone.

But not entirely. On the back side of the King's Palace, along friezes near the ground, and extending maybe two feet high, were lines of exquisitely carved elephants, trunk to tail, each procession not more than a foot high—and a man, a living man, on his knees, counting them, making notations in a book.

"What are you doing?" I hadn't spoken to a human being in several hours.

"Counting the elephants." The young Indian motioned me to silence until he came to a seam in the wall.

"Why?"

"We're doing an archaeological survey."

"Oh. Who?" I looked around. For it was only he I saw at work.

"Most of the people are at the Queen's Bath and at the camp. They excavated the Queen's Bath recently."

I was intrigued. Having an amateur's interest in archaeology, I wanted to know more, but, though helpful in pointing out the beauty and details of the procession of elephants, horses, dancers, he didn't know much about the "dig," and urged me to go on to the Queen's Bath or the camp. I could tell he was very keen on his job, his responsibility in counting the elephants, and wanted to get back to his task.

I walked on. I was on another road that passed through ruined walls; somehow the desert, the dryness, the dust, made it all look so neat, until I came upon mounds of fresh dug dirt, and a huge deep rectangular hole, built of precisely cut stone, magnificent in its proportions. This was the Queen's Bath, awesome in its newly exposed emptiness. There was only one person there, eager to hurry off. It was lunch time, it appeared, back at the camp. "Come there," he urged and walked away.

I sat on the rim of the bath for a while, imagining it full of sparkling water beneath the blue-white sun-filled sky, and the water filled with splashing, laughing, incredibly beautiful, bathing women. The kings were reported to have had thousands of wives.

Or had the bath been reserved for just one queen? I did not know. It was immense, far larger than any modern swimming pool.

Then I started along the road the man had indicated as leading to the archaeologist's camp. It was still a mile or more away. I walked and mused.

It had always been one of my dreams to be part of an archaeological team, to know and understand, first hand, by sifting its dust, an ancient civilization. Since I was in no hurry, only wandering, expected nowhere, I decided, as I walked along, that I could volunteer a few days. I, too, could count elephants, dust stones delicately with a fine brush, record minutiae of which, quite probably, I would never know the meaning. I quickened my stride. I felt buoyant. I entered the camp with confidence, met some charming people sitting on the steps of a ramshackle building and asked to see the director of the site.

The directors turned out to be an Australian and an American, both wearing khaki shorts, as they sat in a tent that stood beside the building where I had inquired. It was hot and dusty, organized, and, under the open tent wings, shaded to a greenish hue— all an amateur archaeologist could hope for. The two young men were most welcoming, in that way that foreigners in a foreign land are pleased to see another foreigner. I made my offer. They turned me down with regret, saying that only Indians could be hired for the project.

"What about you?"

"Oh well," they laughed, "we're just the directors. The Indians have other priorities. They're not interested in investing money in digging up their past, not such a recent past as this."

"Recent?"

"The major ruins date back only to the fourteenth century."

"That seems old enough to me."

"Not in India. No investigation of the ruins has ever been attempted. They're too new, uninteresting, in a land where two thousand-year-old ruins go begging for excavation."

"Why?"

"The government has to cope with the living problems. But

they welcomed our suggestion, stipulating only that our work force must be composed of citizens of India. It's a boon to the economy out here in the desert."

"But I'm volunteering."

"Even then the government asks that we take only Indians, for our volunteers get educational credit—and they are fed."

Without further ceremony, the two men rose, saying it was lunch time and inviting me to join them. I went with them onto the open porch of another building. There I was introduced to seven or eight groups of people sitting at many tables, and ate one of the most interesting lunches of my life. The spicy food was delicious, though, perhaps, by Indian standards rather plain, since they served only two or three dishes. The company was superb, the knowledge I gleaned quite marvelous. Vijayanagar, I was told, had ruled all of southern India off and on from 1336 to 1565. How precise it all was, I thought, for being so unstudied. But it appears the history was known, if not the remains.

There were other visitors from the States, quite a number of Indians, a few Australians. Everyone talked excitedly about the Queen's Bath. It, apparently, was their major accomplishment for the whole dig. Their funds were getting low. The work could not go on too much longer, but, eventually, they hoped a book would come from their efforts. For, to their knowledge, there was only one book ever published about the site, and it lacked pictures. One of their goals was to make a photographic record of the remaining buildings, and, along with their research, publish a splendid coffee-table book. In my mind's eye, I already saw photographs of the Vittala Temple. The book would be breathtaking.

Someone read a passage from Abdur-Razzaq, who had visited the Empire in 1443, "The city," he had written, "is such that eye has not seen or ear heard of any place resembling it upon the whole earth." He went on to describe the palaces, between which streams flowed in "channels of cut stone, polished and even," the bazaars full of merchandise from the world over, and fragrant with flowers, sparkling with jewels: rubies, pearls, diamonds, and emeralds for sale "openly in the bazaar."

"In the King's Treasury," Abdur-Razzaq noted, "there are chambers, with excavations in them, filled with molten gold, forming one mass. All the inhabitants of the country, whether high or low…wear jewels and gilt ornaments in their ears and around their necks, arms, wrists, and fingers."

The gold was all gone, the archaeologists cheerfully acknowledged, by the time they got there. Indeed, the Empire of Vijayanagar was annihilated in a period of five months, the American Director told me, in an orgy of deliberate destruction probably surpassed only by that wreaked upon the Aztecs by the Spanish when they razed every stone and building right down to the ground. The American read from another book, quoting Sewell, "Never perhaps in the history of the world has such havoc been wrought, and wrought so suddenly, on so splendid a city; teeming with a wealthy and industrious population in the full plenitude of prosperity one day, and on the next seized, pillaged, and reduced to ruins, amid scenes of savage massacre and horrors beggaring description." This pillaging followed, the Australian director added, the decisive battle of Talikota fought on January 23, 1565, by Vijayanagar against an alliance of four sultans from the north.

As I walked away from the good company after the good lunch, my immediate path lay past a row of buildings in use. They stood like temporary buildings lightly upon the dust. It may have been the village of Kamalapura. I walked on, thinking about the line, "…the glory that was Greece and the grandeur that was Rome…" Realizing for the first time that India was filled with lost empires as grand or grander than any of those in the West, empires of which neither I nor most Westerners knew even the names.

At the end of the road, the circuit should have brought me back to Hampi, to the market, to the bazaar, but I did not recognize my surroundings. The road did not make a perfect circle was all I could guess, maybe it was a spiral. It did not meet its beginning. But, to my astonishment, there, to my left, higher than anything else in all the landscape, towered the Virupaksha Temple with its eleven-story gateway glistening white in the last rays of the sun. It was so immense, so carved with figures, that surely it portrayed half the population of India upon its rising wedge shaped tower. How had I missed it on my arrival at Hampi? It was in such fine repair that I thought, at first, it might have just been built. I walked down into its courtyard, under the heavy roof to view the three-story gateway that led into the inner temple. I looked about in disbelief. It was not so finely carved as the Vittala Temple, but there was a plaque indicating it was even older than the Empire. It was overwhelming in its extent. How had I missed it?

To this day I have found no books on Vijayanagar.

Unless I return to walk the dusty roads, tap again the singing columns, I may never know more about what I have seen, where I have been. Authors who do mention Vijayanagar say it is just one monument among many which are not even listed in most guidebooks. The Dravidians, you see, always controlled, and still control, the south, while the Aryans, Hindus, and Muslims came in from the north. The present, as in other countries on earth, spars with the past.

Jan Haag also contributed "A Wedding in Mahabaleshwar" to Part I and "Sick under the Bo Tree" to Part III.

✳

The wise old sorceress that she is, India is always at the ready to conjure up other acts when the freak shows wear thin. This land in which people spend lifetimes exorcising the demands of the flesh is at heart a sensual one, celebrating her earthiness with stone carved as finely as lace, rich food, rainbows of shining silks, intricately woven carpets, and exuberant dance. She is, after all, the home of our most graphic depiction of sexual passion, the Khajuraho temples, with delicately chiseled sculptures illustrating every sexual position you've ever fantasized about and then some.

—Cheryl Bentley, "Enchanted"

JULIAN CRANDALL HOLLICK

★ ★ ★

Scribes of Bengal

Calcutta is known for its slums and misery,
but it is also a center of arts and letters,
India's city of poets.

RABINDRANAGAR IS A *BUSTEE*, OR SLUM, IN CALCUTTA, UNLOVED
and unrecognized, home to six hundred men, women and children. It consists of eighty one-room thatched huts, squeezed between a stagnant pond and the main road that leads from the
downtown heart of Calcutta past Salt Lake, a suburb of gray
apartment blocks built just twenty-five years ago but prematurely
aged and yellowing, victims of the constant humidity.

It was dusk, a soft smoky haze punctuated by the wan smiles of
underpowered street lamps. In this entire slum, there was just one
light bulb, jury-rigged illegally from the nearest telephone pole.
My friend Raja Chatterjee and I held flashlights while ten-year-
old Samra Bhaja, sitting cross-legged on a rug thrown over the bare
earth, accompanied herself on the harmonium.

Samra had never attended school. She probably never would.
Most days she helped her mother roll *bidis*, cheap Indian cigarettes—
cut tobacco rolled in leaves and held together with thread. Samra's
voice was pure, untrained, with perfect pitch, full of pale melancholy
as she unfolded her song: "This necklace bruises me; it strangles me
when I try to take it off. It chokes my singing. Take it from me! I'm
ashamed to wear it. Give me a simple garland in its place."

"Who wrote this song?" I asked. Samra was too shy to answer. Raja was astonished: "Tagore! Rabindranath Tagore! Surely you've heard of him?" I hadn't then. But over the past few years, Raja has almost single-handedly educated me, not only about Tagore but also about all of Calcutta's myriad cultures.

Calcutta. The name conjures up an image of poverty and human suffering: the Black Hole, starvation, barefoot beggars. It is a city of somewhere around eleven million people, about five million of whom live in slums, perhaps another quarter-million living on the streets. Yet, ironically, something else is going on in Calcutta, something that doesn't recognize the boundaries of caste or class, education or illiteracy. For if there is any one thing that binds Brahmin and Untouchable, *babu* and domestic worker, slum dweller and rich socialite, it is a passion for culture. Indeed, Calcutta as a city proudly defines itself through this passion.

At the height of its glory in the nineteenth century, Calcutta was called the second city of the British Empire, rivaling London in its riches and social refinement. No surprise, then, that in Asia, Calcutta was regarded as the center of learning for everyone from Peshawar to Hong Kong. What does surprise many people outside India is that, in its own collective mind, Calcutta undoubtedly still holds this position.

It's commonly claimed (although I don't know how these things can be measured) that Calcutta has more poets than Paris and Rome combined; more literary magazines than either New York or London; more theater companies and art galleries than anywhere else in Asia; and undoubtedly more publishers, however small. It's the only city in India where movie theaters have "House Full" signs outside their doors from lunchtime onward. Poetry readings are major events, sometimes drawing more than a thousand people.

Why this hunger for culture? One prominent poet thinks many in the audience at poetry readings are there just to be seen. Filmmaker Satyajit Ray, who admitted he couldn't really explain why so many Calcuttans pack theaters, cinemas, and concert halls, suggested that cultural events are a great way for young people to meet and have a chance "to be alone together for some time, maybe holding hands while the lights are down." Bob Wright, who runs the Tollygunge Club, one of Calcutta's leading social and athletic gathering places, offers a more convincing explanation. "The Bengali," he says, "has always set himself up to think that God put him on this Earth to be a poet or a writer, and other races to do the dirty work."

> ◯ atyajit Ray died in 1992. Just before he died he was awarded an honorary Oscar in America for lifetime achievement by the Academy of Motion Picture Arts and Sciences.
>
> ◆
>
> —JO'R and LH

"Always" is a word that goes back a long way in India. In the Calcutta area, there have been village settlements of fishermen, weavers and priests for at least a thousand years, while Calcutta itself is a mere three hundred years old— young by Indian standards. Established by the British East India Company in 1690 to serve as a trading post, the city is attached like a human ear to the banks of the Hooghly River. The inner ear is the "White Town," the former European city of spacious homes and broad avenues, built around a vast green core of field and wood—the Maidan—Calcutta's answer to Central Park. Beyond that, encompassing the three villages that predate the British settlement, lies the native section, or "Black Town," of narrow lanes, innumerable slums, bazaars, temples, mansions and *godowns* (warehouses). The oldest part of the Black Town is the top of the ear: North Calcutta. This is where Rabindranath Tagore's family lived.

Into this city flowed the influence of Western art forms—the novel, the short story, painting, popular and classical music, theater, and, later, cinema—primarily from Great Britain, but also from other Western countries. Calcuttans took these alien cultural forms and ran with them. In so doing they reinvented and reinvigorated Sanskritic and Bengali culture. One of the pioneers was the early nineteenth-century social reformer Raja Rammohun Roy, usually called the father of the "Bengal Renaissance." Roy believed fervently that Bengal's future lay in producing a synthesis of the best of East and West.

The Tagore family was in the vanguard of this movement. The family included brilliant artists and writers, but all their talents were recombined in Rabindranath. In 1913 he became the first non-European to win the Nobel Prize in Literature. The effect in Calcutta was electrifying, confirming for Calcuttans their self-appointed role as the intellectuals of India. It's hard to escape Tagore's influence in Calcutta, especially that of his songs. He wrote more than two thousand, many in the minor key, most of them about God, nature, and love. You hear them on the radio, in homes, on the train, in schools, and in slums like Rabindranagar.

Every year, Calcuttans celebrate Tagore's birthday with a month-long festival of his poetry, plays, music, and dance dramas, which usually deal with Indian mythology. They also show films made by Satyajit Ray of Tagore's short stories and novels.

Calcutta is, above all, a city of scribblers. It seems that all Calcuttans feel that they have a right to see their opinions and prejudices in print. "There are two things you will find in the middle-class Bengali character," claims Nirmalya Acharya above the din of ceiling fans and animated conversation in his favorite haunt, the coffeehouse on Bankim Chatterjee Street just off College Street. "They try to write poetry—every Bengali considers himself a poet—and they try to bring out one little magazine."

Nirmalya should know. Along with some other university friends he started a literary magazine in 1961 here in the coffeehouse. With Satyajit Ray's help, they came up with the name *Ekshan*, which means "Now" or "Present Day." "We never thought the magazine would last more than a few issues," says Nirmalya. "It's thirty years now. I think the time was right!"

Nirmalya takes me to the office of a fellow publisher, down a narrow side alley off Mahatma Gandhi Road. In one room, a man in a *dhoti* and a rag of an undershirt is cranking brightly colored magazine covers through an ancient and blackened handpress, something more appropriate to Dickensian London than to the era of desktop publishing. Isn't it perhaps a myth that Calcutta is still the midwife of the small literary magazine?

"There are probably two thousand small magazines published here," Nirmalya says. "But it is becoming very difficult these days. Paper costs fifteen times as much as it did when we started *Ekshan*, and printing costs have increased tenfold. My friend here is thinking of winding up this press. It's just not viable anymore."

Only a short distance from Nirmalya's home, up Mahatma Gandhi Road and down Tamer Lane, is the home of Sandip Dutt. Sandip is a schoolteacher, but he's also the proprietor of the Little Magazine Library and Research Centre, twelve thousand volumes stacked right up to the ceiling, occupying every inch of wall space on the first floor of his home.

"I started this in 1978 because no one looks after the small and obscure magazines," Sandip tells me. "It is my love and duty to look after these little magazines and make them available to

Calcutta is like Dickens's aging Miss Havisham, forever the jilted bride. What the white ants don't make off with, the mold ravishes. Buildings blackened with age, yellowed by the sun, and pockmarked by damp sprout trees and crumble, as if trying to return this urban morass back into the swamp it once was. Sagging Georgian mansions, derelict shells too far gone for habitation, still evoke colonial grandeur. England's industrial revolution is reincarnated in the huge jute mills along the riverbanks, no different from the cotton mills of Dickens's time. To walk through Calcutta's steamy streets of Victorian buildings is to know London in the 1800s, a twilight world of cheerless alleys and fetid gutters; of formal, tattered parks, tear-jerking melodramas, and tearooms stirred by debate; of literary outpourings and experimental art; and of the very rich and the very, very poor.

◆

—Mary Orr, "India Sketches"

the people." Four afternoons a week, after he returns from work, Sandip opens his doors and allows students and researchers for an annual fee of 50 cents to come and ferret through his treasures. Sandip shows me magazines printed on banana leaves, rolled in cigarettes and stuffed into matchboxes. With real pride he brings out a rare first edition of *Bangadarshan* from 1872, and a copy of a short-lived magazine published and edited by a domestic worker in the late 1960s.

"Have you ever published a magazine?" I ask, somewhat naively. "Oh yes! I publish three magazines for my public." Sandip continues the tour. "I started this collection with fifteen hundred magazines. Now I receive four or five new ones every day. The problem is space. There's some left in that room," he says, leading me into a third room, christened Poetry Books Library. "What happens when that's full?" I ask. Sandip rolls his eyes upward. "It's going to move up to the next floor, isn't it?" Another roll of the eyes. "I have a duty to these magazines."

As I leave the Little Magazine Library, Sandip takes my arm. "Remember," he tells me earnestly, "Bengalis want to express their ideas. They're not so much interested in material things. They're much happier pursuing intellectual ideas."

None more so than my friend Raja Chatterjee. Raja never seems to have held a steady job. But he has a profession—being a Bengali intellectual. Raja looks the part, clad in a white *dhoti* and top, and carrying a cloth shoulder bag jammed with books, notebooks and pencils. Somehow he finds work, at the film studios, or helping to mount an experimental translation of Anouilh or Brecht or Durrenmatt at one of the city's innumerable small theaters. He's just finished helping his friend Malay produce a series of half-hour television programs of Bengali short stories. Each episode cost three thousand dollars to make, impossibly cheap for any Western producer but a fortune for Malay and his wife, who have put all their savings into the series.

Raja lives in South Calcutta, near the famous Kali Temple, with his wife, Runu, and daughter, Sonali, and Runu's widowed mother, who spent several years in the former Soviet Union as an

A dhoti

interpreter. She speaks and reads Russian, Bengali, Hindi and English. The house is full of books—Tagore, of course, Maxim Gorky, Byron and Shelley, lots of Shakespeare—and an upright piano. Runu has been going blind for several years now but still teaches piano at a private school. "Come round to dinner tonight. We will prepare a special Bengali fish curry for you," she tells me. "My daughter also wants you to hear her play the piano."

That evening, twelve-year-old Sonali plays short pieces by Mozart and Grieg. Then Runu plays the first movement of Beethoven's "Moonlight Sonata" and a Strauss waltz. Runu apologizes profusely for the sound of the piano: "It must be tuned. But when is the tuner coming?" Raja promises to get the tuner tomorrow. But I doubt he can make much of a difference now. The constant humidity has badly altered the sound. Imagine Beethoven played on a barroom piano in the Wild West. The effect is surreal and very Calcutta.

After supper, Raja wants me to meet his friends Dakoo and Kumar at the coffeehouse off College Street, a half-mile of bookshops and bookstalls spilling over onto the pavement, carrying first editions, pamphlets, paperbacks in every Indian language, with more than a fair smattering of books in and out of print from France, Germany, Russia, and England.

Dakoo is a cartoonist. He's drawn a small book of cartoons on Calcutta's three hundredth birthday for me. Sometimes, one of the daily papers publishes his work. The rest of the time he just draws and waits. Kumar works in one of the city's luxury hotels, supervising room service. But every morning he writes a poem. Kumar and Raja both write naturally in English. English is as much a language of Calcutta as Bengali. Kumar has never sought a publisher; he wants to know my reactions to his poems. Raja also writes poetry and has had no problem finding someone to publish five hundred copies of sixty-odd pages of his poetry in hardback.

Raja, Kumar, and Dakoo may never be famous, but they are pursuing the right of every Calcuttan and every Bengali to be an intellectual or an artist. No one snickers. Driving through Calcutta one day, Raja suddenly blurts out: "Chief! What about this Jack Kerouac? You know him? I am very much liking this man." Raja has read Kerouac in Bengali. Romantic images of a foot-loose Kerouac obviously appeal to the Bengali psyche.

At times this obsession with culture seems so self-conscious that one wonders if it isn't really motivated by something else: a fear that Bengali culture will be diluted by the presence of so many non-Bengalis in Calcutta. And also by the Calcuttans' need to reassure themselves that their city still counts on the world cultural stage, when so many in the West and India have written it off as a provincial backwater and worse.

One of Calcutta's most famous indigenous folk forms is an endangered species. *Kalighat,* or "bazaar," paintings are usually water-colors—very colorful, often strongly satirical, sometimes bawdy. They were sold as

*A*void Calcutta's unhealthy monsoon. From June until the end of September over a meter and a half of rain bombards the city. Outhouses overflow and contaminate water used for drinking, bathing, and washing cooking utensils. Many of the eight thousand annual deaths caused by cholera and gastrointestinal diseases occur during the rains. Antiquated, silt-clogged sewage pipes drain only a quarter inch of rainwater per hour. Manhole covers are removed to facilitate drainage, and in nonstop rains (more than thirty centimeters, or a foot, in twenty-four hours), open sewers, hidden under water, become booby traps as pedestrians inadvertently plunge into them and drown.

◆

—Mary Orr, "India Sketches"

cheap souvenirs to the pilgrims who came to the Kali Temple in South Calcutta. But then postcards and mass reproduction spelled their demise. "You want to see *Kalighat* paintings? No problem! There are some in the Metro. Let's go, Chief!" And Raja whisks me out the door of the apartment and down the stairs to the street. It's raining. Raja shouts a command in Bengali and two rickshaw-*wallahs* at a nearby stand pick up their rickshaws and wade through brown water two feet deep to the doorstep.

We cross Chowringhee to what looks like a small ventilation shaft, where we climb out of our rickshaws. Raja leads me down some steps into the world of the Calcutta subway, known as Metro, the city's pride and joy. Each station is decorated with paintings and sculptures. When we reach the *Kalighat* station, sure enough, reproductions of *Kalighat* paintings hang on the walls. Other stations display reproductions of paintings by Tagore or early scenes of European Calcutta. Many Calcuttans, says Raja, ride Metro just to see the artwork. There's another attraction, too: each station has several color television sets, which show popular films or cricket matches.

On Monday morning the Maidan is deserted. Raja and I go back into North Calcutta, to Kumartuli, a former red-light district but also home to the image makers of Calcutta. The easiest way to get there is by taxi. Throughout all the years I've been coming to Calcutta I've been driven by Tivari, a Brahmin from Uttar Pradesh, who lives here with his father and brother. I think my Western habits must have shocked Tivari when I first met him. Highly literate and a devoted follower of Rama, the legendary God-King of Ayodhya and hero of *The Ramayana*, Tivari deter-mined to educate me. On my second visit he had acquired a tape deck in his taxi. He would endlessly play *bhajans*, popular devo-tional hymns to the greater glory of Rama and Krishna, sung by a popular "playback" singer.

In the end Tivari won. I needed a tape of *bhajans* for a radio program. Tivari promptly obliged. In return he asked for cassettes of my programs. Now his customers have a choice: *bhajans* or

National Public Radio, although the speed is seriously off on his machine, and I can scarcely recognize my own voice.

Kumartuli is a rabbit warren of sheds, workshops and alleys where some four thousand potters shape bamboo, straw and clay into life-size reproductions of gods and goddesses. Since Calcutta's unofficial patron is the Mother Goddess, major festivals, or *pujas*, are held each year to celebrate her various aspects. The potters make images for these festivals, including Durga, who rides a lion and destroys demons. She is worshipped for four days, usually in early October. Kali, a more terrifying form of the goddess, with her protruding tongue and garland of skulls, is celebrated a month later.

During our visit, many of the potters are preparing for the upcoming Durga Puja. We watch as one of them, hard at work, smooths gray clay onto a large straw-and-bamboo frame. He learned how to make images from his father; for most of the potters, image making is a caste profession going back several generations.

Others, such as Aloke Sen, a former art student, use images as tools of social criticism. His images of Saraswati, goddess of learning, depict her in chains. "I want to show the slavery of today's education, where children are just stuffed with facts," he says.

Sen's Durga images have become famous because of their ambiguity. Sen refuses the crude depiction of the demons that Durga slays as the epitome of evil. He sculpts them with the faces of ordinary men and women. "They represent the evils in the hearts of every man—lust, anger, vanity, infatuation, jealousy, and greed," he asserts. His tableaus, which show Durga mounted on a lion and slaying a demon, will fetch him about 20,000 dollars. They will grace four of the largest neighborhood stages set up by street committees. For four days and nights of the Durga Puja, people will flock to see these works of art. On the fourth night, each neighborhood committee will take down its Durga images, place them on bamboo stretchers and carry them to the banks of the Hooghly.

Five years ago, Raja decided I must experience my first Durga Puja from the vantage point of the ordinary Calcuttan. He instructed Tivari to drop us off en route to the river, right in the middle of several hundred Bengali musicians. Together we marched through the night to the tune of something I still believe was meant to be "Scotland the Brave," played by Bengali bagpipers clad only in *dhotis*. Once at the water's edge all hell broke loose. Each team bearing a Durga image maneuvered down the muddy embankment and then heaved it into the water, where it would dissolve back into clay, straw and bamboo on its way to the Ganges and the Bay of Bengal.

Durga Puja is Aloke Sen's personal vindication as an artist. But it is also his nightmare: "These images are my creation. They are like my sons and daughters. Now the studio is full. But soon it will be empty, and the suffering will begin. It is unbearable for me to watch them putting my images, my children, into the Ganga!"

On the scale of human suffering, Aloke Sen fares better than most Calcuttans. Yet perhaps, in the final analysis, it's the struggle to survive amid decay and death that gives so many Calcutta artists and writers their subject matter. "With problems you have food for creation. You have your material," said Satyajit Ray. "If you're living in Stockholm all you can do is make films like Bergman does, about human beings and all the psychological this and that."

Raja and Dakoo agree. Their work is obsessed by their love-hate relationship with the city and its problems. This tension is best summed up by filmmaker and actress Aparna Sen, who also edits Calcutta's leading women's magazine. She freely admits she hates the city, then adds, "But I know what it looks like in the morning, in the evening. I know what the streets are like and how the shadows fall...even though I hate it I can't think of working anywhere else!"

Julian Crandall Hollick was the Regular India Correspondent for National Public Radio in the United States from 1988 to 1990. He is a columnist for The Sunday Times of India, *and divides his time between India and the United States.*

＊

The subway system of Calcutta is immaculately clean, runs smack on time, and doesn't reek of urine—this in a country where nothing is particularly clean, nothing runs on time, and pretty much everything stinks of piss. Each station has well-tended plants, murals, and even TV sets playing news or movies. The stop below the Indian Museum boasts irreplaceable marble sculptures in fragile glass cases, all completely unmolested. The fare is one rupee, a little over a nickel, about one-twentieth what it costs to ride New York's filthy, unreliable, crime-plagued sewer.

—Jonah Blank, *Arrow of the Blue-Skinned God:*
Retracing the Ramayana through India

LARRY HABEGGER

The Horns of Kaziranga

Rhinos still roam the grasslands of Assam.

AT 4 A.M. CALCUTTA IS QUIET. THERE IS LITTLE ACTIVITY IN THE streets: a few rats scurry in the gutter searching for food, clambering over the mounds of sleeping people who crowd the pavement. Calcutta quiet is rare. The congestion here seldom permits the city to relax.

The only sounds now are the creaking of the rickshaw, its beaten wood grating like old bones under my weight, and the patter of the *dhoti*-clad rickshaw-*wallah's* feet echoing off the buildings as he pulls me toward the bus stand. He flicks his head sideways to look at me out of the corner of his eye and mutters something without breaking his rhythm.

"I was taxi driver. Taxi no good. Rickshaw good." Then something about rupees. I know he will ask for more money than we agreed upon. *Baksheesh:* as Indian as sacred cows and maharajahs. Then he's quiet again, and I feel the sky. It's crowding down, heavy with rain. But today I don't mind because I'm off to track rhinos.

The rickshaw stops. Without warning the rickshaw-*wallah* sets down his yoke, almost tossing me headlong into the street. "Wait," he says, then walks to the gutter to urinate. I've clearly put him to work before his morning ablutions. Ahead the ghostly hulks of two Brahma cows lurch across the street, stopping to graze on garbage. The rickshaw-*wallah* returns and we move on.

As I expected, he asks for double the agreed fare when he lets me off. I give him a few extra rupees for the early start, smile, say "thanks," and walk away, hearing him grumble only an instant before I hear the creaking of the rickshaw.

The bus to the airport is only half full and goes smoothly, a pleasant surprise. More remarkably, the flight leaves on time and after a short hop over Bangladesh lands safely in Jorhat in the state of Assam. Outside, as I expected, it is raining.

A taxi driver buttonholes me on the tarmac before I even reach the terminal. His English is good.

"Where do you want to go?"

"Kaziranga."

"Ah, you want to see the rhinos."

I nod, smiling.

Kaziranga National Park is

*C*entral Calcutta is the last place in the world with hand-pulled rickshaws. Chinese immigrants introduced them in the late nineteenth century. Somewhere between seventy thousand and one hundred thousand barefoot pullers rent the high-wheeled contraptions by the shift. Most pullers are from Bihar State and they struggle to send a portion of their scanty earnings to their families. Some moonlight as small-time pimps and drug dealers. The strenuous work, poor diet, and grotty living conditions exact a grim toll on pullers' kidneys, lungs, feet, and lives. Owners of rickshaw fleets are often wealthy and influential. Some, according to rumor, are politicians and police.

◆

—Mary Orr, "India Sketches"

the final stronghold of the great Indian one-horned rhinoceros. It has been a sanctuary since 1901, and in 1972 it was declared a national park. Now the government of India finances and maintains it. The official count for rhinos in 1993 was over eleven hundred and the park is home to many other animals including some six hundred wild buffalo, several thousand deer and wild boar, sloth bears, and the occasional leopard and tiger. Poaching, however, is a very serious problem.

Jorhat is an agricultural city in a lush setting. Mostly rice and vegetables are grown here, and the jungle seems to encroach on all sides, squeezing onto fields, forming leafy borders for gardens on the outskirts of town.

I take the taxi to the bus station, and after a wait of an hour and a half am in line to buy a ticket, which in India is always a struggle. You must fight to get to the window, then fight again to get your money to the attendant before all of the other insisting hands. I was hoping it would be different in Assam, but it wasn't.

My seat is on the hump of the rear wheel, by a window that isn't there. In its place has been jammed a rusted piece of sheet metal. The rain flows in and trickles down to the floor. When we start to move it blows in, splashing indifferently on my leg. I slide closer to the man next to me and prepare myself for the next fifty-six miles, or three and a half hours.

We stop for tea whenever the driver is thirsty. He seems to be unquenchably thirsty today, but I don't mind because it gives me a chance to get out of the rain, and a cup of tea combats the chill.

A short while later two seats miraculously open up when we

> Our bus pulls out shakily into the main street honking warnings to all creation. Just then a nonchalant beast crosses, ignoring the bus. For this the bus will stop and wait. The beast, a water buffalo, the divine brake inspector—nothing will divert him from his chosen path. Mythic vehicle of Yamah, god of death, black shiny hide and always casually chewing, he crosses the road and carefully completes his slow examination of our souls.
>
> ◆
>
> —Mark Antrobus,
> "Chasing the Rainbow:
> A Western *Sadhu* in India"

stop near a muddy path. The man next to me slides to the seat across the aisle and smiles at me. I slide to the aisle seat and it feels like shelter. Stretching my legs, I thank him, and sit back, able now to enjoy the scenery.

Assam is intensely green. Flat fields thick with rice run casually to the forested hills in the distance, a fresh, vibrant green flowing to meet the older, richer shade on the horizon. Blazing-white egrets stand idly, occasionally taking their graceful flight like a ballet done against an impressionist backdrop. For many miles we pass the rice fields, interrupted only by occasional clumps of forest where the hills send a delinquent finger toward the road. Then abruptly a tea plantation emerges. The flat, orderly spread of shrubs is speckled in light and dark green. Acacias stand among them like angels in a tranquil land. We roll on, through alternating fields of rice and tea.

The rain continues, heavily at times. The bus is now full, an unfortunate man in rags taking my former seat. His dark, haggard face is adorned in white stubble; his mouth is scarlet, his teeth red and rotting from years of chewing betel nut. He chews slowly now, and from time to time spits the flaming red spittle into the rain. He is not alone. On this bus at least half of the passengers are chewing, and not just the old people, but also young men in Western shirts and trousers, young women with beautiful dark faces wearing silver and gold nose jewelry and wild saris. For the first time, in the closeness of the bus, I can smell it, the slightly sweet rancidity of the betel nut. We bounce along, no one in any apparent hurry.

The monsoon is lingering, like an unwelcome guest. This year it has been especially heavy. The river Brahmaputra has flooded much of its valley, and thousands of villagers have been evacuated to relief camps. The rain continues to blow in on the old man and his scarlet spittle, and I begin to wonder if I'll be able to get into the sanctuary.

A ripple of conversation flows the length of the bus and the man across the aisle tells me with a smile, "Your stop is the next one."

I thank him and prepare to go out into the rain, suddenly

reluctant to give up the security of this rickety bus bouncing through the countryside.

As the bus recedes in the distance I make my way up a narrow road through a tea plantation to a small complex of buildings at the top of a hill. Run by the government of Assam, the tourist lodge is reasonably priced and comfortable. Meals are cheap and adequate, and the friendly Assamese who manages the place assures me I'll be able to visit the sanctuary, if the rain stops. The sky shows no signs of that, and the rain is steady until darkness comes suddenly at 5 p.m.

I have little hope of going into the park when I am awakened the next morning by a rap on the door at 4:30. I rise sleepily and step outside. It is dark and quiet. Water drips from the trees, but the sky is holding. At 5 o'clock it is light, and the sky, still overcast, shows signs of breaking up, lifting on the horizon like the hem of a long skirt to show pale sky beyond. A short while later, without breakfast, I climb into a jeep with six Assamese and we drive off, three miles to the elephant camp.

A cluster of Indians stands around a raised wooden platform, waiting for *howdahs* to be mounted on the elephants. The women are wearing their flowing saris, the men are dressed in slacks and sweaters just as colorful. It doesn't take long to prepare the elephants, and we climb the platform to reach the *howdahs*, clamber aboard, three or four to an elephant, and slosh off into the swampy grasslands, a band of seven elephants.

Our pace is slow, but without warning and barely two minutes into our journey we spot our first rhino. It stands shoulder deep in grass, munching, stopping to stare at us as we approach. Seven abreast, we must be a formidable sight to its tiny eyes. It watches us until we come within thirty feet, then slowly turns and sloshes off. We follow it, cameras clicking, people chattering with excitement.

The rhino looks like an anachronism with its thick hide divided into sections like plates of armor. Its single stout horn and hooked upper lip give it a fierce appearance, but when it flaps its small ears it suddenly seems amusingly docile. Its eyes become sad rather than mean, and I see that it is a peaceful creature despite its prehistoric appearance.

Not far away another rhino is accompanied by a herd of swamp deer and an egret. The deer watch us curiously, while the rhino grazes and the egret rides on its back. Now and then the egret jumps off to snatch a meal, but each time it returns. As we move in their direction, the deer prance away to join a larger herd on higher ground.

We make our way slowly through the swamp, and rhinos appear everywhere. One is submerged up to its chin in a water hole, another peers at us through tall grass. Gray herons and egrets take flight and move in slow motion away from our path. Starlings chatter in the occasional trees. White-headed fish hawks swoop low over the waters, and a pelican, shining white like the egrets, glides effortlessly toward a landing spot in the distance. We see more deer, which panic and thrash through the tall grass as we surprise them, and more rhinos.

When we return to the lodge, the park official tells me the sanctuary will close tomorrow because the high waters are too hard on the elephants. He amiably suggests that I try to come back later in the season, and I smile, thinking of a place on the other side of the world.

Later that day I prepare to leave, to make my way out of Assam. I wait for the bus to Gawahati, hoping the rain will wait for me to get there. I had hoped to get out again to see the rhinos, but I finally decide that they are better off left alone. They seem happy here, and they will have peace for another little while.

Larry Habegger is co-editor of the Travelers' Tales *series. He is co-author with James O'Reilly of* World Travel Watch, *a column that appears in newspapers throughout the United States.*

✳

An oboe trilled softly in the distance. India's gods were stirring. I said good-bye to my friends and let myself be tempted into the darkness. A drum started playing. I ran towards the sounds, becoming part of a large crowd ascending the steps into a Hindu temple. Night and thousands of oil lamps had magically transformed the stone walls of the building. They had become a universe of warm, flickering stars. I had stepped into a Hindu vision of heaven.

Bells began ringing. A central building was illuminated with more oil lamps. A priest circulated a flame, a blessing, a purification from Agni, the Goddess of Fire. The crowd pressed to glimpse within the inner sanctum. Isolated yet visible, surrounded by yet more stars, washed by the hymns of hidden priests, was Vishnu, the center of the Universe, the Preserver.

—Jan Zabinski, "Walking the Length of India"

✦ ✦ ✦

Wheels of Life

Cycling in India is not for the faint
of heart—but it offers unparalleled
contact with local people.

WE LEFT THE GREY, NOXIOUS HAZE HANGING OVER INDUSTRIAL
Delhi and headed for the countryside and Agra. Our escape was
far from peaceful. The spine-shattering roads were a constant blur
of bell-ringing cyclists all rattling and rolling and racing their way
along beside us. It felt like the motorway as we swerved in and out
of a surge of riders with overtaking and undertaking manoeuvres
I never would have believed possible on two wheels. Often a
plethora of people would perch precariously—on a single bike—
fragile, veiled old women side-saddling on rear racks; boys balancing in crazy contortions; children strapped to the crossbar along
with goats and ducks and carcasses. All this and yet they still managed to accelerate after us in hot pursuit. They were addicted to
chasing and racing and no way were they going to let a couple of
fancily kitted-out foreigners glide past unnoticed. We sped up, they
sped up; we slowed down, they slowed down; we stopped to tend
to the call of nature, they stopped to watch. We were constantly the
centre of attention—and that is something you are stuck with in
India, whether you like it or not.

The Indians could be hair-tearingly infuriating but they were
wonderful people, always wanting to help even if they had no idea.

There seems to be only one style and make of bicycle in India—it is a black, single-speed with upright handlebars and fenders. It apparently comes in only one size as well; as I have seen countless Indian boys riding bikes so large, that one slip could dash all hopes of them ever enjoying sexual intercourse.

The problem this homogeneity poses is that riding my multi-colored, twenty-one- speed mountain bike with bar-ends and panniers is the equivalent of the circus coming to town.

Whenever I pass another cyclist there is the inevitable, "Squeak, squeak, rattle, rattle, clunk" as he speeds up to pass (I use "he" because I can count on one hand the number of girls I've seen riding bicycles so far). Once he has successfully passed, wearing a determined grin, he stops pedaling and turns around to get a better look—forcing a radical swerve to avoid collision. This frustrating "leap-frog" can go on for kilometers.

◆

—Willie Weir, "Cycling India: Letters from the Road"

"Which way to Jodhpur?" I asked a camel-man at a fork in the road with no signpost.

"Jodhpur? This way please," he said with arm outstretched, pointing vaguely in a direction somewhere between the two roads.

"Jodhpur," I tried again, gesticulating vividly, "is left or right?"'

"Yes," he said.

"Thank you," I replied and carried on, none the wiser.

Apart from the roads being a swarming mass of everything that moved, there were also dangers of the immovable type. The positioning of road hazard signs was decidedly erratic and I often came across gaping chasms in the road, at least six feet deep, without the slightest warning. It was not just people who suffered from a lack of proper road maintenance but also luckless livestock—I once discovered a scrawny goat bleating listlessly as it lay trapped at the bottom of one such ravine.

Another time, as I was merrily flying along with Peter, the road suddenly disintegrated with a fifty-foot drop into a fast-flowing river. There had been no signs, no warnings, and it was only a good pair of brakes that saved us from plunging over the edge (where, we learnt later, two motorcyclists had died the previous night). A little delayed, we heard an urgent shout from a roadside workman busy with a small task force of men and camels.

"Hello! Mister—stop please!" he cried as he scrambled up the sandy bank. "The road—it is washed far away."

"Yes, thank you," I replied with bemusement, "we had noticed."

As we were riding along one day, a bit of grit lodged in Peter's eye and it puffed up so badly that he could not see out of it.

"What you need is an eye hospital," I quipped, as if such a thing would exist among such ancient and underdeveloped scenes of paddy fields, stone-breakers, oxen-turned water-wheels, human-pulled carts, sari-clad labourers undertaking backbreaking work and men walking with sacks of goat fodder on their heads. As a cloud of thick, choking dust settled from a passing fleet of swaying camels, I read a sign beside us that said:

> *I* have learned the most important rule of the road: THE BIGGER VEHICLE AL-WAYS HAS THE RIGHT-OF-WAY. This puts bicycles at the very bottom of the vehicle caste system. When two trucks converge, and you, the lowly cyclist, happen to be present, you have but one option other than death—head for the ditch! And time and time again, that's exactly what I did on the road to Agra (and I thought being a bicycle courier in Seattle was exciting).
>
> ◆
>
> —Willie Weir, "Cycling India: Letters from the Road"

EYE-SPECIAL HOSPITAL
PLEASE THIS WAY

Alice in Wonderland? No, this was India—a country which never failed to surprise. We followed a bank in the direction indicated by the sign but could see only a bunch of bangled women chattering in a golden aura of sunlit dust with big brass water-pots on their heads as they walked towards a small cluster of mud huts. We stopped a youth wearing a shabby red shirt with "Mr. India" written on the back.

"Mr. India," I said, "do you know the way to eye hospital?"

"Eleven minutes walk this way," he said, pointing in the opposite direction to that of the sign.

"Are you certain?" I asked uncertainly, following his gaze. "All I can see that way are giant haystacks."

"Yes, eye hospital certainly this way."

In India it is not a good idea to ask just one person's opinion, especially as far as directions are concerned. Not wishing to appear discourteous or unhelpful, they will say the first thing that comes into their head rather than honestly and far more usefully admitting that they do not know. It is best to ask as many people as possible and opt for the majority view. This does not mean that you will then be going in the right direction—it just gives you a slightly better chance of doing so.

We therefore asked as many people as possible but we still ended up lost and it was simply by a stroke of good luck that, exhausted, we stumbled upon a ramshackle hut to replenish our water and discovered that we had finally reached our goal. The eye hospital consisted of two dusty, dingy rooms and a bald, bespectacled little man with a magnifying glass. He looked like Gandhi but he was in fact the eye specialist. Peter was laid out on a board. A dim, flickering torch was shone into his eye and then the doctor produced a syringed needle.

Panic-stricken, Peter sat bolt upright and narrowly missed impaling his eye on it.

"Whoa!" he gasped. "Where are you going with that? I don't need any needles, all I need is a cotton-bud."

"You must remain lying. I must anaesthetize the eye."

The thought of an injection near his eye turned Peter rigid with shock. He lay unflinching as the doctor carried out his delicate manoeuvre and successfully removed the offending article.

Peter was pronounced healed, given a bottle of drops and told, "Please Mr. Peter, no charge."

The Taj Mahal was memorable not only for everything that it is memorable for but also for meeting Aiden, a hairy cyclist from Matlock Bath in Derbyshire, who joined us and amused us with his continual flow of unusual "slug poems" and reactions to his own case of dire dysentery. We threesomed it out into Rajasthan—a combination which only confused people further.

"Madame!" hailed a tall Rajastani buried beneath a brightly coloured turban. "I conclude you have two husbands."

"Well, I'm afraid you conclude wrongly," I said. "One's my puncture repairer and the other's my slug-poet."

"Ah yes, of course," he replied and turned tail with a flick of his elaborate mustache.

The sun, a blazing ball of fire, set the walls of Jaipur aglow with a deep, flickering, rosy hue as we arrived. It was easy to see why it is renowned

*M*idway between Delhi and Agra we pulled into a dusty lot behind a clump of bushes and stopped at a run-down teahouse for refreshments. Our driver clearly knew the place well because he bypassed the main entrance, successfully evading a group of men who squatted together in the heat surrounded by a motley assortment of animals. It was a woefully listless scene until we got out of the car and one of the men spotted us. Suddenly the place erupted in a frenzy of music, dancing bears, frolicking monkeys, slithering snakes, squawking birds, and wild gyrations by the men who were at once competing with each other and working as a unified team to win our rupees. We escaped into the restaurant and the scene quieted again until a tour bus pulled in and the show began anew, the same frenetic performance. All day it must be like this, long periods of quiet followed by bursts of pandemonium, all an ongoing attempt to eke out a living.

◆

—James O'Reilly and Larry Habegger, "Fools in Agra"

as the Pink City but things did not stay rosy for long in the clam-
orous congestion that followed. Peter, behind me one moment, was
gone the next, vanishing into the mêlée. India is like that; it can just
swallow you up. Aiden and I spent a fruitless half hour scouring the
teeming streets for him but soon gave up. It was a pointless task. We
knew we would meet him again somewhere along the way: in a
country brimming with nearly nine hundred million people it is
amazing how easily and how often you keep bumping into people
you either know of or know.

Peter was located a hundred miles down the road, eating a
bowlful of banana porridge beside the Holy Lake of Pushkar,
where ash-covered *sadhus* with matted hair and loin cloths sat
cross-legged in a state of hypnotized spiritualism. The devout wandered with blood-red *tika* marks on their brows and garlands of
marigolds, offering coconuts to the sacred waters where they
bathed to wash away years of impurity and to strengthen their
good karma in states of rapt reverence.

Pushkar was a wonderful place to hang up my wheels for a
while and relax. It was brimming with trippies but it was one of
those rare places where an influx of travellers proved an advantage.
After weeks of cycling through small rural villages where no bus-
or train-travelling sightseer would feel inclined to alight and where
we were constantly at the centre of animated and forever curious
crowds who unceasingly pummelled us with questions and inane
gibbering chit-chat, it was sheer bliss to be able to walk around
Pushkar without being hammered or pursued.

The crooked streets were lined with makeshift stalls piled high
with pyramids of bananas, papayas, coconuts and peanuts, chickpeas
and grapes. Next door to a vendor selling second-hand teeth, I
bought some exquisite mangoes and gorged myself silly.

Aiden and I shared a big, airy rooftop room which turned out
to be a popular thoroughfare for the local monkeys. These were
the sort of thieving, hiss-spitting (possibly rabid) monkeys that
you treated with some respect. If they pocketed your bunch of bananas, then you would neither challenge them nor question the
act. "Go ahead," you would say, keeping a wary distance from their

devilishly sharp claws, "please help yourself—you're welcome to anything—the choice is yours." It was better than risking the high possibility of being attacked and bitten.

Sitting on the sun-scorched rooftop overlooking the lake one afternoon, Orwell in one hand, banana in the other, I was dreamily peering down at the pigeons strutting on the waterside steps of the *ghats*, pecking and drinking, when suddenly the soundtrack of *Jaws* filled my head. Down in the murky depths of the Holy Waters I caught sight of a savage-looking catfish—more a shark than a mere fish—with grotesque, evil eyes and a mouthful of razor-jagged teeth. More of them appeared on the scene—huge, sinister beasts, lurking just beneath the surface, scarcely moving but ever watchful of the winged activity on the *ghats*. The clottish pigeons were quite unaware of the impending danger from the denizens of the deep and continued to peck at the water's edge. Then came the moment. A pigeon bent down for a thirst-quenching beakful. In a splashing flash, the monster fish leapt from the water, grabbed the pigeon by its neck, decapitated it, retained the head and dived back down into the holy murk.

Every morning at dawn I would pocket a book and a mango and walk beneath reddening skies, out past the stalls, the temples, the curled, skeletal forms of sleeping beggars, to climb a massive, rugged outcrop of rock. At its top was a golden fairytale temple, perched high above the shifting sands of the desert. Parrots with wildly coloured plumage and crests that jutted like ships' prows would flit and swoop like circus clowns; and eagle-like birds of prey would glide gracefully past at eye level. Way down below was Pushkar, a distant shimmer of Holy Lake and whitewashed roofs gently stirring into life as the sun crept over the sandy horizon. For a couple of hours I would sit, queen of my castle, enjoying the peace, my mango and my aptly titled book, *Far from the Madding Crowd*.

From Pushkar the three of us branched off in different directions. I fancied a while of lone Indian travel and ignored people's warnings, including Naveen's back in Delhi: "Don't travel alone—the village people are uncivilized and dangerous." Peter and I arranged to meet for tea several weeks later at the Lake Palace in Udaipur. Aiden, with his slug poems and dire dysentery, was running out of time and jumped on a train. Before doing so, however, he handed me a "dog stick."

"I think you might need this," he said, "if the dogs of Pushkar are anything to go by."

He was right. It was not the uncivilized people that would terrorize me but the dogs. India was teeming with pariah hounds. Packs of snarling, salivating canines would surge in my wake, hell-bent on sinking their wolflike fangs into a juicy chunk of blurred, revolving calf. There was no way that I was going to play brave, stand my ground, look them in the eye and ward them off with a few lobbed rocks. They bore down on me from all sides, some of them twice my size—huge, frenzied creatures thirsty for blood. In a state of panic I would reach unbelievable speeds in frantic, lung-bursting attempts to outcycle the ferocious beasts. All the while I would whirl and wield my dog stick, every now and then delivering a direct hit which would send one of my tormentors sprawling with a yelp. This was no dog-loving nation and these were rabid beasts.

> *I* stepped out of my hut, and again met the dog, a red-eyed, long-nosed, brown, fruit salad of genes with battle scars, the perfect nemesis for Little Red Riding Hood. Each moment that I thought I may be getting closer to some understanding of Mahabalipuram as a thumbnail sketch of India, this dog would appear; my accuser, one of a class of canines known in India as "pariah dogs."
>
> ◆
>
> —Laurie Udesky,
> "Mahabalipuram Daze"

As I cycled across the Great Indian Desert, people, places and food and water supplies thinned to a trickle. I would pass the desiccated carcasses of camels and macabre, grinning skulls—a reminder of what could happen if things went wrong. All the time, high above in the burnt white skies, were the ever watchful and ever hungry eyes of circling vultures.

My Indian maps were hopelessly inaccurate and gave little help in discerning what might lie ahead. Villages that I had relied on for food or water or accommodation and which looked quite promising on the map turned out to be dismally small or nonexistent. It was no good pointing to the map when seeking directions from a crowd of villagers, either. Most had never travelled further than the neighbouring village, let alone to one fifty miles away. To mention Delhi or Calcutta was like talking of another planet. If I showed them the map a multitude of grappling hands would descend upon it, turning it upside down and back to front in mystification. I gave up trying to extract navigational information from it and wore it on my head as a turban instead, or wrapped myself in it sari-fashion or, when the sea of pressing faces was too overpowering, I used the map to cover my face and disappeared into a glorious but brief respite of crumpled paper where no eyes could meet mine. There I would stand, motionless, among a rabble of hundreds of puzzled people, my features veiled by 1:1,500,000 scale map of India, thinking: is this really happening? I wanted to curl myself up in a dark corner and hide. But the head-shattering din and the treading on my toes made me realize that, yes, it was happening all right. The clamouring crowd would press closer and closer, trying to get a glimpse of this peculiar, map-bedecked alien on a pink bicycle. Then, when I felt they had overstepped their mark and had stood on all my toes, and when a few cheeky types in the front stalls had sneakily tried to peep through the gaps of my mapped disguise, I would suddenly throw it aside and say, "Boo!" It never failed to amuse.

Water supplies were often highly suspect. One night I turned up at a small temple; I asked for water and was directed to a well. I threw down the bucket, hauled it up, added a purifying tablet that tasted of swimming pools and drank my fill. Refreshed, I went to bed. The next morning I returned to the well and discovered, by the light of day, that a family of fat rats had set up base in its murky depths.

On the road to Jaisalmer I met Philippe, a Belgian bus-driver riding a heavy, single-speed heap of Indian-made Hero bicycle. Fed up with crowded trains and buses, he had bought his bike brand new for £28 [about $43] up in Rishikesh, a place the Beatles had made famous for staying there during their hippy phase. He would sell it later in Jaisalmer market at only £4 less— not a bad rate of depreciation for a two-month tour covering more than fifteen hundred miles.

It was a day for meeting cyclists. Down the road I met a white-haired American who had an exquisite brass gear lever. After a collision with a rickshaw in Bombay, he had a new one made up from the shambles of a scrap-metal mechanic's shop. Its precision work surpassed even the like of Campagnolo—and it cost a mere twenty-five pence. Indians are great improvisers; nothing gets wasted and if they do not have it they will make it.

Then out of the heat-haze Peter appeared. That evening we stayed in a small *dak* bungalow (a government-run rest-house) which we found hidden in a compound in Phalodi. Usually these places provided a degree of escape from the inquisitive locals and this one did too—for about half an hour.

I had a shower in our en suite bathroom—a dark, odorous, cockroach-infested space about five-foot square with a cooking-oil drum full of water and a hole in the floor that acted as both drain and toilet. Then I fell on the bed in a state of sweaty torpor. The whirring ceiling fan had two speeds: slow, which was as beneficial as "off," and fast, in which it spun in a frenzy with the ferocious noise and speed of helicopter blades gone berserk, stirring up a hot whirlwind of choking dust and threatening to decapitate you every time you stood up. It was better to sweat in silence.

Then we were discovered. Outside the window a small but determined battalion of twelve-year-olds had sneaked up on us unnoticed and then broke into a giggling torrent of: "Good morning your father name! English is house! What your time!"

We closed the window, closed the door and suffered in stuffiness.

The window was pushed open; a face pushed through. "Book yes not?" We slammed it shut. It opened again (there was no catch): more faces, more giggles, more screams. Then the door was discovered; it was banged on and pushed open to cries of impish laughter and a retreat of scuffling feet. We wanted some peace, we wanted some sleep, but we were not going to get any. I sat up and started shelling peas. Peter sat up in exasperation. He wanted to sort them out—the boys, that is, not the peas.

"Leave them," I said, adding hopefully but unrealistically, "they might get bored and go away."

I should have known better; Indian staying power is remarkable and the squad outside did not go away. They simply became noisier and more excited. Then they took to hurling missiles.

When Peter exchanged his flip-flops for baseball boots, I knew he was preparing for gang warfare. Then he picked up his bicycle pump. Things were getting serious. He crouched by the door like a tensed tiger ready to pounce before the kill, waiting for an over-confident enemy to open the door. I acted as decoy and continued passively podding peas. Peter called me Bait.

THWAACK! The door was kicked open and Peter, emitting a deafening war cry, burst out with such terrifying speed that I dropped a pod in fright. All hell was let loose. He charged into a thick cloud of dust after the panic-stricken stampede. Yells and screams of fear reverberated off the compound walls. The gang leader broke away from the pack and Peter was after him in a flash, accelerating hard as he made a lunge and grabbed him—a blubbering, wailing wreck pleading innocence. The rest of the mob scampered up the boundary wall and made it to their safe haven, but they were still screaming and leaping up and down like a bunch of berserk baboons.

Peter the Great triumphantly dragged his hysterical, flapping prey into our room. The wide-eyed captive was terrified, certain that he was doomed. Locking him in our cell (the toilet), Peter shouted tauntingly through the door: "Boy toilet like? Yes not stay? Time now quiet! Not please shout!"

Our victim yowled away, hammering like a mad thing on the

door and emitting ear-shattering screams which soon brought the government staff and half the village running. Bursting through the door, they found us both sitting on the bed calmly shelling peas.

"Evening," said Peter.

"Hello," I said.

"Aaaargh!" screamed a voice from the toilet. We continued our shelling as if nothing was amiss.

The room became a jam-packed madhouse with everyone shouting and screaming simultaneously. We explained the situation, our wailing captive was rescued and finally the commotion died down. We were left in peace. Bliss.

Later we ventured out to get some *dal* and *chapatis* from a small *chai* house where the owner asked if it was true that Peter had ill-treated a child. Peter relayed the full story.

"That boy," laughed the owner, "is my nephew. Always he is very bad boy indeed. Very spoilt. Much needed to be taught a lesson. Thank you."

Alone again, at Bijolia I stayed at a "hotel" which was half tea-house, half mechanic's shop. My room resembled a scrap yard. There was a bed—grimy-grey with an oil-stained sheet and surrounded by old tins of grease, rusting wheels, lethal scraps of metal, an assortment of shoddy tools and even an old car engine.

I was hungry. I would have to head outside to find some food. But in India things were never that easy. It would take a lot to work myself up for a dive into the scrum of horn-blaring trucks, dust, dirt, filth, scavenging mangy animals, incessant noise, and clamouring crowds which, along with the squads of snarling dogs, would pounce upon me as soon as I emerged from my den. I was exhausted as it was from the cycling, the heat, the lack of peace, the suspect food and water—just from India in general, really— and venturing out on a food-finding mission would exhaust me even more. It was not possible simply to walk out, buy some food and return within moments. To head out into the street-anarchy was a major expedition and needed a lot of willpower.

It was half an hour before I even mustered enough energy to

sit up, and another ten minutes before I succeeded in putting on my shoes, after which I needed a rest and sat for a while, panting, heat-dazed and sweaty, to contemplate my next move. Finally, my stomach willed me to put one foot in front of the other and I hit the town.

Bijolia was a ramshackle place, the streets and gutters full of rotting rubbish and excrement, the "shops" full of shoddy goods. It was a small but noisy place—one big, blaring nightmare that resounded in nauseating waves round my head. The people, as always, were curious but friendly. I did not have my bike with me but they all knew who I was.

"Hello English bicycle! Stop! *Chapati*? *Dal*? You want very best mealing here?"

I chose one of the many bench-lined food houses whose fronts were adorned with the usual grease-engrimed cauldrons. I peered into each one, rejecting mixtures which had unidentifiable bones protruding from them, and chose the old tasty and (usually) trustworthy *dal* before retreating to a rickety bench.

> By our bad habits we spoil our sacred river banks and furnish excellent breeding grounds for flies....A small spade is the means of salvation from a great nuisance. Leaving night-soil, cleaning the nose, or spitting on the road is a sin against God as well as humanity, and betrays a sad want of consideration for others. The man who does not cover his waste deserves a heavy penalty even if he lives in a forest.
>
> ◆
>
> —Mohandas Gandhi, quoted by V. S. Naipaul in *An Area of Darkness*

The mustachioed chef, wrapped in a tea-towel, was a nice man. He shooed away the encroaching crowds as if dealing with a pack of pestering dogs and left me to eat and write my diary. A few moments later an old-fashioned chauffeur-driven Ambassador car pulled up outside. An immaculately dressed Western couple stepped out and surveyed the squalid surroundings with disdain. I felt quite excited to see them—I had not spoken to anyone other than an Indian for nearly twelve days. I smiled their way and called a chirpy, "Hello!"

They looked but did not acknowledge me at all.

"Edward," said the woman in peeved tones, "I'm just dying of thirst. Tell Narayan to bring us a cup of tea, but only if it looks safe. The place is so frightfully filthy. We'll drink it in the car."

The chauffeur dutifully obliged and bought the tea, which I noticed cost a lot more rupees than mine had. He did not use one of the tea-house's cups but a special one the woman had given him, presumably for reasons of hygiene. Edward and the woman drank their tea on the back seat of the car, doors shut, window blinds pulled, insulated from the outside world. They had uttered not a word to any of the curious onlookers. Then they drove away.

"Why did you charge them three times more per cup of *chai* than me?" I asked the owner.

"Tourist," he said.

"But I'm a tourist."

"No, you are travelling on bicycle. This I think is very good. I also travelling on bicycle but car I have not."

When he learnt that I was a cook by trade, he invited me to join in the *chapati*-making—rolling the dough into putty balls, flattening them with a rapid movement from hand to hand, and slapping them on to the sides of the traditional clay oven, its flames fanned continuously by a skinny boy sitting on his haunches. Making *chapatis* looked easy but was not. Each time, mine turned out like mottled cow pats, which everyone found very funny—especially when I put one on my head and got on with diary writing. When I left, the owner gave me a going-home present: a day's supply of *chapati* and *dahi*.

I approached Sawai Madhopur on Holi, a religious holiday during which Indians enact a bizarre celebration that involves hurling brightly coloured paint over each other. Roadblocks of stones and wood and bodies were constructed by gangs of boys in an attempt to slow down the traffic. Covered in their war paint, they danced around ecstatically, demanding: "Rupees! Rupees!" Should you refuse, you found yourself a target for a liberal spattering of paint. The same fate awaited you should you oblige. Being bicycle-bound made matters worse and the only hope was to storm the roadblock at speed. A multitude of waving arms, some clutching sticks, would lash out dangerously in a wild attempt to stop me. Usually I managed to fend off the mob—but never the paint. By the time I arrived in Sawai Madhopur I looked like a moving advertisement for Dulux.

It was in Sawai Madhopur that I was directed, redirected, and finally became lost when searching for the *dak* bungalow. My last request to three betel-nut-chewing men at a junction had resulted in being pointed in three different directions. I ended up at a five-star hotel which happened to be on the edge of the Ranthambhore wildlife reserve—part of Project Tiger and home to forty-six of these biggest of cats. Half a century ago there were forty thousand tigers in India; now there are only twenty-five hundred.

Contrary to popular belief, their demise was not entirely due to the unrestrained tiger-hunting sport so eagerly pursued by maharajahs and officers of the British Raj. Agriculture, poaching, deforestation, rising human populations, army stations, tea-growers' plantations, insecticides, and industrial development have all conspired to reduce tiger numbers.

I asked the hotel manager for directions to the *dak* bungalow and he whisked me up into his jeep. We sped to a remote, jungly spot deep into the game reserve and there stood a tent, in a state of severe disrepair: it consisted of a tattered piece of tarpaulin draped breezily over a bough, beneath which lay a string bed which seemed to have been gnawed by tigers.

"Please," said the manager, "it is my sincerest pleasure that you come to passing the night here and if you have luck tiger may visit you."

Personally, I could not see anything lucky about being stuck at night alone in the middle of the jungle with hungry tigers on the prowl. I politely declined his offer, whereupon he invited me to stay in his hotel free of charge, with meals and tea on the veranda included. This offer I could not refuse.

There was more in the bargain. At dawn the next morning, he escorted me in his jeep into the reserve in search of the elusive tiger. Hours passed as our eyes continually scoured the thicket. I saw warthogs, mongeese, monkeys, crocodiles, and many strange species of deer—but no tiger. I was on the point of giving up all hope when suddenly, rippling through the long, dry grasses, was a real-life tiger of heart-stopping magnificence. Dagger-toothed and jagged-clawed, it was a perfectly designed, burning-eyed, striped killing machine—a mighty vision of pure grace and power.

At a tender age, Josie Dew fell out of a fast-moving vehicle and developed a life-long aversion to cars. Then she got her first bicycle and never looked back. She has cycled through thirty-six countries on four continents. This story was excerpted from her book The Wind in My Wheels: Travel Tales from the Saddle.

★

It had been one of those days—hot and dusty, with trucks and buses honking and a couple of flat tires to top it off. I had stopped on the side of the road to look at my map and get my bearings, when a teenage boy rode up on his scooter and asked, "One minute of your time?" A harmless request—but I have learned in a country of 900 million people, if you give everyone a minute who asks for one—you soon run out of minutes.

In this particular situation I chose to withhold my sixty seconds of attention and pedaled off. Soon came the whine of a scooter as the boy pulled up alongside of me. "One minute of your time?" "Ignore him and he'll go away," I thought and picked up my pace. He caught up and began repeating, "Sir, I am talking," *over* and *over* and *over* again. This went on for five minutes and I imagined with my luck, he had a full tank of gas.

I slammed on my brakes. "OK, you win," I said, "You've got one minute," pointing to my watch, "Go."

He looked me straight in the eye and said, "I am God." I was speechless. What is the proper response when a thirteen-year-old boy confides in you that he is a deity? I AM GOD!" he repeated more emphatically. What did he want? Did he want me to kneel at his feet? To sing his praises? Did he want my Visa card? " I AM GOD!" I turned to go. "Sir, I am talking. Sir, I am talking."

I snapped. I lost my cool. I became unglued. I yelled at the top of my lungs, "Get out of my face! Leave me alone!"...and several other choice phrases.

He took one step back, held out his hand and said, "One hundred rupees."

He must have seen the look of homicide in my eyes, for he quickly hopped on his scooter and scooted off, before I could begin to holler again. Thank Krishna *that* was over.

A mile down the dusty highway I began to laugh. I laughed until tears came to my eyes as I realized what the poor kid had meant to say was, "I am *guide,*" and his fee was one hundred rupees.

                          —Willie Weir, "Cycling India: Letters from the Road"

* * *

Love Has Teeth

In the proper context, there's nothing
quite like a simple meal.

IT WAS A MODEST BEACHSIDE PLACE, NOTHING FANCY AND NOT FAR
from the Charles Correa's Cubist Cidade-de-Goa resort, one of a
handful of such enclaves on Goa's eighty-mile coastline.

We were the only customers and sat at a window table overlooking the ocean. I'd eaten nothing of any interest since my
farewell bacchanal at Bombay's Taj Hotel luncheon buffet (one of
India's most extravagant culinary displays) and expected the worst
in this empty restaurant.

My fears were utterly unfounded.

Two little palate-cleansing bowls of spicy seafood broth known
as *tomyupkung* and a plate of steamed mussels in a garlic, cumin, and
wine sauce appeared within minutes of our arrival, along with two
loaves of crusty Portuguese bread, hot and smelling of San
Francisco sourdough. We obviously didn't eat fast enough. Another
appetizer followed in a couple of minutes—this time delicate slices
of home-smoked mackerel wrapped in little pouches of palm
leaves. Then, with hardly a pause, came slivers of perfectly cooked
suckling pig, crisp-skinned and juicy.

Even Angelo, my hired driver, seemed surprised by the speed of delivery. We considered asking them to slow things down a little, but whoever was creating these magnificent degustation dishes back in the kitchen was well and truly on a roll. We decided to let him be and just enjoy his handiwork.

The chef was tireless. Tiny crisp-crusted vegetable *samosas* redolent with familiar Indian spices were followed by slices of *apa de camarao*, a sort of pie with a golden rice crust over a succulent mix of whole prawns cooked in coconut milk. Then a slight pause before the main dish, *Pomfret Recheiado*, a whole fish filled with a rich pungent stuffing of sour red *masala* and grilled until the skin crackled like cornflakes when you cut it.

This was too much. But whoever it was cooking back there hadn't finished with us. Small bowls of *vindaloo* were accompanied by tiny crushed rice and lentil pancakes and, before we could raise our hands in defeat, out came a *masala* of miniature pink crabs in a sauce brimming with coriander, flecks of chili peppers, cumin, and *garam masala*. All this washed down with *capitos* of heavy Goan red wine, a little like young port but far more pungent. Angelo staggered to the kitchen and returned a few minutes later.

"Oh—she's so beautiful!"

"Who?"

"The cook—it's a girl who is cooking all these things. She is…" he sought the most complimentary adjectives but failed. "You must see her. I will ask."

He vanished into the kitchen again and seemed to be gone a long time.

And then she emerged.

She couldn't have been much more than a teenager. A dark-eyed, golden-skinned Goan madonna, blushing a little, and carrying a round dish of something resembling crème caramel. Angelo was grinning like a gibbon.

"You know what this is?"

"No, but it looks good."

"This is *bebinca*. She can make *bebinca*! This takes hours of work. It's eggs, coconut milk, sugar…what else?"

The girl whispered something in a voice that sounded like a spring breeze.

"I don't know how to say in English. Special spices—a special mix. Every cook makes a different mix. This is a very traditional Goan dish—but very, very difficult to make."

He looked at his love with adoring eyes.

"Isn't she…?"

The girl blushed even more, placed the dish on the table, and scampered back to the kitchen.

And that was the last we saw of her. The *bebinca* was superb—light as a cloud, a melt-in-the-mouth creation that left the palate sweetened and refreshed. But Angelo's only thought was for the girl, and he set off for the kitchen again.

This time he was unlucky.

A large man with a thick black mustache, large by Goan standards at least, stood by the door. Angelo made some complimentary remarks about the food, the man nodded but seemed aloof and wary. My friend returned with the bill. It was for a ridiculously small amount, hardly more than you'd pay at a roadside hamburger joint back home. He looked utterly forlorn and defeated. Love has teeth behind a pair of pretty lips, and he'd been bitten. His plate of *bebinca* sat untouched; his romantic urges had been crushed. The man was obviously guarding the door. Protocols had been infringed, and it was clear there'd be no more dallying with the pretty cook today.

"You can always come back," I said.

Angelo seemed not to hear me and we drove away in silence.

David Yeadon also contributed "A Bath for Fifteen Million People" to Part I and "The Mirage of Life" to Part III. These stories were excerpted from his book The Back of Beyond: Travels to the Wild Places of the Earth.

★

I sat in the Delhi airport and watched the big electric clock in the departure hall that tells passengers when to board. I thought I imagined that

time was moving in fits and starts: 1:12 a.m. for fifteen minutes, then 1:27
for another twenty, 1:47.... Closer inspection revealed that the clock was
not plugged in, and its digits were being flipped manually by a little man
in gray overalls whenever the mood took him.

—Jonah Blank, *Arrow of the Blue-Skinned God:*
Retracing the Ramayana through India

ANTHONY WELLER

Remnants of the Raj

Ghosts of the British past still hover
in the hill stations of the north.

In July, when the rest of India was baking in terrible heat, cursing and hoping for the monsoon that would bring floods with its blessing, I decided to go up above it all, to the cool air and heights of Simla.

Delhi, Old and New, was unbearable. At over 120° Fahrenheit the mind and spirit stop working properly at the body's urging; the air is a recipe of equal parts dust and sweat. This is the curse of the Indian subcontinent and is in part an explanation for the philosophical asceticism so prevalent for centuries. One must simply withdraw into nothingness and accept it all. The monsoon, which beggars all description with its force—I saw it dent the roofs of cars—can be as awful as the heat. No wonder the British in India, early in the nineteenth century, created these oases in the lower reaches of the Himalayas—Darjeeling, Simla, Mussoorie—where the mind could still operate, tiny nirvanas for a master class, with elaborate support systems of numerous bearers from below. They were called, inadequately, "hill stations," and Simla was and is queen of them all.

To get to Simla I took the toy train that begins at Kalka, in the Punjab, and carries one slowly and precipitously up. India has one

234

of the greatest railway systems in the world: it is the efficient bloodstream that keeps the country alive. The toy train, on its narrow-gauge toy track, crept audaciously up through mists and around mountains. Below us lay folded valleys and terraced fields of an extreme green. We passed through forests of pine and cedar and paused at small stations with melodious names like Koti and Sonwara that looked like blue-and-white retirement cottages surrounded by careful gardens. We burrowed through stone tunnels cut in the hillsides, 103 in all, some only twenty yards long. Cows and water buffalo shambled away at the nearness of our train, and the air became fragrantly cool.

We left the wrinkled valleys behind, crossing arched stone bridges; dark hawks heard us coming and swung out over wastrel gorges. And then, after Summer Hill, we came up out of the clouds to the majesty of sunlight burning on Simla.

Furiously packed onto a series of steep, connecting ridges, all Simla looked pre-

So the British loaded their families and belongings onto horses, carriages, and *jampans*, and climbed into the Himalayas. Here they found the cool breezes, the wild roses, the streams, waterfalls, firs, and ferns of distant England. True, the mountains towered thousands of feet into the clouds, monsoon rains drenched the hillsides, and the forests were impassable, but with Queen Victoria's name upon their lips, they dealt with all that. Within a century, roads had been built, with the necessary bridges, tunnels, and aqueducts, and in the cleared forests little English resort towns arose with timbered cottages, rose arbors, tea shops, theaters, churches, and cemeteries. In that farthest and remotest region, the pillars of the Raj constructed surrealistic replicas of the little coastal towns of Devon and Dorset. The hill station became a part of the Indian experience.

◆

—Anita Desai, "Hill Stations of the Raj," *The Armchair Traveler,* edited by John Thorn and David Reuther

carious, a jigsaw-puzzle town. It seemed to tumble across the Himalayan spines, and from afar, set in tall trees, it resembled a British country town that had gone a-wandering, far from home. But for nearly a century, during the summer months, Simla was transformed into one of the most important and powerful places on earth, for it was the summer capital of the British Raj, the play-paradise of those ruling gods, with their idle wives and spoiled children, all outnumbered by servants. I wondered what remained of the Raj now, here on Olympus.

As we approached, the social profile of Simla was rapidly re-vealed. On the highest level, where the town appeared to stroll and bustle even at a distance, stood Simla's most striking emblems of Britain: a Gothic church, a gazebo-like bandstand, a Victorian the-ater, and a Tudor-style stone town hall, all set along the winding esplanade known as the Mall. Dribbling in profusion below, con-nected by cart roads and circuitous lanes and dizzying staircases, was a large community of lesser, chattering structures that was the lower Simla bazaar, called a "crowded rabbit warren" by Rudyard Kipling in *Kim*. The author elaborated:

> A man who knows his way there can defy all the police of India's summer capital, so cunningly does verandah com-municate with verandah, alleyway with alleyway, and bolt-hole with bolt-hole. Here live those who minister to the wants of the glad city—*jhampanis*, who pull the pretty ladies' rickshaws by night and gamble till the dawn; grocers, old-sellers, curio-vendors, firewood-dealers, priests, pick-pockets, and native employees of Government.

Little seemed to have changed, though there were fewer rick-shaws in use. An elevator had been built, however, and it took me up in several stages from the railway station to the Mall; a huffing porter, with my bags strapped by a coarse rope to his back, took twenty minutes to make the same journey. These men are the human trucks of Simla, and I saw them every day staggering along the winding roads, carrying sofas or chests or filing cabinets, glad to have the work. Behind them, always, was the panorama of mountains, and scattered across the dense ridges and rising from the trees were the sloped roofs and weather-vaned spires of private mansions and bungalows, with names like Wingate, Prospect Hall, Knollswood, Strawberry Hills, Holly Lodge, Oakover.

I stayed at the Woodville Palace Hotel, a converted mansion at the quietest end of the Mall. Surrounded by pines, protected by cannons, with expanses of lawn, a gazebo, and chairs outside where guests sat playing cards over tea and watching their children, Woodville still looked like the summer home of Prince Rana of Jubbal, a Punjabi state. His wife, Princess Brinda, had traveled widely in the thirties, and the spacious rooms downstairs were hung not only with swords and tigers' heads and old prints of local scenes but also with autographs of Tyrone Power, Laurel and Hardy, Hedy Lamarr, Clark Gable, and Queen Victoria. There was the largest billiards table I have ever seen and ebony bronzes of Pan and Shiva and a nymph.

The Woodville was still maintained by the grandson, Uday Singh (his family occupied the entire second floor), and his mother, Princess Ourmila, young photographs of whom I mistook for Ingrid Bergman's. I sat outside and watched the Indian families at tea: father and uncles serious over cards, mother and aunts pouring and discreetly spying on the hands, children on the swing or playing around the lawns among nodding flowers. Woodville was five minutes from the activity of the Mall, in its own secret grove, and some days I had the whole mansion to myself. Every morning at breakfast a barefoot servant in round cap and gray Nehru jacket would bring me my newspaper, clasp his hands, give a slight bow, and murmur, "Sir, are you happy?" I always said, "Very happy," and he always looked relieved.

Simla was still a resort, but for the inheritors of an empire, no longer for the empire builders themselves. Families were on promenade all day long on the Mall and along the higher, crescent-shaped ridge, stopping to gossip where the two met at Scandal Point. Men in holiday suits whirled their canes, women in swirling saris twirled parasols, and children happy on ponies were led about by impassive attendants. Simla monkeys, a local kind of rhesus, were everywhere. Nut-brown, with plaintive, concerned faces, they scampered along the streets or from rooftop to rooftop, discussing and disapproving of the human activities below.

My first day on the Mall I fell into step with a well-groomed boy in shorts and knee socks, hand in hand with his little sister. The boy greeted me politely—perhaps he was eleven. I envied him his perfect diction.

"Good morning," he said brightly. "And how are you enjoying Simla? You have seen the Viceregal Lodge? No? You must. They've done quite a good job of keeping it up, I should think. And how do you like these Simla monkeys? A special breed. We don't have them down in Delhi. I should show you my *Star Wars* collection. Do you know, I was up on Jakko Peak with two bags of nuts that cost me five rupees each, and one of those jolly monkeys leapt on my head and grabbed one bag while his friend ran up and stole the other! Naughty fellows, they cost me ten rupees."

His sister, staring after a trotting pony, wasn't paying attention. The boy said to her, "Be polite to the gentleman. Show some manners to the uncle."

The children reminded me of what Ajay, a young, amiable sales representative for a British metalworks firm, had told me on the train from Delhi, the *Kalka Mail*. "Simla is a society that talks," he said. "It always was. Why? Because up there people have time. They look down on the people in the big cities on the plains as being too modern. Always in a hurry. In Simla, in the summer, even if you work there, you go to work late, have a long lunch, and close up early and go for a stroll along the Mall. In the winter you might not go to work at all. You might ring up and say, 'Too much snow in front of my door.' But people there gossip, gossip, gossip. Who was with whom last night on a bench on the Ridge and what X is having for dinner and why Y was not invited. It's a favorite honeymoon place. My parents had their honeymoon there, and their parents." He grinned. "So will I, next August. It's an older style of living. Not like Delhi or Bombay. Like the British."

On the Mall, where no cars were allowed—only horses and

rickshaws—I was able to have coffee in a coffeehouse, tea in a tea shop, buy a sari and goggles, go roller skating, play billiards, sit by a waterfall, hire a rickshaw, feed a monkey, select a carved walking stick, ride a horse, purchase a faded photo of a British hill picnic, eavesdrop, pick up Martial's *Epigrams* in paperback. I was able to have my fortune told, my head examined, and my picture taken in front of the snowy peaks in the distance. Had it been winter I could have gone ice skating.

I'd been wondering if there were any Britishers left, and a gentle antiquarian bookseller named O. C. Sud told me of an elderly lady named Mrs. Montagu, who lived on the Upper Bharari Road. He was busy reorganizing his shop, because a Japanese mountaineering society had recently come through and bought up masses of rare Himalayan books. He seemed, cannily, to have plenty more. "You must meet Mrs. Montagu," he said. "She's a bit of living history, and she's the last one left. She's been here since 1909. Be sure to speak up."

The next day I found my way along the twisting lanes that led away from the Mall. Grand bungalows were perched on the slopes above me, in stages of absolute decay or preservation, and flowers grew around them: zinnias, dahlias, pink cosmos, and others in yellows and whites and purples. The gabled bungalows had country gardens that might have been found in Kent, though the unfamiliar blossoms of the East grew among them, especially where the gardens had gone to abandonment. Some birdcalls, too, I recognized from walks in England: there were thrushes, and the unexpected cuckoo as well, imported permanently by a homesick officer a century ago. All Simla had about it, beneath the memory of cheroots and wine and officers' clubs and dances and flirtations and tattling servants, a profound sense of homesickness. Carved hearts enclasping British names, pierced by arrows, were still on some trees.

I found the dark, gabled cottage behind a green gate, amid the scents of honeysuckle and roses. Stone steps led from the garden into the woods. The cottage would have been at home in

Tunbridge Wells, but the *ayah* who answered my insistent knocking was a skinny Indian woman named Rada who spoke little English.

I was led into a shadowy hallway rich with the odor of newly polished wood and the hollow ticking of an old clock. By a staircase was a many-paned window with lace curtains, and old prints of wild tribes, men on horseback, and palaces on cliffs hung nearby. Upstairs was a sitting room full of books, a tiny fireplace, wicker furniture, and armchairs with handmade cushions. Rada left me mysteriously, then returned five minutes later.

"Come," she said.

I was led into Mrs. Montagu's bedroom, which looked out on her garden. It began to rain very lightly, a falling mist. She lay on a settee in one corner, and she was so old she looked miniature, though her skin glowed and she still had a beautiful, open, Renoir face. She was wearing a square green Indian cap that made her look jaunty, and she was wrapped in a blanket. Near her, in a hanging cage, a parrot hopped from foot to foot, and behind her were several framed photographs of British men in uniform.

Her eyes were squeezed open, but she looked past me. She put her hand out, palm up, on the small table between us; it was an effort. I touched her hand with mine, and she took it and squeezed my fingers.

"I am a hilly-billy," she announced. "I love these hills, I have lived in them all

---

A wisp of the British Raj remained on the evening veranda of the rest house. After dinner I relaxed into a wicker chair, the night air cool and calm, and shared tea with two English couples. Joking, talking of England, it was easy to imagine that, for the moment, it was as it once had been: pretty *memsahibs*, gallant young British officers, confident in themselves, enjoying all that came with being an officer and a gentleman in British India.

◆

—Jan Zabinski,
"Walking the Length of India"

my life, and I will die in them. I have my place already. At Jalore. My grave."

I said, "How old are you, Mrs. Montagu?"

She said with surprise, "I can't remember." She paused. "I'm sorry. I was here in Simla when I was a little girl. It's changed."

"Were you born in the eighteen-eighties?"

"I...think so. I'm very old, you know. I'm a hilly-billy." She loved saying that word—it made her smile sweetly. I said, "What do you remember most?"

She said firmly, "There were so many dances then, and parties, nearly every evening. At Viceregal Lodge. And the Hotel Cecil. I was more beautiful then." She squeezed my hand more firmly. She said suddenly, "Are you married?"

I said I wasn't. "Should I get married?"

"Well, I expect it would be a good idea," she said. "Then you and your wife could call on me more frequently."

I pointed to the photographs. "Was one of those men your husband?"

She blinked at me. "No," she said finally. I saw a memory cross her face like a cloud, but she let it pass out of sight. She said, "I can see you, but I can't read anymore. I ruined my eyes. Have you seen my animals? I've got lots."

I'd seen none but the parrot, and it seemed tired. When I felt it was time to go, I stood up. Mrs. Montagu, still holding my hand, leaned forward on the settee a few inches. She was waiting to be kissed, and when my lips brushed her cheek her skin was as soft as a flower's petal.

"Perhaps I'll see you again tomorrow," she murmured.

Rada led me downstairs in the gloom, past the pictures of old India. Somewhere in the inner reaches of the house a clock struck once. It had stopped raining. Rada followed me nervously out to the gate and closed it behind me, giving a little wave.

One morning I found Viceregal Lodge, at the top of Observatory Hill. It was a tiring climb without a carriage and horses, up a long steep road that during the Raj had been covered, on festive occasions, with more than a mile of red carpet. Now the Rashtrapati Bhavan (the Indian Institute for Advanced Study) the former center of all British power in Asia, looked the same as in old photographs: a grand stone mansion in the high Victorian style, almost a castle, surrounded by carefully manicured lawns with solemn rows of blooming flowers and gardens on many levels linked by mottled stone steps. Ivy still clung to the walls, and a great bell hung in a cradle before the entrance. The inside, all five floors, was entirely of carved Burma teak. Once the ballroom had welcomed nearly a thousand guests at a time, now it was devoted to the natural sciences.

It had been built during the rule of Lord Dufferin, from 1884 to 1888. That viceroy had not been as enamored of Simla as most were: in a letter, he wrote, "That the capital of the Indian Empire should be hanging on by its eyelids to the side of a hill is too absurd." Viceregal Lodge still seemed invested with enormous power. It had an aura of military theatricality, of plumed pomp, and from here viceroy after viceroy had decreed, absolutely, the fate of several hundred million people and the movements of the mightiest army on the entire continent.

I sat outside by a sundial, beneath an oak, and watched the gardeners at work. The entire scene was so British, but for the hypnotic mountains, that it was easy to enter the past. More than the gabled, polite buildings of the Mall, Viceregal Lodge was built as an act of total confidence, authority, and conviction—from balustraded balconies wrapping around every wing, as if waiting for some high officer to perform his morning constitutional, to the shaded walkways with their hanging lanterns, to the smallest detail, the weather vane perched on the highest painted dome. It was a good old British cock, and today the wind was blowing firmly from the east.

On my way back I stopped in at Sidhuwal Lodge, perhaps the oldest building in Simla, dating from 1826—about five years after the town's inception. It nestles just above Christ Church and the Simla Library. There I met the ex-major Bhai Fateh Jang Singh, a stooped old gentleman in a turban with white beard and mustache, glasses, and a steadfast gaze. A Sikh, he was a reservoir of stories. He'd known Simla since the twenties, and I asked him if there was a tale behind the name of Scandal Point.

"Which tale? Which scandal?" he said. "I can tell you several. The best, and don't bother to try and verify it, is that close to the turn of the century a local maharajah was looking for some girls for his harem, scouting around, and one of his servants collected a daughter of the queen's viceroy for him. He had to give her back and move twenty miles away." He shrugged. "I don't think the British would have been satisfied with that."

I asked him what he thought of the British rule.

He rested his hands on his cane and said, "Considering the fact that they were an alien culture and had to do certain unpleasant things to control India…" He paused, "They were all right. It was quite a life we had here in Simla with them. Polo thrice weekly. Other days, train our horses

I arrived in Darjeeling in a dense fog. Above the window in the living room of the teahouse was a panoramic photograph of the most magnificent mountains I had ever seen. I asked where that scene was. The proprietor tilted her head as if I were nuts and pointed out the window. "There," she said.

I looked out at the solid bank of clouds and vowed to stay as long as necessary, to see that sight. Each morning I'd wake up and eagerly look out my window but it was always the same gray mist, until one morning I awoke at dawn and sensed something different in the texture of the sky visible from my bed. My heart started to race. I sat up and there, filling the window and most of the sky was the glimmering massif of Kanchenjunga, dusted a brilliant red by the rising sun and sprawling across the horizon as if embracing the whole world. For many moments I disappeared into it, overcome by the sheer gravity of the mountain. It was the most powerful vision I'd ever seen.

◆

—Larry Habegger,
"Strolling to Sikkim"

in the morning, lunch, three rubbers of bridge, cocktails, dinner, bed. Dances. Hunts. Pheasant shooting—I was a fine shot. And a great deal of tennis."

He preened his white mustache absentmindedly, his memory reaching back. "You must remember, the British never sent us politicians. *I* was a politician—I won my first election in my early twenties. No, the British sent us *statesmen*." He arched his eyebrows at me. "Look around you. Until recently every stick of every building in Simla was put up by the British. Like Folkestone or Sussex, old chap, yes?" He was teasing, putting on an accent. "They all knew how to give fine parties. One viceroy, Lord Linlithgow—had three daughters. We called them Hope, Little Hope, and No Hope."

I said, "Besides the town, what did the British leave behind?"

He grinned mischievously. "The bush shirt."

My last afternoon in Simla I was invited to have tea at Chapslee—"the most beautiful house in the hills," people said. I found it on one of the lanes past the smoky clutter of Lakaah Bazaar, up a flagstone path by a tennis court. It was one of the more discreet old houses in Simla, without the grandiose melodrama of some of the mansions; in the old days it had been a secretariat. Its shrubbery lent it a country cottage aspect, but it was large.

A servant showed me into a hall of carved teak. Paintings of lakeside castles, mountainscapes, and princely forefathers were framed on the walls beside elegant daggers. Gigantic blue and white Mogul vases ushered me into a sitting room of velvet chairs, painted miniatures, silk drapes, and a marble hearth. The carpets were like an ornate lawn. In a farther room were books in glass cases and ivory-inlay tables.

A boy came to greet me, with a sweet, open face that held all the humor and intelligence of Kim himself.

"May I show you around? My father will be along in a minute. My name is Chandrajit."

He caught me staring at a silver-framed photograph on the mantle, from the time of the First World War. The young woman in it was British, and beautiful in a soft-complexioned, spirited way, without fuss or pose. She looked oddly familiar. The photograph was inscribed "From Hermione M. with love" in a flourishing hand.

The boy said, "That was Mrs. Montagu. There's a lovely painting of her, upstairs, as a girl with long, long hair."

His father said quietly, "A very interesting woman," and came into the room. Lithe, calm, misleadingly fierce-looking with his black beard, Ratanjit Singh had a kind of slippered tranquility that put me at ease. He put his hands in his pockets and said, "She was a great friend of my parents, so my wife and I look after her. She was born in 1892, in India, and lived here until she was seven. Then she went back to school in England for ten years. Her father wanted her to stay there, but she threatened to swim back if she had to. A long swim."

"What did her husband do?" I asked. "She didn't talk about him."

"Ah," said Ratanjit. "Very strange. After settling here she went back to England only once, in her early twenties, and she married some handsome young man on a dare. It lasted less than a month. That's when she came back." He picked up the photograph. "She never married again, but she had a great love affair. With an army man here who was already married. It lasted almost thirty years. He went back just before our Independence, in 1947, and she never saw him again. A few years later he died." He shook his head. "She was quite a beauty, as you can see. But she was very vain about her looks. She loved to read, but wouldn't wear glasses, and

> *S*ooner or later the lurking shadow of separation takes definite shape; asserts itself as a harsh reality; a grim presence, whispering the inevitable question; which shall it be?...the rival claims of India and England; of husband and child.
>
> ♦
>
> —Maud Dever, *The Englishwoman in India,* quoted in *Plain Tales from the Raj,* edited by Charles Allen

when her eyes weakened she looked through a magnifying lens. Now she can't read anymore."

I said, "What about her animals? I didn't see any."

Ratanjit nodded. "She used to keep dozens, dogs and cats and thirteen parrots in her bedroom. Now there's only the one."

Over tea we were joined by his wife, Pronoti, and their daughter, Mandira. We talked of foreigners' expectations of India. Pronoti said, "I think it's films that do the most damage. What was the film you talked of, Ratanjit? *Octopussy*? Full of snake charmers and fire eaters. People come to India and expect these things. And beggars, beggars, beggars. Tigers everywhere. And elephants." She sighed wearily. "I've almost never seen a snake charmer."

It was time to go. Ratanjit walked me down the flagstone path, and said, as an afterthought, "Did Mrs. Montagu sing to you? No? It's a shame. Sometimes she sings. She still has a lovely voice." He smiled. "She remembers the old songs."

We shook hands, and he wandered back to the house. I stood there, watching the dusk descend and the lights begin to twinkle across the valleys and around me, making Simla an enchanted place. Voices floated to me, a monkey capered in the road; in a few hours those winding roads would be filigreed by moonlight. It was still day, though, an in-between time, and the bungalows were lordly among the trees. Ravens flew out over the pines and cedars; the mists were lifting. As I made my way back, a dark-eyed girl wearing the navy skirt and white blouse of a British schoolgirl passed me, humming to herself and plaiting her long, long hair.

Anthony Weller is a writer and poet who lives in Gloucester, Massachusetts.

★

An Englishman in India is perpetually brushing against the familiar amid the exotic and strange. The familiarity, though, is almost all nostalgia. The Ambassador, India's favorite car, is a fifties Morris. Mail-boxes are red. The upper middle classes remind you of Shire English, and public-school men. They remind you of the clubland heroes of Buchan and Sapper. They call each other Bunty and Junior and Bobby. They do indeed meet at the

Club. They work hard, play hard, drink stiff ones and use a vocabulary that got shot down over the English Channel in 1942. Even when I spoke to someone my age, I had the impression of speaking to my grandfather as a young man.

—Jason Goodwin, *A Time for Tea: Travels through China and India in Search of Tea*

JOSEPH R. YOGERST

* * *

Slow Boat to the Islands

The Andaman Islands are as far from the mainland
as you can get, but they are a good way
to visit an India of yore.

THERE'S NOTHING LIKE A BANANA BOAT TO GET YOU IN THE MOOD
for the tropics, in this case the *MV Yamuna,* a rusty scow if there
ever was one. Nothing like her namesake, the noble river that flows
past the Taj Mahal, she is part of an old and somewhat decrepit
fleet that serves the Andaman Islands in the Bay of Bengal, India's
most isolated outpost.

The decks of the *Yamuna* were already crowded with passengers
and cargo by the time I boarded her in Port Blair, but I managed
to stake a claim to the end of a rickety wooden bench beneath the
smokestack. I knew I would be covered in soot by the time we
reached Havelock Island, a day's journey to the northeast, but I felt
fortunate to be seated rather than curled up in a tiny space on the
deck like the Bihari peasants at my feet.

We soon cleared the harbor into open waters. My companion
for this journey was an energetic young man with dark hair and a
bushy mustache. His name was Neeraj, and like many Indians, he
offered an eclectic repertoire: he wasn't merely a guide, but the
owner of a fax service and computer dealership, the head of the
student union at the local university, a radio DJ, an aspiring roller-
skating enthusiast in the Andamans. (In Port Blair, Neeraj had

248

rolled up a pants leg to show me his skating injuries. "I am still learning to brake," he had said earnestly.)

I looked around at my neighbors. Sitting next to me was a priest, Father Peter Soares, from the old Portuguese enclave of Goa on the west coast of India. He was on his way to tend to the spiritual needs of eighty Catholic families on Havelock, but he'd done some traveling of his own.

"I've been to Reno!" Father Peter exclaimed. He said that his visit to Nevada was part of a religious tour of America, but I couldn't resist the obvious question: "Father, did you gamble?"

He avoided the question with a sly smile and launched into a sermon on the tribulations of being a priest in the Andamans, where he and two other priests were responsible for more than seven thousand people in twenty-seven parishes on three islands.

Meanwhile on the bridge, a couple of Swedes (blond, tanned, and robust) were hawking a watch (gold, cheap, probably a Bangkok knock-

*F*oreigners need a permit to visit the Andaman Islands. (The Nicobar Islands are off limits to non-Indian tourists.) The permit allows foreigners to stay in South Andaman, Middle Andaman, Little Andaman, (tribal reserves on these islands are out of bounds) Bharatang, North Passage, Neil, Havelock, and Long islands. On North Andaman foreigners may stay only in Diglipur.

Day trips are permitted to Ross, Viper, Cinque, Narcondum, Interview, Brother and Sister islands, but currently there are regular boats only to Ross and Viper islands. Boats are allowed to stop at volcanic Barren Island, but disembarkation is not allowed and, as yet, there are no regular services. All the islands of the Mahatma Gandhi National Marine Park are open except Boat, Hobday, Twin, Tarmugli, Malay, and Pluto.

The permit is valid for up to 30 days.

◆

—Hugh Finlay, et al.,
India – a travel survival kit

off) to the ship's engineer. His final offer was five hundred rupees, the equivalent of about seventeen bucks. The Swedes appeared to waiver and finally accepted, stuffing the grubby notes into their cut-off jeans. They held their poker faces until the engineer departed, then they grinned.

Late in the day we neared the coast of Havelock. Thick jungle covered much of the island, but there were chalk cliffs along the eastern shore, and from a perch high on the palisades, a white-bellied eagle swooped low over the water to snatch a fish from just below the surface.

The *Yamuna* chugged gently around a bend, and the Havelock jetty came into view. As the boat docked, Neeraj leapt over the side and raced into the village ahead of the other passengers. I had no idea what he was up to. Father Soares turned as he began to disembark and gave me the same sly smile. His Reno smile.

Neeraj soon returned and implored me to follow. Our destination was the Public Works Department bungalow, a modest wood-framed building in a grove of coconut trees near the sea. "I have been to Havelock before," said Neeraj. "I know you must run to get a room."

The significance of his little sprint didn't dawn on me until I discovered the bungalow was the only place to stay on Havelock and that it had just two rooms. One was reserved for the visiting commissioner of police. We had the other. Everyone else from the *Yamuna* was turned away. The two Swedes were forced to sleep on the floor of the logging operation's office; a group of Germans bedded down on the beach; a honeymoon couple from Bombay shared space with the café owner and his family.

Transportation was another challenge. A rickety public bus sputtered between the two villages on the island, but we wanted to go deep into the jungle to see work elephants, and that could take days on foot. The ever clever Neeraj, however, came up with a solution. He convinced a local lumberjack to give us a lift in his truck.

The three of us were well into the thick jungle when, rounding a bend, we came face to face with an Andaman mammoth.

The huge animal, named Sultan, was the thirty-five-year-old leader of a gang of five elephants.

Sultan flashed us a typical elephant grin and went about his work, pushing giant logs with the aid of two huge tusks. "Those teeth are worth a lot," said Neeraj, obviously impressed by Sultan's dental work.

Astride the elephant's shoulders was a young *mahout*—a refugee from Bangladesh—who directed Sultan with deft heels and gentle taps of a wooden stick on the animal's forehead. But the elephant hardly needed prodding. He seemed eager to get on with his work and disappointed once the job was finished.

The *mahout* jumped down and grabbed a huge papaya from a gunny sack. Sultan munched it down.

Back at the Havelock waterfront, preparations were under way for a big Bengali wedding. A local girl was to marry a boy from Middle Andaman island, and most of the village women were immersed in the arrangements, fixing speakers to trees, hanging strings of colored lights, and cleaning the local temple.

Neeraj and I ate fish-head curry and rice at a small café. Gas lamps flickered from the rafters, and a steady breeze blew in through the open windows, the portent of a rising storm. Soon it began to pour, a raging tropical rain that pounded its cadence along the metal roofs.

Members of the wedding party dashed in from the dark. Would they be forced to postpone the celebration? They implored a small boy to light incense sticks beneath the picture of Krishna. And just like that the storm passed. There was a moment of silence, and then loud music roared down from the trees. Praise to Lord Krishna! The wedding was on!

The celebration lasted until dawn, with dancing and singing among the coconut palms. Finally we all followed the bride and groom as they made their way to the beach. She was sobbing, barely able to stand, supported between her mother and younger sister.

"The bride doesn't want to leave Havelock," said Neeraj. "She has never been away from this island. But now she must go live with her husband's family."

The honeymooners piled into a canoe with an outboard engine and, with a gentle put put put, headed west, toward the dark green bulk of Middle Andaman island. It was just a half day away, but to the Havelock girl it must have seemed like a distant universe.

I first heard about the Andaman Islands from Sherlock Holmes. That was more than a decade ago, on the London stage, during a performance of *The Sign of Four,* the Arthur Conan Doyle mystery that revolves around the theft of a treasure chest of priceless jewels from British India.

Although he makes but a brief appearance, the key to the mystery is Tonga, an Andaman pygmy who turns up in England with a blowgun on a mission to retrieve the stolen treasure. I knew nothing about the Andamans, but over the years I read what I could about them—which wasn't much. And in the course of my study I learned that Conan Doyle used some poetic license: there are no pygmies in the Andaman Islands, and the people there don't use blowguns.

To set the record straight, the Andamans—the northern part of the Andaman and Nicobar Islands—are a group of about two hundred or so islands and islets stretching south through the Bay of Bengal.

The more settled areas of the archipelago seem like pieces of rural India that have been sliced off and cast adrift in the sea; bucolic scenes with thatched roof huts, naked boys on the back of muddy buffaloes, and women in silk saris with jugs of water perched on their heads who seem to move in slow motion across your field of vision.

But many of the islands remain untamed, diverse landscapes ranging from coral reefs to volcanoes that have recently risen from the bottom of the sea. More than 85 percent of the land is jungle, including some of the more impressive stands of rain forest left in southern Asia, with gargantuan trees growing as high as a twenty-story building. The beaches are among the finest in the Indian

Ocean, picture-postcard perfect, with a fringe of noble palms and fine white sand.

Early accounts of the Andamans are filled with stories about shipwrecked sailors who wound up on the menu of island tribes. Indians from the mainland once called the place *Timai Thevu*— "Islands of Impurity"—because of their inhabitants' reputation for carving up human flesh.

Even Marco Polo (who apparently got his facts secondhand) jumped on the bandwagon: "The inhabitants are idolaters, and a most brutish and savage race, having heads, eyes, and teeth resembling those of canine species. Their dispositions are cruel and every person not of their own nation...they will kill and eat."

With reports like that, it's not surprising that mariners generally steered clear of the Andamans. Finally, in 1788, British officials in India dispatched Lieutenant Archibald Blair to the islands to make the waters safe from pirates and cannibals. Blair, a noted surveyor, established the first permanent European settlement, which now bears his name.

The British were less than impressed with their new subjects: short, stocky, dark people who lived deep in the forest. They were long thought to be related to African pygmies—perhaps shipwrecked slaves. Now, however, anthropologists feel they are "negrito" tribes, more closely linked to peoples of Australia and the western Pacific.

The negritos shunned contact with outsiders and became murderously violent when strangers encroached on their terrain. After a few pitched battles, the British decided to forgo the idea of using them as workers and pretty much left them alone.

Today the Andaman Islands' administration shields the negrito tribes from the traumas of the modern world: pestilence and poverty, as well as tourists and missionaries. "We don't want to bring them into the mainstream," says Dr. Madhumala Chattopadhyay, an anthropological researcher in Port Blair. "We take the position that they should be isolated—for their own good."

Over the past three years Dr. Chattopadhyay has established friendly contact with both the Jarawa and Sentinelese, people who had spurned previous anthropological intrusions with a shower of spears and arrows.

"There had been no recorded contact with the Sentinelese in the twentieth century," she explained, adding that when anyone approached their shore, they fired arrows into the air and shouted threats. But Dr. Chattopadhyay knew that the tribesmen sometimes traded for coconuts with other negrito groups.

"We approached the shore, but no one came out of the forest," she said. "After half an hour we dropped a bag full of coconuts into the sea, and the Sentinelese came to collect them. They were afraid at first. They pointed arrows at us. But eventually they averted their weapons."

On the second trip the Sentinelese waded into the surf and climbed aboard the expedition boat. Soon the researchers were allowed to come ashore.

I had applied for permission to visit the tribal reserves, but each time I was rebuffed with a stock response: I might damage their cultural integrity, and they might damage me.

"How dangerous can they be?" I asked one government official. The man gave me a deadpan look and said: "A Bengali settler was killed last year when he was found hunting on Jarawa land. They ran him through with a spear."

Now, two hundred years after the British first arrived, the Andamans have passed to Indian rule, but much of the island chain remains virtually unchanged from precolonial times.

Only thirty-eight of the islands are inhabited and, in part because of tribal reserves and security concerns of the Indian military, only about a dozen are open to foreign visitors. In fact, you can overnight in only two of the islands—Havelock and South Andaman. That helps explain why only a few thousand foreigners reach the archipelago each year, most of them scuba divers or young backpackers who've heard about the islands by word of mouth.

One morning on South Andaman island, I rose at dawn expecting to have a beach near Port Blair to myself.

But the shore was already teeming with fishermen dragging nets onto the sand and sorting their catch into wicker baskets.

Cows wandered up and down the strand, oblivious to the fish, intent on the hunt for discarded coconut husks, which they devoured with relish.

A little later some early-bird tourists wandered down to the surf, and in the blink of an eye, an ice cream vendor pushed his cart from behind the palms. Not far behind was a distinguished looking man with a beard, crimson turban, and swagger stick in hand, walking swiftly in crisp military fashion, greeting bystanders but never breaking stride. Someone said he was governor-general of the islands on his morning jaunt along the beach.

Port Blair itself is more a cluster of villages than a genuine city, a rambling assortment of low cinder-block buildings and tin-roofed bungalows strewn across a wooded peninsula between the open ocean and one of the largest natural harbors in Asia.

The anchorage shelters a mixed bag of craft—banana boats, tramp steamers, and trawlers—and directly behind the docks is Aberdeen Bazaar, the marketplace and central business district. The narrow lanes are filled with odors—fruits and vegetables, incense and spices, diesel fumes from big belching buses. High-pitched Hindi music seemed to emanate from every crevice, competing with the shouts of merchants.

One day on the outskirts of Port Blair, Neeraj and I came across a crowd of thousands gathered around a shrine to the Tamil fire god. We could hear noise in the distance, chanting drums, and a wave of excitement seemed to surge through the crowd.

"The fire walkers are coming," Neeraj shouted to me above the din. Soon a dozen devotees in a zombie-like trance, gesticulating and spinning, crashed into the crowd, their faces smeared with ash, their tongues and cheeks pierced with sharp metal rods as a sign of their faith.

They danced across a fire pit that had been set up by the shrine, oblivious to white hot coals beneath their feet. Pandemonium broke out as bystanders were drawn into their fervor. I was caught up in a great surge toward the fire, and the worshipers in front of me began to stumble. They were almost trampled before the police intervened, beating back the throng with bamboo sticks.

But then the fire walkers vanished, spirited into the temple, and the frenzied crowd was calm once again, content to collect the ashes over which the mystics had passed.

In the last decade the island administration has established more than a hundred national parks, wildlife refugees, and nature reserves in the archipelago as an attraction for tourists with an ecological bent, and as a measure to save one of the last great wilderness areas of India. The parks are home to a vast array of weird and wonderful creatures, from the robber crab, which can rip open a coconut with its mighty claws, to the rare Nicobar monkey, which in proper top-of-the-food-chain fashion preys on the robber crab.

Many of the parks are secluded and rarely visited, and myriad islands—some with strange names like Snob, Grub, Redskin, Jolly Buoy—float within the park boundaries.

It was on Jolly Buoy that I lost my fear of the jungle. The person I have to thank for this is Neeraj. I can't say he really tricked me into the forest, but he did lure me on a false pretense.

We'd spent most of the day snorkeling and swimming off the north shore of Jolly Buoy, a tiny speck of land off the coast of South Andaman, when Neeraj suggested that we visit a secluded cove on the other side of the island. I asked if I should bring shoes, but he looked at me as if I were being silly.

We walked along the beach at first, but then Neeraj veered into the trees. He gazed around, expecting me to follow. I looked down at my feet. They were bare, and I was thinking: aren't there *things* in the jungle? Like snakes, spiders, and leeches that you can tread on. Neeraj could see the hesitation in my eyes.

"Can't we follow the beach?" I beseeched him.

"The beach soon ends," he responded. "This is the only way to reach the other side. If you don't think you can make it…"

So it came down to a matter of saving face. I grudgingly followed, stepping gingerly through the maze of giant roots and vines.

Much to my surprise the forest floor was soft, almost springy. My pace quickened. I still couldn't keep up with Neeraj, but by the time I reached the far shore I was no longer afraid of the jungle.

One day near the end of my trip I went to Chiriya Tapu, a national park on the southern tip of South Andaman. I walked alone through the padauk trees, great white giants that seem to soar into the clouds, and then I trudged through the mangrove swamp, up to my ankles in mud—with a wary eye for the saltwater crocodiles that lurk in the murky tidelands.

The name Chiriya Tapu means "Bird Island," and thousands of avian creatures reside here, living amid the swamps and thick rain forests. There were times when the sky went pink with parrots,

*P*arasites [worms] are most common in rural areas and a stool test when you return home is not a bad idea. They can be present on unwashed vegetables or in undercooked meat and you can pick them up through your skin by walking in bare feet. Infestations may not show up for some time, and although they are generally not serious, if left untreated they can cause severe health problems. A stool test is necessary to pinpoint the problem, and medication is often available over the counter.

◆

—Hugh Finlay, et al.,
India – a travel survival kit

and other moments when all I saw was a quick flicker of neon blue—a kingfisher plunging through the trees.

All around me was an unspoiled cosmos, hermetically sealed by isolation and now fundamentally preserved in its virgin state. I stood in silence, taking slow, deep breaths of the mulchy air, and remembered Tonga from *The Sign of Four*. More than a hundred years have passed since Conan Doyle conjured up pygmies and blowguns, and yet the Andaman Islands remain veiled in mystery.

Somehow I take comfort in that notion.

Joseph R. Yogerst is a Fellow of the Royal Geographical Society in London who has written or edited several travel books, including the award-winning Land of Nine Dragons: Viet Nam Today. *He is a frequent contributor to* Islands *magazine,* Condé Nast Traveler, *and other publications. He spent the last 14 years living in Africa, Europe, and Asia, and recently returned to Southern California where, without credit, a bank account, or a driver's license, he feels like an alien.*

★

The bazaar in Sindnur was crowded, intense, kinetic beyond belief. Beggars with drums and whips established the tempo. I half ran through the market in response to the rhythm. I whirled past a sadhu with snakes around his neck standing on a bed of nails, Jain women with masks across their faces, a man lying prostrate on the road with a painted water pot balanced on his neck, parrot fortune tellers, cows, vendors. On and on.

I was part of a great human spectacle, and I became almost dizzy, giddy, as I careened along absorbing images.

When some children noticed me and began their game of Fox and Hounds, it was 4:45 p.m. and the sun slid behind a cloud. The vibrant afternoon mood paled, so I changed direction, out-distanced the kids back towards the rest house, and found a cup of tea and a delicious Indian sweet enroute.

It had been a hectic, hyperstimulating hour. Its pace was in radical contrast to the countryside, where the impressions can build slowly. Away from the cities there is plenty of time to think, question, analyze. There is no urgency in the moment. Not so in the Sindnur bazaar. Just take a deep breath and do it. Experience it. Think about it later.

—Jan Zabinski, "Walking the Length of India"

PART THREE

GOING YOUR OWN WAY

MARY ORR

* * *

The Valley of Refuge

Even when cultures prohibit contact with outsiders,
people still find ways to touch.

IF YOU'RE GOING TO MALANA, YOU MIGHT WANT TO BRING A
sheep. It could come in handy if you happen to touch a resident
of this secretive, autonomous village high in the Himalayas near
India's border with Tibet. Most of Malana's one thousand people,
isolated here among the mountains and tumultuous rivers of
Himachal Pradesh, are high-caste Thakurs. They practice
Hinduism tinged with animism (nature worship); they fear the
touch of strangers, whom they consider untouchables. They're so
caste-conscious they believe that if you touch them or their houses
or their belongings, that touch will cause ritual pollution, and
you're expected to give a sheep to be used in purification ceremonies. Since few of the trekkers who find their way here carry
sheep, however, enough cash to buy a sheep will do.

The Malanis' strict observance of their traditions has embarrassed the Himachal Pradesh state government. It spent a fortune
stringing power lines over wild and snow-covered mountains to
this fastness set behind a thirteen hundred-foot pass on one side
and a precipice on the other. But the villagers refused the electricity because the lines went over low-caste houses.

No one could tell my partner, Michael, and me how long it

would take to walk to Malana from Naggar, a village propped high up on the Kulu valley's eastern wall. Our guidebook said it could be done in a day. Our hotelier wasn't so sure, and he warned of labyrinthine paths leading to animal pastures, and of false summits along the five thousand-foot climb to Chandrakani Pass. He recommended that we take a guide, because there was no map. But we'd always been able to find our own way to places before, learning to wait at a fork in the path until someone came along to set us on course. We opted for an early start. Alone.

Almost thirty years ago, Irish author Dervla Murphy wrote that her trek to Malana ("Valley of Refuge") involved "such a remarkable concentration of hazards that the business of avoiding death occupied 90 percent of my attention and the beauties of the ravine impressed me only during our rest halts." I was determined to find and follow her route. Like Hansel and Gretel, Michael and I followed *Frooti* juice boxes and *Amul* chocolate wrappers that littered the trails. Higher and higher we climbed, through pine woods and juniper-sweetened valleys. A counterpane of rhododendrons in party-dress pink, pearl white and valentine red covered the hillsides. From alpine meadows we could see back to the peaks above the Kulu Valley. But six hours of steady trekking in thin, high-altitude air exhausted us, and the pass was still nowhere in sight.

*L*ike her Victorian predecessors, Dervla Murphy had to suspend her travel plans because of family obligations. At fourteen she was confined to the family home to care for her mother and remained there another fourteen years. But since then her life has been lived at a pace true to the title of her first book—*Full Tilt*—in which she recounts a bike tour of India and Europe. The Irish-born author has written thirteen other books, eight of them about travel.

◆

—Mary Morris, *Maiden Voyages: Writings of Women Travelers*

We'd hoped to reach the pass before the rain started, which it did like clockwork at two p.m. We weren't prepared for hail. Descending a ridge ahead of us, a party of India Youth Hostel hikers told us they'd left the pass four hours ago, and Malana was four hours beyond that. Daunted, we decided to rest and take up the final leg the next morning. We had no tent. A shepherd's stone lean-to—the only one we saw along the trail—appeared like a mirage to provide shelter. We whisked the cow dung off the uneven floor and huddled under the leaking slate roof. I triumphantly hauled a dozen large plastic bags out of my pack, taking advantage of a brief pause in the rain to slit them open and anchor them with stones over the breaks in the roof. It was cold, but it was beautiful. We slept well.

We reached Chandrakani Pass the next day at noon, after five hours of hiking. The razor-thin strip of ridge fell steeply off to both sides. Whichever way we spun, snowcapped mountains dwarfed us and kept us spinning, like dervishes, spellbound. We stayed for hours, until clouds gathered and stole our view. Around a simple trailside shrine of pebbles, flowers, and incense, eerie upright stones stood like a miniature Stonehenge. We left a few coins and pressed on. We reached a fork: a goat path plunged to the right, a wider trail meandered left. A crude arrow indicated the goat path.

The goat path turned out to be for goats. It narrowed until it disappeared, leaving us to negotiate boulders and an incline so steep that we had to slide on our stomachs and grab tufts and spiky shrubs to keep ourselves from falling. Just as that afternoon's downpour began, a Malani shepherd girl about ten years old appeared on the trail. We followed her under a rock ledge to wait out the rain. I offered her a biscuit from my pack, then another. When the rain eased she slipped away, back to her flocks.

We reached Malana just before dark. We'd heard we could sleep in the school that doubled as a medical clinic and tea stall, a place already tainted by outsiders. Impassive villagers in rough, home-spun robes tied with cords, caps embroidered in zigzag patterns, and Day-Glo plastic shoes motioned the way.

Malana isn't a valley but a mere shelf on a nine thousand-foot-high mountain, guarded by seventeen thousand-foot peaks. The village outgrew the shelf long ago; now its houses cling to the brilliant green slope. The medieval two- and three-story houses built of stone and hand-hewn timber also serve as mangers and granaries. Intricately carved wooden balconies laced with ancient spider webs and next winter's herbs hold looms and farming implements, with space left over for knots of men to gossip and smoke their hookahs.

Perhaps five thousand years ago, the Malanis' ancestors, a mysterious people fleeing a long-forgotten enemy, migrated over the mountains to this place. Later they may have intermingled with some of Alexander's troops, who found their way here after they mutinied in northern India in 326 B.C. Some linguists link Malani, the villagers' unique language, to Magyar and Finnish; others see similarities to Persian. Almost self-sufficient, the Malanis sell or barter medicinal herbs and hashish, refined from plentiful ganja.

Three low-caste families live at the edge of town. None of these blacksmiths, weavers, and potters interact socially with Malana's upper-caste Thakurs. They exchange greetings, but Ram Lohar, a member of the "untouchable" ironworker caste, said he'd never been inside a Thakur home or shared even a pot of tea. His

The barbarians from Central Asia came as conquerors, and when not beaten back by the Aryan hero behaved as conquerors. Their domination intolerably humiliated the proud Hindu order, and it was in dealing with them that it added to its intense pride of race and culture, that violent xenophobia which henceforward became a fixed trait of the Hindu outlook. The compound of fear, hatred, contempt, and humiliation was embodied in the notion of Mlechchha, *the unclean and uncivilized foreigner.*

◆

—Nirad C. Chaudhuri,
The Continent of Circe

grandfather had brought his smithy tools from Simla, the state capital of Himachal Pradesh, decades ago and never left. This was the only home Ram Lohar had ever known, and he accepted the ostracism. In fact, he benefits from it. Unhindered by the taboo against touch, his family earns money cooking for outsiders, and now he is building Malana's first visitors' lodge. He learned English from travelers, people like Dervla Murphy, who'd slept in his haystack.

Although Thakurs disdain the touch of tourists, they pose eagerly for photographs. From a few feet away, I could show women the little jewelry I had and admire their bejeweled noses and their multi-ringed and studded ears, fashionable centuries before trendy Western youths started piercing. Like most rural Indian women, they coveted the silver ring I wore, shaped like a miniature belt, and could barely contain their curiosity as to whether it unbuckled. Their rules prevented them from trying to pull it off my finger, as women elsewhere had attempted.

Ram Lohar showed us Malana's lower and supreme courts—worn rock platforms—where a rotating jury of eleven men handled disagreements. (Theft is unknown in the village.) State police and government prosecutors are banned from the proceedings, even for rare criminal cases. Jamlu, the Malanis' demongod, decides the verdict for hung juries, making his wishes known through a ritual involving a couple of sheep. Ancient wooden friezes and scores of antlers nailed up at rakish angles cover his windowless temple. The deity is represented by a slab of rock zealously guarded from outsiders' touch. The god forbids leather in Malana. Ram said Malana's first tourists were required to leave their leather hiking boots outside the village gate. The dogs made off with so many boots that, for tourists, Jamlu relaxed the no-leather rule.

The god's pragmatic streak also seemed to express itself in allowing the village to accept mail from outside. In a further attempt to draw Malana out of the dark ages, the state had deemed the village worthy of a post office. No villager had enough education to meet the state's qualifications, but the rules were bent.

Someone who could barely read got the job. That morning in the school building, as I rolled up my sleeping bag, a few Malanis filed in and ceremoniously arranged a box of rubber stamps, a till and a stack of ledgers: I witnessed the painfully slow inauguration of Malana's first post office.

Instead of backtracking over Chandrakani Pass we decided to return to Naggar via Jari, a town at the end of an eight-mile-long ravine through which the Malana River raged. To reach it, the Malanis had chiseled hundreds of steps down a sheer three thousand-foot precipice. Skittish villagers on narrow stairways and around stony bends demanded wide berth. As they pressed against the cliffside to avoid our touch, we coped with the crumbling edge. Blood-red signs painted on rocks at regular intervals proclaimed: "In Jari, stay at Ratna Guest House. Toilet, separate rooms, and homey atmosphere." These garish trail markers led us over rockfalls and to monsoon-soaked steps that leaned precariously over rapids. Following writer Dervla Murphy's hair-raising trail, we crossed the torrent on a primitive plank bridge with gaping holes.

Again and again the trail climbed high into the ravine through damp pines and summer wildflowers, only to plummet back down again. Finally it reached the riverbank and stopped altogether. Before us was a sheer cliff that could not be scaled. We'd made a grave error. In the Himalayas, snowpacks melt in the morning sun, and by late afternoon streams and rivers rise dramatically. We'd left Malana too late and now suddenly understood the concerned gestures of the last Malani we'd passed. The swollen river had submerged a segment of the trail. We had two choices: wait there until morning, or pick our way along the vertical rock face to where the path continued farther downstream. We had no rock-climbing experience but couldn't face a night in the clammy canyon. The twenty-foot traverse presented a handful of slippery inch-wide toeholds, some under water. Our heavy backpacks upset our balance, but we made it to the middle of the cliff, both of us hanging just above the torrent.

Then I moved too soon. For one long minute, with my foot on

top of Michael's, neither of us able to move, I thought I'd fall and drown. I started to panic. I tried not to look down, but I was morbidly fascinated. Would the current bash me against the rocks, or could I paddle to shore? Could I even paddle wearing a backpack? It must have been about this place that Dervla Murphy wrote: "I wondered whether my imminent death would come from a broken neck on the rocks or through drowning…" Tears of fear and self-pity smarted my eyes. Then I remembered to breathe slowly and I imagined I was on solid ground. I lifted my boot, freeing Michael's trapped foot. As I hung over the seething river by just one foot and three fingers, I experienced the greatest concentration of sheer terror I've ever felt.

On the other side of the rock the path started up nonchalantly, almost innocently. We didn't know whether to congratulate ourselves for our daring or to chastise ourselves for our poor judgment, but there was time for neither. For a moment we stared at the river thundering hungrily down its bed of boulders and felt strangely part of it. We raced toward Jari in the half-light, following Ratna Guest House signs. Along the path, we almost stumbled over a party of Malanis, sensibly bedded down for the night. I jumped back, indicating that I understood the rules about touch. Only then did the significance of my first encounter with a Malani dawn on me.

I had offered the shepherd girl biscuits. She had accepted. Both times my hand had brushed hers.

Mary Orr was raised in the wilds of northern Canada. At different times in her life she has worked as a waitress, construction worker, mill worker, radio producer, and at a shelter for battered women. She has been a vegetarian for twenty years and wrote the India Handbook *for Moon Publications. She lives in Portland, Oregon.*

*

> …It is karma that brings joy or sorrow,
> Willing or unwilling, we live by our karma.
> Observe the potter shaping his pots:
> Some break on the wheel,

Some crack after removal from the wheel,
Some spoil when wet, some when dry,
Some burst while being fired
Some after removal from the kiln,
Some shatter in use…
So some of us die in the womb,
Some immediately after birth,
Some a day later,
Some a fortnight later, some a month,
Some after one year, some after two,
Some in youth, some in middle age, some in old.
Their karma determines it all.
This is the way the world is—
So what is the point of grieving?
Swimmers dive,
 then emerge from the water;
So creatures sink into,
 and emerge from the stream of life.

—*The Mahabharata of Vyasa* (The Eleventh Book: The Women),
as quoted by Mala Sen in *India's Bandit Queen:*
The True Story of Phoolan Devi

⋆ ⋆ ⋆

Elephant Man

The author, having earned his place in the fraternity of mahouts by riding
eight hundred miles on his own elephant, Tara, arrives at the Sonepur
Mela, the world's largest animal fair. His presence causes quite a stir.

THE CAVALCADE CAME TO AN ABRUPT HALT. IN FRONT OF US
stretched a mile of *mela* traffic, waiting for the signal to proceed, as
the oncoming vehicles inched across the narrow bridge. Bellowing
cattle stamped impatiently against the wooden floors of their
trucks. More were filled with horses neighing nervously, poking
their heads out of the slatted sides. Some vehicles were unrecog-
nisable under gigantic mounds of fodder, spilling over the back, the
front and the sides. Business was brisk for the hawkers. They pa-
trolled up and down the armies of bicyclists, selling fruit, ice-
cream, newspapers and bags of sticky *ludoos*. We gained a few yards
as the traffic was stopped on the far side and with a crunching of
gears and hiss of air brakes, the procession would move forward.
Tara was becoming impossible. One moment she would be swip-
ing food from the hawkers, the next vibrating in panic at the
horses, forcing me to use the *ankush*. Aditya swung down impatiently from Tara's back.

"We'll be here all day. I'll see what I can sort out."

Half an hour later I caught sight of him signalling to me frantically to come forward. I bulldozed my way through, closely followed by the other elephants who were not going to miss this

269

chance. At the entrance Aditya was standing with a smiling policeman who saluted smartly and waved us on to an empty bridge.

"How on earth did you manage that?" I asked Aditya incredu-
lously, as we lumbered across.

"I told him you were related to the Queen of England and that
royalty did not expect to be kept waiting."

"Really?" I said, impressed by his ingenuity.

"No, of course I didn't," he replied. "I gave him a hundred
rupees."

To our right, a steam engine clanked across the new railway
bridge. To our left, a vast shady grove of mango trees stretched out
parallel with the river under which I could see a few elephants
standing. "Haathi Bazaar!" shouted one of the old *mahouts.*

Urging Tara into a lumbering trot, with Bhim and Gokul running alongside, we reached the end of the bridge and, swinging
left, thundered down into the "Garden of Raja Man Singh." We
jumped off Tara, and to the amazement of incredulous onlookers
the four of us danced a jig around her. Opening a bottle of rum, I
poured half the contents down her throat. Each of us then took a
swig and yelled "*Jai Mata Sonepur!*" We had made it.

It was as well that we had arrived early. As newcomers, we
needed to check the lie of the land and to learn the rules. The area
between each mango tree, in front of which the elephants would
be staked, belonged to a different landlord. We made our way
slowly through the orchard, passing fodder stacked like giant
teepees. Each landlord tried to interest us in his plot, offering dis-
counts and special favours, knowing that Tara would almost certainly attract a large crowd. We settled on a site at the far end of
the orchard which gave easy access to the Gandak River some fifty
yards behind and close to one of the main bathing *ghats.* Situated
amongst the nearest row of trees to the river we would not be
hemmed in. Elephants would stand in front and to the side of us,
but not behind.

Our landlord, Lallan Singh, a delightful, wise old man, a veteran
of fifty *melas,* took us under his wing, bustling and fussing over us
like a kindly matron on our first day at school. I paid him one

hundred rupees, the traditional *mela* rent for the use of his land. (If the elephant was sold, the buyer reimbursed this amount.) Two large wooden stakes were driven deep into the ground and one of Tara's front and back legs were chained to each. An "account" was opened with the fodder and firewood suppliers, who delivered in the morning and the evening of each day. To ensure some kind of privacy, Lallan Singh organised a large colourful *kanat* (a rectangular canvas wall) to surround our camp. Between the two mango trees we draped Tara's caparison, the Union Jack, which hung grandly like a war standard. Tables and chairs were produced and by the time the tents were erected and a fire lit, we could have been guests in some maharaja's grand *shikar* camp, lacking only uniformed attendants, popping corks from champagne bottles and a floor covered in richly embroidered carpets.

To ensure good luck and a good sale, our landlord performed the *Aarti*, a special *puja*. He circled our camp holding a terracotta owl in which a holy flare burned. Then, standing in front of Tara, he raised the flame to her like a toast master, chanting a few solemn prayers.

Lallan Singh then sat down with us and explained *mela* etiquette. "When your elephant is sold, everything on the back legs belongs to the seller, the chain, ropes, etc. It is customary to give the buyer the *gudda* (the saddle), the girth ropes, the bell, and any other decoration on the elephant, like silk cords and tassles. It is most important that your elephant is never unattended at any time, during the day or night. Accidents can and have happened frequently at the *mela* and a loose elephant can cause terrible carnage amongst "five *lakhs*" of people. Be very careful," he warned us, "to keep your money hidden, as the *mela* will be full of thieves. When your deal takes place, it must be done quietly, out of the sight of prying eyes and, if possible, in the presence of a few members of your entourage. A showing of people," he explained, "means power and wealth," as we were to discover when approached by the local *zamindars,* who never went anywhere without a large armed bodyguard.

By now a few more elephants had arrived. In front of us was a large tusker. To our right, attended by two *mahouts,* stood an old female with two terrible wounds in her flanks oozing a greenish pus. The owner, an overly helpful man from Orissa, explained that she had received these injuries while working in his cement factory. He was here to sell or exchange her for another. Looking at the suffering of this friendly, docile elephant I vowed again that I would never let Tara be maltreated.

Behind us, carpenters and builders were busily erecting marquees, fenced in by impregnable bamboo enclosures. These were for the different sects of religious *sadhus* who would soon be arriving. Our little set-up was somewhat dwarfed by the opulence of these encampments, particularly the kitchen facilities. Huge cauldrons and stacks of tin platters were being unloaded and carried inside, in readiness for the great feast on Kartik Purnima, which would feed thousands of devotees.

Further down the Haathi Bazaar rich *zamindars* had been allocated the prime sites, where entire canvas villages had been set up, in front of which stood their richly caparisoned elephants.

---

*M*y friend John Hatt had visited the great annual fair at Sonepur, just across the Ganges from Patna, in which many hundreds of elephants change hands, most of them being bought by *zamindars*—the feudal landlords who outside of industrial areas or cities are in reality in control of the state. John took tea with one of these, who had an elephant for sale. "Two gunmen attended him on either side," he wrote in *Harpers & Queens.* "When being photographed, he insisted on adjusting his dress in order to ensure a clear view of the pistol at his waist. When I asked my host if his elephant had ever killed anyone, he replied, 'Only three *mahouts* and a labourer.' One notorious animal is known to have dispatched eight of its *mahouts*....at last year's fair one of these killed a visitor. Life in Bihar is cheap indeed."

◆

—Norman Lewis, *A Goddess in the Stones: Travels in India*

Behind, surrounded by armed chauffeurs, their cars were parked, highly polished vehicles with blacked out windows; so the arrival of Don and Indrajit in the minibus added a certain cachet to our humble enclosure.

Already our presence had caused a stir and groups of people had started to gather outside. It was easy to discern between those who were merely curious and the professionals. The curious, straining on tiptoes, peered over the *kanat* to catch a glimpse of the *firinghee mahout*. The professionals, tough, bow-legged men with sun-blackened faces and shrewd eyes, sauntered casually past Tara inspecting her with a well-assumed air of indifference. They would stop to have a few words with Bhim, hoping to glean a few tidbits of information on pedigree and price. They would then report back to their bosses. These momentary inspections would take place continuously over the next few days. Unlike the hustling West, where fast decisions are the name of the game, a hasty deal is considered undignified in the East, and a strict etiquette is adhered to.

Aditya and I were worried about Bhim. He was not his usual pragmatic, cheerful self. His spirit had left him and he wandered around lackadaisically. Worst of all, he seemed to have lost all interest in Tara. Perhaps it was due to exhaustion or to thinking that once he had reached the *mela* his duties would be less arduous and he would have time to enjoy the fun. In fact, we eventually realised, he was simply overawed. Used to the relative quietness and routine of a zoo, he had suddenly been thrown into the lions' den, the "Newmarket" of the elephant world, where true professionalism counted and one's knowledge was put to the ultimate test and carefully scrutinised. He was out of his depth and had lost his confidence.

Tara too, was affected. Whereas she should have been in her element, as carts drawn by white bullocks continuously replenished her larder, she stood listlessly, a look of total resignation on her face. I began to think this was all too familiar to her. She had been here before, I realised, and my heart stopped.

At Gau-Dhuli (the hour of the cow dust) that quiet magic

*T*he traveler's mantra, re-cited as one is about to embark on a journey by crossing the threshold of the main entrance of a house, pays homage to Ganesh and Vishnu. The verse invokes Vishnu, the lotus-eyed, rider of the Garuda, to give the suppli-cant blessings, prosperity, auspi-ciousness. The first line invokes Ganesh because he is always wor-shipped before any other gods or goddesses in Hindu *pujas*, his consolation for having his head chopped off and replaced by the head of an elephant.

◆

— Rajendra S. Khadka,
"Hindu Flash Cards"

ॐ नमो गणेशाय

मङ्गलं भगवान्विष्णुः
मङ्गलं गरुडध्वजः
मङ्गलं पुण्डरीकाक्षः
मङ्गलं तनुयाद्धरिः

moment just after sunset when the sky shimmered gold between the branches of the mango trees through the dust thrown up by the elephants, a group of men entered our encampment. Their faces showed a certain relief as they spotted me. The spokesman stepped forward and formally intro-duced himself.

"Mr. Shand," he said, "we are the proprietors of the Shoba Nautanki [the folk theatre]. Thanking goodness we have found you in time. Would you do us the honour of inaugurating our first show tomorrow? Already we have sent out this gentleman in a jeep to find you"—he pointed to a man who looked both exhausted and exasper-ated—"and he has been trav-elling for five days. You will enjoy the show. There are many girls. Our theatre," he continued proudly, "has the reputation of the most beau-tiful women. But first we would like you to garland the statue of our local freedom fighter and then we will proceed to the theatre. Our last guest of honor was a famous *dacoit* [bandit]. Now it is appropriate that the first English *mahout* should open the show. We will collect you tomorrow afternoon."

That evening, when the muddy water was turning crimson

from the rays of the setting sun, we bathed Tara in the Gandak, approached from a steep muddy bank, down which she slid on her bottom, like a child on a toboggan. She then proceeded to queue-barge into the elephant-filled shallows, much to the annoyance of the other *mahouts,* who were waiting their turn patiently. It was dark by the time Tara finished her ablutions. Beneath us, elephants lay motionless, like giant prehistoric boulders. Then, as if infused suddenly by some unseen force, they erupted out of the water and lumbered toward the bank. Under the stars, we joined a silent cavalcade of returning elephants, this silence only broken by the soft shuffle of their feet, the swish of their tails and the flapping of their ears. An old *mahout,* riding the lead tusker, broke into song, swelling louder and louder as others joined in, then echoing quietly away into the blackness of the Gandak running swiftly beside us. I was by now so much part of this ancient brotherhood that my other world seemed like a dream as I felt the coolness of Tara's back beneath me.

Indrajit had built a blazing fire against the chill of the November night. We huddled round it, drinking with the owner of a big tusker. He was a landowner, but unlike most of the other *zamindars,* he himself rode and looked after his elephants. He was an honest straightforward man whom I felt we could trust, with a vast knowledge and love of elephants that bordered on passion. His family had always kept elephants. He remembered, as a child coming to the *mela* with his father and counting over a thousand. The bridge is always closed on the day of Kartik Purnima and he remembered the latecomers trying to swim across the river. Due to the strong current, they had been washed away, *mahouts* and elephants drowning.

He admitted quite openly that his tusker was dangerous and only he could control it. However, unlike almost all the owners in the *mela*, he did not use drugs to quieten his elephant. There were now over a hundred elephants here, but he told us that Tara was the best he had seen so far. To an expert, she was obviously naturally fed and of a good temperament. He was not surprised that we were thinking of asking two *lakhs* for her.

"Bide your time," he advised us, "for her that is not an exorbitant price"—adding that if we needed any assistance he would be glad to give it.

In the middle of the night I was woken by the fierce shouts of *"Mahout!! Mahout!!"*—and running outside our encampment I found Tara, her stakes uprooted, about to escape. Bhim, who was supposed to be on watch, was fast asleep in a pile of sugar cane at the side of the *kanat.* I shook and reprimanded him. He apologised sheepishly and promised it would not happen again. But it was too late, the incident had been noticed. An unattended elephant, as we had been told, is an unforgivable crime in the strict *mahout* law of the *mela* and we had, as it were, lost face.

Awoken early by the urgent shouts of *mahouts* and the chanting of *sadhus,* I walked to the side of the *kanat* and peered over. Though relatively empty last night, it was now as if an army had moved in quietly during the night and surrounded our encampment. The orchard was alive with elephants, swaying, feeding, and dusting, while *mahouts,* wrapped in blankets, squatted beside fires, watching them carefully over rims of little terracotta bowls containing their morning tea. Arcades of hastily constructed stalls, like mini-bazaars, had mysteriously sprung up, selling *paan,* spices, food, cheap jewellery, clothing, and medicines.

Behind us, like flowers in a desert, huddled little groups of families. When the sun rose, the women stretched languidly, turning bejewelled arms, ankles, and tips of noses and ears bright gold as the first rays filtered through the smoke-filled air. Elephants ridden proudly by young, well-muscled *mahouts,* their teeth a brilliant white against the black of their faces, raced each other down to the river. Like picadors, holding an *ankush* in both hands behind their elephants' ears, they showed off their skills and their mounts to the best effect. To the casual observer it would seem like a game but it was, in fact, in deadly earnest. Prospective buyers would be watching carefully.

Lallan Singh arrived with an electrician who ran a cable up one of the trees in our camp to connect a large-wattage bulb. At night it would effectively illuminate Tara and, we hoped, keep the boys awake. I watched shamefacedly, but Lallan Singh consoled me. Three other elephants, he told me, had escaped during the night. It was only a precaution.

Our first buyer offered seventy thousand rupees for Tara. This man, a magnificent actor, almost brought tears to my eyes. He told me of the wonderful elephant he had owned for thirty years, which he only rented out on very auspicious occasions. Just last week, tragedy struck when he was away on business. He had instructed his *mahout* to take the elephant to one of these very special occasions. The *mahout,* a lazy man, did not carry out his orders and when he returned he gave the *mahout* a sound beating. A week later the *mahout* disappeared, not before he had poisoned the elephant, which had just died. I declined his offer.

After Tara returned from her bath, I went shopping. From one of the many stalls specialising in elephant decorations, I bought her a beautiful brass neck bell attached to a bright crimson silken cord. Anklets made of bells and strips of silken material to hang from ears and tusks were also available, but I wanted to keep her looking simple, elegant, like a beautiful woman at a ball, wearing a plain dress, unadorned, except for one astonishing piece of jewellery. She did not need decoration.

I employed a specialist in elephant painting. After drawing a line that sharply demarcated the blackness of her oiled crown from the natural grey of her skin, he created with simple coloured chalks of purple, yellow, white and blue, a series of flowers and lotuses on her ears, face and trunk. In the centre, between her eyes, he traced a dazzling star. Taking down the Union Jack, we draped it over Tara's shoulders and when prospective buyers approached, Bhim and Gokul would dramatically draw it back.

As Don and Aditya had disappeared earlier to take photographs, I set off through the Haathi Bazaar, leaving Tara with the boys. My nostrils were instantly filled with the evocative smells of India—spices, incense, the heavy scent of the tribal woman, mixed with the more pungent odour of urine and excrement, and found myself thinking I never wanted to leave. Passing down the elephant lines, *mahouts* and owners alike called me over—not out of curiosity but because I was part of them, an elephant man, inexorably entwined with their way of life. I sat cross-legged by little fires and shared bowls of tea and *littis*, small balls of hot dough roasted over the ashes. I inspected their elephants, checking their backs for telltale sores and scars, and chuckled disapprovingly when, opening their mouths, I found patches of black on their pink tongues.

Easily now, I mounted the elephants by way of their trunks and tusks. I sat caressing their ears, and barked commands to make them sit. I watched a big male having part of its tusk sawn off, for a legal sale of ivory. The *mahout* first carefully measured the distance from eye to lip. After marking a spot which avoided cutting into the nerve, he sawed through it quickly. In India ivory fetches about five thousand rupees a kilo. Magically, the tusk will grow back, just like a finger nail.

At one encampment stood a huge tusker, excessive in its ornamentation. Richly caparisoned in red brocade, bells hung round its neck and feet, yellow and red silken scarves dangled from its ears and tusks and its tail was braided with silver tinsel. The beast swayed from side to side continuously, its piggy little eyes transfixing everyone who passed, with a stare of pure venom. An old *mahout* warned me to keep my distance. This was a dangerous elephant, he told me. In the last ten days it had killed three people.

I counted a hundred and ninety elephants; last year there had been more than three hundred and next year probably there would be even fewer. It is inevitable that this way of life will, in time, die out.

Leaving the Haathi Bazaar I moved on to the other animal markets. For the first time, the sheer size of the great *mela* struck me. At the horse lines I watched a small snow-white arab, its pink eyes heavily kohled to highlight their dullness, its tail dyed the colours of the rainbow, being put through its paces. The rider urged him along at a furious pace, then suddenly pulled him dead on his hocks, whirling him about to perform a kind of "pas" or, in military terms, "marking time." The horses were even more elaborately decorated than the elephants. Some sported headbands worked in gold thread, others had their legs encircled with brass bangles. One wore a necklace of silver and gold, containing verses from the *Koran*. They came from Rajasthan, the Punjab, Afghanistan, and even Australia, watched over carefully by their dealers, old men with faces creased like parchment paper, shrewd, all-knowing eyes wrinkled against the glare of the sun.

Beyond the horses, stretching for almost two miles, were paddocks crowded with cows, bullocks and buffaloes. Finally, I reached the bull pens, known locally as the "jewel market." Apart from the elephants, the bulls fetch the highest prices.

Making my way back to Tara I entered the shopping centres, a maze of streets lined with booths, overshadowed by the giant Ferris wheel of the fun fair and the Big Top of the circus arena. A crowd surrounded a pair of chained, moth-eaten bears. Goaded by their keeper, they shuffled miserably from paw to paw in time to a disco song. For five rupees you could dance with them.

---

*D*ense clumps of sugar cane had spread through the fields here and provided refuge for numerous cobras. A lot of people were bitten by them, Ranjan said, but forceful eradication was impossible for religious reasons. Instead nonviolent persuasion was traditionally practised. The great event took place every year at the time of the November half-moon when a large contingent of snake charmers appeared on the scene. The snake charmers located the ants' nests in which the cobras had taken up residence and played music to induce them to leave their holes. They were then fed with milk, molasses, and the only recently discovered gastronomic inducement, popcorn, which had become their favourite food. The ceremony of feeding at an end, each cobra was presented with a new *dhoti*, after which the priest would wish them a happy and successful year and beg them to cease to bite members of his community.

◆

—Norman Lewis, *A Goddess in the Stones: Travels in India*

A discordant screeching announced the bird market. Hyacinthine blue macaws from South America sat quietly on their perches, their feathers ruffled, swivelling their heads suddenly, blinking their baleful eyes. Nepalese mynahs chuckled and laughed, and a cage of little rice birds, so gaudy in colour that the owner admitted they had been dyed, hopped nervously from side to side. Outside, a shiny black mynah loaded and fired a miniature cannon, and for ten rupees would play cards.

The inevitable snake-charmers squatted at the sides of the streets, playing their flutes tunelessly to serpents swaying from wicker baskets. One snake-charmer, more enterprising than the rest, advertised "a fight to the death" between a mongoose and a cobra. I hoped he had an unending supply of cobras, for inevitably the mongoose would win. Or perhaps he waited until he had attracted a large enough crowd to make it worthwhile.

Jugglers ferried their way through the crowds performing with extraordinary skill considering all the pushing and shoving. As I pushed and shoved I noticed an exceptionally tall man with piercing eyes bearing down on me. I tried to move, but it was as if I was hypnotised. Dipping a long large finger in a small jar of vermilion, he stabbed it against my forehead and demanded five rupees. I christened him "dot man" and over the next few days, whatever preventative measures I took, he always managed to get me. Once, seeing him approach I slipped behind Aditya as the great finger shot out like a sword. I thought I had escaped. Aditya, obviously a seasoned *mela* veteran, simply ducked and I received it on the end of my nose.

"Your teeth pulled for only twenty rupees. Get a new set. A new look." Dentists did a roaring trade from padded chairs operating foot drills. Naive patients writhed in agony as the dentists dug into mouths with what looked like pairs of pliers. In intervals between the shops bold placards hung advertising eating houses, their cuisine varied to suit the tastes of every caste and creed. The smell reminded me of the observation of the old planter who wrote in his *Reminiscences of Behar:* "I cannot say the dishes look tempting while the smell of bad *ghee* makes you wish you had put a little extra eau-de-Cologne on your handkerchief before you left your tent."

Passing brassière shops and signs advertising "Genuine Siamese Twins" I entered the Bombay Bazaar. The smell of bad *ghee* disappeared in a wave of perfume. Here was everything for the lady. Women, young and old, queued up at scent booths, in which men sat cross-legged behind a thousand different bottles. After twirling cotton-wool onto long silver sticks, they dipped them in and dabbed them on the backs of waiting hands. Glass bangle-sellers displayed their incandescent wares on long tall poles. They fought a losing battle to prevent their eager clients from shattering fragile merchandise as the women pulled and pushed them up and down their arms.

In large mirrors, the ladies coquettishly painted on different hues of cosmetics and lipstick and applied kohl to their eyes, while others tried on gold nose and ear ornaments. Baskets filled with brilliant hues of *sindoor* (the powder used to make the *tikka*) sat in rows of tiny coloured mountains and gorgeous bolts of gauze, silk, and cotton to be made into saris, fluttered like butterfly wings as they were gently unfurled.

As I moved on, persistent salesmen pressed me to buy their products; brasswork from Benares, inlaid boxes and trays and miniature Taj Mahals from Agra, enamel objects from Jaipur, beautifully embroidered shawls from Kashmir, and in one rather modern shop a Hells Angel's leather biker's jacket and a pair of correspondent brogues.

The ingenuity of the beggars knew no bounds. Beside a man sitting near the temple lay upright in the dust what appeared to be a human head—and it was just that. He had buried his colleague up to the neck and rubbed his face with paste to give it the colour of a corpse. Another simply walked around naked from the waist down, with a large padlock clamped through the end of his penis. Yet another had buried himself head downwards to the waist and was managing to breathe through the open ends of two bamboo tubes that just broke the surface of the ground. Unfortunately, he had neglected to hire an assistant. Passersby liberally helped themselves to his begging bowl.

On the other side of the temple, I came across the Naga *Sadhus*, who are fiercely ascetic and protect their privacy zealously. Trained in all forms of fighting they are treated with great respect. Their naked bodies daubed in ash, their faces painted white and vermilion, they resent any intrusion from outsiders, and woe betide anyone stupid enough to try and photograph them. I managed a short conversation with one of them. As a penance, he had not sat down for six years and supported his stiffened and deformed legs by leaning on a kind of wooden swing. He was most indignant when I told him that an elephant belonging to King Louis XIV did not lie down for the last ten years of its life and had worn two holes in the stone buttress with its tusks, on which it supported itself. I beat a hasty retreat.

There were the usual abominable sights of the poor unfortunate cripples. One was more terrifying and heartrending than anything I had ever seen. It was a young boy—or rather what was left of a young boy—just a small torso supporting a head, twisted and contorted by some hideous disease. He was pushed around in a little cart. On it perched a parrot, which took your money in its beak.

As I re-entered the Haathi Bazaar, I witnessed two extraordinary fights. Both had been caused by theft, and

I had seen the physique of the people of Andhra, which had suggested the possibility of an evolution downwards, wasted body to wasted body, Nature mocking herself, incapable of remission. Compassion and pity did not answer; they were refinements of hope. Fear was what I felt. Contempt was what I had to fight against; to give way to that was to abandon the self I had known. Perhaps in the end it was fatigue that overcame me. In spite of all that I had read about the country, nothing had prepared me for this.

◆

—V. S. Naipaul,
An Area of Darkness

both were not without humour. The first was a clash of titans between two female elephants, staked next to one another. One of the females had stolen the other's sugar cane. She turned quickly on the thief and instead of using her head as a battering ram, she tried in the most ludicrous fashion to bite off the other one's tail. They whirled round trumpeting and squealing in a cloud of dust, looking like squabbling schoolgirls pulling each other's hair. Three or four *mahouts*, armed with spears, waded in quickly and put an end to this farce.

The second fight was decidedly one-sided until an unusual intervention stopped it. A thief had been caught and was being punished in typical local fashion. His hands had been tied behind his back and his feet bound together. Two hefty men wielding long bamboo sticks proceeded to give him a sound beating on his head and the soles of his feet until he was a crying, bleeding wreck. The women, I noticed, particularly enjoyed this spectacle and joined in enthusiastically kicking the unfortunate man's ribs with sturdy feet, their toes encircled by gold rings, like knuckle-dusters. He would have been killed but for the sudden arrival of a tall, pale, sweating Englishman, a camera slung around his neck, wearing a floppy sun hat. I looked more closely. It was a friend of mine, a travel editor for a glossy London magazine. He waded bravely into the mêlée holding his hands above his head shouting "*Bas, bas*," the only word he knew in Hindi. When this had no effect, he clasped his hands fervently together as in prayer, fell to his knees and cried "*por favore, por favore!!*" Immediately the beating stopped and the crowd became silent. He called the police, who took the bleeding man away.

There was great excitement in the camp when I returned. Tara's price had gone shooting up, from seventy to ninety thousand rupees. This offer had come from a man, Aditya told me, who had a dishonest face and apparently owned a hotel in Delhi. The man had said his elephants were well looked after and simply took tourists for rides once a day. Unfortunately, one of them had been hit by a bus.

Our procession into Sonepur town to garland the statue of the freedom fighter was most impressive. The grandees of the Shoba Theatre supplied us with a bodyguard and I felt terribly important. Forming a phalanx around us, they spearheaded a path through the gaping onlookers. Our entourage, however, did not quite match that of the Prime Minister of Nepal who arrived in Sonepur in 1871 with a bodyguard of three hundred gurkhas and a harem of pretty, lively Nepalese princesses.

My self-importance now blown out of all proportion, I expected a tumultuous welcome to greet me. Instead, there was an infuriated, sweating policeman, trying vainly to control the traffic, roaring uncontrollably around the monument, and a madman juggling *ludoos*. One of the grandees placed a garland of marigolds in my hand. Self-consciously I climbed over the fence protecting the statue, looped the garland over the marble head, and feeling I should somehow justify this honour that had been bestowed upon me, bowed deeply. As I climbed out, the madman dropped his *ludoos*, grabbing me fiercely in a sticky embrace.

Again cocooned by our bodyguard, we soon reached a large building like a warehouse, constructed from wood and corrugated iron. Its front façade was painted gaudily with ladies cavorting in various stages of undress. Tannoys noisily advertised the delights of the show to an eagerly waiting crowd, pushing and shoving to get nearer an entrance controlled by four large policemen wielding large lead-topped bamboo canes with clinical efficiency.

"Welcome to the Shoba Theatre, Mr. Shand," the spokesman shouted. "As you can see it is very popular. Come. We will go through the back."

Inside it resembled an aircraft hangar. At one end, shrouded by a gauzy curtain, was the stage, the backdrop a grove of palm trees set against a starry night. Below, in the pit, fenced off by large iron palings, sat the orchestra tuning their instruments in a cacophony of discordant notes. Behind the pit were the best seats, costing twenty-five rupees, and separated from them by a triple-stranded barrier of barbed wire, was standing room only, at five rupees per person. The theatre put on three shows daily and could hold a crowd of eighteen thousand people.

We sat sipping tea and eating cakes in the wings. Aditya and I were introduced to the artistes—highly painted, plumpish ladies in sequinned outfits, their male partners squeezed into tightly fitting jumpsuits, brocaded like matadors' costumes. The building vibrated suddenly, as the gates were opened and a surge of people fought their way in.

Behind the curtain, a row of chairs had been placed beyond a large red ribbon. A barrage of arc lights hit us as we sat down. I felt inordinately self-conscious and nervous. Sweat began to trickle down my back. The star of the show, Miss Shoba, whose appearance caused a roar of excitement from the crowd, blessed and garlanded us. Long speeches followed. The Master of Ceremonies, wearing a smart, navy blue blazer with shiny gold buttons and white bell-bottomed trousers, introduced me as the famous English *mahout* and gave a lengthy account of my adventures. The crowd became instantly restless, longing for the show to start.

The band struck up, the gauzy curtains lifted and a pair of scissors were thrust into my hands. I stood up, sawed through the ribbon and stammered a few appropriate words, which Aditya then translated. Miss Shoba reappeared and led me off the stage to a small smattering of applause. I wanted to leave immediately to see Tara but Aditya insisted it would be impolite. We must stay to watch at least one act.

I'm glad we did. A seductive girl dressed in a black, transparent sari worked the crowd into a frenzy. The origins of the dancing girl go back to the Gandharva women, renowned for their beauty and skill in dancing and singing. In the old days when the fair was a meeting place for Rajas, *zamindars,* big agriculturists, and businessmen, the girls made a good harvest. Fees of five hundred or one thousand rupees were a common feature for a few dances. On some of the more noted dancing girls, *lakhs* of rupees used to be spent for more personal services.

The seductress of the Shoba Theatre undulated across the stage, singing a ballad of obviously erotic content. She was singing about her lover, with whom she was in bed, complaining he would not make love to her. Aditya translated: "Why do you not come to me my darling? My breasts are young and firm." There was a groan from the crowd behind us. "My thighs are as soft as satin, my crop green and young, ready to be irrigated." This brought the house down. Turning around I saw the barbed wire bulging outwards as the crowd pressed against it, frantic to reach her, followed by the whacks of the police sticks as they rained down on unprotected heads.

It was a relief to be back in the relative peace of the Haathi Bazaar. Smoke rose in eddies through the rich foliage of the mango orchard from the fires round which *mahouts* were huddled, their animated faces illuminated in the ruddy glow, as they traded tales and secrets of their ancient craft. To reach our camp we had to thread our way carefully across a carpet of sleeping people. Inside, feet and arms protruded from under the *kanat*.

Relieving Gokul, I took the next watch over Tara. She still was not her old self. There was something else, an uneasiness about her, which immediately transmitted itself to me. I felt that sick feeling in the pit of my stomach that precedes impending disaster. She seemed to be trying to communicate with me. When I started to feed her sugar cane, she suddenly grabbed my arm and held it firmly in her mouth. She pulled me even closer and we rested against one another, like lovers in a long embrace. Eventually, she released me and lay down.

All down the orchard, in night air hazy from the smoking fires, elephants lay sleeping. Disturbed by something, one would silently rise up like a monstrous spirit and then settle down again as it realised that all was well. Surrounded by six hundred tons of these huge animals, soothed by their snoring, like a ward of asthmatic old men, I felt for the first time a sense of vulnerability. I had never really given it a thought before, but as I looked back on the journey, I realised how much I had taken for granted. At any stage Tara could have killed me. Or any of us for that matter, as simply as swatting a fly. Now I understood that she had always been in control. My destiny had been in her hands. With that realisation, once again, she had taught me respect.

Mark Shand is a British writer who worked at Sotheby's before competing in the London-Sydney motor race, getting shipwrecked in the South Pacific, and writing a book—Skullduggery—about his search for headhunters in Indonesia. He won the Travel Writer of the Year award at the British Book Awards for Travels on My Elephant, *from which this story is excerpted.*

✳

Ganesh is the god of auspicious beginnings, and one of the most popular gods in Asia. All I could think of the first time I saw him was the Flying Dumbo ride at Disneyland, a passage that remains my very earliest memory from childhood.

Lord Ganesh is the son of Shiva, the great god of Destruction in the Hindu trinity, and of Parvati, Shiva's delicious consort. The story behind the elephant's head varies on details from place to place, but the general scene was this: One day Parvati, taking a leisurely bath, decides that she wants a son, someone who will answer to her and her alone. She scrubs down her skin, collecting together a large lump of saffron, and fashions from this fragrant mass a boy. The moment he attains consciousness, Parvati names him Ganesh and puts him to work. She orders him to stand guard by the palace door, and to let no one—absolutely no one—enter.

Shiva, naturally, picks this precise moment to return home from some messy mythical altercation. Our hero is, understandably, rather single-minded in his desire to frolic with lovely Parvati. Seeing this strange child haughtily blocking the door, Shiva demands to be admitted. Ganesh flatly refuses.

Some say the battle was long; others claim it lasted only an instant. It ended, at any rate, with Ganesh's head lying on the ground, a fair distance from the rest of his body. This accomplished, Shiva strolled into the parlor, but the homecoming wasn't quite what he had anticipated. Parvati was furious, and all thoughts of romance were tabled until Shiva somehow put the situation to rights. Desperate to appease his wife, Shiva raced out and appropriated the head of the first animal he saw: a baby elephant. After the successful transplant, Shiva further sweetened the pot by granting his son special privileges, including extraordinary intelligence and high status among his fellow gods.

Ah, Ganesh! Remover of obstacles, protector of children and thieves, patron of the poets! Ages ago, when the great sage Vyasa was suddenly struck by the inspiration to dictate the monumental epic *Mahabharata* in one sitting, Ganesh volunteered to serve as scribe. Halfway through Vyasa's feverish and unflagging dictation, the pen burst into flame and disintegrated. Ganesh, fearful of missing even a single syllable, snapped off his own tusk to use as a quill. Peerless devotion to the art! What better ally, I ask you, for a writer whose pen is perpetually out of steam?

—Jeff Greenwald, *Shopping for Buddhas*

FREDDA ROSEN

Shalom, Bombay

All religions have a home in the vast cauldron
of spirituality that is India.

TO KNOW INDIA IS TO HEAR HER. VILLAGE ROADS AND CITY streets are stuffed with people and their transport. Horns blare, engines cough. People shout, people scream. I was in Bombay, and I'd been away from home too long. I had a headache from India.

I also had too many hours to wait for my flight home. I'd already seen the Hanging Gardens and shopped myself silly. But I didn't have a gift for my father.

"There's a synagogue in Bombay," he had told me when I left for India. I smiled and ignored the implication. My father has been trying to get me into a synagogue since I left Beth El Academy in 1964. I've had other things to do. But now I shrugged.

"Got nothing else today," I thought. I figured there would be a synagogue gift shop like the one at Beth El, and I'd get him something there.

A local businessman I met at the airport wrote the directions: "Jewish Temple, near Byculla Bridge, opposite Richardson and Crudder, Ltd."

Kuldeep, my driver for the day, scrutinized the paper.

"Many temples in Bombay," he said.

"Not Hindu temple," I said. "Jewish temple. Synagogue."

289

He gave me a blank look, but shifted into gear. We added our horn to the honks and screeches of the city streets.

The sun followed us, searing through the car windows, making my clothes stick to my body. My head reverberated as we crossed a bridge labeled Byculla. Kuldeep braked in front of a snack bar, and consulted in Hindi with the owner and two customers. Arms waived to the left and right.

Kuldeep took off down a tiny alley, scattering chickens and children. He drove through the dirt yard of an apartment complex, turned again, and pulled up in front of a large stone structure.

He looked around and gave me a grin. I sighed. The building was topped with a huge cross.

"Place for Catholics," he said.

---

*I*n Kerala once more, the Jews of Cochin deserve a special mention—their ancestry goes back to the sixth century B.C. They were a highly influential community in their time and the Cochin synagogue is the oldest in the Commonwealth....

A more ancient, larger, and more significant Jewish community called the Bene Israel exists in and around Bombay. It is estimated that there are about four thousand Jews in the whole country but, like Parsis, their community is declining.

◆

—Frank Kusy,
Cadogan Guides: India

I took a deep breath. "*Jewish*, "I said. "Not Catholic, *Jewish*."

We began again, asking at a tailor's shop, stopping a schoolboy. Kuldeep honked through cars, buses, trucks, and bikes. The air was thick with incense, carbon monoxide, and wood smoke. Two aspirins did nothing for my headache or my spirits. We found no synagogues.

We did find a police station.

"Anyone speak English?" My voice was plaintive.

Khaki-suited men gave me the once over. One took the paper I waved and studied it.

"Synagogue," I said hopefully. "Jewish temple."

The policeman brightened. "Oh," he said. "You want *Jain* temple!"

I stifled a hiss and tried a new tact. "Where is Richardson and Crudder? Richardson and Crudder, Ltd.?"

He told Kuldeep, and we entered the fray once more. This time we scored. Kuldeep found the offices of Richardson and Crudder. I looked across the clogged avenue and saw a two-story building. It was adorned with a six-pointed star. A sign proclaimed *Magen David.*

"There it is!" I pointed.

Kuldeep responded with an Indian U-turn: a maneuver that involves crossing four lanes of moving traffic and staccato bursts of the horn. He pulled up to the synagogue entrance. Near the gate, a family had set up housekeeping. A woman chopped vegetables, her son washed his hair. They stared at me as I walked inside.

So did the three gray-haired men who sat on the porch of the synagogue. They were small and brown and wore skull caps. I introduced myself.

"Abraham," said one of the men. He waved at the others. "He's Abraham, too. And Ephraim."

They each gave me a smile that revealed missing teeth.

"You want to see the *safers?*" the first Abraham asked, referring to the *Torahs,* the sacred scrolls.

They ushered me inside the synagogue. Abraham pointed to two plaques. One commemorated the one hundredth anniversary of the synagogue, the other touted a donation from a couple from Great Neck, New York. There wasn't a gift shop in sight.

The sanctuary was lined with simple wooden pews. In the center was a raised platform with two gilded chairs. It was cool and quiet. I heard horns, but they were far in the distance.

Ephraim waved toward a corner where men worked on a scaffolding. He told me in careful English that the synagogue, which is over 120 years old, was being restored. But few people worship here now. Ephraim said they rarely have the ten men required to hold a service.

"We don't make *minyan* much. Sometimes on Saturday," he said.

The other Abraham told me that there are only six or seven thousand Jews in India. "We got the *Torah* from England," he said.

He opened the door to the arc, touched my hand, and motioned to the *Torahs*. They had embroidered velvet covers like the ones at home, at Beth El. I ran my fingers over the soft fabric. Then I remembered. I raised my hand to my lips, just as I'd been taught in Hebrew school. The three men lifted their heads and smiled. I noticed that my headache was gone, but my eyes were wet.

I blinked, and told them that I wanted to make a donation to the restoration work. "In honor of my father," I said.

I signed over a traveler's check. The men passed it among themselves, turning it over and over. Kuldeep, who had joined us, explained in Hindi how to cash it.

Abraham pressed my hand. "I give you my card," he said. He gave me a paper with the synagogue address stamped on it.

"Pictures?" I asked, taking out my camera.

"Oh, yes," Ephraim said.

I took one of the three men standing at the entrance to the sanctuary. Kuldeep took one of me in front of the synagogue. I made a mental note to have it framed as a gift for my father.

After all, his errand had brought me a gift, too. The Abrahams and Ephraim shook my hand as I left.

"See you at home, in Jerusalem," Ephraim said. "Peace be with you."

And it was.

Fredda Rosen has written for many U.S. newspapers and magazines and contributed a series of profiles to A Woman's Place is Everywhere, *published in 1994 by Mastermedia. She lives in New York.*

⋆

When I stopped in London on my way home from India, the city appeared empty, and disarmingly quiet. I felt, most of all, ignored: I actually had to hail the taxis, rather than wait for them to tear up beside me and shout me down with offers. Londoners left me alone, and I was lonely for the first time in months. The streets seemed like dormant movie sets—how I imagined Disneyland would look at five in the morning. Shoppers paid whatever the price tag said; cows were confined to Cadbury advertisements. As the Swedish *sadhu* had warned, I was bored within days. After the novelty of leavened bread and tap water had worn off, I'd grown impatient with the city's pace. I boarded a shiny bus for Hampstead. People sat two seats apart, eyes averted, and coughed silently to themselves. I got off the bus at the Everyman Cinema and bought a matinee ticket for *Salaam Bombay*!

—Peter Jon Lindberg, "The Confounding Allure of India,"
The New York Times

JOEL SIMON

✶ ✶ ✶

Lost and Found in Agra

Our own two feet are still the
best locomotion going.

INDIA'S A BIG PLACE, HUGE TO THE NOVICE TRAVELER, BUT FRANKLY, I was surprised at how easy it was to become lost in even a small piece of it. The piece was Agra, home of the Taj, the Red Fort, and more sleepy pedal cab drivers than cab-driven passengers. Most of the rickshaws were parked in a line, with *wallahs* stretched out on bench seats, as motionless as the air, feet propped up on the handlebars, gazing with half-shut eyelids at the mid-day sky from beneath lofty trees. But amongst drowsy competition, one young driver was awake, actively chatting in Hindi with passers-by. Vibrant, and with a healthy smile, he was aware that he'd caught my eye. He beckoned me with a wave of his hand and then swept back an errant shock of black hair. "My name is Ravi, and yours?"

"Joel," I replied. I hopped on and we were off.

I had arrived in India by ship with a group tour. One of the youngest aboard, I had been hired to photograph the voyage and its participants, individuals of means and plenty of leisure time to enjoy it. I was ready for a little time on my own, and willing to sac-rifice a bite of the continuous feast for the sake of adventure.

So with warm air softly brushing against my face, we were off, the pedal driver and I. Ravi didn't speak much English, but we communicated easily. "Which direction?" or perhaps it was "Where to?" he asked. I replied in time—pointing to my wrist-watch, and pulled out a twenty rupee note to establish the fare. I had four hours before photographing a dance presentation at the Mughal Sheraton. We laughed, and with a smiling glance over his shoulder, he rose and fell with each stride, maintaining a steady rhythm on the pedals as we rolled away from the hotel and into the heart of the town.

Before us the wide avenue curved in consort with the river. We quietly moved past slow ox carts, slower groups of sari-clad women, even slower wagons over-laden with heavy sewn brown bags, and all manner of vehicles parked or stranded in various cre-ative positions. Ravi wove expertly through the meandering traf-fic, while the occasional car or truck careened by with surprising skill. A cluster of cows stood placidly beneath a sign advertising leather goods available at some nearby shop: shoes, purses, and belts. A few minutes later we stopped to allow another group to cross the road as they headed toward the river. They may have been cows, but I saw shoes, purses, and belts with legs.

We came to a bend and Ravi stopped, turned around, smiled, and motioned for me to look back. Nestled between a break in the bushes was the Taj Mahal, distant and exquisite, reflected in the shallow waters of the river.

And yet the Taj is not what I remember most.

We continued on, rounding corners, and entering smaller, crowded streets, many of them dirt or half-covered with broken pavement. Children, some naked, some in tattered, faded t-shirts endorsing the Giants or the Red Sox or nonexistent distant uni-versities, played ball with bottle caps and sticks. Clucking chickens scampered under carts as we rolled by.

This was the India of my dreams, now before my eyes, in my nose, in my ears, at my fingertips. As we rode slowly by open houses, Ravi waved hello to some of the residents and we stopped near a door, once painted green and now almost brown with the native wood showing through. He got off the seat and invited me to follow. I did. We entered the dwelling, probably his home, but I'll never know for sure. In the small dark central room, an aluminum pot of water was heating over a wooden stove. An elderly woman in a clean but subtle rust-red cloth offered me a chair, one of two. A cup of hot tea soon followed. I took both, and sat in quiet joy. "Do you speak English?" I asked. She shook her head, smoothly, from side to side, "We speak Hindi," she said perfectly, and added, "and a bit of English, mostly what we have learned in school and from films. Welcome to our home."

After tea, I thanked the woman for her gracious hospitality. Outside Ravi was chatting with other young men, leaning on the pedal cab, still smiling. In a moment of inspiration, I reached into my pocket, withdrew the twenty rupee note and handed it to him, explaining that this was as far as I wished to go. Confusion turned to comprehension when I made a universally understood symbol, wiggling my first two fingers in imitation of legs walking.

"You wish to walk back?" he exclaimed with his eyes, looking at his friends for confirmation. One of the fellows standing nearby asked me: "You wish to *walk* back?"

---

*W*hat most terrified Bernier [a seventeenth-century French doctor who treated the Mughal nobility] was the notion that his long stay in India would rob him of his cultivated Parisian sensibilities. This fear reached its climax when he saw the Taj Mahal:

"The last time I saw Tage Mehale's mausoleum I was in the company of a French merchant who like myself, thought that this extraordinary fabric could not be sufficiently admired. I did not venture to express my opinion, fearing that my taste might have become corrupted by my long residence in the Indies; but since my companion had recently come from France, it was quite a relief to hear him say that he had seen nothing in Europe quite so bold and majestic."

—William Dalrymple,
City of Djinns: A Year in Delhi

"Yes" I replied, "Why not?"

"Perhaps you will become lost?" this man queried. "And your hotel, it is far from here."

"All the better," I answered. "Which way is it?" He pointed to his right. I thanked everyone, and after shaking hands all around, confidently strode off in the direction indicated, feeling proud, foolish, and happy to be really *in* India.

Walking remains one of the best means of seeing and interacting with a culture. No boundaries exist, other than the ones that you set for yourself. In the tourist world of packaged tours, seen through closed windows of air-conditioned buses, with carefully prepared cultural events, performed daily for tourists, directed through the concientious efforts of hired guides, the genuine "travel experience" becomes increasingly rare. But setting out on foot, on your own, is usually all it takes to uncover the sought-after glimpse of life as lived in a strange place.

Elated to be independent, I strolled past whimpering dogs, curious children, and countless friendly and beautiful faces. Men stopped, or stopped me to chat, and always pointed me in a sure direction. It wasn't, however, always the same direction. Unbothered, I continued, motivated by a sense of adventure.

From not too far away, I heard a sound that echoed from my childhood and movies of the wild west: a steam whistle filled the air, calling out to all within range. This was the India I had come to see. I followed the sound to a bridge overlooking a train station. Beneath the bridge people were still boarding the train as the whistle blew again issuing forth white steam which rose and mixed with black smoke belching from the smoke stack. The old engine began to slowly rumble forward. As the train gathered momentum and passed beneath me the bridge shook, and I shook with it. From atop the crowded wooden cars, people looked up and waved enthusiastically as I gazed down. Smoke filled the still air, slowly dissipating, and with it the sound and motion of the train. I was elated.

Dusk was at hand, and with it came the necessity of getting back to the hotel, the group, my job, and admittedly, dinner. Looking around, the street was full of people, mostly standing idle, talking amongst themselves. I walked slowly first in one direction, then retraced my steps and started off in the other direction. Hopeless, I returned to my place on the bridge and looked out at the train station.

It was only then that I heard a small voice at my feet. I looked down, and from within a shallow cardboard and cloth enclosure a bearded head emerged. From a wizzened wrinkled old head, covered with soot, hair in a tangled mat, emerged two sparkling eyes and a smile: "May I be of assistance?" said a gentle voice. Looking up at me from a crouched posture from within his little tent on the street, sat a man, his head scarcely two feet above the pavement. His speech was impecable, his elocution refined, his accent remniscent of the Queen's English.

"I am lost," I replied.

"You are found now," he said comfortingly. "May I show you my book?" he added, with only a slight hesitation.

"Well, of course," I said, and he spun delicately inward, rotating back with a tattered, loosely-bound sheaf of pages hand written in a script that I could only guess was Hindi.

The bridge guardian

"Here look at this." And I did. "I have written it myself," he said modestly.

"What is it?" I asked.

"The story of my life on this bridge. I have been here for nearly eight years now living in this..." and after a moment's reflection added "tent. You are the first tourist I have spoken with, although I have seen a few pass by. Do you mind being a part of my book?" He carefully opened it to a page only partially full.

"No, not at all," I replied. "My name is Joel, I am from America, this is my first day in India, and I am lost...and happy."

"Please repeat what you have just told me," he asked. I did, and slowly he wrote those words in Hindi, I suppose, with an old black pen.

"Now how may I help you?" he asked.

"I should like to go back to the hotel, the Sheraton hotel for dinner with my group." By this time there was a small circle of onlookers and onlisteners clustered around the crouched man and myself. He spoke some words in Hindi to a man standing next to him. That man spoke to a younger boy who ran off down the street. Soon the boy returned and with him a rickshaw-*wallah*. The crouched man in the tent (I never knew his name), told me that the driver would take me to the hotel whenever I wished. I told him I wanted to stay longer and chat through the evening, but that I was obligated to return to the group. They expected me to photograph a dance presentation.

I slipped my hand into my shirt pocket and drew out my only pen, a cheap ball point pen, but nearly new. With a smile, I offered it to him. With grace he took it into his soot and ink-covered hands. Holding my hands in his and holding my eyes with his, he thanked me for my contributions to his book, and to his life.

In this simple moment I knew I had been found. I had become lost in India. But India had found me.

Joel Simon's photo assignments have taken him to all seven continents, including the North Pole, the Antarctic, and ninety-five countries in between. When not traveling, he's at home in Menlo Park, California, with his wife, Kim, his cat, Ichiban, an itinerant possum named Rover, and a Tibetan rinpoche named Ventul.

✦

Dr. Jaffery was prostrated on a prayer carpet, finishing his evening *namaaz*. Fardine went to join him. Uncle and nephew knelt shoulder to shoulder, hands cupped, heads bowed in the simple position of submission.

When he had finished, Dr. Jaffery rose to his feet, brushed the dust of his pyjamas and came over to Olivia and me. He welcomed us, then added: "You looked at us strangely while we were praying. Do you never pray?"

"I used to," I said, embarrassed. "Now...I am not sure what I believe in, whether I'm an agnostic or..."

"You make God sound so complicated," said Dr. Jaffery, cutting in. "God is simple. To follow him is not so difficult. Just remember the advice of Rumi: 'Follow the camel of love.'"

"But follow it where?" I said.

"To wherever it leads," replied Dr. Jaffery. "God is everywhere. He is in the buildings, in the light, in the air. He is in you, closer to you than the veins of your neck."

—William Dalrymple, *City of Djinns: A Year in Delhi*

MICHAEL BUCKLEY

The Cycle-*Wallah* Does Northern India

The views are different from the
saddle of a mountain bike.

THERE IS NOTHING POLITE ABOUT ROAD SIGNS ON THE LEH-TO-Srinagar road in Ladakh: they are directed at Indian drivers fond of taking hairpin bends and blind corners at full throttle. The roads are high and rough and treacherous: Beacon, the paramilitary organization that constructed and maintains this highway in Ladakh, has erected bright yellow concrete markers along the route or painted signs into sheer rock walls. Signs that range from the cryptic—IF MARRIED, DIVORCE SPEED—to exhortations like GO MAN GO—BUT GO SLOW. A bit below the belt is BE GENTLE ON MY CURVES, later reinforced by DARLING I WANT YOU—BUT NOT SO FAST. And to really tug on the heartstrings: PAPA GO SLOW—OR-PHANAGE NO NO. But the strangest one yet seen offers this stark advice: DEATH LAYS ITS ICY HANDS ON SPEED KINGS.

Fortunately, I was spared the maniacal Indian truck drivers because the road up from Kashmir was blocked by snowfalls at Zoji La Pass. The pass blocks traffic for an inconvenient eight months a year—but I had flown into Leh from Delhi and thus bypassed the pass. When the pass opened, it would be bumper-to-bumper trucks spewing exhaust fumes. For the moment, there were only a hand-ful of trucks and jeeps commuting up to the pass and back again.

Sooner or later I would have to face the problem of actually crossing the pass, but until then, I had the entire road to myself—and my trusty mountain bike.

And what a magnificent road it is. I'd been on it for five days now, breezing along with a string of snowcapped mountains to the right, and Salvador Dali desert landscapes to the left. On the approach to Lamayuru, there is a long uphill stretch nicknamed the "Jalabi Bends" by truck-drivers—*Jalabi* being a kind of Indian sweetmeat with orange twirls. I passed a small roadside shrine that marks the spot of a serious accident, and gives the names of the fallen—these unnerving memorials punctuate the entire route to Srinagar. I tackled the laborious climb up the coiled switchbacks with rockbands of green shale, purple shale; near the crest, I came across some traders with donkeys having a tea break. They motioned me over to their campfire, and foisted Ladakhi tea on me—a horribly salty, pinkish concoction that I knocked back out of politeness. I gave them some chocolate. They examined the bike; I exam-

*B*efore noon I came upon several huts enclosed by a bamboo fence. Several men crouched around two huge tree trunks pushed into a smoldering ash pile, smoke wisping from the log ends. Coached by my stomach, I made a quick decision and pulled around. I squatted with them around the fire, smiled, and felt good when they smiled in return. Soon I was their guest, happily gorging on an endless meal of rice, *chapatis, dhal,* and *subji* (curried vegetables). The rain came again, and the cook valeted my cycle into an unoccupied thatched shack. My hosts then eagerly started up a card game. I lost rupee after rupee while trying to figure out the rules, doubly confounded by a suspicion that the rules were being changed as we played. When I drew the line for betting at my watch they were disappointed. I dared not bring out my camera.

◆

—Michael Sutherland,
"*Rohtas* Riding"

ined their gear; we sat around the fire. These encounters were strange and almost wordless, but somehow very meaningful.

The road continued through a bizarre moonscape of yellowish clay and pitted rocks. Rounding a bend, I caught sight of Lamayuru Monastery, dramatically lit by the afternoon sun—an impossible structure fused to a rocky outcrop, with dark, brooding hills behind it. It seemed to come straight off the page of a book about mythical places—even in its advanced state of decay, this Tibetan fortress exudes an air of majesty and splendor. Lamayuru is set down a valley: monastery at the top, village below, and a stream and barley fields at the bottom. The village is small— perhaps five hundred souls—and has only a rough jeep road in.

I rode the bike down a dirt track to the monastery—travelers are allowed to stay in a wing of the temple. Phuntsak, the monk in charge, is a wheeler-dealer—he runs a small shop, which had the best stock I've seen so far. He had Indian peanut butter, *chapatis,* dried apricots, biscuits, garlic, tea. The monk immediately took a fancy to my pile sweater, a bright monastic red, and inquired about trading food for it.

"You *dhal*? You ricing? You potato? How much you jacket? How much shopping you jacket? You biscuit? You tea?" Phuntsak spoke a variety of English that conveniently eliminated all verbs. I resisted the attempts to buy the sweater, and sipped *chai* while he cooked up some *dhal*.

Two other travelers drifted in for food. Stephanie was from England, and her boyfriend, Wally, was from Portugal. They looked like they had stepped straight out of the 1970s. Stephanie had a hippie headband; Wally sported five earrings in each ear. They rated all their travel destinations in terms of hashish—how available it was, the quality, the price, and whether smoking it was tolerated or not.

"Ah, Singapore, freak me off!" cried Wally. "*Incroyable the policia* there. *Quand* I arrive they search me everywhere. Everywhere. Freak me off!" He took a toke on a hash-lined cigarette. "Kathmandu was the best place—smoking in the restaurants, ma the laws they change. Even in India they change the laws. Goa was

the place—lots of crazy people. Carazey! And then the police arrest me in India—shake me over, you know. *Bastardos!* So we go
up to Tibet. Lhasa was the greatest—lots of good hashish there, ma
then the riots, they close out the place."

"You biscuit? You tea?" asked the monk.

"Yes, both thanks."

Hoping to change the subject, I inquired about Zoji La. They
crossed the pass several days ago.

"Ah yes, we met with one dead man there," said Wally. "He was
lying on the snow, very stiff. Poor bastard."

"It was fucking freezing!" piped in Stephanie. I glanced at
her gear.

"Were you wearing those?" I asked, pointing at her sandals.

"Yes, but with socks," she said.

God spare us—no wonder it was freezing. And they crossed at
night, by the light of the full moon. That way, claimed Wally, there
was less chance of an avalanche.

"How did you get to the pass?"

"Oh, with some Indian soldiers, in a jeep," said Stephanie.
"They were all sex-starved or something—kept asking me about
kissing. Wanted to know how I kissed, and whether I liked kissing
and things like that."

"Freak me off!" cut in Wally.

As I left, they were arguing furiously with the monk over the
seven rupees for the *dhal*. And I was glad I was traveling in the
opposite direction. I stepped outside and found it was snowing,
and I cursed and cursed. The fresh snow had thrown all my calcu-
lations about crossing the pass into doubt again.

From Lamayuru, some very tough climbing. I reached the top
of Fotu La, the highest pass along this road at almost 13,500 feet,
marked by some frayed prayer flags. But my legs weren't tired. I felt
high. I felt like riding. And riding. A rhythm had been set up that
I couldn't break now—nothing could stop me except a sunset.
And so I bounded along, headed for the next pass. After all the
complications of flying into Leh, this part was remarkably simple:
a bicycle, a ribbon of road, and crisp mountain air. And I moved

along in a kind of trance, with a cadence that seemed effortless. Rather than trying to conquer a pass, I found myself somehow integrated with the landscape.

It occurred to me that if meditation can be induced by concentrating on a single action such as breathing, or on the rising and falling of the stomach, then any repetitive action could induce a similar calming of the heart. So if there is walking meditation (that concentrates on the act of walking), there must also be jogging meditation (focusing on footfalls), snorkel meditation (concentration on breathing sounds), ski meditation (honing in on the sounds of skis scraping the snow), and bicycle meditation (my foot is going down, the chain is going around, the other foot is coming up, the chain is going around...).

And so I whipped through to the next pass, Namika La. Then I put on my downhill gear—fox-fur hat, silk scarf—for there was a glorious six miles of switchbacks down into the green, green valley of Mulbek.

There wasn't much in the way of lodgings in Mulbek. I found a family with a spare room. Mulbek was a very small place—I was an instant celebrity. Across the street was a nine-meter-high Buddha sculpted into a granite rockface with a tiny monastery at its base. The monks took turns riding my bike. I was given tea. A townsman took me off to his house for dinner—a double-storied place with animals below, and living quarters on the main floor. His family and neighbors crowded into a courtyard to get their photos taken and I promised to send some copies. One duo especially caught my eye: a grandmother cradling a child. The child had a smooth, pinkish skin; the grandmother was dark and leathery—and when she smiled, a thousand wrinkles creased her face and rows of stumps appeared instead of teeth.

At Kargil, you cross a cultural divide, from Buddhism to Islam. It's only a matter of twenty-five miles away from Mulbek, but there was a very different kind of energy here. *"Salaam Alekum"* was the new greeting. The town has several mosques—and a heavy military presence because Kargil sits right near the border with

Pakistan. I left Dras early in the morning after tea and biscuits, and climbed into a snow and icebound area, steadily up to 11,300 feet. My goal was to get in as close as I could to Zoji La Pass—which meant a stop at Gumri army post. Gumri was a quagmire of slush and dirty snow; gasoline barrels were embedded in the muck, and hundreds of empty tins were scattered around, with flies and crows picking at them. Obviously no collection here—the rubbish of the years just piled up in the snow.

I saluted the platoon commander. He was decked out in a down parka, with heavy snow-goggles perched on his head.

"You're near Zoji La now," he said.

"Can I stay here for tonight?"

"No need—it's only a few hours over the pass."

"It's dangerous in the afternoon—avalanches."

"Soon night will come—it's better to cross at night."

What, and freeze my bollocks off? Not bloody likely—I'll be damned if I'm going over at night—after I've come all this way, I want to see the pass.

"I want to cross early in the morning—at sunrise."

"We have no space for you here."

"All right then, I'll sleep in the snow."

Finally he relented—and I was shown a shed littered with empty rum and whisky bottles. I got some hot water and added a packet of noodles. The hot food lifted my spirits. It had been a rough day. I was glad I'd found refuge here because I didn't have the energy to carry on.

There were a dozen men at Gumri, locked in for the winter—it was an isolation posting. Behind the army huts stood Gumri Glacier, shaped like a gigantic *stupa.* There were about two miles of snow-blockage on the road through Zoji La; bulldozers were working it from both ends so it would be open in four or five days. At sundown the road crews returned. They had blackened faces, and the blackest clothing I'd ever seen. I doubt if any of them had washed their clothing since the date of acquisition. As for them-selves, well, that was hard to tell…. Probably too cold in this region for cleaning up. It all reminded me of a grimy fairytale: the soot-men—back from their grimy stint on the road, going into grimy rooms full of soot from stoves, smoking grimy cigarettes, sleeping in grimy beds in grimy buildings covered in grimy snow. Myself, spattered in mud up to the knees, must've looked immaculately clean to the grimy men. At least I had a few colors to show—red and blue. All their stuff was either camouflage khaki, or diesel-fume black.

In the shed, I slept with every stitch of clothing on, my head in a fox-fur hat, body in a sub-zero sleeping bag, and all of this inside a bivvy sack—and I was still freezing.

I had no idea how I was going to cross Zoji La with a bike. All I knew was that I had to start off at dawn, when everything was still frozen, so less chance of an avalanche. I just hoped the crossing didn't involve any climbing. The next morning I tied down the flaps on my fox-fur hat so my ears were covered, and set off. The track from the army base turned into a roadway with a layer of solid ice, and walls of frozen snow on either side. Great! I got on the bike and started wheeling off—and promptly went for a six on the ice, banging my elbow. I got up slowly—this was not going to work.

Then I saw a group of horses trudging along in the distance. They were up on the snow, naturally the horses could not have got any grip on the road of ice. The horsemen spotted me and pulled me onto the snow bank. The horse track went away from the road, cut a wide arc around it, across a snow-filled basin. I trudged along in the horse tracks. The landscape was exuberant and I stopped to take pictures as the sun came out with blinding force. In the distance, a

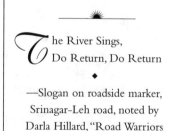

The River Sings,
Do Return, Do Return

♦

—Slogan on roadside marker,
Srinagar-Leh road, noted by
Darla Hillard, "Road Warriors
of the Zoji La"

caravan of pack-horses was dwarfed by a massive peak of snow, ice, and rock. Here was a paradox: Zoji La was stunning yet dangerous.

One half of me wanted to stay and look longer, bewitched by this icy domain, but the other half told me to hurry on before the sun climbed higher and loosened the snow.

The pack-horses were bringing sacks of food across this bridge of snow to trucks waiting near Gumri. As they went along, they dropped vegetables here and there, so I could tell if I was on the right track by following a stray tomato, carrot, or pea-pod in the snow. And horse-droppings. I could only hope I wouldn't fall into a crevasse or a sinkhole. The occasional rough burial site, marked by a pile of clothes, sped me along my way. A few years back, the pass claimed several hundred lives. Toward autumn, a truck had broken down on the pass, backing up traffic behind it; an unseasonably early snowstorm struck the hapless trucks, and the occupants froze to death. It was not till the following summer that road-crews were able to dig the trucks out of the snow.

By late morning I was over the worst of it—an Indian traveler helped me to climb over the last bank of snow, and back onto the roadway. I turned for a last look, then took off. Around a bend, I left the desert plateau of Ladakh behind me. Just like that. The transition was abrupt and complete—and most bizarre. And there was an exhilarating set of hairpin bends down into the Vale of Kashmir. It was as if the gods had spilled green paint over the landscape—spruce and pine trees, lush meadows, alpine vistas, cool breeze. The precarious road I was traveling on had been blasted out of a mountain-side. I raced down the switchbacks—down, down, down to the alpine resort of Sonamarg. From Sonamarg, it was fifty miles of glorious downhill to Srinagar, the capital of Kashmir. I whooped and hollered all the way down, startling Kashmiri shepherds and their sheep....

On the map of Srinagar, I had scribbled some notes: *houseboats, bombs, ice cream, Glocken.* I was to experience all of those things. Srinagar, being ten degrees cooler than places like Delhi, has long been a summer retreat; however, there is no respite from the greed of Kashmiri merchants. They buzz around, droning the same old spiel: *My friend, I have houseboat, you come see. Cheap. You want a carpet? I have excellent carpet. Have tea at my shop. No need to buy, just look.*

At the Glocken Bakery I had a temporary cultural relapse, went berserk, and devoured four apple pies in a row. A traveler I met at the Glocken showed me one of the newest sights of Srinagar: around the corner, along the Bund, was a urinal that had just been blown up. A Kashmiri separatist group had picked this harmless target as a warning, setting off a bomb after midnight when no one was around. The manager of the houseboat I stayed on told me there was no trouble in Kashmir. When pressed—when I told him about the urinal on the Bund—he said "Well, we are having a few bombs, but only *small* bombs." A cycle tour through the dusty, squalid, old town sector revealed a different story: soldiers in full riot gear with shields, Sten guns and 303s. I passed a heavily sand-bagged police station that had a blue paddy wagon and a fire engine outside with steel mesh across the windows.

Srinagar was like a powder keg—ready to go up at any second. I got out quickly, headed for the next destination—Dharamsala. In early June I cycled through the foothills of northwest India, through pinewood forests. I hitched a ride on the open back of a truck for a hair-raising ride through Jawahar Tunnel, which bored two miles through a mountain-side. Then I carried on cycling past the hill resorts of Patnitop and Batote, and dropped down to stony plains with cactus shrubs. I stopped at small lodges for the night, or got myself invited in as a guest at Public Works Department buildings, which had been set up for traveling VIPs and engineers. The weather see-sawed from thunderstorm cool to searing hot. When the sun came out, the road turned to hot, sticky tar. Road workers with black umbrellas and watering cans full of pitch were mending holes one by one in the awful heat. What a hellish job!

My diet consisted mainly of fresh mangoes—the only food available that wasn't booby-trapped with chilies. "Only a little chili," the man at a roadside stand reassured me, motioning to caul-drons of food. Oh yeah? Tell me about it—the last dish just about blew my head off. Stopping in the shade to peel a mango, I looked up to see the doleful eyes of a huge Brahmin bull staring at me. So

I surrendered the skins, and the bull promptly vacuumed them off the highway.

Travel is a kind of sensory deprivation. There's always something you crave—cheese, chocolate, or, on the Indian plains, water. It's not ordinary tap water you crave, but a glass of sparkling-clear, cold mineral water from the French Alps with a slice of lime. In northwest India the choice was between bad colas or mango drinks. I say bad colas because most were carcinogenic—they had cancer-causing additives. Some fizzy drinks were rumored to be used as birth-control devices—used in a douche after the fact. I'd taken to mixing mango drinks with tonic water. I'd order ten mango drinks at a roadside stand, plus tonic water—and for theatrical effect, open all of them. Suspense—a great crowd gathered, gape-mouthed. I consumed two on the spot, and poured the contents of four in one water-bottle and four in another.

> *T*he hill station of Dharamsala became home to the Dalai Lama and his followers when they fled the Chinese occupation of Tibet in 1959. Today it remains his residence and the seat of his government-in-exile. The community has a Tibetan ambiance and a school with an excellent library for studying Tibetan culture.
>
> ◆
>
> —JO'R and LH

Farther down the road, after a long stop in Dharamsala, I cycled on to the Punjab—where the crowds got bigger and more wide-eyed. And the traffic got worse. Trucks careened down the road straight at me, forcing me to pitch myself into the shoulder of the road. Pairs of overtaking trucks even deprived me of the shoulder and made me dive for my life. Here and there an upturned truck or smashed-up car would loom up, left where it lay at the roadside— a kind of monument warning the living to slow down. Those signs up in Ladakh had been right on: Indian drivers *were* maniacs. Bizarre roadside signs still continued: one advertised medical services, depicting the bearded face of a Punjabi doctor—turban, stethoscope around the neck—and, in English, the caption: Sex, Urine, Skin, Stone, Piles.

The highway traffic was thick with horn-happy truck-drivers, the heat oppressive, and the scenery dull, but the Punjabis were a friendly lot, most likely because the place had been closed for the previous five years. Nobody was asking for pens, and the road was sealed, smooth, and flat. The only sign of trouble was the odd checkpoint, where soldiers scoured buses and trucks—presumably for terrorist weapons. My thirst was incredible: I worked my way through an entire fridge-full of mango drinks and bad colas by noon. At each wayside stop, doing my one-man "rehydrating theater" act, I was surrounded by Sikhs who chattered excitedly over the bicycle, squeezed the tires, and played with the derailer.

I clocked up a hundred miles by nightfall, struggling through to Batala, a sizable town full of chaotic traffic. The noise-level threw me off-kilter—horns blaring, people shouting, radios squawking. I got to see plenty of Batala, circling the place three times looking for a guesthouse. Everybody had a different story—even when I was standing ten feet away from the place (no sign out front, windows boarded up) people pointed in five different directions. Finally the guesthouse manager spotted me, and hauled me around the back into a courtyard. Things got better after that—an air-conditioned dining-room in the guesthouse served a fine order of chicken *tandoori* with *nan,* vegetables, glasses of lemon soda, and bottles of Thunderbolt Lager. Beer was the only thing that could quench my thirst.

In the early morning, Batala looked like a battlefield. It was all quiet after the upheavals of the previous day's traffic and commerce. The streets were deserted, piles of garbage smoldered, crows and mangy dogs picked over the garbage, a few beggars rose from the ashes. It was another of those bombed-out looking Indian cities of the plains, with piles of bricks, sand, rubble, car parts, and garbage lining the main drag, shells of storefronts, and dust, and smoky fires. Splashes of color miraculously appeared as the markets stirred to life—bright red tomatoes, the pale orange

of mangoes, and the striking blues, reds, and yellows of the turbans of Sikh vendors.

Droves of turbaned cyclists were moving along the dusty road,
some carrying large brass pots filled with milk. The road was shaded by eucalyptus; farther out were rice paddies and haystacks.
Closer to Amritsar, movie billboards appeared, such as: BEDROOM
EYES—a sensuous mystery—FULL OF SEX.

At Amritsar I joined the Grand Trunk Road. I'd spent the better part of two months in India, and yet managed to avoid India—
Leh and Dharamsala were not "India." They belonged to the high
country—to Central Asia. India was the plains—heat, Hindus,
monsoon. Amritsar didn't seem like India either. It was Sikh, a synthesis of Hindu and Islamic influences, and militarism.

The holiest shrine of Sikhism is the Golden Temple. At the
entrance to the temple was an Indian army post with sandbags,
checking all who entered for weapons. But inside it was tranquil,
with cool marble walkways. The temple combined a sense of
peace, grace, and beauty—a rectangle of double-storied structures
enclosing a large sacred pool. To the center of the pool, connected by a marble causeway, was the main temple—burnished a true
gold at sunset. Some nine hundred pounds of gold leaf were used
to cover the temple exterior; on the interior, delicate frescoes and
glasswork adorned the walls and lofty ceiling. The central cloister
was a perfect acoustic chamber. I lingered here under elaborate tile
work and swishing fans, taking in the hypnotic harmony of the
singers who chanted hymns from the Sikh holy book, the *Granth
Sahib,* backed up by men on drums and accordion-type instruments. I closed my eyes and let my mind empty itself. The music
had the most relaxing effect. This was a bizarre feeling—I'd come
here out of curiosity, as a traveler, but ended up blending in as a
pilgrim at this sacred site.

The Golden Temple Museum evoked a very different mood—
it showed bloody portraits of Sikh martyrs—beheadings, scalp-
ings, bodies broken on "the wheel," babies cut into pieces or
speared—but the displays stopped abruptly in 1978, with nothing
on the Sikh militant attempts to establish an independent state of

Khalistan, "Land of the Pure." And nothing on the horrific sequence of events in 1984: the Indian army raid on the Golden Temple, the subsequent assassination of Indira Gandhi by her Sikh bodyguards, and the mass killing of Sikhs in New Delhi as retribution.

The next day, I set off along the Grand Trunk Road to Lahore. This section of the highway was four lanes, and hardly a truck in sight. But it was Sunday, and the strip was between borders. I remained apprehensive—was this introduction to the Grand Trunk a trick or treat?

The Grand Trunk qualifies as the oldest highway in the world, one small section near Calcutta dates back to 1000 B.C. The handiwork of previous empire-builders was consolidated under the Moghul emperors in the sixteenth century—they forged a route of sixteen hundred miles, connecting Kabul with Calcutta. In the nineteenth century, the British upgraded it as a military supply route, metalling the road and planting trees along its length. The Grand Trunk was a stately, tree-lined corridor through the vastness of India—thronged with ox-carts and grain and cotton wagons. Pilgrims and traders, Hindu and Moslem, walked along in a festive mood, with march music supplied by the tom-tomming of drums; at night, travelers bought food from hawkers and swapped tales around campfires.

In 1886, Thomas Stevens pronounced the Grand Trunk the finest highway in the world. Stevens was in a unique position to pass such judgment: his rear end was mounted on a penny-farthing. He was indulging in the first—and only—trip by penny-farthing around the world. By the late 1880s this contraption had been superseded by a diamond-framed, chain-driven machine, a forerunner of the bicycle in use today. The penny-farthing was heavy and awkward—and a fall from it could be disastrous. There were no tires (the wheels being hoops of metal), no gears, no chain—and most annoying of all, no roads. Stevens had to settle for railway tracks, horse-carriage tracks, or mule-paths. When the going got rough, he had to push the bike along, or have porters carry it. Compared to these tracks, a long, flat, sealed road like the Grand

Trunk was a boon for riding. This was the India of the British Raj—and Stevens fully availed himself of British hospitality.

It's only a short ride from Amritsar to the Wagah border crossing into Pakistan. A blistering wind was blowing, and I was coated in sweat: the humidity was crippling. Herds of water-buffalo, Brahmin bulls, and black goats huddled in the shade of trees to escape the ferocious heat. In the no-man's land between borders, the bank on the Indian side was closed; the one on the Pakistani side was open, but had no money according to the manager.

"Sorry we can only change $50," he said. "We have not enough rupees. It is Sunday." He paused for a while, studied me, and with a frown on his face, asked:

"Why are you so thin?"

"I have been cycling in the heat."

The man's ears pricked up. He suddenly looked quite excited. He went to the door, stared at my bicycle and panniers, turned back, and his face broke into a broad smile.

"You are riding a bicycle!" he cried, vigorously shaking my hand and slapping me on the back. "Welcome to Pakistan! Here—sit down! Aziz—bring the cycle-*wallah* some tea! You are riding a bicycle across Pakistan! You are a brave man! You are a hero! Please, sit down! You will change $100, $200, $500—what you want!"

And thus I availed myself of Pakistani hospitality—and basked in the limelight of being one of the few fools to cross this border on a bike. But what did the bank manager mean by being a brave man to cross Pakistan by bicycle? Was he referring to feral animals? Rabid dogs? Highway bandits? Maniacal truck-drivers? What other road hazards did this new country hold? Pockets stuffed with bright-red one hundred-rupee notes and dirty-brown five-rupee notes, I set off to find out....

Michael Buckley is a writer and photographer from Vancouver, Canada. He is the author of several guidebooks to Asia, including Vietnam, Cambodia, and Laos Handbook *from Moon Publications, and* Cycling to Xian, *a* book about cycling across China and Tibet. He is a firm advocate of touring by bicycle; his favorite sport is mountain bike polo.

*

The sign at the foot of the Nilgiri Hills in Tamil Nadu had read: THIS ROAD CONTAINS SEVERAL HAIR-PIN BENDS AND STEEP GRADIENTS. YOU WILL HAVE TO STRAIN YOUR VEHICLE MUCH. My vehicle showed no signs of stress. I, on the other, hand was a virtual cycling fountain as sweat dripped from the end of my nose, my chin, my elbows and my fingertips. At one point the road was so steep that for forty-five agonizing minutes I was forced to stand while pedaling (They called these hills—the summit was at seven thousand feet). I found myself panting out camp tunes from my childhood to take my mind off my aching legs and the thirty-six switchbacks.

As I struggled with hair-pin number twenty-two and my sanity, a passenger in a slowly passing truck called out. "Why you not take the bus?" On the verge of tears I screamed, "I DON'T KNOW!"

Another eternal half hour passed with no summit in sight and I battled with the thought to give up. It would be so easy to get off my bike and wait for a ride. Then I began to hear the sounds of drums and instruments and through a clearing in the trees I saw a village perched on the side of the hill. They were celebrating the annual festival of the local God, Kalliamma. With new-found strength I sprinted to the top.

Smiling faces and laughter greeted me and I was whisked off my bicycle to participate in a large circular dance. Women in saris and men in *dhotis* whirled around me. Two of the men grabbed my hands and coached me through the steps. The local Brahmin priest walked up and gave me a big hug and the villagers cheered. I couldn't help but feel like I'd been plunked down in the middle of a National Geographic special. My tutors must have seen my shaking legs begin to buckle, for they led me off to sit on the grass and brought me bananas and coconuts to eat.

Surrounded by giggling children, I looked out at the valley below— the home of wild elephants and tigers—where I had begun my climb. A grin filled as much with exhaustion as exhilaration spread across my face as I once again knew what I have always known—the answer to why I didn't take the bus.

—Willie Weir, "Cycling India: Letters from the Road"

KATHLEEN CLARK

* * *

My Wedding at the Ashram

What does she think of the "whole deal"?
The author revisits a holy man
to find out.

I FIRST VISITED BABAJI IN INDIA IN 1979. MY LIFE WAS COMPLETELY changed. I didn't know if it was Babaji or India that did it, but I returned from that trip with a shaved head and a heart completely open. I knew that I loved everyone deeply whether or not I could express it, and I knew that the "truth" was very vast and that each person had his own view of it but no one had it all. Even that is questionable, but it is all I can really have. If I hadn't met Toby that might have been the end of it. Life completely transformed, and then it was back to business as usual trying to create a life in America.

But when Toby went to see Babaji in India he knew that he had seen God or at least someone who carried more of that "God-energy" than anyone he'd ever known, and he did what he always does in those cases, he became an enthusiastic supporter of the whole "trip," forcing me to come to grips with it. So, while we were deciding if we were having a relationship or not, I decided I had to get back to India to see Babaji once more and decide what I really thought about the whole deal. I decided this was top priority for me but I hadn't told Toby when, in the middle of an argument, he suddenly said to me, "I want you to go to India with me in June and we'll ask Babaji to marry us."

"You mean, if he says 'no' we won't have to do it?" I replied.

"Yes," he said.

Well, this was a marriage proposal I could relate to. It showed a person with an adventurous spirit and darn good ideas. Little did I know just what it would be getting me into. No business as usual, but life transforming constantly, and of learning the most difficult lessons of my life.

I have come to know India as the land where one comes face to face with oneself under the most difficult circumstances and is deeply changed. Of course at the center of my experiences is the transcendent force of what the Indians call an

Avatar, God incarnate, a parent to our spirit selves, who shows us what it is we are aspiring to.

In India the line between dreaming and a timeless reality is very thin. I find myself in the Kailash View Hotel, Haldwani, Uttar Pradesh, feeling trapped in a world of my own creation and I cannot get out. I am creating it all and it is horrible. I cannot escape. The smell of tires burning. People on bicycles. The train. Cows wandering in the street. Pigs. Dogs. Chickens next door. Everything strange. Smoke hanging over the city. The sheer terror of it! No EXIT!

Haidakhan Babaji, reputed to be a mahavatar—a human manifestation of God not born of woman—is said to have appeared in June of 1970 in a holy cave at the foot of the Kumaon Mt. Kailash, across the sacred river Gautama Ganga from a remote village called Haidakhan in the Nainital district of Uttar Pradesh. He apparently had no known parents but appeared to be a youth of 18 who possessed great wisdom and divine powers. He passed away in 1984.

◆

—JO'R and LH

Toby has burned his feet. He is in psychic collapse. Unavailable. Worried about how he is going to get up the river to the ashram the next day. The cloud about him is palpable. We are not in "ordinary reality." I am terrified. I go outside. I come back in. I cannot get back to normal. Toby is in the bathroom. I go in and say, "Toby, I love you." It is a lie. I don't feel love for him. It is an attempt to get things back to normal, but it is a failure. No luck.

I remember I must be willing to face my death to get to the next level, to evolve. But I fear that if I truly face this feeling, I will in fact die. Yet I decide I have to do it.

I lie down on the bed in this dark room I have created. A lizard dozes in the corner. Mosquitoes buzz. I pull my shawl over my head and fall back into black certainty of my death. Immediately I pop out the other side and I am back into normal reality. I have survived.

We made it up the river the next day. The first words he said to us after we'd gone up the 108 steps from the riverbed to the ashram was, "You two married?"

There are those who still regard the compass as more than a bauble and persist in asking total strangers, "Where's home?" and "Who's Om?" They may be comforted to learn that their dilemma is not unique.

A century ago Nietzsche was asking in italics,

"Will it be said of us one day that
we, too,
steering westward, hoped to reach an India,
but that it was our fate to be wrecked against infinity?"

To the anxious on both sides of the dark water, I would like to raise a toast: a small cheer for fear.

It's harder to applaud the confident ones who as the Indian cynic says, "Go from zero to hero."

Those who have passed beyond fear can't hear.

◆

—Gita Mehta, *Karma Cola: Marketing the Mystic East*

"No, Babaji, but we will be if you'll marry us."

He said, "Tomorrow, 8 a.m."

So we were married. It ended with a plunge into the river. We were tied together. I was afraid he would drown me and my new silk sari would be ruined. I complained and resisted all the way across the river bed, "Baba said, put our heads in the river, not jump in." Finally I gave up. "Oh, what the heck. OK. I'll do it." We jumped in.

It changed the whole thing. The sacred river that washed away the sins of the world was clear, pure, cold on that hot June day. It cleansed us. We could laugh, relax. We were together again. A white dove landed on our window sill.

Later in that trip, I was sitting alone in our room, a cement structure with one window and a mat on the floor. My head is shaved again. I have yellow paint in stripes on my forehead, the mark of Shiva, put there at dawn by Babaji. I have been bathing in the river twice a day, 4 a.m. and 4 p.m. I have been going down 108 steps to squat amongst the rocks if I needed to use a toilet. I have been carrying rocks to build a new temple on the mountainside. I have been chanting *Om Namah Shivaya* and singing 108 names of God and browning my naked skull in the sun. My body feels new, clean. I still don't know if Babaji is God. I still don't know what's happening or why. People love him. I don't love him, I'm afraid of him, but I'm grateful he lets me stay because I know something extraordinary is happening in spite of my disbelief.

For some reason I decide to sink into myself, to see how I am feeling. I sink down and I become the entire World, the Cosmos. I realize the world is inside of me. That it is an actual literal fact. I can feel the truth of this, the physical truth. I had heard this before, "you are the world," but it had been a concept, an interesting philosophical idea. Now it was an actual physical reality. I could feel the street and the cars of the world within me. The forests, the jungles of Brazil and the deserts of Africa, I contained them all within my body and it was good.

Now I am climbing Mount Kailash. This is the sacred mountain here in the foothills of the Himalayas where Babaji sat for forty days and nights after manifesting his body in the cave at the base. It is very steep. I am in my sandals. I cannot stand up straight. I take a step and stop and breathe. It is very slow going. I am bent completely over. I am pulling myself by the grasses on the side of the path. This is very familiar to me. I have done it many times before. But when? Then I remember: I have done this in dreams over and over again. When I reach the top, I am Home. The air feels creamy and welcoming. I feel comforted. I feel that I am *Home* for the first time in my life. I eat the ginger *chapatis* and taste the sacred ash the priest puts on my tongue. I look out on the terraced mountains and the river valley below.

I am finally at home.

It took me many more trips to India to try to decide what I really thought about the "whole deal." To be truthful I have to say I never have decided what I really think about it, but the grasses, the struggle to climb—I have never had that dream again.

Born and bred for the suburbs, Kathleen Clark has spent the latter part of her life trying to escape. She now lives in Santa Fe, New Mexico and is carrying on a passionate affair with a cello. She and Toby are no longer married but are still housemates and good friends.

★

"India is mad with all the madness of reality," the old poet said. The snake man laughs as he swirls the bag of writhing killers around his head; the maharani sighs and adjusts her pearls as she passes the starving child; the twilight sun streaks the feathers of the murdered peacocks in the back of the Jeep full of tobacco smoke. An awareness of violent contradiction and paradox entered my imagination early and pervaded it. Western rationalizations or secular dreams of progress, however much I tried to share them, were always foreign to me, as were all versions of the Divine that left out terror and destruction. My inner reality was of the skinned panther on my father's veranda, and the mango lying on a silver plate near it, the lapis lazuli lozenges glittering in the doorways of Moghul ruins and the beggars coughing under them, the deer's body I found once in a garden in the Nilgiri hills lying eviscerated, swarming with ants, under a light-riddled display of jacaranda.

—Andrew Harvey, *Hidden Journey: A Spiritual Awakening*

RORY NUGENT

Down the Brahmaputra

*The search for the elusive pink-headed duck—last sighted in 1935—takes
the author and his pal, Shankar, to the far reaches of Assam in a canoe
named Lahey-Lahey, or Slowly-Slowly.*

IN THE MORNING, AFTER PADDLING SEVERAL MILES DOWNSTREAM,
we're back in duck country again. The jungle crawls over the
riverbank; birds reappear; tracks along the shore mark the favorite
watering spots for swamp deer, crab-eating mongooses, wild boar,
and various species of cat. In one two-mile stretch, ducks carpet
every foot of water; I figure there are thirty-one thousand birds
floating within sight.

"How did you come up with that?" Shankar asks.

"Math," I say authoritatively.

As we move through a flock of pochards, several pale red feathers drop from the sky and land near the stern. I keep a close watch
on all the ducks and ready my cameras. Hundreds of storks are
feeding in the shallows, clacking their mandibles. A crested serpent
eagle eyes me from a treetop, and a chestnut-bellied nuthatch almost clips me from our rail as it races by trying to tell me something important. I cock the camera shutter.

Slowly Shankar and I develop a perfect cadence, the rhythm of
our paddles in harmony with the river. Our wake is imperceptible,
barely hinting at our passing. The sun guides us downstream,
marking the way with a slender golden path. We paddle on, our

movement as fluid as the water itself. The sounds of the Brahmaputra have grown familiar, their clarity and intimacy comforting. As I listen, I begin to decipher pieces of the river's timeless message.

"Look out!" Shankar yells as *Lahey-Lahey* clears a bend.

I snap out of my trance to find that we're on a collision course with another boat. I back-paddle frantically, jabbing the water, trying to swing the bow around. Shankar is poised to fend off. The other crew, just as surprised, dig in their push poles. *Lahey-Lahey* misses their stern by inches and rounds up smartly, giving us the appearance of expert boatmen. She stops within an arm's length of their rail.

They're turtle catchers, and the two 150-pounders in their bilge indicate that they're good at their jobs. They were tracking a third when we appeared. The captain apologizes, explaining that they were focused on the bubble trail of their submerged prey. Shankar, wetting his lips at the thought of a turtle dinner, asks for the secrets of turtle hunting. The captain explains that there

After tea the next morning, we start loading Lahey-Lahey. Hayna is there to offer advice.

"Never travel in the rain…Giant fish and crocodiles attack during storms…Pray to Ram when you see a whirlpool. He may hear you and save you…Keep your fire bright. Ghosts fear light. Do you have flashlights?…When the moon is up, sleep with your knives…"

He stops, nodding in approval, when I hold out two pieces of fruit. Shankar takes one and we make an offering to Brahma, invoking his spirit to guide us safely to the sea. The oranges splash and bob downstream, carrying our prayer ahead of us. The people of Saikhoa Ghat wave and shout as we climb aboard. We clear the back-eddy along the bank and enter the main channel of the god.

♦

—Rory Nugent, *The Search for the Pink-Headed Duck: A Journey into the Himalayas and Down the Brahmaputra*

are two ways to catch a turtle: trapping it with a net or wounding it with a trident and roping it by the neck when it surfaces.

Turtles are the basis of his village's entire economy. The meat close to the shell is a delicacy that commands a high price in the city; the shell is carved into combs or decorative objects. The captain shows us some of his own handiwork, mostly combs, which, he notes, are of no use to me [Rory's bald]. They give us small amulets made from turtle shell, and in exchange we offer Michael Jackson lighters. Everyone is delighted with the barter.

Following the shifting main current, we cut all the way across the river to the north bank. When the wind is calm, it's relatively easy to pilot the fastest course: ripples point us to the swiftest-running water. However, when it's blowing hard enough to put whitecaps on the waves, it's nearly impossible to track the current, and we must rely on luck.

Tonight it's my turn to cook. When Shankar goes off to collect firewood, I rifle through our supplies hoping for inspiration. By the time he returns, I've unpacked everything.

"What are you doing?" he asks, kindling the fire.

"Looking for something different."

As the fire catches, flames shooting through the top of the mustard oil tin, I can see the grin on his face. He knows we have plenty of food, but it's all the same. We end up eating rice, *dal*, onions, and radishes again, our standard menu, which varies only by the amount of curry powder or pepper we add. There was no tinned food for sale in Saikhoa Ghat; Moti [a teahouse owner and trader] explained that people won't buy food if they can't smell it or pinch it. Shankar decides to write out a shopping list of items to buy in the next town; he's still at it when I turn in.

Several uneventful days later, as we paddle between two large islands, Shankar yells, "Look at that." He's pointing to starboard, but I can't see anything. I raise my binoculars and scan the island. "Tiger?" I ask. Yesterday we spent the entire morning following the tracks of a Bengal tiger. We gave up after finding nothing but leeches.

"Forget the tiger. Look at the water. There!"

It's too late to avoid the whirlpool, so we hang on for the ride. It's the largest we've seen, almost twice the length of the boat.

Previously we've powered right through them, encountering little drag, but not this time. Around and around we go, spinning clockwise, making tighter, faster circles. The horizon becomes a dizzy blur.

"Yahoo!" Shankar exclaims, his paddle shipped, holding on to the painter like a rein. "Ride 'em, cowboy!"

This gleeful feeling is quickly supplanted by terror as the whirlpool starts to suck us down.

"Sheee-ittt. Paddle, paddle!" Shankar now screams.

Both of us thrust our oars into the swirling water as the foam starts lapping the gunwales. The boat lists, her port rail dipping under. The river pours in. We shift our weight to compensate, burying the starboard rail. *Lahey-Lahey* spins on her nose and threatens to dive. The bilge water surges forward, almost catapulting me from the stern. We stroke like madmen, shouting instructions at each other. Water cascades over the stern. We move aft, straining to regain an even keel. *Whap!* the stern hits the river. *Lahey-Lahey* corkscrews, reverses direction, and cuts across the spirals into calm water. We head for the nearest land.

Shankar and I had heard about these giant whirlpools, but we didn't believe the stories told us by Jodu Das, Hayna, and Moti. In

> *A* dead tiger is the biggest thing I have ever seen in my life, and I have shot an elephant. A live tiger is the most exciting thing I have ever seen in my life, and I have shot a lion. A tiger in a hurry is the fastest thing I have ever seen in my life, and I have shot a leopard. A wild tiger is the most frightening thing I have ever seen and I have shot a Cape Buffalo. But for the sport involved…I would rather shoot quail than shoot another tiger.
>
> ◆
>
> —Robert Ruark, *Use Enough Gun,* quoted by Geoffrey Ward with Diane Ward, *Tiger-Wallahs: Encounters with the Men Who Tried to Save the Greatest of the Great Cats*

Indian lore whirlpools are regarded as doorways to another life. An angry deity is lying at the bottom, sucking in the water, waiting to gobble up some unwitting sailor to appease its wrath. The river gods may not forgive our next mistake.

We reach the right bank without further incident and discover a wide expanse of marshland. In a flash my mood changes.

"This is it, Shankar. We've found the perfect nesting ground for the pink-headed duck. Just look at that marsh."

Shankar is not excited; indeed, he groans as I steer for the wetlands. The air becomes thick with flying, biting insects, as well as a stomach-knotting odor of swamp gas. This doesn't deter me, for I sense that the duck is near. I jump out, eager to survey the area, but Shankar won't leave the boat. I point out a few of the highlights of this wonderland, including the thousands of iridescent dragonflies zipping over the stagnant water, flitting from one earthen mound to another, their bodies glistening like sapphires. Birds' nests are everywhere and the occupants shout their welcome.

"They're telling us to go away," Shankar corrects.

I remain undaunted, sure that the white ibis are grunting hello, that the chestnut bitterns are extending a gracious invitation, confident that the flapping widgeons and terns are applauding our arrival.

"I don't like it here," Shankar whines.

"Come on," I urge. "What's the problem?"

"It's just a feeling. I don't know…. It's the kind of place a *burru* would live in."

"A what?"

"*Burru*. My grandmother told me stories about them. They're bad. Evil."

According to Shankar's grandmother, *burrus* appear in two forms, the most frightening being that of a giant, scaly ogre with the claws of a panther and the head of a frog; the more common variety, I'm told, looks like a brontosaurus. In either case the god-beast regards human beings as tasty hors d'oeuvres.

"She saw one and my cousin did too. I'm telling you the truth…. Hey, man, don't mess with *burrus*."

*M*alevolent spirits are collectively known as *bhuta-preta*. These supernatural beings are souls of persons who could not live out their lives fully, or who died with unsatisfied desires. A *bhuta* (demon) comes from the soul of an adult who died young or violently; *preta* (ghost) is the spirit of a child who died in infancy or was born deformed. Female spirits are ghosts of childless women or unhappy widows. *Bhuta-preta* hover between the human world and the world of ancestral spirits.

Until they have been judged, paid their karmic debts, and are allowed into the ancestral spirits world, *bhuta-preta* seek a human to enter, dominate, and make sick. Many people take these spirits for granted, and encounters with the spirit world are not considered hallucinations. But actual possession does carry a social stigma because the type of people Hindu culture considers especially susceptible to possession include the lustful, idle, impotent, bankrupt, recently widowed, and the relatives of prostitutes and convicts.

◆

—Mary Orr, "India Sketches"

"Ah, come on," I chide.

"Forget it. I'm not going with you.... My grandmother wouldn't lie about something like that. She was too religious to make up a story about the gods."

His grandmother once saw a black beast moving swiftly along the edge of the river. At first she had no idea what it was, but when it raised its head above the treetops she knew it was a *burru*. She ran and hid, saying prayer after prayer. Like a python, the beast eats its dinner, usually an elephant, in one gulp. The earthen mounds in the marsh are its dung heaps, each containing the skeleton of a devoured animal.

"Those mounds are sacred," Shankar says, pointing into the marsh.

"Holy shit!"

"Cool it! This is no place for jokes. The area is taboo, man, taboo. Let's split."

"Give me thirty minutes?" I entreat.

Shankar consents, but he won't participate in my survey of the flora and fauna. I wade into the ankle-deep water and head for the widgeons. After a couple of yards I slip into a trench and plunge up to my neck in water, so I swim to one of the sacred mounds. The birds are shrieking horrifically. What happened to the sweet, inviting chirping? I leap for the next mound, miss, and fall flat on my face, mouth in ooze.

"Had enough?" Shankar calls.

I'm about to concede when my legs start to disappear into the soft bottom. I recall this feeling from a trip up the Congo River years ago. Once the muck is over your knees, it's nearly impossible to get out. I grab frantically for the reeds and slowly inch out on my belly.

"Now I'm ready to go," I confess, spitting out mud.

"Ugh! Look at you. Leeches, leeches, everywhere. Serves you right," Shankar rejoins.

We use cigarettes to burn them off. Shankar attacks those on my back while I go after the suckers in my armpits and crotch.

"Hold still. Don't move," Shankar advises, removing one from my left ear.

A mile farther on, near the mouth of a small tributary, we hear a loud splash. What was that? The answer arcs through the air: it's a Ganges dolphin. We ship the paddles and wait for it to reappear. The mammal is nearly seven feet long with a snout like a barracuda and dull black skin. Ganges dolphins differ form their salt-water cousins not only in appearance but also in behavior; neither playful nor gregarious, they surface only for air, exposing their tiny eyes and chiseled teeth.

Since leaving Dibrugarh, the turtle catchers are the only people we've encountered. But Shankar is quick to remind me that many people are probably watching us. We're in the middle of the Badlands.

"This is where that boat got robbed, don't you think? The captain said they were near the mouth of a small tributary," Shankar recalls, adding that the *dacoits* attacked him not far from here.

As the sky turns purple, we begin to search for a safe place to camp. We don't want to sleep on the shore, and the only islands we pass are too wet, barely a foot above water. We keep paddling, hoping to find other boats or a *ghat* not shown on the maps. After the incident in the whirlpool, we resolved not to travel at night. Yet here we are paddling by the light of a quarter moon, able to see only a few yards off the bow. Every time I'm ready to pitch the tent, Shankar finds something wrong with the place. When he wants to stop, I demand that we push on. We're both hungry and irritable, but our bickering ends when we sight a campfire. We paddle toward it cautiously, trying to be quiet, picking up speed as we discern the lines of a fishing boat, about fifty feet long, with a bluff bow and wineglass stern. The massive rudder is made of a latticework of teak boards. On deck a fire dances above the lip of an oil drum hanging by davits. No one appears to be aboard.

"Hell-o…. Hell-o. Can we come aboard? Hell-o…. "

Silence. I shine my flashlight up the curve of the sheer to the deckhouse. The light catches the eyes of five men huddled in the shadows. I lower the beam and see three knives. I douse the light and we're about to paddle off when someone shouts in Bengali, "Go away."

"Phew," Shankar exhales in relief. He responds, "We're friends, not robbers. Look! Look at him." He takes the flashlight and shines it on my face. "A *firang*. He's a *firang*."

I hear the men gasp. Shankar continues, "We need a place to sleep."

They confer privately while we stand in our boat, holding on to their rail. One man keeps shaking his head. Finally a decision is made.

"You can come aboard…. Leave your knives behind."

A crewman bends over the side and gives us a hand up. None of them has seen a westerner before, and the man helping me won't release his grip. Another crewman holds a kerosene lamp to my face, raising and lowering the wick as he moves the light.

"Hmmm," he muses, adding something Shankar doesn't understand that causes the crew to explode with laughter. Whatever the joke, it breaks the tension.

"My name is Gopal. Welcome," says the captain. "We were ready to kill you. We thought you were *dacoits*."

I thank him for his restraint and present them with Michael Jackson lighters. The captain, wanting to reciprocate, motions for us to sit down. He scurries into the cabin and returns with a small paper bag.

"Dreams," he announces.

The fire is lowered from the davits and brought amidships, where we gather to talk. They're all from Lalgola, a town on the Ganges in West Bengal. Gopal, afflicted with a tubercular cough, is almost thirty years old; the others are in their teens or early twenties. All have thick, callused hands. There are no winches or motors aboard; their arms alone pull in the 150-foot nets.

"This boat," Gopal declares proudly, "our home, was built in 1953, and it's still in good shape. My father helped build her.… He was a good fisherman and we worked the Ganges together for years. I grew up on this boat."

The boat, made of teak, is double-planked below the water line. The mast is a debarked babul tree stepped far forward, like that on a catboat. However, it's used exclusively as a towing stanchion; no sail has ever been hanked to it. An arched roof of thatch, tin, and bamboo covers the foredeck; all fishing is done from the aft quarter, where the deck is flat and open. The boat's name is *Lucky*, but Gopal has often thought of changing it.

"Years ago my father and I

> *M*osquitoes are bad news in West Bengal. Apart from the obvious problems of malaria—the disease was rife in rural areas north of Calcutta—the insects were also an indirect cause of house fires. Due to a sudden plague of mosquitoes in the district of Midnapore, villagers had taken to lighting fires on the floor in the middle of their wood and straw huts. The smoke worked splendidly at keeping the mosquitoes away, but more often than not the fires got out of hand reducing the huts to ashes. It was not unknown for whole villages to be burned to the ground.
>
> ◆
>
> —Peter Holt, *In Clive's Footsteps*

were fishing. Just the two of us. I was asleep and when I got up, he was gone…. My mother cried and cried. She said that is what happens to all fishermen. He heard the river calling to him."

Gopal assumed command at the age of seventeen, and for the first few years he was moderately successful. That was when the fish population of the Ganges was still thriving.

"But each year we caught less. Now there is nothing for the nets in the Ganges."

This is his second season on the Brahmaputra, and it may be his last. As an outsider working the Assamese waterways, he must pay the state a 40 percent tax on his catch. That's the law, anyway; the actual tariff may vary according to the official on duty.

"If Shiva is kind, the tax man will take only four of ten fish. Sometimes he takes six. We have no one to protect us. We are not Assamese, so no one listens to our complaints."

Sunal, a lanky man who should wear glasses but doesn't, recounts an incident from two weeks ago. They were fishing downstream and had brought their catch to Sibsagar market. The tax man took most of their fish.

"We went to the police and they told us to leave if we didn't like it here. The tax man is Assamese, the police are Assamese, and we are Bengalis. That is not good for us."

A hush comes over the boat when I ask about the river pirates. The *dacoits* have left them alone, but the fishermen are superstitious and are afraid that mentioning the *dacoits* will ruin their luck. Gopal does tell us that spies in the market tip off the *dacoits*, identifying which boat has delivered a rich load.

We've dipped into the dream bag three times, postponing dinner until everyone's stomach is growling. At Gopal's command the food is prepared. Lobas, the twelve-year-old cook and apprentice fisherman, takes charge. He greases the pots and reaches into the hold, pulling out five containers of spices: hot chili peppers, green peppers, black peppers, more chili peppers, and curry powder. He takes some of each pepper and pulverizes everything with a porcelain rolling pin.

"The juice," he confides, "you must get all the juice."

While the ingredients simmer in mustard oil, Lobas dices some potatoes as a special treat for us. He adds water and drops in seven small fish called *bhangnon-mas*. After bringing the pot to a boil, he adds two fistfuls of curry powder. A half hour later, when the rice is cooked, we wolf down the food.

"Delicious," I say to Lobas, who beams.

Slowly at first and then with a numbing intensity, the spices release their power. I ask for the water bucket. My insides feel as if they're melting and dripping out through my pores.

"Ah, you really do like it," Lobas says, watching me down a quart of water.

In the morning *Lahey-Lahey* looks woefully small next to the high-sided fishing boat. The crew of the *Lucky* call our boat *Susek*, Bengali for dolphin, but Gopal is more critical: "It's no bigger than a Christian's coffin! May the gods smile on you.... You paddle a toy."

With this encouragement, we bid farewell and head out into the morning mist, hoping to make Sibsagar before dark. Several hours later we near the spot where the *dacoits* had attacked Shankar. For the first time he recounts the details of that day.

"I was lost in those islands over there, next to the bank. I took the wrong turn and followed a stream that led to a sandbank. I saw this guy standing in the shore and asked for directions.... When I got near him, he started running at me.... Two more came out from hiding. Phew, I was lucky. I hit one with my paddle and jumped aboard. Then, man oh man, I rowed like crazy.... The next morning I took the bus home."

The story gives me an idea, and I suggest that we pretend the *dacoits* are closing in for an attack. "How fast can we go?"

We stroke double-time, thrusting our paddles into the river, pulling as hard as we can. *Lahey-Lahey* surges forward. We pour it on and pull triple-time. The boat slices cleanly through the water, no longer staggering between strokes. In rapid fire our paddles punch the surface. *Whack! Whack! Whack!* Shadows barely keep up with us. Everything rushes by—the shoreline is a blur of jungle colors. Faster, I want to go faster. I feel invigorated by every stroke;

all that matters is movement. One moment blends into another. Faster! Ever faster into the unknown. I feel the pink duck is nearby, hiding just beyond view.

"Whoa! Look at that!" Shankar exclaims, ending our sprint.

"Keep going. Faster!" I urge.

"Check it out, man. Ahead," he says, pointing to someone walking along the beach.

I snap back. "Sorry.... oh, yeah, I see him."

Shankar takes the binoculars for a closer look. "Well, dude," he drawls, watching the lonely figure, "he looks like a genuine fisherman. I can see a net, but we keep going and stay away from the shore, right?"

Not noticing us, the man continues walking toward a giant bamboo wishbone with a net strung across it. The contraption is suspended between a pair of thirty-foot poles. He releases a line, sending the mesh down into the water. A few minutes later he grabs a length of jute and uses his body weight as a cantilever to raise the king-size scoop. As it climbs into the air, the net shimmers like a spider's web covered in dew. Slowly the thousands of water droplets fall away, each a prism releasing miniature rainbows. The trap is effective; he catches a half dozen fish while we watch.

Beyond him a herd of water buffalo drinks from the river. The large bulls wear iron bells that clang like buoys. On the bank above the herd a shack is perched perilously close to the edge. As we round a sharp bend below it, we surprise several women bathing. Even though they're wearing saris, they're embarrassed, and we try not to stare. A little farther on we moor *Lahey-Lahey* next to five other boats. A path angles up to the flimsy building we saw from the water. Above its entrance the word "Tea" is scrawled in white paint.

The owner of the teahouse is hastily sweeping the dirt floor. He saw us coming, but he's not quite ready.

"Just one minute more.... Please be patient," he says.

"It looks fine. We don't care," I reply.

"You should care," the shopkeeper tells me. "Just a few more seconds.... "

Finally he allows us to enter his neat shop. He tells his son to leave the cook fire and alert the village that a *firang* has arrived. We sit down just as the water comes to a boil. On the wall near the kettle are postcards of exotically colored Hindu saints in various coital positions.

"They look happy," I observe.

"And we know why," he says, rubbing his fingers inside two cups.

"Where are we?" Shankar asks.

The man thinks for a moment. "Ahhh, yes. Rupahimukh Ghat. That's it. Rupahimukh Ghat."

The village is not listed on my map. He sees my confusion and adds, "Kalitas Town. That's what we call it." That name isn't listed either.

"How many people live here?"

"Several hundred. It changes. Sometimes more, sometimes less. It all depends on the blessings of the gods," he says, eyeing my notebook suspiciously.

As we drink our tea, the little shack fills with villagers of all ages. We're especially honored when the Village Council appears. Every time I ask someone's name, the answer is the same: "Kalitas." In this remote village people share food, chores, and a name.

"We are all Kalitas. We come from Kalitas. Our children are Kalitas," Kalitas tells me.

"Don't you use initials?" I ask, remembering how the Gurkhas lessened the confusion.

"What for? We know everybody. I am Big Kalitas. Over there is my father, Old Kalitas, and there is my daughter, Baby Kalitas."

I take out my Polaroid and line up the Kalitas clan for a portrait. Pleased, Big Kalitas grabs my hand and leads me away from the teahouse.

"Come, you must meet Mother Kalitas."

Only half of the village buildings survived this year's flood, and those that are left bear scars from the deluge. The high-water mark on his house touches the eaves, and sections of plaster are missing from the façade, exposing the bamboo lathing. The left side looks as if the breeze is the only thing holding it up.

"We are starting to rebuild, but we have no money." Big Kalitas sighs. "Our cows are all gone, lost to the river. Look at our fields covered in sand. It will be a year before the next harvest…everything must be tilled three, four times."

Once we're inside the two-room house, villagers crowd around the openings, vying for a good look at us. Outside the back door I can hear the *splish-splash* of milk squirting into a metal bucket. Baby Kalitas stares at me with large black eyes. She giggles when I smile at her but recoils when I go to pick her up. Mother Kalitas stands nearby, ready to strike a match the second her husband lifts a cigarette.

"During the flood," our host tells us, "the government made us leave. They took us to the hills on buses. Hundreds of us, all from different villages were kept like goats…. They promised help when we came back. Since then one helicopter has come and unloaded six bags of barley. Six bags of barley!"

As the Village Council leader, this Kalitas must deal with the complaints of all Kalitases. "Sleep is something I want but don't get," he says wistfully. He's unsure whether relief will ever come.

"Several years ago a calf was born with two heads. That was a good sign, we thought the gods were pleased with us. But you know, when I think back, the calf never knew what it was doing. One head wanted to go right, the other left. It died after a couple of months."

Daughter Kalitas, a slender teenager, brings us a tray with two cups of fresh milk and a bowl containing bread and sugar, the traditional offering of hospitality. After eating, we're led to the village center, a vacant lot where the temple once stood. The elders sit in chairs, with the oldest at the head of the group. Two men come from a nearby house with instruments, and a holy man follows, carrying an urn of water. The musicians set up and begin playing cymbals and a *khol* (drum); Priest Kalitas chants, "Water cleanses, water creates, water redeems." He digs his heels in the sand. From the depression he scoops up a handful of dirt and tosses it into the air. "This is the earth. This is our home. May Shiva bless us all."

The music grows louder as the tempo increases. Our host asks us to stay, but with several hours of daylight remaining, we decide to push on. After we have shaken hands with all the villagers, an informal procession escorts us back to the river, led by the holy man. A young girl presents me with a bouquet of wildflowers, and I bend down to kiss her cheek. Shankar puts several of the blossoms in his hair, to the delight of the Kalitases. The cymbals sound farewell. As we move downstream, a figure bolts from the crowd and runs along the bank, waving and keeping pace with *Lahey-Lahey*. It's the girl who gave us the flowers....

That night I dream I'm a bird, the wind lashing my face as I race over the water. I spot the silhouette of a fish in the water and I dive for it. *Splash!* The water cradles my body as I plunge. My form changes and scales appear; a tail develops; my gills strain for air. I can suddenly turn, dart, hover, or glide. I swim to a sunken canoe with half its planking rotted away. A school of small fish live in the stern, and I ask them about the pink-headed duck. Yes, they've just seen it and wonder how I could have missed it. Minutes ago one was dabbling along the far shore. I'm off, cutting across the river, wending my way through the islands. At the shore I crawl up the bank like a salamander and slowly regain my human form. I awake with a start, my body chilled. The campfire is out, Shankar is snoring, and the river droning. Falling back asleep is easy; I'm learning where to look for nature's prize.

Rory Nugent also contributed "The Calcutta Fowl Market" to Part I. Both stories were excerpted from his book The Search for the Pink-Headed Duck: A Journey into the Himalayas and Down the Brahmaputra.

✳

"We in India do not think the gods are far. They are all around us. They walk our streets; they come to us in dreams."

—Adilakshmi, quoted by Andrew Harvey, *Hidden Journey: A Spiritual Awakening*

Breaking the Fast

*Of pigeons, kites, and the end of Ramadan
on the rooftops of Delhi.*

IN THE LAST HOUR BEFORE THE BREAKING OF THE RAMADAN FAST, the courtyards and rooftops were filling with people. Some were lying in *charpoys*, snoozing away the last minutes before their first meal for thirteen hours. Others sat out on carpets beneath the shady trees enjoying the cool of the evening. Nearby, little boys were playing with brightly coloured diamond-shaped kites which they flew up into the warm evening breeze. They pulled sharply at the strings, then released the kites so that they flew in a succession of angular jerks, higher and higher into the pink evening sky. While most of the fliers were quietly attempting to raise their kites as high as possible into the heavens, some of the boys were engaged in battles with their neighbours. They locked strings with the kites of their enemies and attempted, by means of the ground glass glued on their strings, to cut their opponents' kites free.

Yet, on the rooftops, the kite fliers were easily outnumbered by the pigeon fanciers—

Charpoy

the *kabooter baz*—who stood on almost every terrace, hands extended into the air calling to their pigeons: *Aao! Aao! Aao!* (Come! Come! Come!) Above them, the sky was full of the soft rush of beating wings, clouds of pigeons dipping and diving in and out of the domes and through the minarets. The flocks whirled and wheeled, higher and higher, before nose-diving suddenly down towards their home terrace on the command of their flier. Some came to rest on the bamboo pigeon frames—horizontal slats of trellising raised on a pole—that several of the fliers had raised above their roofs.

In England the mention of pigeon fanciers brings to mind Geordies and flat caps and Newcastle Brown Ale. In Delhi the sport has very different associations. It is remembered as the civilized oldpastime of the Mughal court. Its laws were codified by Abu'l Fazl in the *A'in-i-Akabari* and its delights and dangers were illustrated by the Mughal miniaturists. Its arts were mastered by, among others, the last of the Great

We were admiring the towering minaret of Jami Masjid when two Belgian women asked if we'd accompany them up the tower, since women alone were not permitted. Up we went, through a claustrophobic stairwell, wondering if we'd ever reach the top. When we did, the view was stupendous. The Red Fort shimmered nearby in the setting sun, golden clouds hovering like halos. But kids kept emerging from the stairwell like termites; within minutes the tower was jammed, people pushing, arguing, getting edgy. We were pressed close to a knee-high railing with nothing between us and the plaza below but 120 feet of that golden light. We began to worry that someone might go over the edge, perhaps an infidel or two. We squirmed back to the stairwell, finally slipping into the center of the crowd and down. We emerged, immensely relieved. Outside the mosque we discovered a man selling bullwhips. We wished we'd seen him on the way in, but we bought two anyway.

♦

—James O'Reilly and Larry Habegger, "Fools in Delhi"

Moguls, the Emperor Bahadur Shah Zafar. It is still one of the great passions of the Old Delhi-*wallahs*, and one of the many habits which distinguishes them from their Punjabi neighbours in the New City.

Fardine took us to the edge of his terrace, where his own pigeons were kept in a large coop. He opened the wire-mesh door and scattered some grain in the floor. Immediately the pigeons began to strut and flutter about, billing and cooing with pleasure. As they emerged from their coop, Fardine pointed out the different varieties in his collection.

"These are the *Shiraji*," he said pointing to two birds with reddish wings and black chests. "They are the fighter pigeons. This is a very good pair: they have won many battles. And you see these?" He was now pointing at some large pigeons, coloured very light blue-grey. "These are the *Kabuli Kabooter*. They are the strongest pigeons in Delhi. They are not very fast but they can fly very high and for two to four hours—sometimes more. And these red ones: the are *Lal Khal*, along with the *Avadi Golay* they are the fastest of all *kabooter*."

With a swift movement he picked up one of the *Lal Khals* and kissed it on its head. Then, turning it over, he pointed at the miniature bracelets he had fixed to its ankles. "Look!" he said. "They wear *ghungroos* like a dancer!"

Fardine took out a tin can from a cupboard beside the coop. In it was grain mixed with *ghee* (clarified butter). This was obviously the pigeons' favourite delicacy: at the sight of the tin can, the pigeons leapt in the air and fluttered above us waiting to dive down on the first grains; others landed flirtatiously on Fardine's arms and shoulders. The boy threw the sticky grain up into the air and the pigeons swooped down after it. The birds on Fardine's shoulders maneuvered their way down to the edge of the can where they sat on its rim, greedily pecking at the grains. Others sat on Fardine's open palm eating from his hand.

When the birds had eaten their fill, Fardine stood back and shouted: "Ay-ee!" Immediately with a great flutter of wings the pigeons rose into the air and circled above the terrace. When

Fardine whistled the birds shot off in the direction of the Jami Masjid; another whistle and they returned. Fardine waved his arms and the birds rose high into the air; at the cry of *Aao! Aao! Aao!* they obediently returned. With another flutter of wings, the birds came in to land on their coop.

"These tricks are easy to learn," Fardine shrugging his shoulders. "But to become a master—a *Khalifa*—can take twenty years of training. A master can teach his pigeons to capture another man's flock and drive it home like a herd of sheep. He can make his birds fly like an arrow—in a straight line, in single file—or can direct them to any place he likes, in any formation. There are perhaps five thousand *kabooter baz* in Delhi, but there are only fifty *Khalifa*."

As Fardine spoke, there was a sudden report, like a loud explosion. Seconds later the muezzin of a hundred Delhi mosques called the faithful to prayer with a loud cry of "Allaaaaah hu-Akbar!" The sun had set. The fast was over. It was time for the *iftar*.

William Dalrymple also contributed "A Sufi Spring" to Part I, "The Other Raj" to Part II, and "Beyond Turkman Gate" to Part IV. This selection was excerpted from his book City of Djinns: A Year in Delhi.

★

In the middle of the afternoon in Delhi it simply poured, the hardest rain of the year. I discovered that Jimmy, who is only nine, had taken the big black umbrella and gone for a walk! When he came home an hour later, by which time I was getting worried about him, the streets were so flooded, he was soaked to the bone, of course.

"Where have you been?" I asked, relieved and irritated.

He said, "I went down to the *nullah* [open drainage] by the bridge and the corn parcher's son—he's about my age—was sitting all huddled up and his fire had gone out. So I sat down beside him and we both got under the umbrella and sat there. Then his father and his mother and his little brother came. His mother was the most pregnantest lady I ever saw. His little brother didn't have anything on and he got under the umbrella, too. And they were all shivering so hard. I wasn't shivering. Then they all went away so I came home."

—Betty Ann Webster, "Sharing"

THALIA ZEPATOS

In the Ladies' Compartment

The community of women is alive
and well in India.

A MANGO MOON RIPENED AS THE DAY'S HEAT DRIFTED INTO THE
South Indian night. I fidgeted on the noisy train platform at
Ernakulum Junction, alongside the northbound express that was
to carry me on the overnight journey up the west coast of the subcontinent to Bombay. Under the watchful eyes of a six-year-old
vendor, I drained the last of the *chai* and returned the glass to his
waiting hands.

The platform buzzed with now-familiar railway station life.
Indian travelers lugging parcels of all shapes and sizes picked their
way between sleeping figures huddled under shawls. Wealthier
travelers paraded before their hired coolies, who calmly balanced
metal suitcases and trunks on their red turbans as they followed in
single file. Men and women lined up at water stands, washing away
the heat and dust of the day. *Chai* and coffee *wallahs* bellowed their
wares, each toting a huge aluminum kettle in one hand, a bucket
of repeatedly rinsed glasses in the other. Food vendors chanted
their way alongside the train, exchanging fruit and chili-laced
snacks for one- and two-rupee notes pushed between the metal
bars that crossed each window of the ancient train cars.

I'd traveled over five thousand kilometers by train during six months of wandering India. The second-class trains were always hot, the seats often crowded, the air dusty. Riding down the east coast and up the west, I bounced babies on my lap, practiced new words in Telugu, Malayalam, and Kokkani, and traded fruit for homemade meals. Tiny villages ringed by rice paddies and banana plantations passed outside the window in an unending panorama of rural Indian life.

Trains in the south provided an unusual treat—a small "ladies' compartment" at the end of each car, designed to carry six or eight women traveling without the protection of a male. They seemed unneeded for these strong Indian women who dealt matter-of-factly with numbing adversity. I was thankful, however, that the Indian Railway system had provided me an exclusive place to meet Indian women without hovering husbands, fathers, and brothers edging in to control the conversation. My previous journeys in the "ladies' compartments" had been the scene of some of my most delightful and instructive encounters.

On one twelve-hour ride across the shimmering heat of the Thar desert to the fortress city of Jaisalmer, I was surrounded by fierce-looking, bejeweled, Rajasthani women. They frankly reviewed my foreign looks and dress, their black eyes wandering slowly from my wavy brown hair to my ringless toes.

I returned the interest, pointing to their red and blue patterned skirts and the scores of ivory bracelets that climbed past their elbows and under the sleeves of their tight-fitting bodices. With shy smiles, they admired my silver ankle bracelets and, one by one, displayed theirs. They removed their necklaces and earrings with girlish giggles and adorned me like a doll. Riotous laughter met my polite refusal of a tattooed matron's offer to pierce my nose. Heads shook with approval as a young woman with high cheekbones and a lustrous smile combed and oiled my hair. As we approached Jaisalmer, we scrambled to return jewelry and sandals to their owners.

Days later, as I wandered through the walled town, these same women drew me into their houses, painting elaborate designs on my palms and feet with henna that lasted for weeks.

$\mathscr{A}$ man in a white coat comes by to take dinner orders. There are two choices: vegetarian or nonvegetarian *thali*, the Hindi word for the steel trays that the food comes on. A *thali* really means that rice, lentils, and bread will be served along with a main dish or two.

The orders are wired to a station ahead, and the *thalis* are picked-up during a stop and distributed. After dinner the trays are collected and off-loaded further up the line.

Recently I've been on a train where the *thali* system has been replaced by food in tinfoil dishes. After dinner, I wondered what to do with the trash. Normally I don't balk at throwing it out the window, since food is usually served in leaf-dishes and tea often comes in disposable clay cups. But tinfoil? Go right ahead, said my two Indian seat mates, one of them a botanical scientist who preserves endangered plants for a living; it will be recycled.

◆

—Cameron Barr, "Night-Train Glimpses of India," *The Christian Science Monitor*

A shrill from the steam locomotive jolted me and urged me inside for the long trip to Bombay. This "ladies' compartment" was crowded, with eight or nine women sharing seats for six. We smiled and nodded greetings in Hindi; no one offered a word of English. As a wiry young woman in a tattered green sari closed the door that separated the compartment from the rest of the train, I glanced around and wondered what new play would unfold during this night's ride.

While the train pulled out of the station, I was preoccupied with the necessity to transfer in Mangalore in the middle of the night. With sign language and a few words, I indicated that I was headed for Bombay. A confident, middle-aged woman with silver streaks highlighting her thick black braid alternately pointed her finger at my chest and hers, repeating "Bombay" with each movement. Yes, yes, we both had the same destination. She then started the process anew, this time saying "Mangalore" while using sign language to pantomime that we would get down and change trains there. I hoisted my pack and followed it up to the overhead bunk. I folded myself into sleep, hoping to keep her in sight during the late-night transfer.

Dozens of jangling bangle bracelets sounded a tinny alarm as a brown hand shook me repeatedly. It was 3 a.m. and I struggled awake as the slowing of the train's momentum signaled the approach of Mangalore station. My protector picked up her own small bag, pulled my backpack from the overhead rack, grabbed my hand and hauled me down from my berth. It seemed that keeping her in sight would not be difficult.

We wandered up and down the platform in a zigzag pattern to avoid sleeping travelers. Carrying her cloth bag without trouble, she headed straight for the corner where the red-shirted coolies were dozing and negotiated with one until he accepted her offer. He then led us along an empty track until we came to a spot that looked to me like any other. His fee paid, he floated away

We'd been traveling for hours in fits and starts, lurching from station to station, stopping in the middle of nowhere for no apparent reason. The steam locomotive spewed ash and bits of coal which blew through the window on the wind, soiling the seats, our clothing, our bodies. As darkness fell I saw sparks flying with the grit, something I'd never noticed on these ancient Indian trains. At night the smoke was alive with fire, whole constellations of stars riding off on the breeze.

A short while later we stopped again, the locomotive shut down, the smoke and ash cleared, but the sparks continued, and as I leaned out into the sticky heat I realized they weren't sparks at all, but the air was thick with fireflies.

◆

—Larry Habegger,
"To the South"

as she triumphantly smiled and pulled me down to squat beside her. She indicated that we would wait in that spot for the Bombay train.

I decided to put my faith in her, discarding the notion of finding a railway employee for official verification, and settled down to wait. Other travelers emerged from the night and spread their bundles to claim sections of the platform. Their low murmurs were silenced by the deep rumbling of the approaching train. As the steam-belching locomotive screeched into the station, people and luggage multiplied around us. Suddenly we were at the head of a pulsating crowd. Madame, as I thought of her, firmly stood her ground and barked at anyone who tried to usurp my spot. I knew that none of us transferring from other trains would have reserved seats; now I realized that many might not even make it into the train.

The air brakes hissed and we bounded up the steps of the car still lumbering slowly before us. I stopped short as we entered the corridor; every spot was already filled, there was simply nowhere to go. Madame propelled me forward as I struggled to keep my pack from battering other passengers. The first compartment we passed had twelve or fourteen women sardined into a space designed for six. As we pushed our way forward I realized that *every* compartment was a ladies' compartment. The entire train car was packed with hundreds of Indian women—matrons, teenagers, and tiny grandmothers shushing girl and boy children. The ultimate Ladies Compartment.

My advocate moved ahead of me, regally examined the two benches that faced each other in the next section and parted the women on one bench with a sweep of her mighty arm. She parked me firmly between those on one bench and inserted herself opposite me. A howl went up from the women on both sides. Color rose to my face, and I started to relinquish my place, but Madame pushed me back down and answered each argument with a quick retort. A quiet woman wrapped in a blue sari edged in gold brocade murmured in clipped English, "She is informing everyone that you are a visitor to our country and we must show you hospitality." Grateful for a translator, I implored, "Please apologize for me and explain that I will sit in the corridor."

As the argument proceeded, a growing faction seemed to be urging acceptance. To make more room, some of the children were sent to join the luggage in the upper berth. The train moved out of the station, and everyone became resigned to our presence. Arms and parcels were adjusted for the most comfortable fit; several women lifted the ends of their saris over their eyes as they prepared for sleep. I tipped my head to get a better view down the corridor; it looked like a refugee train, a scene from a movie where all the men were gone and only women and children remained.

Then a single masculine figure began working his way toward us from the opposite end of the car. A grizzled old man dressed for colder climes in a green wool army-surplus coat, he lumbered down the aisle, a vintage musket resting in the crook of his arm. Stopping before each compartment, he peered nearsightedly at the faces crowded inside and then moved on. As he inspected our section, I questioned the English-speaking woman again. "Who is he?"

"A guard hired to protect the women."

Incredible, I thought, and smiled at him. He stared. Perhaps he didn't encounter too many foreigners in the second-class train.

Then he said something

*F*or all its frustrations, life in the subcontinent could never sink to dullness. What is more remarkable is India's capacity to make even the most absurd incidents seem perfectly plausible—my Swedish friend selling off his belongings, for example, to meditate beside the Ganges. Such transformations appear quite natural after only a few weeks under the Indian sun. The sight of an ox munching on the rug in your hotel lobby might not merit a flinch.

I began to worry, in fact, that my eyes were adjusting too much, that I'd return home to find the light muted, and everything a shade less interesting than before.

◆

—Peter Jon Lindberg, "The Confounding Allure of India," *The New York Times*

urgent, lifted the gun, and pointed it straight at me. The women around me all started chattering at once, with Madame trying to yell louder than the rest. My translator tilted her head to one side as she listened, and then said in a low voice, "He thinks you are a man and has ordered you out of this car." A moment later, she added, "The others are arguing whether you are a man or a woman."

I laughed briefly at this turn of events, until he jerked the gun at my insolence. I wore neither the long braid, nor the sari or knee-length tunic over trousers of the other women on the train. My close-cropped hair, baggy pants, and collarless white cotton Indian man's shirt were chosen for comfort, ease of travel, and to help me avoid harassment. I stood and rocked steadily among the jumbled feet and discarded sandals of my travel-mates in the narrow space between the two facing benches. Momentarily turning my back to the old fellow, I pulled the baggy shirt taut under both my arms and showed the women the outline of my chest. They roared in laughter and approval, and pushed the old man and his gun away.

As dawn approached, food and hot *chai* were produced from among the folds of bags and parcels. The story of the guard and the foreigner passed in waves up and down the train, the punch line always enacted amid gales of laughter. Madame seemed especially proud of me as women and girls craned their necks or shyly walked over to see me in person.

When we reached Bombay, Madame was reluctant to turn me loose. She walked me to the front of the station and negotiated fiercely with the autorickshaw driver for my fare to the General Post Office. Then, she gave me a long lecture in rapid dialect. Her accompanying gestures advised me to be careful of men driving rickshaws, on the streets, in buses, or just about anywhere. Despite the language difference, her message was clear. She seemed to be saying that if I got scared or had a problem, I should always rely on women for help.

Thalia Zepatos is a political consultant and writer who lives in Portland, Oregon. She is the author of A Journey of One's Own: Uncommon

Advice for the Independent Woman Traveler, *from which this is excerpted, and* Adventures in Good Company: The Complete Guide to Women's Tours and Outdoor Trips, *both published by Eighth Mountain Press, Portland, Oregon.*

★

She spent hours trying to teach us how to wear saris. It looked so easy the first time she demonstrated. She held the six metres of cloth in her delicate hands, showing us how to determine which side should be the border. She then tied a knot in the opposite side and tucked it under her skirt. Deftly she wrapped the cloth around her waist. Resembling a goddess in the temple statues, she held the length of cloth out like the wing of a butterfly in her left hand, and with swift finger movements folded it until it fell in perfect folds. This section she draped over her left shoulder then, with the same graceful finger movements folded the remainder of the cloth, tucking it around near her waist. The pleats flowed like a waterfall down to her feet.

It looked simple, until we tried. The knot was easy enough to make, but draping the full length of cloth around our waists and trying to keep it from falling while attempting to make folds was difficult, to say the least. About sixteen ladies stood in the room dripping with perspiration. Our fingers did not move gracefully like hers. I could not understand. I use chopsticks, I knit and sew, but I never did learn to drape the sari. With incredible patience she explained the process again and again. "Don't worry, it took us a long time to learn, and we have been wearing them since we were sixteen."

—Nesta Rovina, "A Love Story"

✦ ✦ ✦

Reading the Leaves

Do you really want to know the future?

I HAD ONE FINAL MISSION BEFORE I RETURNED TO MADRAS. Ramesh suggested that if I wanted to discover more of the secrets of India—and, indeed, myself—I should go to a Nadi reading.

The Nadi is the world's most mysterious system of astrological prediction. The Nadi dates from around two thousand years ago when a *rishi* called Brighu produced a vast series of personal horoscopes on palm leaves called *saraswathi*, after the goddess of knowledge. He dictated his predictions to a team of scribes, who wrote them down in Mundu Tamil, the ancient form of Tamil.

Rishi Brighu is said to have had the power of divine insight and he was able to write down the past, present, and future lives of individuals, who would make their stay on this planet in years to come.

It seems difficult to believe, but the Nadi readers claim there is a palm leaf for nearly everyone in the world. It seems mathematically impossible that Brighu would have had the time to write down the past, present and future of billions of people. But the Nadi readers counter this argument by saying that many people share the same palm leaves. Therefore, on that basis there are perhaps thousands of people out there with the same past, present, and future as yourself. Likewise, Brighu based his philosophy on the fact that when a person died his or her spirit would pass to another person.

The Nadi differs from other horoscopes in that it uses no intuitive, instinctive skills of clairvoyancy. First you provide your date of birth and an impression of your thumbprint—the right thumb for males, the left for females. Then you are asked a few questions as a sort of index: Are your parents still alive? Do you have brothers and sisters? Then the reader looks for the palm leaf corresponding to you. All the Nadi reader does is relate exactly what is written on the palm leaf. Nothing else. Ramesh was able to read the ancient Mundu Tamil script. When his Nadi was read a few years ago, he asked to look at the palm leaf afterwards. "What the man had just told me was exactly the same as what was written down," he said. "Just from my thumb print, the palm leaf got my whole family history absolutely accurate as well as my life to that point. As to whether the future was accurate, I have yet to find out."

If you don't believe in horoscopes, then all this will sound like nonsense. But it must be said that the Nadi is one of the great mysteries of India. And Indians take their readings very seriously indeed.

The Brighu Samhita, or collection, was duplicated 150 years ago. And one of the sets of inscriptions had ended up in the little town of Vaithishwaran Koil, thirty miles south of Pondi. The palm leaves were kept in a small terraced house in the centre of town.

When I turned up, a minibus load of rich Indians from Madras were crowded on the verandah waiting to have their leaves read. A man in the office seemed amazed that an Englishman had heard about the place. He arranged for me to see a reader immediately. The problem was that no one spoke much English. Help appeared in the form of a well-to-do tea-planter and his wife from Ootacamund, the hill station on the western boundary of Tamil Nadu. They had travelled 250 miles specially to have their fortunes read. They spoke good English and they agreed to sit in on my reading and translate what the reader told me.

We sat down on the floor in a large room with shuttered windows. It was dark and gloomy and lit by a single candle. The Nadi reader was called Mr. Chellian. He sat on a cushion behind a low lectern. He took my thumbprint and asked a few questions about my family. Then he disappeared into a backroom and returned with a set of palm leaves. They were long strips, measured about one inch by a foot, and tied together with leather thongs. They were covered in the neat, tiny script of Mundu Tamil.

Mr. Chellian flicked through the leaves and came to the one that corresponded to me. He began reading it. I have to admit that although he was not entirely accurate about my childhood and immediate past, he got most of it right. It galled me to be reminded, for example, of my lack of academic study at school. He also correctly identified my father's occupation—farmer—and informed me, correctly again, that my sister was an actress.

Mr. Chellian moved to my future...and then to the end of my future. And this was the bit I had not wanted to hear.

He lowered his voice. My interpreter, the tea-planter, did the same. Suddenly everything had become very solemn. I had a nasty feeling about what was going to happen next. The Nadi reader continued. The tea-planter translated: "At the age of...you will leave this life. It will be in a hospital on the...of...and you will go peacefully." That was enough for me. I stood up, thanked everyone for their time and handed Mr. Chellian his fee. He looked puzzled. Why was I in such a rush to go? I muttered something about needing a breath of fresh air. Not for a moment had he thought there was anything wrong in telling a person when and where he was going to die.

And that put an end to my metaphysical meanderings. It was time to return to Madras and get stuck back into Clive's trail. Bala was preparing to leave his yoga studies to fly back to Australia and I promised Ramesh that I would look him up again before I left India. I was sad to leave Pondicherry. The place had given me an insight into what India could offer the world. That nothing should be clear-cut; that we should take nothing for granted; that it is too easy to explain events as mere coincidence; that the forces of destiny are guiding us all.

Peter Holt is the great-great-great-great-great-grandson of Robert Clive, who defeated Siraj-ud-daula, the Nawab of Bengal, along with his French supporters at the Battle of Plassey in 1757. Clive's victory ushered in almost two hundred years of British rule, and Holt's book, In Clive's Footsteps, *from which this story is excerpted, is a journey in search of his ancestor. He lives in London, where he has worked as a reporter and editor at several newspapers.*

✳

There exists in India a secret knowledge based on sounds and the differences of vibration according to the planes of consciousness. If we pronounce the sound *OM,* for example, we clearly feel its vibrations around the head centers, while the sound *RAM* affects the navel center. And since each of our centers of consciousness is in direct contact with a plane, we can, by the repetition *(japa)* of certain sounds, come into contact with the corresponding plane of consciousness. This is the basis on an entire spiritual discipline called *"tantric"* because it originates from sacred texts called *Tantra.* The basic or essential sounds that have the power to establish the contact are called *mantras.* The *mantras,* always secret and given to the disciple by his Guru, are of all kinds (there are many levels within each plane of consciousness), and may serve the most contradictory purposes. By combining certain sounds, one can at the lower levels of consciousness, generally the vital level, come in contact with the corresponding forces and acquire many strange powers: some mantras can kill (in five minutes, with violent vomiting), some mantras can strike with precision a particular part or organ of the body, some mantras can cure, some mantras can start a fire, protect, or cast spells. This type of magic or chemistry of vibrations derives simply from conscious handling of the lower vibrations. But there is a higher magic, which also derives from handling vibrations, on higher planes of consciousness. This is poetry, music, the spiritual mantras of the *Upanishads* and the *Veda,* the mantras given by a Guru to his disciple to help him come consciously into direct contact with a special plane of consciousness, a particular force or divine being. In this case the sound holds in itself the power of experience and realization—it is a sound that makes one see.

—Satprem, *Sri Aurobindo or The Adventure of Consciousness*

★ ★ ★

Serenity 101

A lesson in self-understanding.

BEFORE HEADING NORTH, I HAD SEVERAL MATTERS TO TAKE CARE of, a few chores, things to buy. I especially wanted to visit the yoga school near Bombay, where I had studied years before. I bought my ticket for the evening train to Lonavla and made my way to a compartment. Of the three seats inside, one was occupied by a bald heavy-set mustached burgher, who, it was obvious, would not wake up until his station. Another man sat at the opposite end of the brown upholstered seat, reading a newspaper.

"May I sit here?" I asked.

"Yes, by all means," he said, reading.

After several minutes, he put the newspaper on his seat and went out. The train was not yet ready to leave. Shortly afterward, another man entered the compartment.

"Is this seat taken?" he said, pointing to the empty space.

"I don't know."

"Then I will join you. You are American?"

"Yes."

"My name is Akram. What are you doing in India?"

"I am interested in the Ganges and in Indian culture."

"Have you studied yoga and meditation?"

"A little, but...not enough."

"That is very good, that you avail yourself of our great traditions. I myself am a student of Krishnamurti. Perhaps you have read some of his holy books; he writes in English."

"No."

"He is a holy man, but a secular holy man. He wears western clothes and travels around the world giving talks. Basically, his message is: to develop the awareness of yourself—of your moods and the habits that control you. By doing this, a person overcomes his anger and loses all of his antisocial behavior."

"How long have you been a follower of Krishnamurti?"

"All these many years," he said.

At that moment, the man who had left the newspaper returned to the compartment. "Excuse me," he said, "but that is my seat. I left my newspaper there to reserve it."

"I'm sorry," said Akram. "I didn't realize. However, this is a friend of mine, and I would like to talk to him for the journey. Perhaps you could find a place elsewhere."

"My luggage is already up there in the rack, so if you don't mind..."

"I *do* mind," said Akram, crossing his legs.

"Look. Here is my newspaper and that is my valise. What more proof do you want?"

"I don't care," said Akram standing up. "Find another place."

"This is my seat," reiterated the other man.

"Off," shouted Akram, his tiny black eyes flickering like a snake. "Get off or I'll throw you off!"

> "*I*'m losing my serenity," I hissed at a bank clerk after having spent all day trying to untangle currency problems which would have taken ten minutes to solve at home.
>
> "Madam," he answered, "it takes many years to attain serenity. One does not lose it in a day."
>
> ◆
>
> —Cheryl Bentley, "Enchanted"

At that point, I offered to leave. But before I knew it, Akram had laid his hands on the other man, and the two then set about punching each other.

I managed to pry them apart, whereupon the other man scooped up his newspaper and valise, and left the compartment.

"I am sorry," said Akram, smoothing out his white shirt and brown trousers. He sat down beside me and resumed his composure. "We were talking about..."

"Krishnamurti."

"Yes. It is very difficult to develop self-understanding. But once a person does, he loses his selfishness and egotism and becomes free of anger."

And so we spent the next two hours, talking about Krishnamurti and the serenity one achieves through self-understanding.

Steven Darian has been to India several times to pursue his studies in Eastern and Western thought. He studied Indian religion and languages at the University of Pennsylvania and has written articles on Indian culture. He is currently a professor at Rutgers University, Camden, New Jersey. This piece was excerpted from his book, A Ganges of the Mind: A Journey on the River of Dreams.

⋆

Before my visit to the ashram in Southern Kerala, my knowledge of yoga consisted of browsing through manuals with photos of people bent into positions that looked downright frightening. Was the human body really meant to be able to perform like Gumby? Yet here I was in India attempting (without much success) the cobra, the locust, the plow and the wheel. These positions as interpreted by *my* body, could be renamed the pain, the torture, the agony, and the defeat.

The days were full at the ashram and the structured schedule left very little free time. Squeezed in between 5:30 a.m. and 10 p.m. were four hours of yoga (or *asanas*), three hours of meditation and chanting, two hours of lecture, one hour of "Karma Yoga" (otherwise known as chores), two meals, and two tea breaks. It all had the feel of summer camp, including a pristine lake for swimming (watch for crocodiles) and a corner café outside the ashram where you could often find desperate yogis sneaking a smoke or indulging in a large fruit salad.

—Willie Weir, "Cycling India: Letters from the Road"

NORMAN LEWIS

To the Tribal Heartland

*Few know about the many millions of tribal people living
in the forests of India's interior. The author travels
deep into these regions to visit them.*

TAPTAPANI WAS THE FRONTIER WITH SAORA TERRITORY, HOME-
land of about 400,000 members of one of India's most populous
and successful tribal peoples. They had been spread through
Orissa since before the Aryan arrival, although continually
pushed back out of the fer-
tile plains, first by outright
invasion and conquest and
later by various forms of ex-
propriation masked by legal
skulduggery of the kind still
generally practised. They
were notable for their collection over the centuries of
innumerable gods (a principal one being the earth-
worm), and for the compli-
cation and cost of their
ceremonies. It is their custom in the case of death to
conduct two funerals, the

*T*he 54 million tribals in
India are roughly the
equivalent of the combined
metropolitan populations of
New York City, Calcutta, Rio de
Janeiro, London, and Shanghai.
Put another way, this is nearly
the entire population of France,
or Italy, or Egypt, which all
weigh in at about 57 million.

◆

—JO'R and LH

second of which, a protracted affair known as the Guar ritual, had bankrupted many families.

The ladies we had seen in search of fruitfulness at Taptapani were Saoras, and the unnamed fertility god, too, was in all likelihood from their vast collection. The local girls from nearby villages belonged to a division of the race known as Sudha Saoras—*sudha* meaning clean—in recognition by their Hindu neighbours of the fact that they no longer ate the meat of the cow. At the far end of the Saora country where the high mountains had discouraged Hindu penetration, the Lanjia Saoras clung wholeheartedly to the old ways, and Ranjan said that the opportunity would arise to see them too.

We left Taptapani at dawn, climbing among the misted forests into and over a low mountain range, held up for a moment by another of India's great vistas, with yellow morning light flooding the plain streaked with the brush strokes of shadows cast by the tall palms. The first Sudha Saora village gathered shape by a stream curling through glowing fields, and we stopped, left the car and walked to it.

It was another page of an atlas turned. On the road to Taptapani India had imitated Mexico; here were laid out the softer splendours of one of the countries by the China Sea. Here were the sago palms, first sighted from above, now seen to have pots fixed to their trunks below incisions from which dropped the sweet sap in which fermentation would begin on the same day. Something of the kind was to be seen in Indo-China of old where as here no serious obligations could be undertaken, no troth plighted and no contract sealed without ceremonial imbibings. Generally among the Saora the bride-price includes twenty pots of wine, and none of their innumerable ceremonies can be completed without libations. The theft of alcohol is their most serious crime, resulting in mortal retribution.

At this hour in the morning the village was the scene of intense activity, with men, women, and children at work doing odd jobs and tidying up round the houses, or out in the fields pumping up water, weeding, hoeing, grinding millet, twisting sisal fibre into rope, cleaning out irrigation ditches, and bringing in bundles of long, feathery grass with which to make or repair thatches. The place swarmed with animals, with puppies, piglets, and bantam chickens, kept—since the Sudha Saora were vegetarians—as pets.

The villagers showed their excitement at the sight of new faces, and were eager to show us round. One thing about their village stood out—its spruceness. Being outside the caste system had left the Saora with no alternative but to clean up for themselves. It was a cool place in a hot country. Unlike the Hindus, who, being basically migrants from the north, had only been on the scene for two thousand years, the Saora, having been obliged from time immemorial to defend themselves from the sun, had learned how to do it. They built themselves windowless houses with thick walls of wooden trellis plastered with mud, and two doors in line at back and front kept open to pass the air through. The thatch came as low as three feet from the ground, and was deep enough to accommodate a spacious verandah on which the family spent much of the time. The Saora took pleasure in pointing out and explaining the merits of these architectural features. They were proud of their decorative skills, leaving their walls coloured the rich maroon of the local earth and free of ornament, but carving woodwork, doors, door-posts and lintels in lively animal shapes: rampaging elephants, peacocks in flight, strutting roosters, and an occasional whimsical and inoffensive-looking tiger.

The village *Gomang*—the headman—now trotted into sight, a pleasant, twinkling little man who, said Ranjan, had taken time to slip on his ceremonial gear: a hat with white plumes, tunic, tasselled loin-cloth, training shoes, and a species of silver codpiece, worn in this region perhaps as a badge of office. He had a frank and ready answer for questions. Modhukamba, he said, contained twenty families, totalling two hundred people. They lived on cow's milk, various *pulses* they grew and the income from the sale of tussor silk cocoons—all such production being equally divided in the presence of the village god. The elections at the end of last year had provided a small cash windfall, for he had been able to negotiate a fair price for the community votes. When I showed surprise that such a transaction could be openly discussed, Ranjan explained that vote-selling was the normal practise in all such backward areas, and a vote cast without receiving a cash reward would be unheard of.

Nodding his agreement the *Gomang* added that the settlement in this case had been unusually generous, for the candidate who had visited the village in person had even presented him with nine pots of *mohua* flower wine, considered much superior to the liquor of their own production. This would be utilised in the big Guar ceremony, to be held as soon as enough funds had been collected to buy a buffalo for the sacrifice. I raised the question of the Sudha Saora's vegetarian diet, and the *Gomang* said that this was a rare case when departure from the rule was tolerated.

> *T*he mythological relationship between trees and women descends from the prehistorical inhabitants of India, when people propitiated the spirits which inhabited the jungle, sensing the deep connections between plants and human beings. To illustrate this mutual dependency, early tribal myths tell of women fertilizing trees. The asoka is supposed to burst into flower when kicked by a virgin's foot, the mango tree at the touch of her fingers.
>
> ◆
>
> —Naveen Patnaik, *The Garden of Life: An Introduction to the Healing Plants of India*

The village priest, a Hindu, would abstain from the ceremony, to be performed instead by a *kudan*, or shaman. It was by the performance of such rituals, he pointed out, that the village's health and prosperity were maintained. On the topic of health he added that the Hindu priest dealt with minor ailments with considerable success. As for the rest, he capped his ears with his hands in what Ranjan said was a gesture of resignation. Most of the villagers, he said, had never seen a doctor. The nearest town was many miles away, for which reason no child went to school. The whole village was illiterate.

The *Gomang* was suddenly surrounded by women who made it clear by their gestures that they had a serious problem to discuss. It turned out that they were suffering from the attentions of officials operating the Intensive Tribal Development Programme and, said Ranjan, had first assumed that we had something to do with the scheme. The programme starts off from the premise that tribal people's unsatisfactory existences can only be improved by government interference. This often takes absurd forms. V. S. Naipaul recalls a project designed to provide farmers of India, whether tribals or not, with bullock carts fitted at unimaginable cost with pneumatic tyres and ball-bearing wheels. Bastar, along with Bihar, is considered as being one of the most exploited and wretchedly backward areas in the world, yet the *Illustrated Weekly of India* reported that a start had been made to improve the situation of the region by the installation of solar lights in some villages, "which of course do not function."

In Modhukamba the government Micro-Project seemed even more lunatic in its inspiration. In such communities cow dung is as highly valuable as we had found it to be in Bihar, above all as an ingredient in an ointment applied to sores and for mixing with vegetable dyes. The ITDP had turned up, built a large underground concrete chamber, ordered the villagers to fill it with their precious manure, and closed and sealed the lid, through which a number of copper tubes led into the village houses. The villagers were told that this arrangement would supply gas for their cooking fires—they only had to turn on the tap. This they did, but there was no issue of gas. "None of the projects worked," said the magazine article. "Every programme is ill conceived and found to be utterly irrelevant in a particular context." In the case of Modhukamba there was no wood to be had in the neighbourhood, the women said. No other fuel but dung. What were they to do?

Every experience of this journey contradicted the picture of rural India as presented by the films. India has always been shown as overbrimming with people. Here it was lonely. Having left the main coastal road with its unceasing procession of lorries, there was no traffic at all, and on this and succeeding days we drove all day without encountering, except in an occasional small town, a single private car. The fact is that there is virtually no travel in the interior of India. There is nowhere to stay, nowhere to eat, and it is not particularly safe.

We were now making for the area of Gunupur on the Vamsadhara River close to the border with Andhra Pradesh, where the main concentrations of so-called primitive Lanjia Saora are found in high mountains and thick patches of forest. Once again the scenery had undergone an almost theatrical change: a harsh Indian version of the Australian outback: red rocks tumbling through a wood, the black, bustling untidiness of hornbills in the high branches of trees with sharp, glinting leaves and orange trunks, terracotta earth, the copper faces of Saoras cutting wood with the sound of metal striking metal in a forge.

A *dhaba* in this isolated spot offered no alternatives for the mid-day meal: a narrow hut with crows fluttering over the scraps at the entrance and a three-legged dog licking at something splashed on the floor. This possessed its own landscape in miniature of eroded hills and dales—even a river in the form of a black dribbling from the kitchen area. Plates made from leaves stitched together with something like toothpicks were stacked on a shelf and a man in a dirty singlet with a bad skin condition of the forearms took down three of them, and wiped away the red dust using the rag with which he had just pushed the sodden rice left by the last customer from the table top. Onto each of these leaf-plates he ladled a dollop of rice then went off to return with earthenware saucers containing fiery mixtures of vegetables cooked with chillies.

The moment had arrived once again, after so many years of lack of practise, to eat soggy rice with the fingers, an operation never at best elegant in the eyes of the onlooker and intolerably messy until the knack has been acquired. The local method was to pick up and compress the gobbet of rice with the tips of the five fingers, raise it to the lips, then propel it into the mouth with a sharp upward thrust of the thumb. Thereafter—and this was new to me—the diner would dislodge the grains of rice adhering to his fingers with a jerk of the wrist scattering them about the floor where the three-legged dog awaited.

Discreetly I studied the performance of Ranjan and our driver, watching for fine points. Both, as to be expected, were excellent. The rice I scattered went in all directions; their scatterings were contained within the circumference of a circle no more than a foot across. The meal was conducted in total silence on our part, that of the *dhaba* staff, and the two Saora woodcutters, with fine, aqualine, slightly predatory faces, seated in a far corner and flicking their fingers free of rice with graceful, patrician gestures. At the door the man in the dirty singlet waited to pour water over our hands. The crows were trying to get at a silver lizard that had taken refuge from them under the Ambassador.

Suddenly we were in an area of Christian missionary effort and conversion. The Indian government had consistently opposed the presence of missionaries in wholly Hindu areas, but tolerated Christian evangelism in tribal country such as this, persuaded that the integration of the tribals into the national society can best be effected by the demolition of tribal customs and religious beliefs. The Catholics and Lutherans have long shared the harvest of souls and continue, often in fierce competition, to confuse potential converts who find it hard to understand why the same God is to be reached by such widely fundamentalist sects of the kind involved in recent years in Latin-American scandals in which they have been charged with forcible conversion and genocide.

The first indications of missionary presence and success were graveyards with large white crosses planted in the red earth on the outskirts of tribal villages. Cremation, said Ranjan, had always been practised except in cases of persons dying from unnatural causes, whom it had been customary to bury. Burial was thus associated with tragedy, calling for discussion among the elders as to the extra funeral rites required to succour and appease an unhappy soul. In all parts of India, Ranjan said, it was the same. The missionaries bought conversion with food and medicine. They were the only source of antimalarial pills in the anopheles-ridden mountain villages of the Saora country. If the Saoras were only required to say, "Yes, I believe in God," before receiving the handout, he thought it would have been an excellent thing. It turned out that much more than that was expected in exchange to complete the deal. The Saora had to convince the good father, or the Christian evangelist, that they no longer believed in the Earth Mother, the gods of fire and water, the gods and goddesses in charge of the fertility of a whole assortment of crops, in the Lord of Thunder, the Guardian of Roads, in Thakurani, the blackened pole under its thatched roof defending the village, in the goddesses of each individual household, the cobra god to be placated with flute music and fed with rice and milk, and Labusum, Divine Earth Worm and Creator of the World. The Saoras saw no objection to adding the Christian deity to the others, but even with the magic tablets within their grasp were profoundly troubled at the obligation of doing away with all the rest.

Back in the rainy season when malaria reached epidemic proportions the *Gomang* of another Saora village had discussed his problems with Ranjan.

"We Saora have many gods," he said.

"You do," Ranjan agreed.

The *Gomang*, like the rest of his people, was innumerate. "Could you help me to work out the number of these?" he asked.

Ranjan and the *Gomang* totted up the various names, adding two or three who were considered too powerful or dangerous to be mentioned by name, and could only be alluded to in a

*M*alaria is endemic in tribal areas of the interior, and treatments to prevent it change from year to year as mosquitoes become immune to drugs. The best way to prevent malaria is to avoid being bitten by mosquitoes. Wear clothing that covers the arms and legs, sleep under mosquito netting, and use good insect repellent.

—JO'R and LH

roundabout and placatory fashion. A total of twenty-three was agreed upon.

"Most of them have always been kind and useful to us," the *Gomang* said. "The missionary is asking us to exchange twenty-three for one, plus a month's supply of Nivaquin. It seems unreasonable."

Potasing, a Lanjia Saora village built on a hillside thirty miles away, was recommended by Ranjan as one of the least afflicted in the zone by the government's efforts to uplift the tribal peoples and guide them along the paths leading to national integration. He found it—as I did—mysterious that the main targets chosen so far for these endeavours should have been remote mountain villages, most of them difficult to reach. In these areas the teams had made a start by knocking down cool, solid and practical Saora houses and replacing them with rows of concrete cabins with corrugated-iron roofs, located normally without access to water or refuge from the sun.

Incomprehensibly to Ranjan, Potasing, which would have been easy to reach and demolish, had so far been left alone. It was a village of eighty-five families, one of a group described in a recent government report as "in a real primitive stage, nevertheless of instant visual charm." The low houses with their plain, immensely thick walls of red mud had been fitted into the contours of the hill in a way that recalled the harmonies of Taos. As in the case of Modhukamba, doors, door posts, and lintels were richly carved and painted with flower and animal motifs, and like the lowland village it gave the impression that daily routines of house-scouring and sweeping went on. Here mountain rivulets ran down through the lanes with butterflies by the hundred at their edge, opening and closing their wings as they sucked at the moisture.

Someone had run to fetch the Post Master, who appeared in Potasing to have taken over the function of the *Gomang* of old. He was pleasant and eager to be of assistance, a young man in well-pressed slacks, a wrist watch with a metal band, a button lettered PM pinned to his white shirt, and a fair amount of English. His official duties, he said, occupied little of his time and left him free to pursue his spiritual studies. He announced that Potasing was now a Christian village, and that he himself in the absence of a resident Catholic priest was empowered to act as deacon in charge of the welfare of the religious community.

The mass conversion at Potasing—so close to the road and the Hindu sphere of influence—had been a major achievement carried out in five years. In other cases where Christians had allowed their guard to drop—"Christian inspiration slackened" were the words he used—the Hindus had moved in. "But now we are giving battle on this front," the PM said. The battle was to be against illiteracy, which impeded access to the Scriptures. We were informed that there were twenty-four places for pupils in the new village school. And how many attended classes? I asked. "One," he said, in no way abashed by what would have seemed to me a melancholic truth. "The teacher is sent by the government. He is to teach in Hindi," he explained. "This they are not understanding."

The Saora were famous for their ikons, as they are generally termed, although known locally under the name *anital*. Charming and vigorous examples of folk art of the kind are to be found with local variation among most of the tribal peoples of India. There was a recognisable affinity with the vast painting with which the housewife of Hirapur covered her walls, although ikons were limited in size to a few square feet. In Hirapur inspiration of old had been diluted by custom, and by the sheer necessity of employing space-filling patterns to be finished in a matter of hours in between odd jobs about the house. At Potasing the artist sat alone in silence, families in a darkened place, waiting for a vision to form. Only a few families—the Brahmins of art—were allowed to paint ikons, thereafter made available to the general public in exchange for a small gift or service. An ikon was painted in commemoration of a recent death, in honour of an ancestor, or to celebrate a festival when, like a magnificent Christmas card, it was often offered by the artist to a friend. It was also employed in the treatment of illness by a shaman who might prescribe the dedication of an ikon to the village deity, together with, say, a course of massage and the sacrifice of a white cockerel.

For the PM the ikons had become meaningless, and therefore slightly boring. The Church of Christ did not require such paintings, nor, he added, did the new generation of the village. "They are looking," he said, "another way." And the carvings in and around the doors? I asked. Were they to come to an end, too? That was to be expected, he said. The few carvers left would find other things to do. Some were learning to carve toys for sale. People no longer wished for carvings on their new houses. They were a sign of backwardness. And were the new houses to be made with concrete and corrugated iron? When these materials could be had, he thought.

For all that—for all his distaste for those things in which Ranjan as well as I showed what must have been such inexplicable interest—he was an impressively tolerant man, and ready to help us in any way he could. It was at his suggestion that we set out to scour the village for any ikons that might have survived. A small hitch arose. Most of the villagers were out, he explained, working in their fields, and nowadays when they left their houses they locked up after them. Even the PM seemed surprised to encounter this sudden intrusion of untribal practice. In a land in which, by my experience so far, all doors were open, this indeed was a break with the past. The PM led us to several houses known to belong to notorious conservatives who might have had an ikon about the place, while a few villagers who had joined us, including a young man in a Toshiba t-shirt, scampered up and down side lanes in search of a household that might not have moved with the times. In the end one was found, and an elderly lady festooned with bangles and beads invited us in to inspect her ikon. It was painted in Saora style in white upon a red background, recalling aboriginal rock drawings, or palaeolithic hunters on the walls of caves, or even more the figures and scenes woven into the *huipils* of the Indians of Central America. Here Saora manikins pranced and capered in ceremonial hats and under ceremonial umbrellas, rode elephants and horses, pedalled bikes, and were carried by fan-waving attendants in procession. They played the musical instruments of the past but shouldered the guns of the present. Gourdfuls of wine awaited their pleasure, displayed like Christmas gifts on the branches of palms. The flaming sun illuminating this scene might have been copied from an Aztec codex, as might the Saora medicine men too, who had conjured it from darkness with their feathered wands.

The PM, watching us, smiled at our pleasure. He was happy for us. "We are lucky to find this," he said, "it is belonging to one old lady. I am thinking it is the last." I tried to match his face with the faces of the Saoras who had crowded into the dark room after us, but they seemed to belong to a different race. "Can he really be a Saora?" I had whispered to Ranjan. "Yes, he is a Saora," was Ranjan's reply, but centuries of evolution miraculously crammed into five years had produced an astonishing metamorphosis. The PM had leaped out of the stone-age of Saora art and belief, and the change seemed even to have paled his skin among the deep mountain complexions of the men at his back and to have smoothed his face. He had stripped away the credence that inspired paintings and carvings. Life, as he tried to explain, above all had become simple. "Too many gods," he said. "Too many processes. Now one process only." The concrete and corrugated iron shack was all part of the process of simplification.

The village of the Sudha Saora had swarmed with people. Potasing, with about three times its population, seemed strangely deserted; as many as four houses out of five were locked up. I asked why this should be.

"They are working in the fields," the PM said. "They are very active in employment."

"But this is an in-between season with not much to do," I suggested.

"If there is a willingness to work it is always to be found. We shall be growing new crops which now they are planting. One government inspector was here. He is sending us pineapple to try. In the old times people were lazy. They were drinking much wine. Even the young children were drinking wine. That was bad. We have cut down those palm trees which were giving the wine."

"But what do they do to amuse themselves? Do they drink at

all, dance, go to harvest festivals, stage the Ramayana, put on cockfights? Surely it is not all work? I know they've stopped painting."

"Well, we cannot say it is all work, but we are not wishing to do these other things. I am telling you that everything is different now. On Sunday we are attending church. Practising also to sing hymns. They are telling us that soon a bus will be coming on Fridays for the cinema in Gunupur. This is something for which we are all very glad."

The PM had turned his back on art, and art had forsaken him.

After several days without access to newspapers we had picked up a collection at Rayagada, one of which, coincidentally, contained an article on the Saora. It was particularly concerned with the problem of bringing them, along with the other tribal minorities, into the mainstream of Hindu society.

"We must turn our back on this talk," Ranjan said. "For forty years they are talking

---

*T*he tamarind tree is of greatest use to the poor tribes who inhabit the forests of India. In times of famine they husk the tamarind seeds, which are then boiled and powdered into flour to make bread. Both the leaves and the flowers of this tree are edible, and the tamarind tree is much revered by its dependents.

In the *Tribal Myths of Orissa,* retold by Verrier Elwin in 1954, it is said:

When God planted the tamarind tree and tended it, it grew long finger-like fruit. He tasted it and found it good. He decided to share it with men. When vegetables run short, He thought, they could eat it as chutney. But I shan't tell the birds about it, He decided, otherwise there won't be enough for men.

God called Man and said to him: Guard this tree well. Plant it on your hills. It will be greatly to your profit.

◆

—Naveen Patnaik, *The Garden of Life: An Introduction to the Healing Plants of India*

368 Travelers' Tales ★ India

but nothing is done. Are they wishing these people to be Hindus? For this they must have caste. A man who is born a Saora cannot have caste."

One of the rickshaw men down in the street had found a customer. An immensely corpulent man, helped by a small friend, climbed in. The rickshaw man stood up on a pedal, bringing all his slight weight to bear, and they moved off.

"Is that a Saora?" I asked.

"That is a Hindu. When a Saora becomes a rickshaw-puller it is end of road. They speak their contempt for working for pay. 'I am a farmer,' they will say to you. 'I am not a slave.'"

I read on. "It says here that the Saora are exceptionally primitive."

"Primitive, yes. Backward. Most people are seeing it in that way."

"But in their villages there is no real poverty."

"That is my personal opinion. They have no possessions, but no one is hungry. No, they are not poor."

"Would you say they are devoid of personal ambition, and that crime is unknown?"

"They have no ambition. It is safe to mingle with them. You will not be robbed."

"Do they work in each other's fields, as it says they do in this paper?"

"That is automatic. They are also helping to build each other's houses. They are very democratic. Not even the *Gomang* may give them an order. He will say, 'Let us sit down and talk.' Then he will say, 'This is my advice.'"

"And this is backward?"

"The government says it is. The government tells us it is backward. I am very much liking these people but they are backward in all the things they do. Our national society is requiring from them the opposite of all these things."

Beneath us another customer—this time of average size—had turned up for a rickshaw, and Ranjan called my attention to the transaction taking place. The slender boyish rickshaw-puller at the head of the line waved the fare to a grey-haired man waiting behind him.

"This young man is passing an easy fare to the old man who is following," Ranjan said. "He is a Saora. I think only a Saora will do this. They have a goddess who tells them they must help, so they are eager to behave in this way."

"Are they going to survive?"

"If they learn to use money they will survive."

"How does that affect the situation?"

"Because if they are not understanding money they will be cheated."

"By who?"

"Everyone who comes who is making business with them. Always it has been their custom to barter the things they make or grow. They know how many bags of rice to a goat; they cannot handle rupees. If a tribal man cannot barter he must sell to a merchant. He cheats them with his weights and with his money. When the merchant has robbed him it is the turn of the moneylender. Maybe the Saora's crop has failed and he must buy food, but he does not understand what is meant when the moneylender speaks to him about interest. So this man cannot pay and he must give up his land and go to be a labourer and break stones or dig coal for all his life."

"How often does this happen?"

"All the time. Who can tell you? Now we have industries more labour is wanting. Also politicians and landowners are desirous of obtaining more land. This is happening thousands of times every day."

Norman Lewis has written thirteen novels and ten nonfiction works. His A Dragon Apparent *and* Golden Earth *are considered travel classics, and* Naples '44 *is considered to be one of the best books written about World War II. He lives with his family in Essex, England. This story was excerpted from his book,* A Goddess in the Stones: Travels in India. *His most recent work is* An Empire of the East: Travels in Indonesia.

✳

As we entered Konarak the first rays of a glorious sunrise were illuminating the Black Pagoda, a temple of such solitary grandeur yet of such sensuality that my first impression was one of shock. I had been fortunate once, many years ago, to have visited an empty Taj Mahal on a bright moonlit night and had thought that nothing I would ever see could surpass it for its beauty. But the Taj Mahal is a mausoleum, a tomb, silent in its splendour while Konarak is alive, a constant motion of stone—celestial nymphs with swelling breasts and rounded hips, the rhythms of the lovers and the ecstasy on the faces of the erotic statues. Its energy is manifest in scenes of royal hunts and military expeditions, with infantry, cavalry, and elephants marching in full regalia, speaking of the dream of an ambitious and mighty monarch.

Conceived as a celestial chariot of the Sun God, pulled by seven exquisitely carved horses and supported by twenty-four monolithic wheels, each of which represents the division of time, the temple was constructed by King Narasimha Deva the First of the Ganga dynasty of Orissa in the mid-thirteenth century A.D. Twelve thousand men toiled ceaselessly for twelve years to complete this masterpiece, and it was named the Black Pagoda by the captains of coastal ships who used it as a landmark. Konarak is the peak of Orissan architecture about which it was said that the artisans "built like Titans and finished like jewelers."

—Mark Shand, *Travels on My Elephant*

Encounter with a Rajah

Appearances can be deceptive.

I WAS LED OUT OF THE PALACE AND ACROSS THE COMPOUND AT THE back, where the dogs now lay prone and panting under the trees. We walked towards a low range of buildings that looked as if they might be stables, with a Land-rover and what could have been the original Willys Jeep parked outside. A number of men seemed to be waiting for something to happen, but stirred involuntarily as we approached, then saluted and grinned at one and the same time, with the mixture of affection and subservience that usually char-acterises the inferior greeting his master in India. Ram gestured to an open doorway, then turned and left me to fend for myself. I walked into a spacious area where a nondescript figure in slacks was bent over a piece of machinery under neon lights. I was about to ask him where I could find His Highness when he heard my step, straightened up, wiped his hands on an oily rag and came for-ward to greet me.

It was not quite the setting I had expected for an encounter with Sri Brihadamba Das Raja Rajagopala Thondaiman Bahadur; nor did the ninth and last Rajah of Pudukkottai look at all like an antique. This elderly Indian, with grey stubble where a beard might have been, was slender and supple, and he moved easily across the floor. He was surrounded by lathes, jigs, drills and all the tooling that would have fitted nicely into any small industrial workshop in the Black Country of the English Midlands. The maker's name on the biggest pieces was, in fact, Willson of Birmingham. The place smelt of engine oil and warm iron fittings.

"It's amazing," I said. "This is your hobby?"

His head wobbled fractionally, almost apologetically. "I get a great deal of pleasure from it." He spoke perfect English with the merest trace of accent, but very softly and diffidently. Every gesture he made was restrained, until he touched his machinery. Only then did he seem utterly sure of himself.

"Come, let me show you," he said, leading me out into the yard with something approaching authority. He raised the bonnet of the Jeep and contemplated the engine with a gleam in his eye. "Yes, it is one of the first production models. I have restored her and converted the engine from petrol to diesel. That is more economical." We went back inside. "And that is a four-kilowatt generator I have just finished for the estate up at Kodaikanal. It will run when my windmill is becalmed. I installed that last year." He really was proud of having made these useful things. He was the very model of the shy and obsessive inventor, the one who is teased for blushing if a girl so much as speaks to him, but is pursued by the most attractive and kindest of them, who is desperate to mother him and gets him towards the end of the script. I couldn't imagine him behaving regally anywhere, certainly not issuing edicts from the throne to a council of apprehensive courtiers. Gandhi used to call him Rajah Rishi, the Ascetic Prince.

He led me to a corner of the workshop, where a number of Hindu deities in gaudy bazaar colours were framed on a tin wall. An incense holder stood on a toolbox before them. His Highness bore Lord Shiva's mark in grey ash on his forehead. He indicated that I should sit on a wooden chair after he had laid a clean cloth there, then drew up another one opposite.

I dared to say what had gradually been dawning on me. "You really would rather have been a mechanic than ruler of a princely state, wouldn't you?"

A sweet smile crept over his face, and for a moment his eyes seemed less tired, less pouched with wear and tear. Then came the diffident inclination of the head again. "My mother was a very old-fashioned lady and it would have broken her heart."

Geoffrey Moorhouse has written several books on a wide variety of subjects, including the highly acclaimed Calcutta *and* To the Frontier. *This story is excerpted from his book* OM: An Indian Pilgrimage. *He is a Fellow of the Royal Society of Literature and lives in North Yorkshire, England.*

*

Sometimes it's hard to tell if an Indian is nodding "yes" or shaking his head "no," because typical Indian body language includes a loose wobbling of the head that looks like a simultaneous nod and shake. The wobble means "ok," "I hear you," "sure," but not necessarily "yes." A clear nod is a "yes"; a clear shake is a "no." The head wobble says many things, including, in conversation, "right, right, go on."

—JO'R and LH

DAVID YEADON

* * *

The Mirage of Life

A long border to border journey reveals
nothing and everything.

CLOSE YOUR EYES AND IMAGINE THE UTTER EMPTINESS. A WHITE nothingness—a brilliant, frost-colored land—flat as an iced lake, burning the eyes with its whiteness. Not a bump, not a shrub, not a bird, not a breeze. Nothing but white in every direction, horizon after horizon, on and on for over two hundred miles east to west, and almost one hundred miles north to south.

This is the Rann of Kutch (or Kachchh), the largest area of nothingness on the planet; uninhabited, the ultimate physical barrier, separating India from Pakistan along its far western border. Only camels can cross these wastes, and at terrible cost. During the monsoon seasons it's a shallow salt marsh, carrying the seasonal rivers of Rajasthan slowly out to the Arabian Sea, just south of the great Indus delta of Pakistan. Then for months it's a treacherous quagmire of molasses mud under a brittle salt skin. Periods of safe crossing are minimal. Occasional piles of bleached bones attest to the terrors of this place. Tales of survivors, reluctantly told, are unrelieved litanies of human (and animal) distress. There is life out here—herds of wild asses the size of large dogs and vast flocks of flamingoes encamped in mud-nest "cities"—but very hard to find.

"It is a strange place." An old man in one of the baked-mud villages on the southern edge of the Rann had finally agreed to talk about the place through a local interpreter. "I crossed the Rann many times when I was a young man. Now the only people you will find on it are people carrying drugs or guns. The army tries to stop this trade"—he flung out his small, cracked hands—"but what can they do? The Rann is so vast, the army cannot always use their trucks or their jeeps. They get stuck in the mud, even in the dry season. You can never trust the Rann. Every year it is different. It is very hard to know which way is safe for a crossing. One year"—he paused and studied the endless horizon—"many years ago, I lost my brother and eight camels. He was not so experienced as I was and we had a disagreement. I told him we had to go the long way because the monsoon had been late and the mud was not dry. But he was in a hurry. His family was very poor...." The old man smiled sadly, "We are all poor but he wanted to buy land and build his own house...he was in a hurry."

He paused again and we all sat staring at the shimmering whiteness. Even the sky was white in the incredible heat. "He was a good man. I was his older brother. He should have listened to what I told him." Another long pause.

"What happened?" A stupid question. I knew the answer.

The old man shaded his eyes. "He had his eldest son with him, twelve years old. A fine boy..."

There was a wedding in the village. We could hear the music over the mud-walled compound. Later there would be a procession and a feast of goat, spiced rice, and sweet sticky cakes.

"He went a different way?"

The old man looked even older. His face was full of long gashed shadows.

"You must go to the wedding," he said. "They will be proud if you go. Not many people like you come to this place."

"I've been already. But I think it made people a bit uncomfortable. I seemed to attract more attention than the bride and groom. One man looked quite offended, a man in a bright blue suit."

He laughed. "Ah! Yes. I forgot he was coming. He is with the government—very important. He likes to take charge of things...just like my brother."

"So what happened to your brother?"

The old man shrugged. "He took the wrong path. We found two of his camels on our way back. They were almost dead but we brought them back home to our village."

The music of the wedding faded. It was hard to find shade from the sun. I looked across the Rann again. Almost one hundred miles to the other side, with no oasis, no water, no shade, just this end-less salt-whiteness.

"He could have reached the other side. Maybe he decided to stay for a while?"

"His family is here. His wife and his children."

"Maybe the army arrested him?"

"No, this was nine years ago. The army was not here so much at that time."

"So you think he died."

The old man drew a slow circle with his finger in the sandy dust.

"He became a 'white,' like so many others."

"A 'white'?"

"We call that name for men who do not return from the Rann. Part of their spirit remains in the Rann. There are many, many of them. Who can tell. Maybe hundreds of men. Hundreds of whites."

"Back home we call them ghosts—the spirits of the dead still trapped on earth."

"Yes I know about your ghosts. Here it is a different thing. We are not afraid of the whites. When we cross the Rann we remem-ber them. They protect us. Sometimes they guide us."

"But you never see them?"

The old man smiled and spoke quietly. "As I told you, the Rann is a very strange place and you can see many strange things...it is difficult to explain. The Rann is not like other things on earth—not even like other deserts. It has its own nature and if you listen and look and think clearly, you will be safe..."

"Your brother didn't listen?"

"He was a good man but much younger than I. And he had many worries. His mind was full of many things. He could not hear clearly."

"Do you think about him a lot?"

"He was my only brother. We had five sisters. But he was my only brother."

"So, in a way, he's still here."

"Of course. He is a white. He will always be here."

My long (very long) journey to the Rann began on the Nepalese-Indian border, in the gritty, noisy little town of Birganj. Sixteen hours of bone-crushing bus travel had brought me south from Kathmandu, over the passes and down through the gorges, and deposited me at this nonentity of a place.

All I wanted when we finally arrived in Birganj was a simple bed and sleep. A simple bed came easily enough (a square of plywood and a sheet in a freezing cold $3.00-a-night hostel), but sleep was hard to come by in a room also occupied by an enormous Australian earth

The monotony of our safari was shattered by a frightening experience. We approached a village in the early morning hours. I was looking forward to stretching my legs. As we entered the village, a group of men gathered before us. They shouted, "*Pagal, Pagal!*" in threatening voices. One old man appeared with a rifle and made nasty gestures. Abdul did not utter a word. He prodded our animals to move quickly out of town. The men followed behind our caravan screaming insults until we were far from their town. Abdul explained to me that the villagers felt that apart from locals, only lunatics would come to such a remote place. A lone woman could only mean trouble. She must therefore be a witch. They wanted no part of us and our bad luck. Most likely I would never again have such an honour. I had been labeled mad and then banished as a witch.

◆

—Marybeth Bond,
"Solo in Asia"

gypsy whose snoring seemed to shake plaster off the walls and
made the windows rattle. Haggard and dizzy with fatigue in the
early dawn, I tried to sort out my papers for the border crossing
while he insisted on telling me hard-luck tales of his injuries, ill-
nesses, and illicit dealings, all the way from Darwin ("best place in
the land of Aus, mate") to Dar es Salaam. His pessimism and
chronic dislike of almost everyone he'd met and everything that
had happened to him made me wonder why he bothered traveling at all. His ultimate tirade was directed at "that bunch of bastard
wogs" in Bombay who had managed to relieve him of all his
worldly possessions except his sleeping bag and had even run off
with his money belt crammed with dollars from some emerald-
smuggling escapade in Malaysia. The air was purple with his pro-
fanities, and I was tired of him.

"Isn't there one single place you've enjoyed?"

His mood changed. The swearing and cursing subsided, and this
hairy giant of a man became almost teary-eyed as he told me about
Bhuj, the idyllic Gujarat coast ("Not a bloody soul for miles. The
best beaches in India, mate. No one ever goes there.") and the mysteries of the Rann of Kutch.

So thank you whatever your name is; I forgive you your snoring and your jaundiced outlook on life and your self-pitying
tirades, and will remain ever grateful for your introduction to this
truly fascinating corner of India. Now the only thing I had to do
was get there....

Bus travel seems endless. People get on, people get off, but the
journey goes on forever. The only thing that changed were the
occupants of the seat beside me. So far I'd had three Indian companions, each of whom had slept through all the noise, heat, and
confusion. I envied them their tranquility.

Then came a spritely young woman, a nurse from Eire, with a
wonderful singsong way of talking. All her sentences ended in an
upswing of Irish brogue. In spite of five months of backpacking
around India from ashram to ashram, she still retained that bright-
eyed enthusiasm of the novice traveler. Nothing seemed to phase

her. She was totally in love with her life on the road—not a bit of the tired TET [Totally Exasperated Traveler] anywhere. I envied her too and was sorry to see her leave.

And then Dick Davies arrived, a young Welshman with a prematurely old face, deeply lined and flecked with dark scars. He wore an old suede hat, Australian style with one brim turned up, baggy green corduroys, and a torn leather jacket so stained with grease, food, blood, and mud that it was difficult to tell its original color.

At first I thought that he too would sleep out the journey like my three Indian companions, but our conversation became animated when we compared notes on Kathmandu and the Himalayas.

"I'm a real white-water nut," he told me with a grin that made his old face suddenly look very young. "Himalayas, Central America, New Zealand, Africa, you name it. I've been kayaking there."

He was a true world wanderer, who had spent most of the last decade of his life seeking out white-water wonderlands all around the globe. I felt envious once again.

"I've never done any white-water stuff," I said. "Somehow I don't think I'd enjoy it that much."

He laughed. "It doesn't make that much difference what you do really. Like anything good in life, you end up pretty much in the same place."

"And you get there by kayaking."

"Yeah. Listen, I'm not one of the religious types. Y'know. You've met them. Nepal, Ladakh, the south. They're all over India. They're all looking for something that makes everything make sense."

"Centering?"

"Centering? Okay—that's your word. Call it anything you want. It's all the same. You know what it is when you get there."

"And kayaking. That's what you do."

"Yeah. But it could be something else—anything...."

We both sat quietly for a while. Something he'd said brought back a memory.

"Y'know, I almost drowned when I was a kid," I said. "Near a waterfall. I fell under and couldn't get back up. I'm sure that stupid experience put me off the idea of messing around on white water."

"Oh yeah. Well—that can do it."

"You never got close to drowning?"

He nodded but didn't seem to want to talk about it. The smoke from his cigarette curled around his hat.

"One time I think I did drown." He spoke slowly.

"Meaning?"

"Well, I don't know really. Something strange. Still don't know what happened...."

I knew he wanted to tell me so I just waited. He lit another cigarette.

"Ah—it was a long time back. When I first got started. I'd only been doing it a few weeks. And I was lousy. I mean lousy. I couldn't get the hang of it. I wanted to, but I couldn't. It wouldn't come right. Anyway, this one day I was up in Scotland by myself, the Cairngorms, trying to get it right, and everything's going okay until, hell—I was under the boat and then out of it and I couldn't touch the bottom and I didn't know where the hell I was. And jeez, was it cold! Real brass monkey stuff and churning away like mad. Currents all over the place, and I was flippin' over like a hooked fish. I'd sucked in a lot of water, I couldn't find the surface. It was black as pitch. I'd got no air left. I knew I was drowning. And all these weird things were happening. You get flashbacks like they tell you—I was crying because I'd broken my mother's best plate. Then I was on a soccer pitch with the mates. All kinds of stuff. Coming home down the lane from church past the pub and hearing them all singing...and then it all sort of went quiet and it wasn't like I was in water or anything...it was just okay and there didn't seem to be much to worry about anymore...."

His cigarette trembled in his fingers. The afternoon sun flickered through a filigree of tree along the roadside.

"And then. Well everything got weird. I wasn't in the water. I was on the bank, sitting on some sand, and the boat was right by me and it looked fine and I felt fine...I wasn't even coughing or anything."

He shook his head and grinned.

"Hell—I dunno what happened. Still don't. I thought I'd drowned, lost it. Into the great yonder and all that. Weird. I don't know how the hell I got to be sitting like a Sunday afternoon fisherman on a riverbank with the boat and everything—all together in one piece."

My spine was tingling. That was my story. The accident that had happened but never happened in Iran, twenty years ago. One of the strange events that changed my life and my way of looking at life. We sat quietly for a long time listening to the hiccupy rhythm of the bus engine....

> *There* is an indefinable mysterious Power that pervades everything. I feel it, though I do not see it. It is this unseen Power which makes itself felt and yet defies all proof, because it is so unlike all that I perceive though my senses. It transcends the senses. But it is possible to reason out the existence of God to a limited extent.
>
> ◆
>
> —Mahatma Gandhi, *Young India*, October 11, 1928

On the long bus journey south from Jaisalmer to Bhuj, across miles of deserty wastes, I did some homework about the Rann of Kutch. The owner of the hotel had very generously lent me a few books on Gujarat, and I scribbled away, delighted by one descriptive passage from a booklet by a Lt. Burns in 1828:

> ...Rann comes from the Sanskrit word "*ririna*" meaning "a waste"... a space without a counterpart on the globe, devoid of all vegetation and habitation....Its surface shines with a deadly whiteness; the air, dim and quivering, mocks all distance by an almost ceaseless mirage. No sign of life breaks the weary loneliness. Stones and bones of dead

animals mark infrequent tracks....Passage at all times is dangerous, travelers being lost even in the dry season. Because
of the heat and blinding salt layers, passage is made at night,
guided by the stars from dawn to dusk.

Just my kind of place for a dry-season ramble!

Gujarat has also been a "land apart" on the Indian subcontinent.
Ruled for centuries by powerful and fierce Maharaos, the
"Kutchis" have long had an outward-looking attitude to the
world. Their fame as seafarers, merchants, traders, and even pirates
has made them a major presence in East Africa, Arabia, and the
Persian Gulf. Recent development here by the Indian government
of the new port of Kandla is beginning to increase Gujarat's links
with the rest of the country, but the Kutchis still value their own
history, traditions, and independence.

The ruined castles of feudal chieftains, set high on the crags of
Gujarat's Black Hills, are still revered places. So too are the remote
shrines of local saints, whose pious meditations and fierce penances
(*tapsia*) were said to give them power over gods and the local war-
rior-kings.

You can see that power here in the bleakness and broken ridges
of the hills. Fragments of ancient fiefdoms still dot the sun-
bleached desert and, as Bhuj suddenly appears—a gray, solemn bas-
tion of towers and high stone defense walls—I wondered how
much had really changed in this remote region since the wild ram-
pages of a ferocious duo known as Mod and Manai in the ninth
century A.D., and the cruel vengeances of the warrior Ful in the
next century.

Tales of cunning, intrigue, murder, and massacre are the very
stuff of Gujarat legend. Our contemporary scandals and conspira-
cies of financial finaglings and political philanderings seem like
schoolboy pranks when set beside the tangled complexity of regal
power plays in and around Bhuj....

The following day brought another unexpected series of
incidents.

"Please, sir, do not forget, if you wish to visit the Rann, you will be required to carry a permit," the hotel manager advised me.

Getting a permit. Okay—no problem. I was more familiar with Indian behavior now and foresaw no difficulties....

"It is best, sir, if you will get to the office early," he advised. It was not even two o'clock in the afternoon. Plenty of time.

But I should have known better.

The process required visits to three separate government offices; endless filling out of forms (and filling them out twice due to a clerk's inability to spell my name correctly); languorous pauses for betel nut chewing and tea; returning to previous offices to "clarify" form entries; minute inspection of every detail of my passport (including the binding!); an impressive display of seal-making using a stick of red wax and a candle (only to have the seal snapped into half a dozen pieces a few minutes later by the next official on my list— in the next room); constant confusion over the forms themselves, which were all in English, only hardly anyone spoke English; meticulous compiling of papers (at one point I carried fourteen different sheets of paper from one department to another held together by sewing pins); a warning from the next to the last official that if the forms were not all completed by closing time at 6:00 p.m. I would have to start the whole process

*A*llow lots of time for paperwork. Procedures may prove more costly if officialdom senses that time is at a premium. If you're willing to sit it out in offices (take a thick book along) you may win out. Also, try again. I've gone back to exactly the same office the same afternoon (hair combed differently, different clothing) and the same official has not recognized me. It has sometimes happened that the second or third time I've been successful. Go back on a different day, or try another city for your permit.

◆

—Michael Buckley, "Getting the Run Around," *Great Expeditions*

over again the following morning; and finally, at five minutes to six, waiting for the last signature from a man who looked very imperious and sat on a tall chair raised on a carpet-covered dais and seemed to be far more interested in the condition of his fingernails than in my pile of wilting, ink-stained forms.

But I was proud. Throughout the whole four-hour ordeal I had never once raised my voice or played the arrogant colonial (whom I'd discovered deep in my psyche while traveling in India). I smiled. They smiled. They shared tea with me. They offered me betel "*pan*" and I accepted (it took hours to get all the little pieces of nuts and spices and whatever else goes into its elaborate preparation out of my teeth). I offered them *bidi* cigarettes, which they accepted (but on one occasion politely mentioned they would have preferred Marlboros). And then—clutching my precious papers like winning lottery tickets—I returned to the hotel for a traditional vegetarian *thali* dinner (usually the only food available in Bhuj hotels).

Tomorrow I'll finally be off to the Rann, I told myself. I celebrated by ordering a second enormous metal tray of *thali* and was just finishing off my rice, *dhal*, vegetables, and *paratha* when someone started beating on my door with the urgency of a fireman in the midst of a blazing inferno.

"Police. Open."

Now what? I opened the door.

Two neatly dressed policemen stepped promptly into my room with the worried manager trailing behind, shrugging hopelessly.

"Passport."

Keep calm, I told myself, don't blow a fuse. Be like you were earlier on at the government offices.

So I was.

I answered all their questions, let one of them search my luggage, smiled as they meticulously inspected all my permits, and smiled again as they saluted smartly and left. The manager was very apologetic.

"They very nervous, sir, of people going to Rann. Much trouble with drugs and weapons."

He couldn't seem to stop shrugging his shoulders.

"That's okay. I'm just a tourist."

"Yes—I am knowing that, sir. But they..." His twitching shrugs completed the sentence.

"Honestly. It's okay. And thank you for looking after me."

He left, bowing and shrugging simultaneously.

Five minutes later, another knock on the door. This was becoming an Inspector Clouseau nightmare. I opened it. And behold—another enormous tray of *thali* with two bottles of Thumbs Up Cola.

"Complimentary manager," the young boy said.

What a nice way to end the day. Three dinners!...

The drive north from Bhuj began as sensations of diminishing stimuli, leaving the city and then the Black Hills behind, easing further and further out into a flattening desert plain. I paused in one of the few villages on the edge of the Rann and was entertained by the headman while his wives and daughters paraded past me in brightly embroidered jackets decorated with hundreds of tiny mirrors. I watched them sewing and sifting rice in the shade of their mud huts and among the circular granaries topped with conical roofs of reed thatch. Out under the thorn-bushes beyond the village, herds of white cud-chewing cattle sat in statuesque groups, guarded by naked, gold-skinned boys.

Further on, way out across the salty flats, a herd of over three hundred camels were being led by a group of *raiskas* to a market near the coast. *Raiskas* have a notorious reputation as fly-by-night seducers of village women as well as their more traditional roles as balladeer-historians, news carriers, and nomadic traders....

A little later I met the old man whose brother had been lost in the Rann many years ago. After his sad tale of the terrors of the place and the spirits of "the whites" that haunted it's barren wastes, I was anxious to drive on deeper into the blazing nothingness, past the sun-cracked skins of stone mountains, peeled off like onion layers. I wanted to see the herds of wild asses said to roam the eastern portion, the Little Rann, and the vast gatherings of flamingos living and laying their eggs in "cities" of conical mud nests way out in the whiteness. So I drove on, leaving the village far behind.

Now there was not a tree or a shrub or even a single blade of grass anywhere. Nothing but an endless eye-searing blankness in every direction. The track was a vague incision in the salt, but beyond that was what I'd come all this way to see—nothing at all. Twenty thousand square miles of perfect flatness. No clouds, no movement, no life. Nothing.

It was like vanishing into some vast realm beyond the mind, way beyond thoughts, beyond feelings and sensations and all the convoluted tangles of consciousness. Even beyond awareness itself. A space so colorless, so silent, and so infinite that it seemed to be its own universe. And I just simply vanished into it....

The sun was so hot in the dry air that I almost felt cold. I noticed this odd sensation at one point, about twenty-five miles into the whiteness, when I got out of the car and walked out across the cracked surface of the salt. After a couple of hundred yards or so the heat shimmers were so violent that I could no longer see the vehicle. I couldn't even see my own footprints due to the hardness of the salt and the intense shine radiating from it. Then I noticed the shivering, similar to the sensation of a burning fever when the hotter your body becomes the colder you feel. It may also have been flicker or two of fear. I realized that I had done something rather stupid. Two hundred yards away from my landmark was the same as a hundred miles. I didn't know where the hell I was. I was lost!

I remembered tales of arctic explorers caught in sudden blizzards and dying in frozen confusion a few blinding yards from their tents. A few yards in a blizzard is infinity. This was infinity.

In retrospect the whole incident seems ridiculous, but at the time I sensed panic and the horrible reality that if I didn't retrace my steps within the next half hour or so I'd become a raving sun-sacrificed lunatic lost in this utter nothingness. Given shade I could have waited for the sun to drop and the shimmers to dwindle. But shade was as impossible as alchemist's gold here. There was no shade for two hundred miles.

And then, as suddenly as they had come, the shivers ceased and I felt an unearthly calm. I was neither hot nor cold now. The purity of the silence rang like a Buddhist bell, clear and endless. Here I was in the loneliest, emptiest place on earth, smiling inwardly and outwardly, utterly at peace, as if in some sensationless limbo state between life and death.

I burst out laughing at the zaniness of the whole predicament and my feet, without any prompting and guidance from the conscious part of me, walked me surely and certainly right back through the shimmers and the vast white silence to the car.

The Rann is still with me now. In times of silence I return to its silence; in a strange way I find it comforting and reassuring. We should all carry a Rann somewhere in our minds. A place of refuge and utter peace. A place of the mind but far beyond the mind.

I never did see the asses or the flamingoes or anything else out there. If I'd taken a camel rather than a car I could have continued further and deeper but, as it was, I was hampered by thick mud below the salty crust about thirty miles in. The monsoon had been late that year and the Rann had not yet been thoroughly baked by the sun to make it safe for my way of traveling. But that was fine. I'd found what I'd come looking for. Absolute nothingness.

David Yeadon also contributed "A Bath for Fifteen Million People" to Part I and "Love Has Teeth" to Part II. These stories were excerpted from his book The Back of Beyond: Travels to the Wild Places of the Earth.

*

What have you gained if you have not gained yourself, the immortal, the infinite? What have you gained if you have never tasted in your life the deep longing for deliverance and supreme emancipation? And what have you gained if you have not tasted the joy of self-surrender, if your heart has not longed to make of you a flute in the hands of Krishna, that master musician of the universe, and if you have not been able to sweeten all your miseries with a touch of God?

—Dr. S. N. Dasgupta, quoted by Tim Malyon, "The Seeking of Emptiness," *World Magazine*

PART FOUR

IN THE SHADOWS

BRIDGET MCCOY

✦ ✦ ✦

The Boys' School

Misogyny is strong in India, raising the question:
Are women the lowest caste of all?

LONELY PLANET'S GUIDE TO INDIA CONTAINED A CRYPTIC PRECAU-
tion for women travelers. In Bharatpur, near Agra, it warned against
passing near a boys' school alone when the students were being let
out. There was no explanation or anecdotal material. Simply this
warning. Experience told me that their advice was rarely frivolous
or unfounded. However, today I was not to be deterred.

India had posed difficulties from the start. During a twelve hour
bus trip from the Nepal border, we had only stopped twice. And
even then, there were no bathroom facilities. I had to squat in the
fields, and had bled on my clothes.

In Varanasi we saw very few women on the streets, certainly not
the number of women merchants we had encountered in Nepal.
And there continued to be no public conveniences for women.
Higher caste women only relieve themselves in their own houses,
and low caste women must use gutters and alleyways like the rest
of the poor in India. A Westerner who wants privacy must find a
hotel or restaurant that caters to Westerners, or hold back nature.

After spending the morning viewing the museum at Ramnagar
Fort, I was desparate to pee, but, as usual, there were no public toilet facilities. I discovered the unofficial toilets on the vast stairs

that ran behind the castle down to the river. Climbing giant stone steps to reach a discreet, hidden spot at the top, I felt dried human excrement crunch under my feet. It covered every inch of the stairway. Richard distracted the kids who were intent on following me.

While lack of bathroom facilities is inconvenient and embarrassing, it is not ego threatening. Richard made a young friend one evening who offered to show us Varanasi by moonlight. Or rather he offered to show Richard. I trailed along like a shadow, a complete nonentity as far as this fellow was concerned. I might as well have been dressed in black and veiled. He led us through the narrow alleys of the old city, up the cobblestone streets and down steep steps, picking our way through the spots made slick by cow manure and urine until we reached the *ghats*. He took Richard by the hand, fussed over and protected him lest he slip or get lost. I could have fallen in a great hole, and I don't think he would have noticed.

---

*I*ndian women, who suffer both sexual frustration and the humiliation of abuse in intimate relations, are routinely told that they live on pedestals, adored as goddesses by men. Psychiatrists and women's rights activists say otherwise—that most young women merely bear up until they can gain stature by producing a son—but the fantasy persists.

◆

—Barbara Crossette, *India: Facing the Twenty-First Century*

Traveling west to Khajuraho and Agra I found a more contemporary and less sexist India. These places attract many Indian tourists as well as foreigners. The bus and train stations offered public conveniences for both sexes, and I saw contemporary, cosmopolitan Indian women dressed in modern, less constricting fashions. Still, there were places where I was leered at or physically accosted without warning. In the old part of Agra a man on a bicycle squeezed my arm roughly as he sped by. I was furious, but had no recourse.

And only twenty-five feet down the street a boy of ten or so imitated him.

I was careful not to provoke these incidents, dressing modestly and traveling with my husband. Probably the best explanation came from a young man we met in Delhi who asked "Isn't it true that American women like to have lots of sex with a lot of different men?" I was seen as a whore by virtue of nationality.

On the bus from Fahtepur Sikri I was seated next to a man and his youngest daughter. He showed us a pen from Denmark, a picture of a pinup who lost her clothes as you turned it upside down. His hand brushed my breast as he reached out to exhibit the pen to Richard while his wife and two older daughters twittered in the seat in front of us. I was left wondering about the experience.

A kindly soul on the train to Jaisalmer was full of similar misconceptions. He was a gray-headed father of four daughters and grandfather to three. He struck up a conversation with us. He said that his "Auntie" lived in the United States and worked for the Indian Embassy in Washington, D.C. She had told her nephew that all women in the United States are married to three or four men.

"Oh, no," Richard and I protested, "that's not true."

"Oh, not at the same time," replied our friend, "but Auntie says all American women have three or four husbands, one right after the other. But Auntie tells the Americans she has only one husband for life."

"No, this is an exaggeration," we both reiterated, probably to no avail. Misconceptions about the United States are rampant, fed by U.S. movies full of gratuitous violence and sex.

He asked very direct questions. Were my tubes tied? What kind of birth control do we use? The old fellow was pleasant and amusing, but by this time I had become somewhat wary of all men. When he offered me a handful of the crunchy snack food that was sitting on a paper on his lap, I was suspicious of his motives.

I had become sensitized to physical contact between sexes, since it is so strictly prohibited here. I had difficulty reading people's intentions towards me, had often found myself off balance, becoming more guarded.

After a few weeks in northern India, the country was beginning to wear on me heavily. I have always been an independent woman. I have traveled alone, camped alone, backpacked alone without fear in my own country. I have always been a proud woman, certain of my own invulnerability. Now, traveling with a man, I felt more physically vulnerable than I ever did in the United States. I was like the experimental monkey who received random and erratic shocks. My stress was much greater because I had no idea when the next assault would occur.

These events strained my relationship with Richard as well. He wanted to help by championing my cause and challenging my antagonizers. One day I was ogled and grabbed at by a group of teenage male students as I bicycled past in a park. Richard whirled his bike around and pulled up in front of them, blocking their path.

"How would you like it if I treated your wives, mothers, sisters like this?"

The group twittered with nervous embarrassment. Even the teacher stood dumb. They looked at their feet and avoided eye contact until a spokesman muttered an apology.

I was grateful that Richard had spoken up for me. I hadn't known how to deal with this affront, and would have kept going. Yet I realized later that I was furious that I needed him to fight my battles. He had become guilty by gender association. My champion was haplessly part of the group that was conspiring to strip me of my power. When I explained this to Richard, he was surprised but empathic. Now I had managed to put him in a bind as well. Or India had put us in a bind, leaving us both puzzled by a culture that we didn't understand on many levels.

Of course I met men who treated me kindly, courteously, and respectfully. The old tailor in Delhi who sewed my Punjabi suit took great pains to maintain decorum as he fitted my new outfit. The singer in Jaipur with the beautiful dancing hands smiled at me guilelessly.

In Jaipur a young man named Madho befriended us. We rented bicycles and pedaled into the center of town. Stopped in a busy intersection, Madho suddenly rushed after two adolescent boys and confronted them angrily. We were astonished. A moment later he returned to us and pointed to the built-in lock that passed through the rear tire spokes on my bicycle. One of the boys had engaged it as a prank. If I had moved, I would have tipped over in the midst of heavy traffic. Madho had run after the boy because he thought he was trying to steal the key as well.

"Ugly," Richard said.

Madho agreed. He understood that men his age treated women cruelly. It was not his way. Twenty-one years old, he told us that he would never marry. He didn't want the sort of relationship that his father had with his mother. She always came last he told us. It is wrong for a man to love his children but not his wife. His parents had given him a sense of hopelessness about his own prospects.

Some of his despair arose from Madho's own relationship with his mother which lacked communication and touching. Although they oc-

*F*emale infanticide is commonly practiced, said the social investigator in Rajasthan, where traditional antifeminism is more solidly entrenched than elsewhere. In other northern states including Uttar Pradesh, Haryana and the Punjab girl children were permitted to survive, although with reluctance. Dr. Surander Jaitly of Banaras Hindu University, who questioned a number of village women, found a sinister predominance of women who had lost daughters through accidents ("they fell down"), but never a son. Lakshmi Lincom of the Tata Institute of Social Sciences found that if a girl avoided outright infanticide she could expect discrimination right from the cradle, being weaned before a boy and liable to suffer from malnutrition. She would be taken out of school and introduced to child labor much earlier than her brothers, and was four times more likely than them to be employed in the rural hard-slogging labor that comes so close to the definition of slavery.

♦

—Norman Lewis, *A Goddess in the Stones: Travels in India*

cupied the same space, there was no contact. He took two fingers and drew parallel lines passing and moving off in opposite directions.

The Indian pyschotherapist Sudhir Kakar points out that the male child is totally indulged and protected by his mother in the first four or five years of life. These ties are abruptly cut when the child is turned over to a stern father for initiation into the male world. Kakar contends that these circumstances create an individual who is self-centered, distrustful, and disrepectful of women, the result of having been so violently torn from an overly-indulgent maternal haven.

So when I encountered the boys' school as it was letting out, I decided to keep walking. What could I possibly fear from a group of thirteen-year-olds? I was in the wrong place at the wrong time in the wrong country. An Occidental woman looking ahead to the twenty-first century confronted by an India that was clinging to the past.

The boys saw me and rushed out to the street. "Hey, lady, kiss my penis," taunted one of them. The rest of them took up the chant, "Hey, lady, kiss my penis."

I kept my gaze down and walked rapidly toward the market, but I was quickly encircled by a wall of pubescent males shouting insults. Boys on bicycles surrounded me like savages around a wagon train.

"I love you," they shouted. "Kiss my penis lady."

All my frustrations with India rose up in an insuppressible shriek. "Pigs, you're just little pigs! You should be ashamed. Go away!"

My shouts only whetted the crowd's appetite for mass hooliganism, and they pressed against me, pushing and grabbing. The circle of bicycles tightened until metal was almost scraping me. They smelt blood. I was scared. I noticed an elderly *chai-wallah* at a nearby stand and made a pleading gesture at him. He shouted something to the boys. In this class and caste conscious culture the old man could not have much status, but they reluctantly started to disperse. I was surprised that they obeyed him. However low his status, it was evidently higher than mine.

I touched my hands to my forehead in thanks.

As I turned to walk off, the boys had one final say. A large stone hit me directly between the shoulders.

Bridget McCoy is a long-time resident of Sonoma County in Northern California. Periodic attacks of wanderlust have drawn her to near and faraway places. Her other passions are photography and riding her horse, Taxi.

✳

At passport control [in the Delhi airport], the Indian official, who obviously thought he was "a bit of all right," wobbled his head in quaint Indian fashion and said, "No allowing you to passing."

"Why not?" I said.

"You stay in my country. You are making me fine wife."

"Sorry," I told him, "but you should have thought of that earlier. I have to go home now."

"No problem."

"What do you mean, no problem?"

"No problem you staying in India. You making me very fine wife indeed."

"It's a nice idea, but I'm afraid I'm fully booked. I already have another twenty-seven husbands dotted around. I'd like to fit you in but, you know—you have to put your foot down somewhere."

"No problem," (wobble, wobble), "you fine wife."

"If you'd like to take a look at my passport, I'll be on my way."

"Please, first one kiss as you are hurting my heart."

"Now look here, Sunny Jim, you're supposed to be a sensible passport official. I don't want to hear about your personal emotional upset."

"One kiss."

"No one kiss. Passport look."

"One kiss."

"Good grief!"

"Good grief?"

"Yes, good grief—you're working your ticket."

"One kiss."

"Look! Passport—is good yes?"

"One kiss no problem."

"Okay. One kiss, but on passport picture, okay?"

"No problem."

With that, he delivered a wet one on my photograph and, casting a woeful look towards me that would no doubt linger until the next Western female came along, he let me go.

— Josie Dew, *The Wind in My Wheels: Travel Tales from the Saddle*

STEVE COLL

✦ ✦ ✦

The Die is Caste

*Human greed and cruelty do not
respond well to legislation.*

I DO NOT KNOW THE NAME OF THE MAN I ADMIRE MOST IN INDIA.
He may have left a business card but I did not retain it.

He showed up unannounced at my front door in New Delhi
one afternoon in the midst of the 1990 caste riots. An affirmative
action plan promising reserved government jobs to a wide tier of
India's lower castes had sparked a violent reaction in the north.
Mobs of upper-caste university students fearful of losing opportunity through reverse discrimination roamed New Delhi's wide
avenues, trashing cars and grocery stores stocked with smuggled
imports from the West. Lower-caste students and farmers staged
their own demonstrations, battled with police, and erected
makeshift roadblocks on the highways out of the capital, where
they burned buses and pelted cars with stones. Hysteria about the
riots and the divisive consequences of affirmative action sang daily
from the Indian national newspapers which are owned, edited, and
written by members of the upper castes. Fueling the apprehension
was a spreading wave of ghoulish self-immolations by aggrieved
upper-caste teenagers and preteens. The burnings had been
sparked by Rajiv Goswami, an obscure, quiet upper-caste student
at Delhi University who stood one afternoon on the perimeter of

a street crowd of chanting protestors and then, in circumstances which remain unclear, doused himself with kerosene and set himself alight. Soon Goswami, wrapped in gauze and fighting for his life in a New Delhi hospital, was being hailed as a tragic but noble paragon of self-sacrifice in a worthy cause, namely the development of a society based on "merit," not caste or feudal identity. Seeking to emulate Goswami's reputation, and perhaps to resolve troubles unrelated to political dilemmas such as affirmative action, dozens of other upper-caste teen-agers in New Delhi and elsewhere began to soak themselves with gasoline and set themselves on fire. Panic and dread spread among parents of the upper-caste urban middle class—accountants, clerks, bureaucrats, and businessmen born to social privilege but struggling under varied pressures in an increasingly competitive political economy. In my neighborhood, which was dominated by such relatively wealthy but insecure households, parents kept a sharp eye on their matches.

In this atmosphere I opened my door and stared in disbelief at a smiling young man on my front stoop who clutched a cigarette lighter, a bottle of kerosene, and a fire extinguisher. He was perhaps twenty-one, clean-cut, dressed in pressed slacks and a knit shirt. He announced that he was a salesman, appointed representative of the finest manufacturer of fire extinguishers in India. He said that if I would spare a minute of my time, he would provide a demonstration that would not only amaze me but would convince me of the immediate need to stock my house with his fine safety products.

"Sir," he asked, "shall I set myself on fire?"

As he began to pour kerosene onto his forearm, I recovered my voice in time to object. I noted that as a foreigner, I had no great worry that my children would immolate themselves over a caste-based affirmative action plan. But I did wonder whether this sales pitch was working very well elsewhere in the neighborhood.

"Business, sir, is booming," he answered.

I invited him in and asked about his background as he unpacked demonstration fire extinguishers and promotional videotapes. He said that he was lower caste by birth. His father was a peasant farmer who owned and tilled a couple of acres, meaning that he was better off than those at the very bottom of the rural ladder, the landless. Still, his parents had worked mightily and saved scrupulously to put him through school, he said. Now he was at university, an undergraduate in engineering. He hoped eventually to study abroad. Meantime, to earn money for school and to keep himself in style, he was moonlighting as a fire-extinguisher salesman, tromping door to door through upper-caste neighborhoods offering to rescue the privileged from themselves at twenty U.S. dollars a pop. It was a very good franchise, he said.

Though uncertain about the quality or utility of his extinguishers, I told him that I would buy three, strictly on the principle that such audacity must be rewarded if India is ever to realize its ambitions. I think the salesman wasn't sure what I was talking about, but he remained polite enough, no doubt on the principle that the money of lunatic foreigners was just as good as the money of frightened Brahmins.

I tended to invest my hopes in such quixotic characters because otherwise it would be easy to give in to despair about the legacy of feudalism and caste in South Asia. Even in Pakistan and Bangladesh, where casteless Islamic ideology has helped to decouple feudal economic arrangements from spiritual tradition, the old system clings to the land like glue, trapping all sorts of ambitious people in place. The system finds a thousand ways to perpetuate itself, including forms of religious sanction, as in the exploited tradition of living Islamic saints in the Pakistani countryside. As with race in America, it is difficult to be certain when you care too little and when you care too much about feudal and caste discrimination. But if you believe in virtually any version of the egalitarian ideal, and if you confront with open eyes what this discrimination means in South Asia today and how it operates, the enormity of the problem can be staggering.

In India, ancient caste identities remain very much alive, despite the determined efforts of Nehruvian policymakers to kill them off. If you could produce a satellite photograph of India with different colors marking the prominence of different castes, the result would

*C*aste was created by force, it is true. About three thousand years ago India was invaded by the Aryans, a race of light-skinned warriors from the harsh foothills of the Caucasian mountains. The conquerors built a thick wall to separate themselves from the land's subjugated natives, a wall that stretched the length of the subcontinent. It was a solid wall of ideas, a wall unbreachable by any weapon because it existed in people's minds. The Aryan men-at-arms became the Kshatriyas, the priests they brought with them became the Brahmins, and the indigenous multitudes who now served them became the Shudras. Later, once trade joined war and farming as a major way of life, the new class of merchants and shopkeepers became the Vaishyas.

Once the sting of invasion faded to a faint memory, caste developed into a central tenet of the nascent Hindu faith. The children of victors and vanquished alike subscribed to the evolving belief.

♦

—Jonah Blank, *Arrow of the Blue-Skinned God: Retracing the Ramayana through India*

be an indecipherable patchwork. There are thousands of castes and subcastes sanctioned by Hinduism as divinely ordained earthly stations from which one cannot escape except through death and reincarnation. Some castes are large, such as the superior Brahmins or the inferior Untouchables, but even these have regional subdivisions notable as much for their differences as for their shared status. Other castes are tiny groups, confined to a single clan of artisans or laborers in a single village. The overall stratification is roughly symmetrical. About 15 percent of India's population are reckoned to belong to the upper castes at the very top. About 20 percent belong to the very lowest castes or to oppressed indigenous tribes at the very bottom. (Untouchables are in this group, though technically they are not a caste at all, but a spiritually homeless group of "outcasts.") This lowest tier is designated by the government as "scheduled castes and tribes" and has been targeted in various affirmative action programs since just after independence. In the middle, some 65 percent of the population belong to what is known these days as the "other backward classes", lower and lower-middle castes and minorities such as Muslims and Christians. Within this grouping are some clans that have done very well since independence, some that have done very poorly, and some that have simply remained in servitude to their landlords. It was a doomed attempt by India's crusading prime minister V. P. Singh to initiate for these other backward classes a new, sweeping affirmative action plan in public employment that sparked the caste riots of 1990, including the upper-caste self-immolations that brought the fire-extinguisher salesman to my door.

For decades now, South Asian politicians and activists have been attempting sporadically to untie the hierarchical binds of history, religion, and culture through land reform legislation, speeches, symbolic acts, marches, electoral campaigns, industrialization plans, welfare programs, and government hiring schemes. Many of these efforts reflect the noblest aspirations of the Nehruvian state: social mobility and an end to caste distinctions through universal education, full employment, widespread health care, and a benevolent, leveling bureaucracy. That Indian society continues to honor these ideals is evident in the way it can still be shocked by dramatic instances of their breach. Indian newspapers, magazines, and video news programs controlled by the upper castes report regularly and prominently on the continuing murder, rape, and arson attacks carried out in the countryside by upper-caste landowners against the lower-caste landless. But often implicit in such reporting is the idea that these cases are archaic exceptions, abhorrent to the enlightened sensibilities of the cities, where castes and creeds mix freely and can stake their claims to the future. What the opinion-making upper-caste elite does not often wish to reckon with is how the Nehruvian state itself has been constructed to preserve caste roles—and especially in the cities. Too often what the state has created is not a level playing field but a series of interlocking, competitive clan- or caste-based mafias—vote banks, as they are called by Indian politicians—where the organizing principle is not merit but patronage. And patronage flows not only from the state machinery but from the advantages of birth. Upper-caste networks are enriched and often protected from challenge by inheritance of land and state-sanctioned business franchises obtained from the precolonial princes, and later, the British imperialists.

The independent Indian state has partially undermined the strength of upper-caste networks. In the cities and in such institutions as the bloated military, old caste and feudal identities are dissolving. A younger generation is rising with attitudes significantly more egalitarian than those of their parents and grandparents. New lower-caste mafias have attached themselves to the state, mainly through affirmative action and electoral politics, and have built up their own networks of patronage and wealth, lifting some of their members to new social and economic heights—in some cases, even overthrowing local upper castes who used to hold them down.

Yet progress toward the creation of a casteless society has been much slower than the Nehruvian idealists promised. One bit of anecdotal evidence was what Indians would say when I asked whether the old caste and feudal identities really made any day-to-day difference in their lives. I asked this question of hundreds of people in cities, towns, and villages. Almost invariably, those of high birth said that feudal and caste origin mattered less and less in swirling, modernizing South Asia. Younger Brahmins and Rajputs would say that they had lost their parents' ability to determine the caste of a stranger with a few subtle, well-chosen questions about family background. But not once did a person of low birth tell me the same. They knew exactly how to determine the caste of a stranger and did so regularly; to them, caste and feudal identity made all the difference in the world.

It was not difficult to see why, even within a square mile of my supposedly exclusive neighborhood of "luxury" concrete-block three- and four-bedroom homes inhabited by upper-caste Indian bureaucrats and multinational businessmen. Just a few hundred yards from my driveway, on a sheltered hill up a dirt alley, lived a colony of untouchable "ragpickers" who made their living from the refuse of the Delhi rich. Their small compound, perhaps two acres square, consisted of a dozen low tar-paper shanties; a "school" constructed from a canvas canopy, rope, and wooden pegs; and heaps upon heaps of steaming, stinking garbage, which the residents collected, sorted, and sold off to Delhi scrap dealers. Flies and mosquitoes swarmed through the colony, far outnumbering the residents. Unwashed, unclothed children chased one another through the trash as their parents squatted beside the great piles, picking and sorting. In economic terms, the ragpicking colonies—there are scores of them nestled into major cities—are carefully integrated into urban life. They serve as partial substitutes for municipal garbage collection. There is little public refuse collection in India, in part because there is little household waste that

the larger economy wants to dispose of entirely. One man's scrap is another man's house. One man's newspaper is another's shopping bag. One man's lawn trimmings are another's donkey feed. Ragpickers are intermediaries in these recycling transactions. But while they operate in a market-based, cash-driven subeconomy, they cannot be thought of as free agents. The roles they played centuries earlier as bonded, landless peasants in the rural villages, many of them now play again in the new cities, despite the job set-

> *I* have always found it uncomfortable to travel in a group in which a member, whether a driver or otherwise, is excluded at mealtimes. In India with its complex caste separations the situation was more tricky than in England, for people who seemed to mix easily enough when working together sometimes appeared to withdraw into a strange dietetic *purdah* when mealtimes arrived. I had already noticed that when we stopped for tea at one of the *dhabas*, Devi refused to eat and our driver immediately disappeared from sight.
>
> ◆
>
> —Norman Lewis, *A Goddess in the Stones: Travels in India*

asides and education schemes that have brought a relatively small number out of the trash heaps and into the dimly lit offices of the bureaucracy. The exploitation these urban Untouchables face today is more complicated than it used to be, but to the ragpickers themselves it does not seem different because it arises not merely from poverty but from the stigma of low birth.

I drove up to the ragpicking colony one afternoon and sat on rope cots with a dozen residents to talk about caste and politics. Surely, I argued to them, despite the timeless degradation and poverty, there were scraps of progress here in the colony as well— the school provided by the government, for example, or the fact that they had escaped from the isolated oppression of the villages to a city where they could better protect themselves and their children. Didn't it seem likely, at the least, that some of their children's children might find a way off these heaps, propelled in part by the hard work and willingness to migrate of their courageous grandparents?

But it was difficult to find anyone who held this view. They understood my argument well, they wrestled with it privately themselves—they just did not believe it.

"I've been here since 1974," answered one emaciated man, Om Prakash. "I haven't seen anyone rise out of this. We have all stayed poor. Not a single person has become big. We only watch after our own children. I had a brother, he came to New Delhi and did a bachelor of arts degree. Now he's back in Haryana working as a ragpicker. This is the place for us. We can't get out of here. We hope and we try. There's always hope, but we never reach anything. I'm sure my grandfather hoped, too. Even if I work hard, if I go forward one step, there are ten people pushing me back again."

A few hundred yards from the ragpickers hillock lies the rutted entrance to an even more oppressive world: a colony of stone crushers. I first noticed them while landing at New Delhi's international airport. In certain air traffic patterns, the planes sweep low over a vast scarred landscape of eroded red clay rock quarries just outside the airport grounds. If you peer down carefully into the pits, you can see small bands of shirtless men and scarved women and even children smashing rocks by hand with picks and axes. In summer, they do this work in temperatures of up to 120 degrees or more. There are about five thousand of them, mainly landless Untouchables from neighboring, drought-stricken Rajasthan who are collected by unscrupulous labor contractors, forced into debt, and then set to work in the quarries for decades, even generations, until their loans are repaid. The workers live in shanty colonies on the rim of the pits. Shortly after dawn each morning they carry their picks and sledgehammers on their shoulders down into the quarries and begin smashing against the walls. When piles of rock accumulate at their feet, they lift the stones and hurl them into flatbed trucks that arrive to haul the rocks away. A family earns about $1.50 per truckload at present exchange rates, after commissions and expenses deducted by the quarry owners. On a good day, a fit husband and wife

*I*t is easier, far easier, to accept a humble position if it is divinely ordained. To a Hindu, each person's place in the world is not determined by chance. A Brahmin is a Brahmin as a reward for the virtues of a previous life, and a Shudra is a Shudra for past sins. It is all perfectly just. Over the course of several incarnations, even the lowest peasant can rise to the top of the heap.

Until the present, this belief made social inequities tolerable. But when the order of the world is no longer changeless, it is no longer divine. Class is increasingly determined by money rather than by God. Indians have traditionally seen caste as a means of cooperation, a way of structuring society so that all members can work together in harmony. But if the system is stripped of its religious meaning, class becomes a struggle of each person against every other. If stratification has no basis in morality, it becomes a prison.

◆

—Jonah Blank, *Arrow of the Blue-Skinned God: Retracing the Ramayana through India*

working hard together can fill two or three trucks. The pits are divided up among families until all the stones on a given wall are crushed. Typically, a single family will smash rocks on the same wall in the same pit for seven years or more, day after day. Sisyphus could not have known worse than this.

Before climbing down into the pits one day to talk with the crushers, I visited the manager of the quarry "labor society," which skimmed a percentage of the crushers' wages and in theory invested the money in housing and water. We talked for a while about how the quarry system works. I asked casually why all the crushers were either Untouchables or tribals. "It's the nature of the work," the manager answered, laughing. "You wouldn't expect a Brahmin to come and do this, would you?"

God forbid. Wandering that afternoon from pit to pit, dodging stones as they fell from hammers, I asked the crushers whether any of the Brahmin-born, socialist-bred labor organizers or politicians who lived in the big flats and houses just a few hundred yards away had ever accomplished anything for them. Nobody shied from the opportunity to complain.

"In the morning, you can't work because of the heat and at night you can't sleep because of the mosquitoes," said Lal Chand, squatting on a pile of rocks in the shade. "We've got no electricity. The nearby slums have electricity, but we don't. There are all sorts of people who come here and say you will get electricity. They want something from us—votes, money—then they go away. Nothing changes. They tempt us with a lot of things, but then they disappear." He has been crushing rocks for six or seven years, he said. I asked Chand how he occupied his mind while swinging his sledgehammer. He said mainly he thought about riding the bus to buy liquor and get roaring drunk in Haryana, a journey he could afford to undertake about once every twenty days.

In a neighboring pit I found a young, attractive, muscular married couple, Choti Devi and Bahwaral Lal, rhythmically hacking at a wall and loading a truck with stones. They were born and raised on the rim of the quarry—their parents work in the same pit— and were married fourteen years ago, when he was twelve and she was eleven. They have two sons, two daughters. They have been chopping at this same wall for ten years.

"I keep thinking about food all day—that's what makes me work," he said, glistening with sweat.

"What about your kids—will they do the same job?" I asked.

"My son will do the same thing," she answered, hoisting stones to her head and heaving them into a parked truck. "I'll send him to school, but there's never enough money, so he'll do this as well. This work is nothing difficult. I have the strength."

"What's so special about kids?" her husband asked, smashing stones for Devi to lift. "I was a kid and I did it. If there's no alternative, why not? I studied math and science, but now there is no alternative."

"He gets mad in this heat," said his wife. "Two years ago he got mad and ran away. We both blame it on the heat. We've got to live this life. If we fight, it's because of the heat. We've got to take our anger out on somebody."

"It helps when she comes and works," he said. "It helps a lot."

I asked about New Delhi's various labor organizers and socialist activists. What did they think of them?

"They come and tell us to become one," he answered. "How can laborers become one? We've got pressures from the masters. If we get into the union, we'll lose our jobs."

"What worries you the most?" I asked.

"Tuberculosis."

Silence. Then the rhythm of hammers on rocks, rocks falling on rocks, rocks landing in trucks. A jet flew overhead, banking low on approach to Indira Gandhi International Airport. I asked Lal what he thinks about when he sees the planes.

"We want to go there," he said, stopping now to lean on his pick. "I feel angry when I see them. They're looking at us. Even I want to fly. I want to sit on an airplane and see the world."

"Perhaps it will happen," I mused, foolishly.

"The only time I'll fly from here is when I quit the world," he answered.

Steve Coll is a Pulitzer Prize-winning journalist and author of four books, including On the Grand Trunk Road: A Journey into South Asia, *from which this story is excerpted. He has been a reporter and foreign correspondent for the* Washington Post *since 1985 and is currently based in London.*

★

I was watching the activity at Kali's shrine one day when a crowd of foreign tourists came through. Their guide had not even finished explaining the significance of the goddess and the form of worship practised by her devotees, when one of the party went to the priest in charge of the water tub, bought two pats of *ghee* and with caricatured movements hurled these in slow motion at the bronze, so that his wife could capture his bravado with her cine-camera. Many of the foreigners roared with laughter, while the nearest Indians managed to look disdainful and disapproving without moving a muscle or uttering so much as a sigh.

I hurried away, ashamed by the man's vulgarity and the colour of my skin, to sit on the steps near Meenakshi's shrine. A small boy came past with a basket of flowers on his head, and when I smiled at him he tried to wink at me by closing both eyes at once. Shortly afterwards he returned with a girl of about the same age. She thrust a flower at me and I, mistaking her purpose, declined it as gently as I could.

She held it out more urgently. "No money," she said. "Take."

So I did, and prayed that she and her brother might have a long life.

—Geoffrey Moorhouse, *OM: An Indian Pilgrimage*

WILLIAM DALRYMPLE

Beyond Turkman Gate

The author enters the strange world
of the hijras, *India's eunuchs.*

TURKMAN GATE LIES ON THE SOUTHERN EDGE OF OLD DELHI. Most of the ancient city walls were pulled down twenty years ago and the gate now stands alone on a traffic island like a great beached whale washed up on the edge of the city.

One morning in mid-January I jumped over the railings and climbed up to the parapet of the gate. It was a little before dawn; the Old City was just getting up. Sweepers raked the dirt and dung away from the front of stalls; a *muezzin* called from the minaret of a nearby mosque; *chai- wallahs* pulled their blankets closer around them and lit their burners to boil the first tea saucepan of the day. It was still very cold.

I waited for a full hour before I caught a glimpse of the sight that I had come to see. Just as the sun was rising, a solitary bicycle rickshaw jolted out of the labyrinth of the Old City and trundled underneath the gate. Inside were three figures. They were clad in brightly coloured silks and muslins, flowing saris edged in glittering gold brocade. They were heavily made up, with painted cheeks and scarlet lipstick; each of their noses was pierced with a single diamond stud. They were dressed for the *nautch* [type of dance performance popular in the early nineteenth century], dressed as

411

women, yet they were not women. Even at a distance of twenty yards I could see that their physiognomy was very different from the delicate features of Indian girls. Their faces were too strong, their arms were too thick, their shoulders were wrong. They smoked. Physically, they resembled painted men, yet they were not men. Like Dargah Quli Khan's friend Taqi, the figures in the rickshaw were all eunuchs.

Eunuchs were once common over the width of Eurasia. They are fleetingly referred to in ancient Assyrian and Babylonian stelae and became popular as servants—and as passive sexual playthings—in the degenerate days of the later Roman Empire. In the Muslim world their impotence made them perfect harem guards and they rose to power as chamberlains, governors, and even generals. They were slaves in Anglo-Saxon England and survived in Italy well into the nineteenth century, singing castrato roles in opera as well as in the Vatican Sistine choir.

Yet today eunuchs have apparently died out everywhere except in the subcontinent. Here they are still not uncommon figures in the poorer parts of the larger cities. In all there are thought to be some three-quarters of a million of them surviving. Modern Indian eunuchs dress as women and arrive uninvited at weddings and birth celebrations. They dance and sing and make bawdy jokes. From the poor they extract money in payment for the good luck and fecundity that their blessings are supposed to impart. From the rich they take larger sums by threatening to strip naked unless paid to leave; terrified middle-class party-givers will give them anything as long as they go quickly. They are volatile, vulgar and can sometimes be violent.

Yet despite their frequent appearances in public, very little is actually known about the Indian eunuchs. They are fiercely secretive and of their own choice inhabit a dim world of ambiguity and half-truths. They trust no one, and hate being questioned about their lives; if they are pressed, at best they will slam their doors in your face. Only occasionally does a scandal—a stabbing during a territorial dispute or rumours of a forcible castration—throw them into the headlines and into the dear light of day.

For ten days after that first sighting from the top of the Turkman Gate, I trawled the teeming alleys of Old Delhi, trying to identify the houses of the eunuchs and attempting to persuade one of them to talk to me. Sometimes I would receive a mono-syllabic answer to a question, but generally my enquiries were met with either blank silences or, more often, with graphic expletives.

One fruitless morning, after an unusually rude dismissal from a eunuch's house, I retired dispirited to a nearby *dhaba* for a cup of *chai*. There I finally decided to throw in my efforts at making con-tact with the Delhi eunuchs; it was taking up a lot of time and there was still no hint of a breakthrough: after ten days I still knew as little about them as I had when I had begun. While I was sitting there, sipping my glass of hot, sweet Indian tea, I was approached by a shifty-looking man who asked me whether I could help him; he had seen me with my camera; could I help him mend his? I had nothing better to do, so I agreed to try. He led me to his house and in a few minutes I had diagnosed the trouble—a flat battery. Zakir thanked me and then quietly revealed that he had been watching me for several days. He knew what I was looking for; and he indi-cated that he might be able to help.

He was, he said, a jeweller. His family had always been Delhi jewellers—his ancestors had served the Mughal emperors and before them the Delhi Sultans. At the court they had made the jewellery for the Imperial eunuchs. When the British evicted the Mughals from the Red Fort in 1857, some of the court eunuchs had come to live nearby, a few minutes' walk from the Turkman Gate. There his family had continued to serve them. He said that he had known all the local eunuchs since his childhood, and that he still made all their jewellery. I had helped him, he said, now it was his obligation to help me. He instructed me to meet him the next day at the Turkman Gate, soon after dawn. He would see what he could do.

I was there on time, and Zakir was true to his word. He led me through the narrow alleys of the Old City until we came to a lane barely two feet wide. At the end of the lane, round a chicken-leg turn lay a large *haveli* of the late Mughal period. He knocked three times, and the door swung open.

Like most things in Delhi, the curious position of the eunuchs in Indian society can be explained by the head-on collision of two very different traditions, one Muslim, one Hindu. *Hijras* (eunuchs) are referred to in the very earliest of Hindu texts, the Vedas, written in the second millennium B.C. Here castration was seen as a degrading punishment meted out only to the very lowest in society. An Untouchable who was caught urinating near a Brahmin could be castrated, as could any lower-caste Hindu who had sex with a Brahmin woman. The act of castration brought the criminal to a level even lower than the Untouchables. By the time of the Mahabharata, one thousand years later, the position of eunuchs had improved very little. To be a eunuch was a curse; even the sight of them was defiling to a Brahmin. No one was allowed to accept alms from them, no one was allowed to consume food prepared by them, they were excluded from all sacrifices. As a solitary concession, non-Brahmins were permitted to watch them dance.

The position of eunuchs in Islam was always very different. Although the Prophet Muhammad forbade castration, eunuchs were always common in Muslim society and because of their sterility were considered free of the taint of sexuality. They were thus especially suitable to guard sacred relics and great sanctuaries. The shirt of Muhammad in Cairo was guarded by eunuchs, as was the Great Mosque in Mecca. Pilgrims—*hajjis*—would kiss the eunuchs' hands on their way to see the Ka'ba, the most holy shrine in all Islam.

Dedicated courtiers, undistracted by families, they soon rose to powerful positions, first in Mameluk Egypt, then in Ottoman Turkey, but most prominently of all in Mughal India. "The kings, princes, queens, and princesses place great confidence in these people," wrote the Italian traveller Niccolao Manucchi. "All people of quality have eunuchs in their service and all the other officials, servants, and slaves are bound to account to the eunuchs for all they do." As officials and as singers, dancers, and conjurors they were still prominent figures in Safdar Jung's Delhi; according to Dargah Quli Khan, Taqi was a favourite of the Emperor and had access to His Majesty's private apartments.

When the Mughal court was disbanded, Muslim *hijras* were exposed for the first time to the other, Hindu, tradition of eunuchry. In typical Delhi fashion the two traditions merged, and the *hijras* became subject to a very Indian compromise.

To give birth to a hermaphrodite is still considered by simple Indians to be one of the most terrible curses that can befall a woman. At the same time the blessing of a *hijra* is considered to be unusually potent. It can make a barren woman fertile. It can scare off malevolent *djinns*. It

> The extraordinary accomplishments of Muslims—builders of the Taj Mahal and scores of palaces, weavers, landscape designers, and painters of great skill—are often undervalued by Hindu India, whose temple architects, lacking the arch and dome, built dark, massive towers often distinguished only by their sculpture and friezes.
>
> ◆
>
> —Barbara Crossette, *India: Facing the Twenty-First Century*

can nullify the evil eye. In the streets *hijras* are jeered at, sometimes even pelted with rubbish. Yet at a poor family's most crucial and most public celebrations, at a marriage or at the birth of a male child, the absence of a *hijra* would almost invalidate the whole ceremony. The eunuchs themselves have aided the merging of the two traditions. They no longer guard harems; instead, as in the Mahabharata, they dance for a living. They no longer dress like men as they did in the Mughal court; instead they deck themselves in jewellery and cosmetics and wear saris. Nevertheless, they retain many of the characteristics of their courtly forebears.

Manucchi gives a rather patronizing description of characteristics and temperaments of the eunuchs of Mughal times. "Among the qualities of this sort of animal is their extreme covetousness in collecting gold, silver, diamonds, and pearls," he writes. "They are afraid to spend money even when it is necessary, fond of receiving, niggardly in giving. Nevertheless they are anxious to appear well dressed. They are foul in speech and fond of silly stories. Yet among Mohammedans they are the strictest observers of the faith."

Manucchi obviously disliked the Delhi eunuchs: "They are baboons," he wrote, "insolent, licentious baboons." Anyone who comes across them casually today can easily see why he was so rude. Yet you do not have to spend very long with them to appreciate how India, then as now, has turned them into what they are, how it has brutalized them and forced them to anaesthetize their own sensibilities.

Thrown out of their homes, rejected by their families, they come together for protection. In the streets they affect the manners of a pantomime dame to gain attention: they pinch men's buttocks, purposely make buffoons of themselves, but are quick to take offence. With little possibility of much fulfilment in this world, they look to the next; they are for ever visiting temples and mosques (for this they are required to revert to their male clothes) and going on pilgrimage to Hindu and Muslim shrines over the subcontinent. In this strange mix of piety and bawdiness, they directly recall the world of Dargah Quli Khan and the Muraqqa'-e-Dehli.

The house was a late Mughal *haveli* off Gulli Mr. Shiv Prasad. A pretty young eunuch in a canary-yellow silk sari led Zakir and me through a vaulted passageway and out into a small courtyard.

Under a wooden veranda lay a spread of carpets and divans. Sprawled over them were two more eunuchs; one was staring at herself in a mirror, applying lipstick, the other was combing her hair. Nearby sat two effeminate-looking men; there was also a baby in a cradle. Despite the early hour, the eunuchs were all dressed and painted as if they were about to go out to a late-night *nautch*. They greeted Zakir warmly, but frowned at me.

"Who's the *gora* (white)?" asked one.

"This is my friend Mr. William," said Zakir. "He's a writer."

"Why have you brought him here?"

"He would like to meet you all."

"You know we can't talk to any outsiders," replied the *hijra*, "unless Chaman Guruji gives us permission."

"And she won't," said the other *hijra*, pouting defiantly at me. "She doesn't like *goras*."

"Where is Chaman?" asked Zakir.

"Upstairs. She's sick."

We climbed the rickety wooden stairs that led up to a balcony; as we did so, one of the eunuchs blew a kiss at me and the others burst out laughing. At the top of the stairs, Zakir knocked at the door. A gruff voice commanded us to enter.

As we stepped through the portal, we left the late Mughal *haveli* behind and entered a very different world: inside we were confronted by a gleaming pink boudoir that could have been the dressing-room of a 1950s Hollywood film star. Mirror-glass tiles covered the end walls and the ceiling; pink plastic carnations peeped out of brass vases; cut-out pictures of actors and actresses were pasted into a frieze over a glass bookcase filled with Hindi videos. The pink chintz curtains matched the pink chintz bedspread; underneath it, prostrate yet fully dressed in a woman's blouse and man's *dhoti*, sprawled the figure of Chaman, the guru of the household.

Chaman's fingernails were brightly painted and her hair was long and straggly; she had huge sagging breasts. Yet her face with its heavy jowls, hangover eyes and early-morning stubble was entirely that of a man. As we entered the bloated face nodded us a silent greeting.

"Chamanji," said Zakir. "You are unwell?"

"I'm dying," said Chaman. Then, groaning: "Oh! The pain!"

"What is wrong with you Chamanji?" asked Zakir.

"Nothing works any more. This body..."

"Is it your knees again?"

"My knees. And my teeth. And my breathing."

"Have you seen a doctor?"

"I had an injection yesterday. For the asthma. It's like trying to breathe through a thick *chador*."

Chaman held up the pink bedspread against her mouth to demonstrate what she meant.

"I'm in pain, I'm probably dying, and all my little *chelas* (disciples) are leaving me. I had seven, now only three are left to look after their old mother. Remember Maya? She went off last month and married a boy from Pakistan. Promised she would come and see me, but you know what these little *chelas* are like..." Chaman suddenly began to look rather sad. "I can't even see properly any more. And as for my teeth..."

"What's happened to your teeth?" asked Zakir.

"I had them all out last month. Got new ones put in. Look."

Chaman pulled out her dentures and flourished them at us. As she did so she seemed to notice me for the first time.

"Who's your *gora*, Zakir?"

"This is my friend, Mr. William."

I smiled. Chaman frowned.

"Is he your boyfriend?"

"No," said Zakir. "He's married. To a girl."

Chaman wrinkled up her nose in disgust.

"He has brought you a present, Chamanji," continued Zakir.

From the bottom of my pocket I produced a silver *ta'wiz*, the Sufi charm Zakir had suggested I purchase as a gift for Chaman. I handed it to the guru. A fat hand shot out from the covers and snatched it from me.

"Who gave you this?" asked Chaman.

"Pir Hassan Naqshbandi," I said.

"Naqshbandi, eh?"

Chaman bit the corner of the *ta'wiz*. This seemed to satisfy her as to its authenticity.

"It will make you well again," I said hopefully.

"Nothing will make me well again." The old eunuch fixed me with a sharp eye.

"Are you American? From the land of Hollywood?"

"No. I'm British."

"From London?"

"From Scotland."

"You know Sean Connery? I read in a magazine that he was from Scotland."

"You're right. He is."

"In the old times we *hijras* used to be like your zero zero seven. We were called *khwaja saras*, not *hijras*. We used to live in the king's house. In those days we never danced. Our job was to listen and tell things to the king. We were just like your Sean Connery."

Somehow I couldn't imagine Chaman and her household taking on Goldfinger or seducing Ursula Andress, but I let this pass.

"I love the movies," continued Chaman. "When I was a girl I wanted to be an actress. Look!"

From the bedside table Chaman produced a black and white photograph. It showed a beautiful, heavy-boned girl in a European dress. She had heavily rouged lips and painted eyebrows. A velvet choker was tied around her neck; massive gold earrings hung from her lobes. The tone was sub-Garbo; only the *tikka* mark between the eyebrows gave away that the image was Indian.

"That was me when I was twenty-five," said Chaman. "I was beautiful, no?"

"Unique," I said.

Chaman blushed with pleasure: "You mean it?"

"*K*nowledge can make you old. Compassion is a river of youth that will never run dry. Knowledge can make you tired—bathe in the water of compassion and you will be refreshed."

◆

—Rinpoche Thuksey, quoted by Andrew Harvey, *A Journey in Ladakh*

After the breakthrough with Chaman it still took two months of regular visits with Zakir before I got to know the other eunuchs properly. I used to arrive early in the morning before the household had left on their rounds. They would always be busy putting on their make-up and brushing their hair. Often there would be some drama: Razia, the loudest and most ebullient of Chaman's *chelas* would be wringing her hands and weeping because her new boyfriend had gone off to Ajmer or because Chaman had called her a tart or because her pet goat had gone missing; she always suspected her neighbours were planning to slaughter it.

Another source of worry was the baby girl that Panna, another of Chaman's *chelas*, had adopted; if ever it wheezed or coughed or refused its food, Panna would work herself up into an opera of agitation. The only *hijra* who always kept her calm was Vimla, the prettiest and quietest of Chaman's *chelas*. She was in charge of the kitchen and by seven in the morning would be busy chopping up chillies and onions ready for lunch.

Razia, Panna, and Vimla were all very different—in their backgrounds, their characters, and their looks. Razia was the most unlikely of the three. A Kashmiri Muslim, she claimed to have been to the Doon School (the Indian Eton) and to have completed a Master's degree in English at Bombay University. I was never able to establish whether she was telling the truth—virtually all the *hijras* I talked to shrouded the facts of their lives in a thick wrap of fantasies—but she was certainly from a middle-class background and spoke fluent English.

"I became a *hijra* very late—in my mid-twenties—after my mother died," she once said. "I was born with a body that was masculine but my heart was always feminine. I never fitted in anywhere, but now I feel good with these people."

"Was it very difficult when you first joined the *hijras*?" I asked.

"When I arrived it was very strange. Everyone lived together; there was no privacy. The six other *chelas* were all illiterate and came from villages. Before I used to be a real reader; but here there was not one book in the house. None of them even read a newspaper. But Chaman was very protective and supportive; it was as if I was still living with my mother."

She added: "Sometimes I wanted desperately to go home, to see my sisters. Once I went all the way home—but I never went in. I just looked in the window then went away."

"Did the other eunuchs accept you?" I asked. "Didn't they mind your posh background?"

"Not at all. Thanks to Chaman they were kind to me. Besides

I was useful to them. I was able to talk English and to read and write. We are all happy together. Sometimes when I see Panna with her baby I wish I was a woman and had a husband and a child. But Chaman doesn't like us to have partners. She doesn't like men in the house—at least not corrupt men. She's very jealous of her daughters."

Panna, Razia's friend, was a very different creature. She was a very large *hijra*: nearly six feet tall. Her face was covered with the scars of smallpox and she had a huge protruding belly; a shadow of light stubble flecked her chin. She would never have won a beauty contest. But she was one of the shyest of all the *hijras* I met, and one of the most gentle; her life revolved entirely around the baby she had just adopted. Her story emerged only after I had got to know her very well.

It seems that Panna was born asexual—with no visible sexual characteristics—into a poor family who lived in a village near Varanasi. When Panna was just twenty days old, the village midwife disclosed that she was neither male nor female, that she was a *hijra*. The news spread like wildfire. Panna's mother, fearing the consequences, left the village with the baby and went to stay with a cousin fifty kilometres away.

"In the village, my deformity had become the sole topic of conversation," Panna told me. "The rest of my family were ostracized. It was said that we were cursed. The following day a relative came to the village and said that my mother had died of shock soon after reaching her cousin's house.

"I was brought back along with the body of my mother. The death did not move the village. Instead they sent a message to Chaman, who used to visit the village every so often. The curse on the village had to be removed. Chaman came with two *chelas* and took me away. I grew up to be the *chela* of Chaman, and Chaman became my guru.

"Being a *hijra* was the only possibility for me; there was no other career I could have pursued with the body that was given to me at birth. Sometimes I used to be lonely and unhappy, but now with the baby my life is complete. Now I don't care what people say: at times I look at the child and I am so happy I can't sleep at night. When she is older I will send the child to a good girls' school and see that she is taught English. Maybe one day she will be beautiful and become a model or film star."

Panna is unusual in that she was born asexual. The vast majority of eunuchs, and almost all those I met, were born physically male. In Europe they would probably describe themselves as transsexuals and have a full sex change. But in India the technology for this does not exist. The only choice is between a brutal—and extremely dangerous—village castration, or, for those who can afford it, a course in hormone pills followed by an anaesthetized operation. The operation is illegal in India, but there are several doctors who, for a fee, are willing to take the risk.

Vimla, the most feminine-looking of the eunuchs, did not have the money for an operation and voluntarily underwent a village castration. The son of a Jat farmer outside Delhi, by the age of thirteen she was already refusing to work in the fields, saying that she felt more like a woman than a man.

"I was sure that I did not have a place in either male or female worlds," she told me. "My body was that of a man but deep down I had the heart of a woman. At puberty I started thinking of myself as a *hijra*.

---

*E*n route we picked up our first hitchhiker, a young tribal who displayed great excitement on seeing a large dead snake in the middle of the road.

"What on earth was that all about?" I asked Aditya.

"Our friend has expressed a wish that the snake would come alive and bite him."

"What...!"

"He believes that it belongs to the lowest caste of snakes. It is, in fact, an Untouchable. Therefore once our friend bears this mark, all other snakes will avoid him."

♦

—Mark Shand,
Travels on My Elephant

"One day a *hijra* named Benazir came to my village. She was very beautiful and I fell in love with her. When I was on my own I would feel sad and would not eat properly. Only when Benazir returned did I feel happy. My family began to suspect that I was in love, but they did not know with whom. But in the village people who had seen Benazir and me together began to gossip."

A lucrative marriage settlement that Vimla's family were negotiating fell through as rumours began to spread. In frustration and shame, Vimla's father beat her up. The following day Vimla ran away to Delhi to look for Benazir.

"For days I searched for my Benazir, but I did not have an address or know the name of her guru. I knew no one in Delhi and had no money. I had to sleep on the pavements and beg for money. Occasionally I got a free meal from the *pirzadas* (officials) at the shrine of Khwaja Nizamuddin, but often I would go to bed hungry."

Eventually Vimla met and was adopted by Chaman Guru.

"In those days Chaman was very rich and beautiful. She became my guru and gave me lots of beautiful saris and gold bangles. I started to wear women's clothes and to put on make-up. The following year I was taken to a village in the Punjab. I was dosed with opium and a string was tied around my equipment. Then the whole lot was cut off."

"I knew it would be very painful and dangerous, but I got cut so that no one would taunt me any more. After I was cut all my male blood flowed away and with it went my manhood. Before I was neither one thing nor the other. Now I am a *hijra*. I am not man or woman. I am from a different sex."

I once asked Vimla if she ever missed family life.

"We are a family," she said. "A *chela* must obey her guru like a bride obeys her mother-in-law. We *chelas* must work hard, do the cooking inside the house, and most of the dancing outside. We have an obligation to look after our guru when she grows old, just like we would look after our own mother. In return, when we first become *hijras* Chaman Guru teaches us *chelas* the ways of the eunuchs."

The longer I spent with the eunuchs, the more it became clear that the whole system was highly structured, both within the household and outside it. Just as every household of eunuchs has its strict rules within its walls, so each household also has a well defined "parish" where its members are allowed to operate. Violations—poaching in another household's area—is referred to a special council of eunuchs from all over India and Pakistan which meets once a year.

There is even a Central School of Dance for the *hijras*. It occupies a shady campus dotted with bushes of purple bougainvillaea in Panipat, fifty kilometres to the north of Delhi. Here Prem Hijra, a bad-tempered old eunuch with a bun and beady black eyes, offers courses in dancing (folk, *Bharat Natyam*, Arab belly dancing, or disco) and singing (traditional, *ghazals*, or modern film songs) to new recruits. She also runs refresher courses for those who want to perfect a particular style of dancing or learn the latest film songs.

"She's very strict," Vimla once told me, "But they say that in her youth she was the best dancer in North India."

I pressed Vimla to show me her dancing and eventually, after first consulting with Chaman, she invited me to join the household on their rounds, or "going on tolly" as they call it. Every household of eunuchs has a network of informers—sweepers, *dhobis*, midwives—who report back the imminent births and marriages in their district. Every day, before setting out on tolly, the guru of the household prepares a detailed itinerary of addresses to be visited, and the eunuchs adhere strictly to this list.

We set off at seven in the morning after a particularly frantic bout of making-up: all three *hijras* cleaned their teeth with *neem* twigs, smudged on great quantities of lipstick and dusted their faces with blusher. Then we all took a convoy of rickshaws to Lajpath Nagar, in south Delhi.

At Lajpath Nagar we met up with two musicians, a pair of elderly men, one of whom played a harmonium, the other a pair of *tabla* drums. After a quick breakfast we set off to the first address on the list. As they walked along the streets, the eunuchs clapped their hands and made bawdy jokes, behaving quite differently from the way they did inside their Turkman Gate *haveli*. Vimla in particular underwent a radical character change. Sweet, shy, and doe-eyed at home, she would rush up to complete strangers in the street, grapple with her skirts and shout: "*Sardarji!* You with the beard! Give me money or else I'll flash!"

The first house on the list was a small ground-floor flat belonging to a carpenter. The eunuchs piled into the entrance hall, the musicians started up the music and Vimla led the dancing by stamping her foot and ringing her little anklet bells. Things were just getting going when a neighbour appeared. Yes, she said, there had just been a birth in the house, but the family had gone to stay with cousins in Haryana; there was now no one at home. Disconsolately, we got back into the rickshaws and set off to the next address.

This was a far larger, middle-class house a few blocks away. Here there had been a marriage three days before, and the bride had just been brought to her new house

*T*he *hijras* of Rajasthan [once known as *nazirs*] believe that their tradition will be passed down through their disciples. "This house and the land we own were given to us by the rajahs. It has been handed down for generations by our gurus. We cannot destroy it," said Shardabai, the guru *hijra* of Ajmer. Unlike the urban *hijras*, these dignified, courtly *hijras* make their livelihood from farm produce and the rent they receive from their tenants.

When Shardabai walks through the streets of Ajmer, people come and touch her feet in respect and receive her blessings. Mothers bring their sick children to be cured by Shardabai's prayers. Her disciples are invited to dance and sing at marriage and birth ceremonies. "People love and respect us because we live a traditional way of life according to custom. My disciples cannot break these rules. They have to toe the line," said Shardabai with quiet authority.

◆

—Aruna Har Prasad, "Uninvited Guests," *World Magazine*

that morning. The old men started up the music and the eunuchs began to dance. A crowd of beggar children gathered to watch beyond the garden wall, but from the house itself there was no response. After a while a toothless old woman peered nervously round the door and smiled. Then she went back inside again.

Meanwhile Panna, despite her bulk, was putting on a fine display. She wobbled her head one way, wobbled her bottom the other, all the while singing an Urdu verse which Zakir translated as follows:

> God bless you,
> You are very sweet,
> You are very lovely,
> God will give you long life.

This classy poetry appeared to do the trick. People began piling out of the house: two daughters-in-law, several small children, some unmarried daughters, two old grandfathers and the new bridegroom. The new bride, required by Hindu etiquette to be blushingly coy for several weeks after her marriage, cowered beyond the open window, twitching the lace curtain. Vimla now took centre-stage, while Panna grabbed an unwilling daughter-in-law and whirled her around in a waltz for a few steps.

As Vimla pirouetted, pulling her sari over her head in a parody of the Dance of the Seven Veils, Chaman Guru put down the cymbals and got down to the serious business of collecting money. The grandfathers both put fifty-rupee notes in the plate, while one of the daughters-in-law presented Chaman with the traditional gift of a plate of flour. But this clearly was not enough as far as Chaman was concerned. She signalled to Panna to carry on singing. A few more fifty-rupee notes were offered, but again Chaman shook her head. Eventually, as the song wound on to its thirtieth verse, the bridegroom presented Chaman with 1000 rupees. Bowing and scraping, the eunuchs withdrew.

It was a strangely farcical routine, and must be extremely tedious to enact day after day. But when society closes off all other opportunities there are only two choices for the eunuchs: dancing and prostitution. Of these, going on tolly is probably preferable—and possibly more lucrative.

I was always struck by the eunuchs' lack of bitterness. Through no fault of their own, through deformity or genetic accident they found themselves marginalized by Indian society, turned into something half-way between a talisman and an object of ridicule. Yet in their own terms they seem fairly content with their lives, and they do not rail against the fate that has left them with this role. In the rickshaw on the way back from that morning's tolly I asked Vimla whether she would like to be reborn as a *hijra* in her next life. She considered for a while before answering.

"Do you have any choice how God makes you?" she answered eventually. "I pray for our welfare in this life. But the next? It is in the gods' hands."

William Dalrymple also contributed "A Sufi Spring" to Part I, "The Other Raj" to Part II, and "Breaking the Fast" to Part III. This story is from his book City of Djinns: A Year in Delhi.

*

At a dark, deserted Delhi intersection, an army officer with a pot belly and a bruised nightstick approached me. I visualized myself held incommunicado for several months in a dank jail cell or sold off into the Bombay cages. When the officer turned on his walkie-talkie I knew I was finished. "Madame," he said, "you will never get a scooter this time of night, I will do the needful." Within minutes he escorted me into an auto-rickshaw, the driver sullenly turned on his meter, and I pressed my palms together in *Namaste*.

—Mary Orr, "India Sketches"

JAN HAAG

✦ ✦ ✦

Sick under the Bo Tree

Illness is everyone's worst fear, but the author finds peace
through healing in a sacred place.

I CAN'T IMAGINE WHY BUDDHA, TWENTY-FIVE CENTURIES AGO, chose this unutterably forsaken spot to sit under a Bo tree. For this is not the identical Bo tree under which Buddha sat, but its progeny. The present tree was brought back as a sapling from Sri Lanka where a cutting of Buddha's Bodhi tree was taken by the nephew of Emperor Ashoka before the original tree died.

Getting to Bodh Gaya is one story, being there in the crucifying sun is another. It takes more than five hours from Patna to Gaya by train, a distance of not more than seventy-five miles. Arriving at the Patna train station at dawn, I was early enough to have a choice of train car. I chose a car half-drenched by water leaking from the roof onto the seats opposite me, thinking it might mean the car would remain cooler and stay less crowded. Not so. Bit by bit, even before we left the station, people encroached onto the wet seats, sat on the wet floor absorbing the water into their clothes and, soon, the heat had dried the residue. Before we had gone ten slow stops on this slowest of all local and stopping trains, we were, as is usual in India, packed tighter than any American can realistically visualize. The ceiling sprouted fans in all directions. Not one of them worked. I sat in the doorway, my legs hanging down over the metal plates of the stairs, just above the gravel, grit, and shit of the railway embankment, grateful for the wind when we were in motion.

The searing heat and the inhuman crush never overcomes the patient good cheer of the ordinary Indian. But I was ill, in a torment of loose bowels, and hungry. I feared to eat the cucumbers which were the only edibles available on the train. But after I ran short of my tepid, supposedly "good," water obtained from the last hotel, an Indian—Indians are always kind and observant—offered me half a long, pale, English cucumber. Cut lengthwise and sprinkled with chili, I could not in all politeness refuse to eat it. So, I let go of the fear of his dirty hands, the dirtier hands of the vendor and the filthy basket in which the cucumber had rested since it had been taken, no doubt, unwashed from the earth. The heat is so intense in India, I told myself, it makes all clean. I felt momentarily refreshed. I had been in India years before and not been sick. Indeed, I had just come down from Kathmandu specifically to recoup my health, to steady my bowels, to find something I could or wanted to eat.

After the five hour train ride to Gaya, it took another hour to get from Gaya to Bodh Gaya in a three-wheel motorized rickshaw. I didn't know it then by name, but I arrived in the town of Buddha's enlightenment the day the pre-monsoon heat struck. Each year, a month or so before the monsoon begins, the heat jumps, from one day to the next, by ten or fifteen degrees. It is expected. And it is welcomed. It is a sign that the monsoon will be good this year.

Arriving at the gates of the Burmese monastery at noon, with the sun firing down its incinerating blasts, I wept to find a sign on the locked metal fence announcing that it would not be opened again until 2:00 p.m. Tears ran down my cheeks as I banged on the gate, rattling its chain, rocking its hot-as-a-branding-iron frame. Finally the ubiquitous young Indian lad appeared (on my side of the gate), gleaned my story and disappeared. Within a few minutes a toothy old man—four teeth stuck straight out like individual canopies over his lower lip—came and opened the gates. Dressed in a *dhoti*, he spoke a bit of sing-song English and was, for many days to come, as kind as a grandfather to me.

He led me out of the blazing sun into a room that seemed cool by contrast even though it must have been well over one hundred degrees. Electricity for the fan was temporarily off then, as I found it was to be at least half the time for the duration of my visit. The room was thick with dust, and the undersides of the shelves of the whitewashed wall recesses were blackened by soot from naked candle flames and their surfaces encrusted with wax—this should have been a warning about the electricity, but I was too ill to recognize it at that moment. There were two hard pallets with clean white sheets folded across them and yards of greyed mosquito netting. I lay down exhausted, ready to vomit, begging for water which the fellow with the teeth got, tepid, from a garden faucet. I tried to ascertain, as any already indisposed tourist would, by asking impolite questions, whether or not it was safe to drink. He assured me the monastery

*I*t is necessary, in the first place, to realize that though a reformer, and perhaps from a priestly point of view a heretic (if such a word can be used in connection with a system permitting absolute freedom of speculation), the Buddha was brought up and lived and died as a Hindu. Comparatively little of his system, whether of doctrine or ethics, was original or calculated to deprive him of the support and sympathy of the best among the Brahmins, many of whom became his disciples. The success of his system was due to various causes: the wonderful personality and sweet reasonableness of the man himself, his courageous and constant insistence upon a few fundamental principles, and to the way in which he made his teaching accessible to all without respect to aristocracy of birth or intellect.

◆

—Ananda K. Coomaraswamy and The Sister Nivedita, *Myths of the Hindus & Buddhists*

had excellent water. This was confirmed by others on the following days, though where it came from in that parched landscape I never knew. Up from the ground somehow. Was it a well? It was good water they said—but nothing could keep it from being tepid. I, who do not like ice-water, longed for the clink of just a few civilized cubes against a sparkling clean glass. I slept and woke and slept again.

Was I close to death? I might have been. Probably I suffered from heat stroke. Certainly I suffered from hunger. They served no food to guests in the monastery. It was more than a mile into town—what was I to do?

Two days later I persuaded the ancient one to get me some food. He brought two small watermelons for me from the town; he, no doubt, had sent the lad. One I ate straight down, for the water and for the sugar; by the next day, the second had began to sour in the heat. I ate it anyway, not knowing when I would get another bit of food. It was a mistake. Diarrhea began again. On the third day I bought a plate of rice across the road at the grass and bamboo shack that seemed to be home to the lad and a considerable number of other family members. I ate two spoonfuls before I carried it home, and then it, too, spoiled before I was hungry again.

If diarrhea or heat overcomes you, one way to revive yourself is by taking the locally available Vijay Electrolyte (a mix of salt and dextrose) with water. Of course, if you have the misfortune to face something like the September 1994 outbreak of pneumonic plague in Gujarat state, this won't do you much good. Antibiotics, flight, and prayer are in order.

◆

—JO'R and LH

The incandescent sun circled in the sky which was pure white, as if the heat had burnt up all the blue. Across the road was the Falgu River, a mile wide, flatter and drier than the Sahara. Palms, gone pale in the light, shagged its edges. Almost no one moved from mid-morning to twilight. On my bed, I lay wondering if this was where I would leave this world. I didn't care.

Though I rarely read novels any more, a desire to reread Thomas Mann's *The Magic Mountain* had recently come over me while I was sitting in Korea in the three month's silence of Kyol Che (the Buddhist winter practice).

When I could stand a bit better, and needed something to do other than feel the pulsing of my despair, I asked about the English Library that was mentioned in my guidebook. From the porch of my room in the separate dormitory, a fellow pilgrim pointed toward the farthest corner of the second floor of the main hall. I mounted the back stairs into an emptiness of grit more desolate than the river beyond the road. One or two bits of English furniture lay about and parts of an old four-poster bed, a broken chair. Otherwise there was nothing on that vast second floor of the monastery.

Below the library, on the ground floor, in the long darkness of their refectory, the handsome, bronzed, young (they were actually in their forties but looked twenty), orange-clad monks watched television all day. At night, returning on their motorcycles, I knew not from where, they slept on the refectory floor or on *charpoys* in the garden. They were delightfully friendly and hugely enjoyed the tourists-cum-pilgrims like me—when I began to appear after the worst of my illness. The dozen or so of us staying at the monastery were a motley crew. There was one regal, young Anglo-Indian woman who, with a Spanish companion, was helping to build the first small structure for a Tibetan monastery, out in some field. There was a young English girl, named Teresa, tall, round-faced, who was planning to return to England to study law after some two years of wandering. She, more or less, saved my life. There was a lovely, smiling Indian woman by the name of Jesse, who called herself a Christian *sadhu*. She went about doing her version of good which did not necessarily jibe with the monks' idea of good. She had, apparently, quite out-stayed an originally warm welcome. There were also a Korean lad with his Japanese friend; several portly nuns from Thailand who spoke only Thai; and still others whom

I saw only in passing in the mosquito-filled nights when the fans stopped their indolent turning, went dead along with the twenty-five-watt light bulbs, and we all wandered out, candles in hand, from our suffocating rooms to dodge and swat the insects.

I stepped across the dust and desertion, tiptoeing my way to the farthest corner of the monastery's shadowed upper story, and there, on the slanting-like-a-teeter-totter shelves of what had once been a piece of nineteenth-century furniture, was a crazily tumbled collection of books: mostly novels, detective stories, a few scientific treatises, almost nothing to do with the spirit, less to do with literature, obviously stuff pilgrims had unloaded from their backpacks rather than carry onward. To my amazement, and thanks be to Buddha, there was a densely printed, translated-into-English paperback of *The Magic Mountain*. Was I surprised? I suppose so. But the heat under the uninsulated ceiling was rising. I grabbed the book and fled.

In my room, through the days that followed, I read it slowly, interspersing my heavy-headed lack of enthusiasm for Mann's ponderous Germanic analysis of the world before chaos—or just when chaos was beckoning—with visits to the ladies' room, thick with mosquitos and crackly with lizards. I tried to catch the water in the shower and the sink and garden faucets when the water was on. The whole system apparently worked by an electric pump and went out as often as the fans. I drank and drank and drank the tepid water. Nothing slaked my thirst. Jesse taught me to toss a bucket of water onto the composition stone floor and to hang sheets, in my case, two sarongs I had bought in Thailand, dripping wet from a line so that the evaporation of all this water cooled my room—if ever so slightly.

Over maybe a week's time I got better, and I got worse. I became friends with healthy Teresa who had worked for six months on a sheep ranch in Australia and as a nanny in the outback. She brought me an egg that Jesse cooked and bitter black tea which is an excellent way to stablize the bowels. Finally, I asked for a doctor. He came and prescribed electrolytes, just as they do in the USA, and almost in the same form: a sickishly sweetened liquid like Gatorade,

which I tried to drink but couldn't. The doctor also gave me medicines, also abominably sweet. But the doctor, a most sympathetic
Indian man, with medicines—he threw in some antibiotics in mer-
cifully swallowable pill form—and house visit included, cost only
about five dollars—better odds than a health care plan.

I wondered, I wonder still, why I didn't just let myself die. Not
sadly, or for any reason or lack of reason, but simply because I did-
n't know where to go or what to do. I had no interest whatsoever in living. Indeed, one night when a funeral procession carrying
candles and branches came walking along the road and out across
the river bed, I quite envied the corpse, draped and asleep on a bier
of wood, decorated all around with withered palm fronds that rattled in the wind.

Eventually, however, with the help of Teresa, I shook off my
ennui enough to stagger, at twilight, into town to eat omelets on
chapatis. She took me to a rather magnificent lean-to built of
stripped young saplings and palm fronds at a wide place on the dirt
road in central Bodh Gaya. She had been in town for several
months and knew a good many of the people, all the paths, and
most of the restaurants.

Bodh Gaya.

How can I give you a sense of it? It's actually a pretty little town
and must be beautiful in the rains. It's flat but surrounded by fields.
It's animated because enough tourists and pilgrims come here to
have inspired the entrepreneurial spirit in some of its inhabitants.
But the friendliness is still genuine. There are monasteries housing
monks of many nationalities scattered all over the town and fields.
At this season, it was May, they looked closed-up and deserted even
though, with a search, one could always find a door open and a
monk, at last, to lead you to the *dharma* hall.

After a few days of omelets and *dharma* halls, I found my way,
very early one morning, to the Mahabodhi Temple. I entered the
sacred ground. The dawn was already losing its crimson hue above
the horizon at what?—4:30, maybe 5:00, in the morning. I was
alone. I stepped through a little low wrought iron gate into the
complex, or maybe it was wrought copper, for it was turquoise-

green with age. Beyond this decorative barrier, a rather wild, somewhat jungle-like garden grew among pillars and *stupas*. There were shoulder high flowers, some green things I didn't know, and lilies. One had the feeling it was watered here. I stepped into the temple. It was silent, gray, stone, and lonely. Statues and carvings stood about in shafts of early light. But I knew this wasn't where I wanted to be. It was the Bo tree I had come to see. There was no one around to ask where it might be.

I went back out into the morning dazzle and I walked to the right around the vast temple building. Soon, scattered at my feet, near the temple's back corner, were elegant, heart-shaped leaves with long curved points. They were scattered everywhere, and the wind blew more, green and golden, to the ground. I looked up. There was the vast tree. I didn't need to ask or look for a plaque.

I stood for a long time, watching the gentle wind scattering the leaves. The Bo tree, though larger by far, reminded me of the balm of Gilead trees I have seen in the American desert, quivering and shimmering in the overwhelming light.

Facing the sun, I sat down with my back to the tree. My mind went blank. I tried to think about Buddha. But I had no thoughts. I tried to think about enlightenment, but no images came. The leaves scattered and I watched. There was no joy. There was even no disappointment. Just a vast neutrality. I watched the leaves fall. There was no lightning bolt of insight, no great awareness to record. The sun rose a little higher. A few more leaves fell, and soon they stopped falling as the wind stopped with the coming of the hotter part of the morning.

I never take mementos home when I travel. I carry no packages, trinkets, or works of art from place to place. Even the most temptingly beautiful sea shells and stones I have learned to leave where they lie. But the idea came to me to pick up a whole, maybe half-inch-thick, packet of the Bo tree leaves. Gently, one by one, I laid them one atop another on my hand.

Then I walked on through the garden at the back. India's gardens are different from Western gardens. They are sparser and each plant, shrub and small tree is very individualistic. There's little landscaping, and no decorator feeling at all about most Indian gardens. Just as each human is to be taken on their own terms, so is each plant. There is a plan, you can tell, but no cohesion.

When I got back to the monastery, I did not know what to do with the leaves. Though turning toward the gold of autumn, they were still fresh and succulent, and fragile. I finally decided to put them between the leaves of my Lonely Planet Nepal guidebook—Buddha, after all, born a Hindu in Lumbini, by the new drawn borders of today, would be a Nepalese. There, between the pages of the book, a few leaves, half a dozen maybe, beautifully molded, remain to this day. The others, a dozen or two, I gave away to friends, family, some to strangers, human beings all, briefly met and briefly loved. But each of those, too, those given leaves, have left their greenish-gold-brownish mold in heart-shaped patterns on the pages of my book.

This image of a young woman and a tree constantly recurs in Indian art, and trees are supposed to increase both desire and fertility in a woman. But the asoka also contributes to the health of men. Asoka bark is noted for its astringent and styptic properties and a lotion made from the bark is used to heal open wounds. Its flower buds, which are highly nutritious, are eaten in the last month of the year by men and women alike, to remove grief.

The very name asoka means "unsorrowing." It is said that when her time was near, the mother of the Buddha went deep into the forest of Lumbini. There, clinging onto an asoka tree, she gave birth to the Enlightened One.

◆

—Naveen Patnaik, The Garden of Life: An Introduction to the Healing Plants of India

One day, soon after the day I sat under the Bo tree, Teresa and I, because I felt I was as well as I would ever get in the heat, decided to take the bus to Sasaram, on our way to Varanasi.

On our last night at the Burmese monastery, the monks took us to visit their new monastery where each private room had its own flush toilet. Still under construction, it was out on a plain about three miles from town. They served us tea—that murky, spicy, sweet, boiled-with-milk-and-sugar Indian *chai* which I happened to love, but which makes me immediately sick. I was about to decline, but thought, for politeness sake, ah! one more stomach ache, what does it matter? and tasted it. It turned out to be, of all things, Ovaltine!—shades of Captain Midnight.

The next day, in their old car that spat and sputtered, the monks drove us, against their better judgment, "nobody takes the bus from Gaya," (everyone takes the train, those infinitely slow monsters the British left, that for some esoteric reason the Indian national pride has become enamored with) to the bus station in Gaya. From there, we two women, squashed into a rumbling bus, headed out across the dryness of the Gangetic plain where all color had long ago been leached from the land.

Eventually, we came to the British built Grand Trunk Road, now one solid traffic jam lined with lorry stops and truck repair shops, across the north of the subcontinent. Wedged in by families and bundles and baskets of foodstuffs, sacks of rice and wheat, a certain amount of small livestock, we squinted through the dusty windows—and I knew, again, why I had come to India. Heaven must be like this, I thought, at least the scruffy kind of heaven in which I would like to abide forever.

Nothing appeals to my soul more than a rocking, lurching bus ride, pressed all around by hundreds of patiently beautiful Indians. As I look out at the pale landscape of rocks and stones and dryness and dust and an occasional tree—always with a bullock cart and white clad driver beneath its branches—India bewitches me. It is, to me, the rarest of opiums to move through that sacred land, whether by bus or, when I felt better, on foot. It in itself is a *raison d'etre*. What did I learn in Bodh Gaya where Buddha sat under the Bo tree? I got up off my bed and moved on. No more. But no less.

Besides, how else would I have found out that the most holy city in India, the sacred city of Varanasi, the "city of light,"—some say, the oldest city in the world—exists only on one side of the Ganges? Across the river it is empty sand.

Jan Haag also contributed "A Wedding in Mahabaleshwar" to Part I and "A Vision of Vijayanagar" to Part II.

★

In their gentle way, Indians have a way of blurring the boundaries of my sharply honed American individualism.

I once walked next to a stooped old woman on a three-day pilgrimage with thousands of others high into the Himalayas. With every painful step, she panted, "Shiva!" Sometimes she lovingly patted my hand, as if to give me, a stranger and her junior by at least thirty years, encouragement.

I remembered my thoughts before the trip. They were a jumble of worries and fears about myself. Could I make it physically? Where would I go to the bathroom? Would my period come, and how would I handle that in the midst of so many people?

With the majestic Himalayas at my feet and the tiny gnarled old woman at my side, I became very small.

I cried nonstop every one of the three days.

I left India that trip too humble to separate myself any longer from the dazzling, deep stream of life around me.

When the distances between self and living again grow great, and my ego starts to flaunt itself, I return to India.

She works her magic every time.

—Cheryl Bentley, "Enchanted"

STEVE COLL

✦ ✦ ✦

Shifting Gears on the Grand Trunk Road

Mortal peril and rampant corruption are everyday facts of life
for India's long-haul truck drivers.

AFTER TRAMPING THROUGH MUD AND POOLS OF OIL, WE FOUND
Bhajan Singh, asleep in a mosquito-infested back room beside his
trucking company's East Delhi office. He was a long, bony, bearded
Sikh. A soiled white turban draped his eyes. Rousted from his nap,
he led us wordlessly through the fetid night smoke spewed by East
Delhi's factories.

He climbed into the ten-ton Tata truck that was his home. He
seemed less than overjoyed about my plan, concocted upon arrival
in South Asia in the summer of 1989 and partially appropriated
from Kipling, to saturate myself with
India by taking a nine-hundred-
mile truck journey from New
Delhi to Calcutta along the Grand
Trunk Road, which spans the
breadth of northern India. Later,
Bhajan Singh grumbled to my
translator, a portly high-caste
Brahmin with a waxed mus-
tache who I will refer to here
as Vinod, that prior to our

Tata truck

departure the trucking company boss had pronounced it essential that we reach Calcutta uninjured, and that, furthermore, if this was not achieved, Singh would lose his job. It was hard to tell whether the demand ticked Singh off because he thought it an unreasonable expectation or because it meant that to keep up appearances along the way, he could not drink as much whiskey or smoke as much opium while driving as he might otherwise do.

"These drivers—Muslims, Jats, Sikhs—are very rough, very rude," Vinod explained in a condescending tone that night. "They are subjugated by everyone—bosses, financiers, police, tax authorities. So they fight back."

Anyone who has weaved through the chaos and carnage of South Asia's phantasmagoric intercity roads might reasonably be nervous about riding shotgun in a Tata truck—a two-axle, six-wheel, top-heavy steel box that looks to drivers of oncoming cars like one of those carnivorous contraptions from the *Mad Max* movies. But after I climbed into the cab, the butterflies subsided. Looking down through the panoramic windshield decorated with swirling stickers depicting Sikh gurus, roses, and fish, I suddenly realized: it was not we who should be nervous about careening down the highway in this metal monster. It was everybody else on the road who should be worried about us.

Singh jammed his gears and pulled out from the mud lot, weaving down the night road through dust and diesel smoke blasting his horn to overtake cows, taxis, camel carts, bicycles, motorcycles, three-wheeled motorized rickshaws, water buffalo, dogs, zippy Maruti economy cars, and pedestrians. The animals, objects, and people meandered backward, forward, and sideways in what seemed a continuous choreographed dance of near-miss. Singh did his bit and managed not to hit anyone.

The unlit, unlined, undivided road fell in small receding patches beneath the Tata's headlights. Tall stands of eucalyptus trees flanked the highway on the flat stretches. Roadside restaurants with illicit bars and brothels attached flashed past. Chimneyed brick kilns loomed in the moonlight. To the sides, we could sometimes see sleeping villages nestled in the shadows. Not only did the truck have no seat belts, it had no doors, so we leaned to and fro in the rushing air, gripping our seats on the heavy bends. Eucalyptus, industrial effluent, burning dung, spices and incense assaulted our nostrils. Horns—ours, theirs, everybody's—blasted all around.

Inside our spacious Tata cab, Singh kept his distance and projected a hard, lonely demeanor. He deferred to Vinod and myself and worried about our comfort. At the same time he bullied his assistant driver, a poor Bihari named Santosh, unmercifully. This seemed to reflect the unspoken hierarchy of our traveling party, with myself at the top by virtue of being a foreign guest, Vinod next by virtue of his Brahmin birth, which he advertised at every opportunity, then Singh, and at the bottom, Santosh, who was of a caste similar to his boss's but earned one tenth his salary and suffered in apprenticeship. Whether one chose to see this hierarchy in terms of old identities such as caste or new identities such as economic status, there was no denying its palpable presence inside our truck. Among my three companions, groveling deference from below and spiteful bullying from above seemed to be the guiding principles.

Hunched with hooded eyes over the steering wheel, Singh spoke laconically about his past. He said he was born as a Jat Sikh, an unruly subset of India's minority Sikh religious group, whose male members traditionally wear turbans and never cut their hair. (Jats are a peasant farming caste group that can be either Sikh or Hindu.) On the small farm in rural Punjab where Singh grew up, his status was ordained by tradition but his opportunities were defined by modernity. His ancestors had been farmers and soldiers, but after dropping out of high school, he took to trucking because the money was good. Now he was independent, even upwardly mobile. He wore a shiny gold watch and said he sent one hundred rupees a month home to Punjab to his wife, whom he wed in an arranged marriage in 1984. Those he left behind in the village were trapped now in the Sikh separatist insurgency, in which more than five thousand people, mostly Sikhs, die in shoot-outs, bomb explosions and police killings each year. In any event, apart from the war, farming bored him, Singh said. He preferred to be on the move. "I'll drive until my body quits."

Or until the road kills him. Daring and reckless behind the wheels of their massive vehicles, India's truck drivers are modern heirs to the traders, conquerors, robbers, and religious seers who have traveled the Grand Trunk Road for centuries. Several hundred years before the birth of Christ, Mauryan emperors laid the first tombstone-shaped mileage markers between Kabul and Calcutta. In some ways, not much has changed on the highway since then. As ever, the road is vividly dangerous. More than one thousand truck drivers, passengers, and pedestrians die in accidents along the highway each year. Its shoulders reveal an almost surreal display of wreckage: trucks lying smashed and upside down in ditches every thirty to thirty-five miles, buses wrapped around trees, vans hanging from bridges, cars squashed like bugs. Sections of the road are controlled by bandits who hijack trucks several times a month, sometimes killing the drivers. Corrupt policemen demand bribes at every checkpoint and throw drivers in jail if they don't oblige. And in rural areas, if a cow or pedestrian is run over, mobs of villagers attack, burn trucks, and lynch drivers in revenge—a peril of which Bhajan Singh would twice be reminded on the road ahead.

In some ways, the Grand Trunk depicts what is unsettled and unfinished in South Asia. The road is the backbone of commerce in the northern subcontinent, and commerce is perhaps the most powerful force churning up change in the region these days—raising expectations, dashing expectations, rearranging old caste, class, political, and religious orders. V. S. Naipaul traveled around India recently and described what he saw and heard as "a million mutinies now." At least half a million of them concern money.

We paid our first bribe almost immediately. An inspector waved us down and demanded tax papers. In India's Nehruvian, "mixed socialist" economy, taxes on commercial goods are supposed to be paid by truckers at every state and city border. The system is partly a legacy of the old European feudal idea, carried abroad by the European colonialists, that whoever controls the road—bandit, prince, thug, foreign imperialist—takes his tribute. In India, the tax goes back to the nineteenth century. More recently, the Nehruvian state has claimed authority but has shared its booty with the bandits and thugs, some of whom are in its employ, others of whom just rush in where the state has left a void. Modern truckers, like the traders of old, have adapted nicely to the system, foraging inexorably toward profit wherever it can be found. Since following the official rules and paying all the official taxes would bankrupt most transporters and bring commerce to a halt, the trucking companies have developed an intricate, shifting system of bribes paid to bureaucrats and police to keep the wheels turning. Private tribute has been substituted for public tribute. The Nehruvian state may be going broke as a consequence, but its employees and their allies are doing rather well.

Our first inspector glanced at the truck's papers and asked for a modest five rupees. Santosh, the assistant driver, slipped him the note

In the 130 years or so since the Mutiny—the last 90 years of the British Raj and the first 40 years of independence begin increasingly to appear as part of the same historical period—the idea of freedom has gone everywhere in India. Independence was worked for by people more or less at the top; the freedom it brought has worked its way down. People everywhere have ideas now of who they are and what they owe themselves. The process quickened with the economic development that came after independence; what was hidden in 1962, or not easy to see, what perhaps was only in a state of becoming, has become clearer. The liberation of spirit that has come to India could not come as release alone. In India, with its layer below layer of distress and cruelty, it had to come as disturbance. It had to come as rage and revolt. India was now a country of a million little mutinies.

♦

—V. S. Naipaul, *India: A Million Mutinies Now*

while leaning out the doorless cab into the enveloping darkness. Bhajan Singh didn't even bother to slow the truck as Santosh handed out the cash.

Some miles on, a policeman waved us down with a flashlight. Singh leaned out and shouted the name of his trucking company, whereupon the policeman stepped aside and waved us through. "The boss pays him eight hundred rupees per month for all vehicles," Singh explained, driving on. "If you are a newcomer, it would cost one hundred rupees—for nothing, just so he will not inspect."

Vinod elaborated. "The trucking companies all pay about forty thousand to fifty thousand rupees to the police per month, handled from the home office, so they do not check for sales tax. He pays because he can't afford not to. There are massive systemic bribes to avoid sales-tax checks. That's why we're waved through.... A friend of mine in Agra has become a multimillionaire mostly because his savings are on sales tax. Bogus permits let you save. That is where the money lies. Freight is nothing."

Besides keeping an eye on me and translating, Vinod had another purpose in traveling to Calcutta. His regular job was as a repo man who chased down truck drivers who defaulted on loan payments. If a driver "absconded," in the Indian phraseology, Vinod tracked him down and tried to get the truck back. Two absconders were believed to be hiding out somewhere in Calcutta and Vinod intended to find them. Normally a few threats and shoves were enough to get the job done, he said. But sometimes he had to go to court. He explained his craft, telling a story about a repo man he knew, whom I will refer to here as Rajiv. Once, traveling by rail to a provincial capital where two repossessed trucks were tied up in seemingly endless litigation, Rajiv found himself by chance in a first-class compartment with two senior judges from the relevant court. Sensing opportunity, he broke out a bottle of whiskey, poured generously, and then explained his legal predicament, gently asking the esteemed judges if they had any advice for a man in his position. The judges cited a few vague statutes. Later, asleep, Rajiv felt himself being shaken awake by one of them, who summoned him to the corridor. The judge handed

Rajiv a slip of paper containing the name of an attorney in the provincial capital and told him to contact the lawyer. Within a week, he had funneled a fifty-thousand-rupee payment through the lawyer to the judge and he had his trucks.

While office mavens like Vinod handle the systemic bribes, Singh takes care of the petty cash out on the highway. Throughout any journey small bribes must be paid to uninitiated tax inspectors and policeman encountered at random. Singh said he works on an incentive-bonus plan. His regular monthly salary is two thousand rupees, or about seventy dollars at present exchange rates. But at the start of each trip, the boss hands over an estimated bribe allotment of about two hundred to three hundred rupees, depending on the going rates. Then, it is up to Singh to make it to Calcutta without spending more than this allotment on actual bribes. Whatever he doesn't pay out to police and bureaucrats, he keeps. Some months, he said, he earns an additional one thousand rupees this way, plus more for fees charged to hitchhiking passengers and kickbacks from truck repairmen.

Shortly after midnight Singh paused to rest at a bustling *dhaba*, or truck stop, beside the moonlit highway. Santosh jumped down quickly and began to dig mud from the truck's tires with a stick. Two dozen or so Tatas surrounded us in the pale light. Boy waiters wandered among the trucks carrying clear glasses filled with milky tea. Singh took a glass, stretched his legs, and pulled out a flask of whiskey.

"We can't live without it," he said, dumping the tea and filling his glass with malt. "The time is short—so I like to drink the whole bottle at once."

As he did, I asked about life on the road. He said he spent much of it sitting in truck stops. "These places are run by the powerful people of the area—*goondas* [thugs]. You have to be a powerful *goonda* to handle these truck drivers. You will find drugs, liquor, opium. Everything is available.... Generally, everyone is available on the road. Calcutta is famous for prostitution. In Bengal [the state surrounding Calcutta], a beetle is more expensive than a prostitute. Drivers are homosexual. They enjoy each other, prostitutes, whiskey, drugs, and beer. Before I got married, I did the same thing."

The difficulty, he continued, is that "there's no respect from the police, no respect from the drivers. At least in Bengal they respect the driver and call him 'sir.' You can drive the whole state and pay one rupee. In other areas, even if the papers are all right, they will arrest me without a bribe. We pay on the spot, officially and unofficially, so I've never been arrested. But there are bandits, too, working with the police, and sometimes those people try to find a way to stop the truck. But I find a way out. The fleet owners and drivers travel in convoys in some areas. Bihar is notorious. There are night robbers. Even here. If we wanted to go past Etah tonight, we would have to drive in a convoy."

> *P*eople in urban areas are just beginning to talk about homosexuality, and gays don't broadcast their preference. One of the first gay men's magazines didn't come out of the closet far enough to print its address on copies that just "appeared" at newsstands in cosmopolitan Bombay. But in the guise of a religious experience, homosexuality is perfectly alright. At a festival in Tamil Nadu, men dressed as goddesses wed male "gods" and the presiding deities aren't content until the "marriages" are consummated.
>
> ◆
>
> —Mary Orr, "India Sketches"

Singh runs this gauntlet in his Tata truck six times each month—five days down to Calcutta from Delhi, five days back, three round trips per month. No holidays, no sick pay, no overtime. Yet he feels in some ways a privileged man. "The road is my house," he said that night in the truck cab, belting down his whiskey. And then, smiling and gesturing to the trucks parked around him in the dark: "We are the road kings."

At dawn the countryside awoke. Bullock carts and horses rattled down the road. Goats wandered through the dirt courtyard where the trucks were parked. The air was heavy with mist, dung, and spice. Even before the sun struck the treetops, men and women trudged by the dozens from nearby villages to the surrounding fields and back, bent under the weight of wheat, sugar cane, and corn. Purple *bahya* flowers rose in a pond across the highway. Cranes and herons bathed among them.

Singh lay passed out on an exposed wooden cot, sedated by his whiskey. Beside him a Muslim truck driver filled bucket after bucket of water at a well, carried the buckets to his truck, hoisted them by rope to the top of his trailer, and dumped the water into the bin. I watched this for half an hour, sipping milky tea, before finally asking Vinod to inquire why the driver seemed so determined to fill his truck with water. The Muslim explained that he was carrying coal from Calcutta to Delhi and wanted to add some weight to his load before he arrived. He gets credit for the extra weight on delivery, he said. On the Grand Trunk Road, everybody has an angle.

Impudent goats woke Singh, who shouted abuse at Santosh, who scrambled to bring tea and hustled to wipe off the driver's seat inside the truck. Soon we were rumbling east again. On a five-kilometer stretch, we honked our way past the following: one small boy hitchhiking, a bullock cart out of control, two cows running amok, bicyclists toting heavy burlap sacks, a horse-drawn rickshaw carrying a smartly dressed family, nine cows and two boys swimming in a muddy water hole, a bullock cart carrying a load of sticks, one behind it carrying a family, three men sleeping at the roadside with their heads protruding onto the asphalt, a herd of goats grazing on the road, a herd of cows crossing, dogs, pigs, bicycle rickshaws, and camels.

A police constable flagged us down, climbed in, and demanded a free ride to the office. As we rumbled along, I asked why all the cops we met wanted a handout. "It should not be that way," he said sheepishly. "But they only pay us eight hundred rupees a month and we have to work twenty-four hours a day. That is not enough money."

As we weaved ahead Santosh leaned out of the cab, waving to the other drivers to move aside. Sometimes they did. The policeman fell asleep and began to snore. When we reached his office, Santosh shook him awake and helped him down.

The partnership between Santosh and Singh was uneasy. Most of the drivers and assistants on the Grand Trunk Road are Sikhs or Muslims—outsiders to mainstream Indian society. But Santosh is a Hindu. He was raised in Bihar state, a poor region traversed by the highway, where banditry is endemic. Fleet owners sometimes hire Biharis as assistants in the hope that their local knowledge will lessen the risk of hijacking. For this, and his ability to pry mud from truck tires with a stick Santosh earned about seven dollars per month. When we had parked that afternoon at a truck stop called Hotel the Great Papa, whose shabby sign bore the motto "Love Is Sweet Poison," Santosh said that he was worried that his boss, whose friends and colleagues are mainly Sikhs, might never teach him how to drive the truck, and that he would be stuck as a poorly paid assistant for years to come. "My main motivation is to be a driver," he said, glancing nervously at Singh, who was asleep on a cot below him. "If he won't give me a chance, I will go someplace else. A good driver must have sympathy with his assistant, must give him a chance and teach him."

Santosh, eighteen, also confessed to a series of romantic entanglements not unlike those of truck drivers celebrated in American country music. Two years ago his family arranged a marriage to a thirteen-year-old girl in his Bihar village. But he said he had not seen his wife since the wedding—she was too young to consummate the relationship. Meanwhile, Santosh said, he had been having an affair with a fourteen-year-old who had recently been forced into marriage with a fifty-five-year-old Calcutta man. He said he saw the girl on his three-day stopovers. "She needs me," he remarked.

No matter what, he said, he would never return to village life or to the small farm tended by his family. With all its risks and hardships, the road was a better living. "Some day," he mused, "I know that I will die in a truck."

Steve Coll also contributed "The Die Is Caste" to Part IV. Both stories were excerpted from his book, On the Grand Trunk Road: A Journey into South Asia.

✶

She is a Punjabi woman, formidable, with callused hands, a "don't fool with me" temperament and a blunt conviction that women are routinely discriminated against in India, and certainly in Calcutta. She decided she would do what she could to break down a few walls.

"My husband and I owned a taxi that we would lease to drivers to drive," she explained. "One day, I had an argument with a driver and he refused to drive. I got angry and said, "OK, I'll drive.""

While many women drive their own private cars, not so much here in Calcutta but in New Delhi and Bombay and in other cities, it's unheard of for a woman to be a chauffeur, a bus or truck driver, or a taxi driver. Assumptions about a woman's place, about what she can or cannot do, especially when it comes to manual labor, are deeply rooted.

Women can haul sand and cement in baskets on their heads to construction sites, but they cannot lay the bricks. Women can sweep gutters with stoop brooms, but they cannot drive the trucks that spray water on the roadways. Women can use hand hoes in the fields, but they cannot drive the tractors.

"Often when passengers get in the cab and see me," she said, "they say: 'Oh, sorry, sorry madame. Oh, madame, sorry, please.' I laugh. I say, 'Don't worry. I'm the taxi driver.'"

—Edward A. Gargan, "A Back Seat to Nobody in Fight against Sexism," *The New York Times*

JIM LANDERS

* * *

The Suffering of Eve

Laws which protect women in India fail
under the weight of its culture.

BHANWARI DEVI LEARNED ABOUT LIFE AS A VILLAGE WOMAN OF India wrapped in dust, cooking smoke, and faded garments meant to last a lifetime. She was engaged before she was born, married at age seven and the mother of four when she was about twenty-five.

In 1985, a strong personality won her the start of a very difficult education. Social workers took her to Jaipur, the capital of the state of Rajasthan, for two and a half weeks of training in the rights and privileges the law offers Indian women.

Bhanwari came back full of ideas. She urged the women of Bhateri to learn to read. She warned the men that child marriage is illegal. When she told the police about the planned wedding of a one-year-old girl to a two-year-old boy, the men of the girl's family vowed that Bhanwari would never again raise her head in the village.

Five of them came after her on a September evening as she was weeding her field.

"They raped me," Bhanwari says. "They made my husband watch."

In a determined, sad voice, she tells a story that says much about violence and women in India, a country where discrimination is deadly and perhaps 30 million females are "missing."

Bhanwari says she doesn't know her age. Her husband, Mohun Lal, guesses that his wife is thirty-six or thirty-seven years old. Their youngest daughter, Rameshawari, is thirteen. Seven years ago, she married a boy who is now a laborer at a nearby village.

"I was not a social worker then," Bhanwari apologizes. "If I had this awareness then, I would not have allowed it."

India's consitution requires equal pay for equal work by men and women. Its laws ban wife-beating and mental cruelty, child marriage and dowry, sexual enslavement, rape, and sexual harassment, known as "Eve teasing."

> *B*hanwari Devi, the woman at the heart of this story, saw her struggle for justice vindicated in 1994 when the men who raped her finally were arrested. Their families asked her to drop the charges; she refused.
>
> ◆
>
> —Jim Landers

But much of the law fails under the weight of three thousand years of celebrating sons and despising daughters.

Sons inherit. Sons bring parents wealth, a dowry worth as much as four years of a bride's family's income. A son is also essential in a Hindu family to light a parent's funeral pyre and open the way to heaven.

Daughters bring financial hardship, then leave to become servants of another family.

Some female infants are killed: smothered beneath a placenta, fed poison or abondoned in the wild. More often, they simply get less than their brothers of the food and medicine needed to survive. Among children younger than five, the death rate is three times greater for girls than for boys.

British demographers who conducted India's first census in

1901 found whole villages with no girls. They called them "blood-red villages." The census counted 972 females for every 1,000 males.

Across India, it has since gotten worse. The sex ratio in the 1991 census was 929 females for every 1,000 males. (The U.S. ratio is 1,050 women for every 1,000 men.)

Tradition and technology combine today so that a female in India is in danger from the moment she is conceived. Hundreds of thousands of Indian parents use sex-determination tests to plan families of sons. Amniocentesis or ultra-sound tests showing a female fetus are followed by abortions.

The practice began in the late 1970s. The number of abortions performed because of sex-determination tests since then is un-known. By June 1982, *The Times of India* estimated that 78,000 such abortions had taken place.

The practice became a national issue in 1982, after the male fetus of a prominent Bombay official was aborted by mistake.

The birth of a girl may bring regret, even grief, to her parents. One New Delhi mother of two girls described it as giving birth to a stone.

Discrimination is such that the Indian government's 1992 action plan for girls declared "She has the right to survive" as its first premise.

The plan says mothers are more likely to breast-feed sons than daughters. Boys are more likely than girls to get treatment for the diarrhea that kills 1.5 million Indian children every year. Boys are more likely to be inoculated against disease and much more likely to go to school.

The typical Indian girl lives her life in a farm village. She grows up illiterate and with two-thirds the calories she needs to achieve her height and weight potential.

One in four dies before age fifteen. The others marry in their teens. They have eight or nine pregnancies, six live births and raise four children before dying at age 59.

More than five thousand Indian women are burned to death each year by husbands and in-laws seeking higher dowries. (A widower is able to remarry and collect a second dowry.) Dowry itself has been illegal since 1961, but the practice is increasing.

Women's rights advocates say they had hoped Indira Gandhi would act vigorously to enforce the laws protecting women during her tenure as prime minister. But Mrs. Gandhi, who dominated Indian political life until her assassination in 1984, was unsympathetic to the feminist movement. She joked about her male colleagues that she was "the only man in my Cabinet."

Mrs. Gandhi's son, Rajiv, was more active as prime minister in bringing women into government before his assassination in 1991. He created a Ministry for Women and Social Welfare, and supported the grass-roots programs that ultimately led Bhanwari Devi into government service as a village worker in Bhateri.

Bhateri sits behind a range of red and chalk bluffs, its small huts spilled in the hollows. Goods come to Bhateri in carts pulled by camels or on the backs of elephants. Trucks are rare. A car attracts a crowd of gawkers.

---

*A*s if dowry deaths weren't enough, another abomination still practiced, though illegal, is *sati*, or widow burning. As Elisabeth Bumiller writes in her book *May You Be the Mother of a Hundred Sons: A Journey Among the Women of India:* "*Sati* had once been common in India, particularly among the Rajput feudal warlords who built the palaces and forts that still rise from the rocky landscape of Rajasthan. Scholars are not sure of the origin of the practice, although there are early references to it in the historical accounts of the ancient Greeks and Scythians. In India, references to *sati* first appeared in the Hindu epics, dating from about two thousand years ago. Five of the god Krishna's wives were believed to have immolated themselves on his funeral pyre; four of Krishna's father's wives had done the same. The custom is named after Sati, the wife of the god Shiva."

◆

—JO'R and LH

Bhanwari and Mohun Lal, her husband, have a two-acre field and a milk cow. Their oldest daughter, married when she was fourteen, lives in another village. Daughter Rameshawari and her two brothers still live at home.

Each year, following the counsel of astrologers, villages throughout Rajasthan arrange mass weddings among brides and grooms as young as one-year-old.

Bhanwari says she does not remember her wedding to Mohun Lal.

"She was seven, and I was nine," Mr. Lal says with a smile. "We were engaged even before we were born."

They began living together when she was about fourteen.

Since 1955, India has required a girl to reach age eighteen before she can marry.

Rajasthani village children are usually married by their tenth birthday. A girl continues to live in her father's house, at least until her first menstrual period. Then it is the father's duty to inform the boy's family that his daughter is sexually mature and ready to live with her husband.

"When a girl's sent away for marriage at such a young age, she'll start having children very young as well. That means more mothers will die giving birth, and more babies will die from premature birth

---

*M*uch of Hindu India's legal literature—most of all the *Manu Smrti*, or *Lawbook of Manu*—provokes fierce controversy among other Indians because of its institutionalization of caste and other socially retrogressive behavior. In an age of equality, the Manu code is unacceptably male chauvinist on the role of women. "Her father protects her in childhood, her husband protects her in youth, her sons protect her in old age—a woman does not deserve independence," it says. If women are permitted to run around unguarded, it adds, "they would bring grief to both the families."

◆

—Barbara Crossette, *India: Facing the Twenty-First Century*

or other weaknesses from having such a young mother," says Kanchan Mathur, one of the social scientists who sponsored Bhanwari and other village women in Rajasthan's Women's Development Project.

"Some of these girls are just ten years old. Their education comes to a halt when they're married," Mrs. Mathur says. "And what do these girls know of sex? They have no idea what's happening to them."

Jim Landers led the Dallas Morning News *team that won a Pulitzer Prize for international reporting in 1994 for a series of articles on violence against women and human rights. He now works in the Washington D.C. bureau of the* Dallas Morning News *as international affairs correspondent and travels frequently to Asia. He lives with his wife Susan and daughters Nicole and Jessica in Centreville, Virginia.*

✳

Sujata was working. She squatted beside a woman in front of her mud-walled home. They conferred in low voices and drew figures in the dirt. Messages would be passed from person to person; there were no telephones. In the time I might have made forty or fifty phone calls at home, we walked two villages and met with three or four women. I was awed by the slow pace and wondered how long it would take to get these things done. What could they accomplish on foot with no telephones?

Quite a bit.

Thrift societies, organized by village women, have broken the stranglehold of the money lenders and enabled families to buy their land and invest in farm animals and basic equipment. Child-care centers and nutrition programs crack the cycle of illiteracy. Wasteland development projects reclaim eroded land and return it to productive use. Appropriate technology projects, such as windmills and biogas, make use of precious natural resources.

—Thalia Zepatos, *A Journey of One's Own: Uncommon Advice for the Independent Woman Traveler*

PART FIVE

THE LAST WORD

GEOFFREY MOORHOUSE

Kanya Kumari

There is no better place to get a sense of India's many-leveled
vastness than from its southernmost point,
a spot of power and purity.

THIS IS WHERE INDIA BEGINS. ON THIS CURVE OF LAND, WHOSE
strained shore is washed by the jade green sea, an entire subcontinent is poised as if upon a sharpened point. Navigators rounded it
in ancient times when extending the boundaries of the known
world, among them the Greeks, whose geographer Ptolemy identified this extremity as Κομαρια ακρον—ultimate Komari.
Behind those early voyagers was an emptiness of ocean, separating
the subcontinent from Africa; ahead, the tear-drop shape of
Taprobane, which we now call Sri Lanka. Yet this was no barren
headland, valuable only because it gave mariners their bearings. Just
offshore, beating their way home against high winds and curling
white water, are fisherman whose ancestors have worked this coast
for centuries. Their craft are the same today as they always have
been: a few tree trunks lashed together, with a bamboo pole bend-
ing to the pull of a swollen brown lateen. A line of them cant at
such an angle to the waves that their shapes are transformed, so that
from the shore they have the appearance of beetles crawling across
the stormy sea. Men balance on these vessels like acrobats, gripping
the slippery logs with fiercely splayed toes. And slowly they make
their way into the lee of the land, to the beach lying beside the

459

subcontinent's most southerly point, and the huddle of white-walled houses rising in terraces above. The sand is well studded with rocks which, at low tide, become increasingly coated with yellow slime, as the fisherfolk squat on them and empty their bowels. As the sea flows into and over the shore, all is miraculously cleansed, so that with the ebbing of the tide the illusion of purity is established again.

Purity matters here. This is a holy place, and the most ardent of the pilgrims who travel the length and breadth of the subcontinent to reach it are obsessed, above all, with what is pure and what is impure. Such considerations can shape their whole lives, everything they do, all that happens to them from conception to the pyre. And yet they live by paradox, as do no other people on earth; so that anyone utterly and shamefully defiled will only be made acceptable again by consuming a potion made from five substances emitted by the cow, including its dung and its piss. Urine is seen as the best purifier of any uncleanliness by the very people who speak of the left hand—in the Tamil tongue native to this holy place—as "the hand of filth."

The pilgrims come by train and by bus, entering the sacred precincts down a narrow road lined by hoardings which clamour to sell accommodation, handicrafts, gimcrack souvenirs, food. Another exhortation more soberly advises them to Beware of Thieves. People pause beside stalls offering bananas, ugly plastic toys, and seashells which have been gaudied with paint and glued together to resemble rabbits, elephants, butterflies, and boss-eyed fish. Persistent young men waylay each newcomer and attempt to press postcards, transparencies, sunglasses, beads upon all who do not wave them aside contemptuously. Beggars position themselves artfully where they are almost impossible to avoid. The air swirls with dust blown up by gusts of wind off the sea, and it tantalises the hungry with promising smells of woodsmoke and spicy things ready to eat. It is deafening with sounds that are neither Indian nor musical, merely amplified noise which mutilates the ears.

At the bottom of that road rises a wedge-shaped *gopuram* above the principal shrine. This is dedicated to Parvati, who was betrothed to Lord Shiva but lost his hand in marriage through some trickery of the gods, who required her to slay the demon king, a feat that could only be managed by one destined to remain for ever *kumari*—virginally pure; in another version of the myth, Parvati came here to do penance in order to be worthy of her god but, being nevertheless rejected, she vowed to embrace celibacy to the end of her days. Endlessly the crowds do homage to this immaculate deity, where she sits on her temple throne, her diamond nose-rings glittering in the lamplight, her visible features embalmed in sandalpaste.

Then most of them board a hazardous old bucket with its wheelhouse aft, which lurches across the short space of tumultuous water separating the land from an enormous rock. This is surmounted by a domed building of much more recent origin than the temple of Kumari. It marks the place where the Swami Vivekenanda meditated for several months in 1892 upon the syncretistic teachings of his guru Ramakrishna, lately dead, until he reached the conclusion that he must take enlightenment to the West; which he did the following year at the Parliament of Religions in Chicago. The West, holding narrower views than his, had much earlier staked its own claim by building a Portuguese church above the pink pantiled roofs of the fishing village, which faced the Bengali sage as he sat and pondered possibilities before making eagerly for the impressionable warmth of America. Hundreds every day cross the water to be with the spirit of Vivekananda, and to make their obeisance to the sacred Sanskrit characters graven in stone; while in the all but empty dolly-blue interior of Our Lady of Ransom, a woman does the Stations laboriously on her knees, after prostrating herself before the Disney-coloured altar with her arms outstretched to their fingertips.

Few come here without cleansing themselves ritually from the *ghats* below the seafront. A squad of noisy youths stripped to their Y-fronts splash water at three shrill girls dressed in the *shalwar kameez* of North India. A young South Indian with his head shaven, apart from a small pigtail at the back, picks his way carefully across some rocks beyond the *ghats* until he comes to a lonely pool, where he bathes in solitude, before rearranging his *lunghi* round his hips. A trio of well-fleshed men descend the bathing steps and jump in boisterously, one of them a Brahmin with the confirming thread of the twice-born slung over his right shoulder and under his left arm. A fourth man stands on the edge of the water nervously, while the others dare him to take the plunge. Eventually and tentatively he does, with a weakly inane grin: whereupon the Brahmin, most pot-bellied and loudest of the others, wades heavily towards him, seizes his hand and leads him to the deeper part, as gently as if the fellow were his infant son.

When the pilgrims have completed their rituals of hygiene and prayer, they saunter along the promenade running above the *ghats* and below the most substantial hotels. They do not investigate the adjacent fishing village because that would involve intrusion into caste, which would certainly occasion astonishment and might even result in catastrophe. The ones who have planned their visit after consulting the lunar calendar can savour a unique spectacle, moments before twilight begins: the pale disc of a full moon rising from the waters as the molten sphere of the sun lowers itself into the self-same sea. These reverent people regard this as another form of holiness. So did Mahatma Gandhi, who also came here to meditate, and whose memorial on the seafront strangely echoes pre-war British cinema buildings, a 1936-ish Odeon, perhaps. With the exception of its fishing village, there is something about Kanya Kumari as a whole, especially along its promenade that conveys a whiff of Herne Bay, or some other English watering place that has known distinctly better days.

But this is where India begins; and she is inimitable. The land rises very shallowly from the sea, its sandy scrub soon giving way to palms and other trees, and plots of irrigated land which villagers till. Presently the first high ground rears above the coastal plain, a ridge of barren rock running northwards in a series of swerving pinnacles, all flaring with heat so intense that they are effectively unclimbable. The scenery is being assembled for topographical drama. Barren rock is soon clad with vegetation and the Western Ghats barricade the occidental seaboard against the rest of the country, shielding lush Kerala from the harsh and bony landscape further inland. Eventually the Ghats subside into the deserts of Rajasthan, which themselves give way to the mighty rivers of the North, that in one season will confer life on millions, and in another cause disaster and death on a frightful scale. When the rains come and the rivers swell there is nothing on earth like the sight of them, running torrentially, a mile or more wide, sweeping everything out of their path. Yet the greatest drama the eye can see is saved for the last and lies well above the Gangetic plain. Foothills rise from the rasping dust of early summer, and shimmer in a palpitating haze, which suddenly lifts when these tops, forested with rhododendron and deodar, have climbed to the point at which snow is a real possibility rather than a lowland fantasy; to reveal the mot sensational range of mountains in the world, white and gleaming and utterly impregnable, as improbably as any theatrical backcloth in their operatic grandeur. They fill the horizon and half the heavens when first seen from any of those foothills in upper Garhwal. If there is such a thing as a terrestrial abode of the gods, then it will surely be there.

Stand with your back to the sea at Kanya Kumari, which is two thousand miles from that stupendous barrier, and sense the weight, the full immensity, the huge variety of this subcontinent bearing down upon you. Beyond this scrubby littoral a tale unfolds such as no other land can tell in such measure as this. No other nation has ever known such a natural diversity of tongues, the result, for the most part, of slow evolution since the beginning of mankind. No other country has lived with so complicated a past so equably, assimilating everything that has happened to it, obliterating naught, so that not even the intricate histories of European states have produced such a rich pattern as that bequeathed by the Mauryas, the Ashokas, the Pahlavas, the Guptas, the Chalukyas, the Hoysalas, the Pandyas, the Cholas, the Mughals, and the British—to identify only a few of the peoples who have shaped India's inheritance. Nor is there another land that constantly provokes in the stranger such elation and despair, so much affection and anger, by powerful contrasts and irreducible opposites of behaviour; wickedness and virtue, caring and indifference, things bewitching and disgusting and terrifying and disarming, often in quick succession. India has nuclear power and other advanced technology close by some of the most obscene slums in creation; she has never failed to hold democratic elections at the appointed time, yet those too frequently elevate men whose own votes can be bought with rupees and other emoluments; she has a high and mighty self-esteem and a taste for moral posturing which equals anything suffered by her people when the British were here; she has been capable of unparalleled generosity to her last imperial rulers, but she bickers endlessly and meanly with her closest neighbour and twin; she gave birth to the creed of massive nonviolent protest and once practised this effectively, yet in the first generation of independence she has assassinated three of her own leaders, starting with the begetter of *satyagraha*.... Such contradictions and anomalies as these run through India from end to end and help to make her incomparable.

As does another characteristic. Religion, too, flourishes here as it does nowhere else. Other lands may surrender themselves totally to a particular faith, but in India most creeds are deeply rooted and acknowledged fervently. Virtually the whole population practices some form of devotion: the Indian without the slightest feeling for the divine, without a spiritual dimension to his life, is exceedingly rare. By this means the wretched can entertain the possibility of improvement, and are sustained in their wretchedness until something better comes their way in another form, or until they are even more blessedly released from the cycle of life and death. The comfortable find in it a justification of their prosperity and an assurance that their submission will continue to bring them rewards. The most truly spiritual merely hope that with perseverance they will one day achieve enlightenment.

Incomparable and inimitable she is; but in this as in much else, India is also our great paradigm.

For a quarter of a century, the great subcontinent had captivated me. I first came to it out of simple curiosity and was almost overwhelmed by that introduction, in which everything was so much more powerful and intense than I had been led to expect. For a moment I was tempted to retreat from it to some bland place where all the senses were not so relentlessly assailed, to some less harrowing society where one's spirits were not so regularly lowered by human misery, to a more restful haven in which it was not so necessary to be forever on guard against persistent and unwanted attention. Plenty of Westerners do not survive their initial experience of the subcontinent, fleeing in anxiety, in disgust, and with indignation from its darkness, condemned never to know it properly. But many more are vouchsafed in that first encounter a glimpse of something so enchanting, so inspiring, so utterly and attractively outside all previous experience, that they know they will return as often as possible, to be thrilled by it afresh.

I was one of these fortunates, and I had many times revisited the subcontinent in order to increase my understanding of it, once in a journey across Pakistan, otherwise repeatedly in India. In the beginning I had chiefly been interested in the local history which, through the coincidence of my English birth, was part of my history, too; to that extent I was trying to find something of myself in this strangely compelling land, even though I was the first member of my family ever to set foot in Asia. But gradually I became more fascinated by the texture of society here, by its very complexity, and especially by the way it had been formed from and was still dominated by religious attitudes, notwithstanding its secular democracy. My earliest visits to India had been confined to the North, which is where most of the great historical events associated with the British took place. When eventually I went south, I discovered a region that was never less than subtly different, and was sometimes obdurately so. It had not been shaped as much as the North had once been by a mighty zeal for Islam, but continental Europeans had left a greater impression here than elsewhere, especially the Portuguese and the French. It was possible to envisage the South as Hinduism's centre of gravity, and I had concluded that this was the reason why a high proportion of the foreigners wandering the southern states were not merely sampling an alien culture, but were more intently looking for spiritual nour-ishment. This, it seemed to me, distinguished them from almost all the outsiders criss-crossing other parts of India, except those who took themselves to Ladakh and similar anchorholds in the more mountainous recesses of the far North.

In a way, I had become one of them. And here I was again, on a further stage of my own Indian pilgrimage, hoping to understand something more of the great subcontinent. Also, trying to find an-other part of myself.

Geoffrey Moorhouse also contributed "Encounter with a Rajah" to Part III. Both stories were excerpted from his book OM: An Indian Pilgrimage.

★

WHAT YOU NEED TO KNOW

WHEN TO GO/WEATHER

While most countries have two, three, or even four seasons, India claims six, but that is because India is not just an ordinary nation but a sub-continent. Roughly, the Indian seasons are: Spring (March-April), Hot (May-July), Wet or Monsoon (July-September), Autumn (September-November), Winter (December-January), and Cool or Pre-Spring (February-March). Like urban sprawl, the boundaries are blurred. And the only way to tell if it's cold Winter or fragrant Spring or the dubious Pre-Spring may come down to your outerwear. Will it be a pullover or a down jacket, if not both?

Given the challenges and subtleties of the weather conditions just mentioned, we nevertheless boldly state that India may be visited any-time, depending of course upon where *exactly* you want to go. The best time to visit India is usually after the wet, clammy, humid Monsoon season, anytime after late October until just before the dry, searing Hot season, which would mean in the vicinity of late April, early May. But if you want to visit some of the towns and villages of the Indian Himalayas, then the best time is April through August when the mountain passes are most likely to be open. While your skin can turn blue in the December cold of Dharamsala in the north, the southern peninsula can be most pleasant. You can even work up a tan as you take that slow train (or a boat, perhaps) from Madras to Kanyakumari to Kovalam.

VISAS AND PERMITS

Visas

Almost every traveler requires a visa to enter India. Once inside the country, be prepared to fill out all sorts of official documents, forms and special permits so you can visit certain "sensitive" areas.

The sub-continent is several thousand years old and has seen the rise and fall of more civilizations and dynasties than historians and archaeologists can document or dig up. Therefore the art of red tape and bureaucratic subterfuge has been refined to a maddening degree.

You can get a six-month **tourist visa** or a one-year multiple-entry visa, both valid from the date of issue. You can also obtain a one-year student or business visa. Your application should be accompanied by a letter from the business or academic organization that is sponsoring you.

You can also get a **transit visa** that should be used only to pass through India in order to reach your ultimate destination. It cannot be used for purposes of tourism.

You must obtain your visa before you arrive in India. The rules regarding visas change frequently. Always check with the consulate or embassy.

Permits

India has fought wars with its neighbors Pakistan and China; it intervened militarily and helped create Bangladesh, which was part of Pakistan; currently, there is a civil war going on in Sri Lanka, its southern neighbor. Internally, various ethnic and religious groups, such as in Kashmir, are constantly on the warpath, demanding to become independent. It is not surprising therefore that India has certain areas that are either totally off-limits or require a special permit to visit them. These include politically sensitive border regions, tribal areas of the northeast, and the Himalayan regions to the north, especially the disputed area of Kashmir. Even if you are supposed to get a special permit to visit restricted areas, such as Nagaland or Mizoram in the northeast, you may discover that it might take weeks if not months to get one, or you may be told that you were supposed to get it from the Indian Embassy in your own country. Many of the islands that comprise the Andaman-Nicobar and Lakshadweep islands are also off-limits or require special permits. In that inimitable bureaucratic twist, you can fly into Port Blair, the main port of entry in the Andaman-Nicobar Islands, and receive a permit at the airport, but if you plan to arrive by boat (from, say Madras, these days known as Chennai) you must get your permit *before* you arrive at the shipping office where you arrange your boat journey or at the Foreigners' Registration office.

Permits are also required when you want to trek. A government-approved trekking agency in India can obtain it for you within a few days. Carry your passport and trek permit with you at all times as there are check posts along the trek routes.

Don't gnash your teeth or tear your hair. India is a hugely diverse country. If bureaucracy and permits do not allow you to visit your destination of choice, find another area to visit. However, if you have time, persistence, and practice your patience, you will usually achieve success. Learn to meditate as you wait.

*C*USTOMS AND ARRIVAL

Duty-free, you are allowed to bring one liter of whiskey, 200 cigarettes (50 cigars), a camera and binoculars, but if you are dragging more sophisticated electronic gadgets such as a laptop computer, special camera equipment, a video cam, or you are loaded with jewelry, then these items must be registered on a Tourist Baggage Re-Export Form. Be sure you know where the serial numbers are located, as these must be noted on the form. But the most important thing to remember is to: **GUARD THESE COMPLETED FORMS WITH YOUR LIFE BECAUSE THEY MUST BE SHOWN TO THE CUSTOMS AGENTS WHEN YOU ARE READY TO DEPART!** Losing these forms will be worse than languishing in purgatory.

Most international flights arrive at major cities such as New Delhi, Bombay (Mumbai), Calcutta, and Madras (Chennai). If you don't want to go into the city itself, connecting flights are available to other major Indian cities. If you are in transit at the Delhi airport, do not go through the Green Channel as you will not be allowed to return for four hours.

Some intrepid travelers arrive overland from neighboring nations such as Nepal or Pakistan. Be warned! It can take almost five hours to clear customs if you arrive on a train from Pakistan.

THE NEXT STEP

GETTING INTO THE CITY:

To get into the city of New Delhi from Indira Gandhi International Airport, a distance of about 23 kilometers, your choices are a bus, taxi, or auto-rickshaw. The quickest and most comfortable journey will be in a pre-paid taxi. The trick is to find the right one. The cheapest one is managed by the Delhi Traffic Police Pre-Paid Taxi service. There are other taxi services available, of course, and all of them will promise you "best price." Be very careful, especially if it is your first time in India. Unscrupulous taxi and auto-rickshaw drivers are notorious for trying to rip off the traveler. They will bargain with you at the end of the trip even though you thought you had agreed upon a price before you got into the vehicle; some will try to divert you to a different hotel even though you have a reservation at a hotel of your choice. Be prepared to haggle fiercely and fight vocally (the louder one usually wins). Note: Taxis will add a legitimate 25% surcharge between 11 p.m. and 5 a.m.

The cheapest but inconvenient mode of transport into the city is the bus. Reliable bus service is provided by the Ex-Servicemen's Air Link Transport Service (E.A.T.S.). Its booth is on the right as you exit the international terminal building. The bus takes you to Connaught Place, the city center, and will drop you off at your hotel if it happens to be on the way. Other local bus services are also available.

Auto-rickshaw is a compromise between the slow but cheap bus and the fast, expensive taxi. If you like to bargain, don't mind feeling harassed, and like to brag about having "been there, done that, Jack!" then go for it.

In Calcutta, pre-paid taxi service is again recommended at Dum Dum, officially know as Netaji Subhash Bose International Airport. Airport buses and minibuses are also available, but local public buses are terribly crowded and not recommended. A way to cut cost and diversify your trip is to cab it to the Metro station 3 kilometers away and take the underground train as close as possible to your destination.

At Meenambakkam Airport in Madras (Chennai), your choices are train, taxi, bus, and auto-rickshaw. A cheap and convenient way to reach the city

center, 16 kilometers to the south, is to take the suburban train. The station is 1,500 feet across from the airport terminal. The train service begins soon after 4 a.m. and closes at 11:45 p.m. Pre-paid taxi and minibus counters are located in the international arrival terminal. It's a thirty-minute taxi ride, but much longer on the minibus since it makes several stops. The public bus will be slow and crowded, but if you have a single piece of luggage, it's the cheapest way to get into town. Then there is the auto-rickshaw. The driver will not use the meter. You will insist that he must. Do you really want to do this to yourself, especially if you've been flying for twenty hours or more?

At Sahar, the international airport in Bombay (Mumbai), do *not* hire an auto-rickshaw. This vehicle is not allowed into the city center. You will be dropped off at the outer suburban area, at the mercy of rapacious taxi drivers who will take maximum advantage of your unfortunate situation. Instead, once again, head for the pre-paid taxi booth which has set fares to various destinations in the city. Since the city is approximately 30 km away, and the traffic is horrendous, it can be a long, tortuous drive even in your own private, pre-paid vehicle. Just like at Delhi airport, there is a bus service provided by the Ex-Servicemen's Air Link Transport Service (E.A.T.S.). Departures are irregular, especially at night, when most international flights arrive.

In general, no matter at which international airport you arrive, first look for the pre-paid taxi booth, then the airport bus service. If you have traveled in India before or feel confident doing things your own way, go ahead and explore the local bus or train services, the freelance taxi drivers, and last but not least, the auto-rickshaws.

If you are arriving at night, book a hotel room in advance.

Finally, a note of caution if you are taking public transport such as the local bus: **Be Aware of Pickpockets.**

HEALTH:

Given its geographical diversity, India encompasses every kind of climate

THE NEXT STEP

and weather condition. You must prepare for the freezing cold of the mountains, the sweltering humidity of jungles and swamps, and the dry, searing heat of deserts. But the most common health hazard is probably the notorious "Delhi Belly," like "Montezuma's Revenge" in Mexico.

If you require medical attention, first contact your hotel staff. Upscale hotels normally have a doctor available on call. Even moderate and modest tourist hotels can recommend a doctor, a hospital, or a clinic.

India has some world-class medical institutions, but for minor illness or discomfort, "mission" hospitals (normally run by Western missionaries) are your best bet. The government-run hospitals are cheap but the wait is interminable and medical care may not be satisfactory.

Many Indian doctors have their own private clinics and they are very good at what they do. Do not hesitate to visit one if recommended by a reliable source, such as your hotel or embassy staff.

Finally, do not hesitate to contact your embassy for help.

Before you depart, check with the Centers for Disease Control (888-232-3228 or online at: www.cdc.gov.) in Atlanta for the most updated information about inoculations and other medical concerns you may have.

Some Helpful Tips:

• See a doctor and dentist prior to departure for general health checkups.
• Depending upon where you are (trekking in the Himalayas, a jungle lodge, a remote village) you could be far from a hospital or any kind of medical help, so be sure to consult a doctor about recommended immunizations before you leave home. Opinions vary on what is necessary, but it's a good idea to have current immunizations for tetanus, polio, and typhoid, and to consider immunization for hepatitis, meningitis, Japanese B encephalitis, and rabies. Except for the Himalayan areas, malaria is a risk throughout India. Bring along anti-malarial drugs, but consult your physician first for possible side-effects.

- Record all current immunizations on your yellow International Health Certificate and carry it with you.
- Don't drink the water or ice, purify first.
- Peel your fruit and do not eat raw vegetables.
- If you wear prescription glasses, bring an extra pair.
- Rehydrate, rehydrate, rehydrate.
- Pack a medical kit which includes: aspirin or acetaminophen, anti-histamine, antibiotics, Lomotil or Imodium for diarrhea, rehydration mixture, antiseptic such as iodine or Betadine, Calamine lotion, bandages, bandaids, tweezers, scissors, thermometer, cold and flu tablets, insect repellent, sunscreen, chapstick, water purification tablets, and possibly even sterile syringes with needles, dressings, and gloves.
- If you plan to trek in the mountains, make sure you have acetazo-lamide (Diamox) and dexamethasone, drugs recommended to prevent acute mountain sickness (AMS).
- Also consider taking a travel kit of basic homeopathic remedies and a homeopathic first aid book. Such remedies can provide rapid relief from common travel ailments including gastrointestinal problems, fevers, and many acute conditions. Books and travel kits are available through your local health food store. If you come home with any serious tropical diseases, including malaria, effective treatment is available from homeopathic medical practitioners.
- Bring along ear plugs because India is a noisy country. Stray dogs bark at all hours but especially at night; shopkeepers turn their radios on to full volume; motor vehicles honk constantly; rickshaw-*wallas* trill the bells and holler at pedestrians, who holler back; megaphones, "loudspeakers," and other amplifiers of sound are used for secular (political campaigns and demonstrations) as well as religious reasons (a *puja*, a religious procession, even a funeral). Sometimes, all of the above are happening simultaneously. Life in India, literally, is on the streets, which is great when you are a wide-awake and wide-eyed tourist, but total torture if you are trying to sleep or rest.

Travel Insurance and Assistance:

Several companies in the U.S. and Europe provide emergency medical assistance for travelers worldwide, including 24-hour help lines, English-

HE NEXT STEP

speaking doctors, and air evacuation in extreme cases. Travel agents and tour companies can recommend policies that can work for you.

TIME

All of India is in one time zone. It is 5 1/2 hours ahead of Greenwich Mean Time (GMT) and 10 1/2 hours ahead of Eastern Standard Time. **I.S.T.** stands for the official Indian Standard Time. (The old joke is that it's Indian Stretchable Time.) Thus, when it is noon in Delhi, it is:

10:30 p.m. yesterday in San Francisco
1:30 a.m. in New York
6:30 a.m. in London
7:30 a.m. in Paris
2:30 p.m. in Hong Kong
3:30 p.m. in Tokyo
4:30 p.m. in Sydney

BUSINESS HOURS

Government offices are supposed to be open anytime from 9:30 or 10 a.m. to 5 p.m., Monday to Saturday, but are closed alternate Saturdays; banks are open from 10:00 a.m. to 2 p.m. Monday to Friday and until noon on alternate Saturdays. Shops and offices are closed on Sunday and public and religious holidays. Bazaars keep longer hours. These official hours vary according to which part of India you are in. Remember also the reality of Indian Stretchable Time.

MONEY

The Indian currency is the rupee. One hundred paisa make one rupee. Paper money comes in denominations of 10, 20, 50, 100, and 500. One, two, and five rupee notes also exist but are being phased out.

Merchants will refuse to accept torn or worn rupee notes. Check your paper currency carefully and reject any that has a hole or in any way looks

much too abused. Conversely, if you do get one, slip it in the middle of a bundle when you are preparing to hand over a large cash amount.

It is not unusual for a shopkeeper or a taxi driver to claim he does not have enough change when you give him 50 or 100 rupee notes. This is another way of getting a "tip." Carry small denominations of rupees and coins, especially if you are traveling in smaller towns and villages.

You are not allowed to bring in or take out Indian money. However, you may bring as much foreign currency into India as you wish. Amounts over $10,000 U.S. must be declared at customs.

Most, but not all, major travelers' checks are accepted. Thomas Cook and American Express are the more popular brands. Keep your receipts because when you want to change your rupees back into dollars, you may be asked to show proof of having changed money legally, i.e., from your hotel or bank. If you stay longer than four months in India, you may have to get an income tax clearance, when receipts will come in handy.

The exchange rate is set by the market and not by the government, thus there is not much to be gained by going to the "black market" (shady guys in dark alleys whispering "change money? want girl? what you want, eh?!"), but you may still get a few rupees more than at the bank or especially your hotel.

To cash your travelers' check, arrive at the bank at least a half-hour before closing time—and prepare for a long wait.

Credit cards are also becoming increasingly accepted, such as when buying airplane and train tickets as well as in mid- to upscale hotels and shops. With a major credit card, such as Visa, you can also get a cash advance.

Unless you are in fancy hotels and restaurants, tipping is not the norm in India, but everyone in the service industry appreciates a few extra rupees or loose change left on the table after a lovely meal or a safe and comfortable taxi ride.

The ancient Indian version of tipping is "*baksheesh*," a loaded word that

*T*HE NEXT STEP

can mean anything from a token of thanks to bribery to extortion. It is that amount of cash (judiciously considered) that is given to anyone from a religious mendicant to earn religious merit, a beggar out of compassion or annoyance, a lowly clerk to shorten your wait, a reservation agent to secure your airline or train ticket, an industrialist to seal your million-dollar deal.

*E*LECTRICITY

India runs on 220-240 volts AC, 50 cycles. Some villages, large towns, cities and most tourist destinations have electricity, although power cuts and voltage fluctuations are common due to supply-and-demand factors. Sockets are the European-style three-round pins, but the fit may not be exact. It is advisable to take your own universal adapter. You can also buy various kinds of adapters in Indian stores.

*M*EDIA: NEWSPAPERS, RADIO, TELEVISION

India is justly proud of the freedom of its press and other media outlets. There are several English-language newspapers and magazines. Some of the best known newspapers are *The Indian Express, The Times of India, The Hindu,* and *The Statesman.* Weekly newsmagazines include *India Today, Frontline,* and *The Illustrated Weekly,* among others. Some special interest publications available are *Computer Today, Auto Indian*; and for those missing their peek at the centerfolds, they can check out racy but earnest *Debonair* magazine; women can catch up with *Cosmopolitan.*

Time, Newsweek, The International Herald Tribune, and other magazines and newspapers from Europe and England are available in major cities, but are very expensive compared to the Indian papers.

Even villagers are tuning in, turning on (and dropping out?) as satellite dishes beam in distinctly non-Indian television fare such as BBC, Murdoch's Hong Kong-based Star T.V., Sports Channel, CNN, and a local version of MTV called ZTV, leaving "Doordarshan," India's national television network, wilting in the heat and dust.

If you prefer radio, listen to the government-run All India Radio, which offers news in English, among other entertainment.

*T*OUCHING BASE

Snail mail is quite reliable, albeit slow, in India. It can take anywhere from one to three weeks to receive mail, depending upon where you are. The same time frame applies when you mail a letter to your loved ones back home. Letters written in aerogrammes are almost certain to arrive at their destinations.

Avoid mailing a parcel from India. If you must, you will come into intimate, infuriating contact with the redoubtable Indian bureaucracy. If you do not send your parcel by registered mail, it may "stray" and fail to arrive at its destination.

Old-fashioned mail is rapidly being replaced by fax, e-mail, and international direct dialing services. Calling home has never been easier. Just look for signs that say "STD/ISD," and they are to be found almost everywhere, usually as a side-business being conducted by a merchant who sells shoes or saris. To cut cost, you can call home and have your loved one(s) call you right back.

Cybercafes are now cropping up in Indian cities and sending and receiving e-mail is a better and more reliable alternative to snail mail; it's more economical than international phone calls.

CULTURAL CONSIDERATIONS

*L*OCAL CUSTOMS: DOS AND DON'TS

Although India is legally a secular nation, the majority of its people (nearly 80%) are Hindus. The rest are Muslims, Christians, Sikhs, Buddhists, Jains, and others. In India, religion often is a way of life. Most cultural considerations, therefore, are determined by an individual's religious faith. Listed

⟨HE NEXT STEP

below are some tips which will help you avoid committing the foreigner's
faux pas:

- *Namaskar* is the traditional Hindu greeting used throughout India.
  It's a simple and graceful gesture of putting your palms together
  with a slight bow of the head. It means hello as well as goodbye.

- Public displays of affection between the sexes are frowned upon,
  but you will often see men holding hands and women walking
  arm-in-arm. This is a sign of friendship and nothing more. Kissing,
  even in Bombay movies, is rare.

- The left hand is considered dirty because it is used in the toilet to
  clean oneself (water, instead of toilet paper, is used in the bath-
  rooms). The right hand is used for eating.

- The horrible Hindu legacy of caste and "untouchables" still persists
  in pockets of the nation. As a foreigner, you may be considered an
  "untouchable" and certain Hindus may refuse to serve you food or
  mix with you. Befriend a Muslim, Buddhist, or an Animist instead.

- Public thoroughfares—streets, lanes, sidewalks—are often dirty.
  Therefore, remove your shoes at the door before entering a room
  or a home. But do not be surprised when you see someone bowing low and touching an individual's feet. It's a sign of respect.

- Women should dress modestly. If nothing else, it will cut down on
  so-called "Eve teasing," or unwelcome comments and gestures
  from men. In a mosque, women cover themselves from head to
  feet; in a Sikh temple, women cover their heads. Non-Hindu
  women (and men) are barred from entering certain temples or the
  inner sanctum.

- Nudity, even on the beaches of more "open" cities such as Goa, or
  when cooling off under a waterfall off a remote mountain trail, is
  still a no-no. You'd be surprised how quickly the locals find out
  that a naked white person is in the neighborhood. Wear a bathing
  suit or a sarong, otherwise you will be stared at loooong and
  sloooow.

- Personal space, privacy, and other Western norms of individuality
  disappear in India. People will barge into your room without
  knocking. They might sit uncomfortably close and when convers-

ing, they can be close enough to you so that you can count their nose hairs.

- You may also find that total strangers in buses or trains will ask you very personal questions, e.g., "Your good name?" "You are from?" "Married?" "Children?" "Your monthly salary?" and even "How may times a week you are conducting sexual intercourse?" etc. Try not to scowl. They are just trying to be friendly and put you at ease.

- Be careful when you photograph people or temple deities. Ask permission first.

- If you realize you've made a mistake or offended someone, just smile, wag your head left-to-right in the Indian style (which means everything and nothing) and say loudly, "Sorry."

EVENTS & HOLIDAYS

The joke is that India has as many gods and goddesses as it has people— and that's only counting the Hindu pantheon! Once we factor in the Buddhists, Muslim, and Christian saints, secular public holidays, and other assorted deities of local villages and regions, well, at any given moment, someone somewhere in India is celebrating an "auspicious occasion," as newspapers like to note. The exact dates of festivals and holidays change every year because many of them follow the lunar calendar. Some of the festivals that are celebrated by most throughout the country are:

January-February (Maagh)

Pongal is a Tamil festival celebrating the end of harvest season. It falls on Maagh 1st, around mid-January. It lasts for four days and includes washing of cattle, processions and feeding *pongal*, a mixture of boiled rice, sugar, *daal*, and milk. In other parts of India, the festival is known as *Makar Sankranti*.

Vasant Panchami occurs on the 5th of Maagh and honors Saraswati, the Hindu goddess of learning. Women and children dress in traditional yellow. School children and even college students visit Saraswati's temples and touch the image of the goddess with pens, pencils, musical instru-

*C*HE NEXT STEP

ments, and other tools of further academic, intellectual, and financial advancement.

Republic Day on January 26th commemorates the next bold step in India's break with its colonial past when in 1950 it became a republic. There is a military parade in Delhi, naturally, and other related activities. Do not confuse this with Independence Day, which falls on August 15.

February–March (Phalguna)

Holi is similar to the water festivals of other Asian countries. It is the climax of spring and is also an exuberant celebration of exploding colors (literally). Anyone is a target of balloons filled with clear and colored water. Colored powders are thrown, smeared, and rubbed on people's faces and clothes. Wear your dirtiest and most expendable clothes, as sometimes the stain may never go away. A word of caution to women: on this day, because of its bacchanalian nature, all the prudish restraints are loosened and men try to take advantage of their close and intimate proximity to women. They can be quite aggressive and present a threat.

In these months, Tibetans mark their new year, *Losar.* Try to be in Dharamsala, the seat of Tibetan government-in-exile.

Shivaratri belongs to the Hindu god Shiva (Lord of Dance, Creator-Destroyer, hashish inhaler). Observe especially his human groupies, the ash-smeared, trident-wielding *sadhus,* who will crowed every Shiva shrine large and small.

March–April (Chaitra)

Mahavir, the founder of Jainism, was born during this time. His followers are the strictest adherants of non-violence. They try to make sure that not even that stray ant is crushed under their feet or a wayward bug enters their mouths or noses. Mahavir was a contemporary of Siddartha Gautam, the Buddha.

Ramanavami is the birthday of one of the most important Hindu gods,

Ram. He is the hero of the epic *Ramayana* which is commemorated as far away as Bali and Thailand.

Christians recall the resurrection of Jesus. Good Friday is full of festivities and good cheer.

April–May (Vaisakha)

Buddha Jayanti, the day when Buddhists throughout the land give thanks that their founder Siddartha Gautam was born, attained enlightenment, and gave up his earthly body on this day and attained nirvana. Monks as well as lay people take joy and pride in being who they are. The best spots are Sarnath near Benares, where Buddha gave his first sermon after attaining enlightenment in Bodh Gaya, the other place to be hanging out on this glorious day.

Meanwhile, on *Id-ul-Zuhara,* Muslims reach far back into history to remember a more somber occasion, Abraham's attempt to sacrifice his son because God told him to. Nowadays, usually a goat is sacrificed.

May–June (Jyaistha)

Muharram, another Muslim festival when the followers of the Shia sect honor the memory of their martyr Hussain, the grandson of Prophet Muhammad. Faithful followers parade carrying replicas of Hussain's tomb, called *tazia*. The cities of Lucknow and Hyderabad are especially famous for these processions.

June–July (Ashadha)

Rath Yatra or the Chariot Festival occurs in Puri (and other places, especially in southern India) where a grand temple chariot of Lord Jagannath (another name of the Hindu god Krishna) is wheeled around.

Raksha or *Raakhi Bandhan* is a day when the bond between brother and sister is recognized and strengthened. On the day of the full moon, sisters tie a colorful amulet on their brothers' wrist and brothers reciprocate with gifts.

THE NEXT STEP

July–August (Shravana)

Independence Day commemorates August 15, 1947 when the British finally "quit" India. It is the nation's most important secular holiday. Politicians give speeches, the flag is raised and saluted, and special events take place. But bureaucrats and children are happy to have one more day off.

August–September (Bhadra)

Ganesh Chaturthi is dedicated to the elephant-headed Hindu god Ganesh, son of Shiva. It is most lovingly celebrated in the state of Maharastra in the west. Clay images of the god are made. Firecrackers are exploded and at the end, the image is brought out of the home and ceremonially immersed in a pond, river, or sea.

September–October (Ashvina)

Dusshera is probably the most important Hindu festival. It symbolizes the victory of good over evil. During this ten-day festival (two-day public holiday), the goddess Durga is worshipped and thanked for getting rid of the demon Mahishasura. In West Bengal, this festival is known as Durga Puja. The life of the god Ram is recited and acted out by amateurs and professionals (called *Ram Lila).*

October 2nd is Mahatma Gandhi's birthday and is a solemn affair. Prayers and devotional songs are the norm. Visit Raj Ghat in Delhi where this courageous founding father of India was cremated after he was shot by a fanatical Hindu.

October–November (Kartika)

Diwali (or Dipavali) is probably the happiest Hindu festival. This five-day festival is especially delightful because at night oil lamps are lit, supposedly to guide the return of god Ram from his fourteen-year exile in the forest. Firecrackers are set off. This is also a time when the goddess of wealth, Lakshmi, is worshipped. On the other hand, it is also an occasion to gam-

ble openly. On the fifth day, brothers visit their sisters and exchange sweets and gifts.

The Jain new year coincides with the celebration of *Diwali*.

November–December (Aghan)

Two famous fairs are devoted to animals. The state of Bihar in eastern India hosts the month-long Sonepur Mela in Sonepur, the largest cattle fair in Asia, if not the world. Besides cattle, other animals are also bought and sold. The star attraction is the *Haathi Bazaar,* the elephant market.

In almost exactly the opposite direction, the desert of western India in Rajasthan, the Pushkar Camel Fair takes place. It's a wonderful opportunity to observe and mingle not just with camels (and cattle) but also the desert folks of the region as well as pilgrims, ex-rajas and maharajas, tourists, and members of the world media.

Guru Nanak Jayanti is the birthday of the founder of Sikh religion, Guru Nanak. The best place to observe and celebrate this occasion is in Amritsar, the most important city for Sikhs and the location of their most important shrine, the Golden Temple.

December–January (Pausa)

December 25, Christmas Day. There are between 22 and 23 million Christians in India. One of the first missionaries to arrive in India was none other than one of Christ's disciples, Thomas, in 52 A.D. Indian Christians, like Christians all over the world, celebrate the birth of Christ by attending services and mass at midnight. It is an official holiday in India.

IMPORTANT CONTACTS

New Delhi has most of the foreign embassies in the Chanakyapuri neighborhood. Several consulates are also located in Bombay (Mumbai), Calcutta, and Madras (Chennai).

THE NEXT STEP

FOREIGN EMBASSIES IN DELHI: ───────────

Australia	688 223
Canada	687 6500
China	600 328
France	611 8790
Germany	688 9144
Israel	301 3238
Italy	611 4355
Japan	687 6581
Nepal	332 8191
Thailand	605 679
UK	687 2161
USA	600 651

TOURIST OFFICES AND THEIR PHONE NUMBERS: ───────

India has a national (Indian government) tourist office, a state government tourist office, and an outfit called Indian Tourism Development
Corporation. The result, not surprisingly, is confusion rather than clarity.
The visitor will no doubt contact one if not all of these organizations,
and probably simultaneously, in order to get the best information if not
the best deal. The phone numbers below are for national tourist offices
in India:

Bombay
123 M Karve Road, Opposite. Churchgate, Bombay 400 020,
  Maharashtra
Tel: 2032932, 2033144, 2033145, 2036054

Calcutta
Embassy, 4 Shakespeare Sarani, Calcutta 700 071, West Bengal
Tel: 2421402, 2421475, 2425813; Telex: 021-8176; Fax: 2423521

Jaipur
State Hotel, Khasa Kothi, Jaipur 302 001, Rajasthan
Tel: 372200

Madras
154, Anna Salai, Madras-600 002, Tamil Nadu
Tel: 8269685, 869695; Telex: 041-7359; Fax: 91-44-8266893

New Delhi
88, Janpath, New Delhi-1 10001
Tel: 3320005, 3320008, 3320109, 3320266, 3320342

Varanasi
l5B, The Mall, Varanasi-221 002, Uttar Pradesh
Tel: 43744

In USA:
3550 Wilshire Boulevard #204, Los Angeles, CA 90010
Tel: 213.380.8855

1270 Avenue of the Americas #1808, New York, N.Y. 10020
Tel: 212.586.4981.

ACTIVITIES

*C*WENTY FUN THINGS TO DO

- You must try *paan* at least once. Usually taken after a meal, it works as a digestive as well as a mild narcotic. *Paan* is a leaf of the betel tree which has an assortment of spices and condiments wrapped inside it. *Paan-wallahs* will prepare it to your specifications. As a beginner, request *mitha paan*, the sweet kind. *Paan* snobs in India, like wine snobs elsewhere, will pay astronomical sums of money for the right *paan*. Do not swallow the liquid as you chew but spit it out—and add yet another ugly red splash on the sidewalk or railway station.

- Go see a Bombay film in a local theater, especially if it's hot and dusty outside. Most modern theaters are air-conditioned and the movies are at least three hours long. You can order snacks, tea, and in some theaters, even beer.

- Take an evening stroll on Chowpatty Beach in Bombay (Mumbai).

THE NEXT STEP

It's a carnival, circus, bazaar, street theater, and a Fellini movie set all rolled into one.

♦ If you have lost your wallet or your pocket has been picked and you are afraid you may starve to death, visit a Sikh temple (*gurud-wara*) in the evening. You will enjoy a most delicious hot meal for free.

♦ If you begin to feel claustrophobic because of the press of human-ity all around you and you fall into that Garbo mood ("I vant to be alone") visit a graveyard. Christian cemeteries in Calcutta, such as the South Park St. Cemetery, and the Jewish one in Cochin are two precious spots to cultivate your solitude.

♦ You've just trekked across a Himalayan range and still feel frisky? Why not ski down a slope! Auli in northern Uttar Pradesh is the top ski resort. You can also ski at Manali in Himachal Pradesh.

♦ If you prefer a less risky sport, go golfing. The Royal Calcutta Golf Club was opened in 1829. Nowadays there are so many golf clubs you can tour the country playing golf.

♦ When you get tired of all the running around, check in for a tradi-tional Ayurvedic massage with herbal oils. Since there are many masseurs of suspicious skills, get a recommendation from a trust-worthy source. After a massage, you must emerge feeling calm and ethereal, not pissed off because you feel you were mishandled.

♦ Losing sleep in bug-ridden beds? When in Kerala, visit a tribal area and go climb a tree—and live in a tree house with modern conveniences.

♦ If you don't want to feel isolated in your aerie and would prefer to be in the swim of things, take a "backwaters" tour of coastal Kerala. Navigating through an intricate network of rivers, canals, lakes and lagoons, you can travel quite far inland and observe the traditional, dynamic life along the waterways.

♦ If you want to feel extra-suave and sophisticated in the pulsing metropolis of Mumbai, stride into "licensed dance bars" like the Bombay film star that you are. Your dream girls will be swaying, sashaying, dancing to recorded disco music or popular Bombay film songs. Dress well and look good. Carry tons of money! And

you may still be denied entrance if the bouncers don't like your looks. Snacks and drinks are available at three times the price of a five-star hotel. And it's all clean fun. It's not a strip joint, and "Please do not touch."

- If you want more fantasy, take a tour of the studios of "Bollywood" in Mumbai.

- Tea is to Indians what wine is to the French. A beverage to be drunk at all hours and for all occasions, good or bad. You are in Darjeeling to view the famous Himalayas. Instead it is covered with clouds. Your whole day may go to waste. So why not take a tour of a tea garden? Afterwards, you may even give up on 'latte or a 'cap.'

- Ballooning and hang-gliding in India are becoming increasingly popular. World Ballooning Festival has been held in New Delhi.

- Go fort-to-fort camping in the Rajasthan, the land of Kings. Acquaint yourself with the 1000-year history and culture of the Rajputs, a proud warrior clan who fought with each other when not fighting the Moguls and later the British. As horses transport you from one hill-top fort to another, you also get a glimpse into the daily lives of local people.

- If you love antiques, or faultless reproductions, Chor Bazaar ("Thieves Market") in Bombay is worth checking out. Like any respectable American flea market, you can find almost anything here. But don't be disappointed if an appraiser later informs you that your "antique" sword was made perhaps only a few hours before you shopped.

- After you've visited a Hindu temple and a Buddhist *gompa*, visit a mosque. In some mosques, you may not be allowed during the times of prayers. And dress appropriately. Compare and contrast your visit with your visits to the other houses of religion. And how do you yourself feel about being inside a mosque? Do the worshippers all look like crazed fanatics or just normal, ordinary folks doing what people do in places of worship?

- If you are feeling lucky and on a roll (or down-and-out) challenge your luck at the horse races. Darjeeling's race course is the smallest course while Calcutta's is one of the largest and most popular.

THE NEXT STEP

- Another escape from heat and dust is to go diving in the islands of Lakshadweep and Andaman. Goa is a good mainland choice and has well-regarded diving schools.
- Well, you've "done" India and it's time to head home. Feeling a little bit uneasy what the future holds? Consult an astrologer, palmist, birth-chart reader. If you know the exact day, time, and date of your birth, you may be astounded by what some of these "futurologists" may predict for you. Go ahead, try it. You have nothing to lose, do you—except your future, perhaps?

NATIONAL PARKS/CONSERVATION AREAS/ HUNTING RESERVES:

India is renowned for its wildlife. Once a paradise for hunters, India today has over two dozen national parks and sanctuaries scattered throughout the country where fauna (and flora) are protected and have a chance to flourish rather than diminish. October to June is the best time to visit. Most parks are closed during the monsoon. Listed below are some parks and sanctuaries you will enjoy:

- Corbett National Park in Uttar Pradesh is the oldest (opened in 1935) and one of the most popular parks. Besides tigers, there are leopards and elephants as well. In 1973, "Project Tiger" was launched here to protect this species which was disappearing fast.
- Sasan Gir Lion Sanctuary, a forested oasis in the desert of Gujarat in western India, is famous as the final home of the rare Asiatic lion. No more than 250 survive. Crocodiles are to be found in Lake Kakaleshwar.
- Periyar Wildlife Sanctuary in Kerala in the southwest is well-known for its elephant population which can be seen while boating on a man-made lake. There are also tortoises, otters, wild dogs, boars, and black langurs (monkeys).
- If you're a birder, you must visit Vedantangal Bird Sanctuary in Tamil Nadu on the southeastern coast. Its marshland is an amazing breeding ground for egrets, herons, pelicans, storks and other Indian water birds. At the height of the breeding season, it is estimated that you can see over 20,000 birds at once.

- Kanha National Park in Madhya Pradesh in the interior of central India is renowned for its variety and abundance of wildlife. It is also a better spot to view the tiger. Other animals include varieties of deer, leopard, boar. The park is also noted for its birdlife.
- If you're in Calcutta, set aside time to visit the Sunderbans Wildlife Sanctuary where the elusive but deadly Royal Bengal tigers prowl among the mangrove swamps and impenetrable forests of the Ganges delta. Crocodiles and other reptiles creep and crawl about. You might also observe the "fishing cat" at the water's edge trying to grab its meal.
- Kaziranga National Park in Assam in the northeastern corner of India is the best place to view the one-horned rhino. Like the tiger, also present here, the rhino is on the brink of extinction because poachers want it for its horn which is prized for its Viagra-like qualities. Leopard, buffalo, elephant, and bear are some of the rhino's neighbors.
- If you prefer wild flora to fauna, head for the northeastern alpine valleys of Uttar Pradesh near Badrinath, a Hindu pilgrimage site at an elevation of 11,000 feet. This is one spot you want to arrive during the monsoon months of July and August, but you will quickly forget the rain, mud, heat, and humidity when you come upon this Valley of Flowers National Park and observe the wildflowers in bloom in "the garden on top of the world."

ADDITIONAL RESOURCES

GIVING BACK

If you want to work as a volunteer while in India, get in touch with the organization first. Despite your best intentions, you may simply get in the way if you arrive at the door without prior appointment. Several organizations have offices in countries such as the USA and you should contact them first before approaching the local offices in India. Local and international organizations also prefer someone who has specific skills, e.g. nursing or carpentry, in addition to genuine goodwill. Most Indian cities and large towns have local chapters of Lions and Rotary clubs which will happily help you in your desire to do the right thing. Meanwhile, some organizations we recommend are:

♦ *The Fund for the Tiger* is a nonprofit, tax-exempt organization dedicated to saving tigers in India and Nepal. Its funds go directly to people and groups (such as Wildlife Protection Society) working in anti-poaching efforts. *Contact: P.O. Box 2, Woodacre, CA 94973; tel: 415-488-0410; email: Jaibagh@aol.com.*

♦ *The Seva Foundation* welcomes inquiries from those who want to work in India. Through its association with Arvind Eye Hospital in Madurai, it not only provides eye care to the local people but also trains an international group in surgery as well as administration and management skills. Seva encourages you to drop by Arvind Eye Hospital when you are in Madurai and take a tour of its facilities. Nine out of ten visitors return to work as volunteers. USA *Contact: 1786 Fifth St, Berkeley, CA 94710; tel: 510-845-7410; fax: 510-845-7410; web site: http://www.seva.org; email: admin@seva.org. In Canada contact: Seva Service Society, 200-2678 West Broadway, Vancouver, B.C. Z6K 2 G3, Canada; tel: 604-733-3248; fax: 604-733-4292; email: sevacan@axionet.com.*

♦ *India Literacy Project (ILP)* is a U.S.-based non-profit organization dedicated to make India 100% literate. It raises its funds in the USA and supports Non-Governmental Organisations (NGOs) working for literacy in India. You can help by making tax exempt contributions and participate in its cultural events. *Contact: India Literacy Project, P.O. Box 361143, Milpitas, CA 95035; tel: 408-937-5383; email: venki@cadence.com.; website:wwwplateau.cs.berkeley.edu/people/radhika/ilp/ilp.html*

♦ *Save a Female through Education (SAFE)*—According to a UNICEF report, in India girl children receive less food, education, and healthcare than boys. Thus, the risk of dying between ages one and five is 43 percent higher for girls than boys. Fortunately, a dedicated group at Duke University and elsewhere are working with a non-profit

organization in India called Sri Ramakrishna Tapovanam, to help fund the education expenses of girl students. Funds will only be used towards education or related expenses. SAFE has assisted schools in getting new books and provided scholarships to deserving students. It welcomes a one-time contribution or a monthly commitment, no matter how small. *Contact in India: The President, Sri Ramakrishna Tapovanam, Tirupparaitturai, 639115, Tiruchirapalli District, India. USA contact: Surendar Chandra, Department of Computer Science, Duke University, Durham, NC 27708-0129; tel: 919-660-6556; email: surendar@cs. duke.edu*

- *Oxfam in India* works in emergency relief, development projects, and advocacy to focus on two broad aspects faced by poor communities: their basic rights and their sustainable livelihoods. Its goal is not just to increase productivity in agriculture and other local resources, but also to make sure that major decisions, such as the location of a major dam, are taken in consultation with communities so that their years of effort are not disrupted overnight. The emphasis, therefore, is not only on transferring financial resources to poor communities, but to empower them with the rights which will enable their advancement. *Contact: Oxfam India, Sushil Bhavan, 210 Shahpur Jat, New Delhi 110049; tel: 011-6491774, 6491775; fax: 011-6186646;email: oxfam@oxin.unv.ernet.in or oxindia@ giasdl01.vsnl.net.in Address in U.K.: 274, Banbury Road, Oxford OX2 7DZ, U.K.*

- *India Development and Relief Fund (IDRF)* is a tax-exempt organization started in 1987 by Dr. Vinod Prakash, a retired World Bank economist, to find solutions to the problems of poverty, illiteracy, malnutrition and natural disasters. It wants to create self help, rather than "welfare dependence." It accepts direct donations, contributions through United Way, stocks and bonds, and gift certificates can be used in lieu of cash for purchases in grocery stores such as Lucky and Safeway. Five percent of your bill will be donated. *Contact: IDRF, 4433 Othello Drive, Fremont, CA 94555 tel: (510) 797-5601 or IDRF, 5821 Mossrock Drive, North Bethesda, MD 20852-3238*

$\mathcal{T}$HE NEXT STEP

- *Madras Institute To Habilitate Retarded Afflicted (MITHRA),* a non-profit voluntary and charitable organization catering to the rehabilitation of the mentally retarded and physically handicapped children. It was established in 1973 by Sister Mary Theodore, an Australian nun, under the guidance of the Archbishop of Madras-Mylapore. Its multi-disciplinary team consists of an orthopaedic surgeon, psychiatrist, occupational therapist, physiotherapist, social worker, counselor, orthotist, special educators and vocational instructors. It has all diagnostic facilities at the center. There are 70 children in the residential unit and around 200 children attend the special school and therapy units. MITHRA would be very happy if various professionals in the field of rehabilitation could come voluntarily to share their knowledge and experiences. It will provide boarding & lodging. *Contact in India: Sr. Mary Theodore, O.A.M., MITHRA, D 171, R.V. Nagar, Anna Nagar, Madras, 600 102, South India. Australia address: Mrs. H. Mahanoy, 9 Soden Street, Greenslopes 4120, Queensland, Australia.*

For a comprehensive list of social service organizations in India, visit the web site: http://www.indiacharitynet.com.

$\mathcal{I}$NDIA ONLINE

The Internet has many different web sites on India. The recommended sites below are good starting points, but by no means comprehensive of what the World Wide Web has to offer. Use your favorite search engine to specify the kind of information you are looking for.

Discover India: http:www.indiagov.org/
Discover India Magazine: http://www.pugmarks.com/d-india/
India Travel Network: http://www.inetindia.com/travel/index.htm
India Travel Promotion Network:http://travel.indiamart.com/
Welcome to India: http://www.welcometoindia.com/
Destination India:http://www.destinationindia.com
Government of India Tourist
Organization:http://www.tourindia.com/
Indiacity:http://www.indiacity.com/

India Express:http://www.indiaexpress.com/
India Buzz:http://www.indiabuzz.com
Travel-India:http://www.travel-india.com/
India Insight:http://www.indiainsight.com/
India World:http://www.khoj.com

RECOMMENDED READING

We hope *Travelers' Tales India* has inspired you to read on. A good place to start is the books from which we've made selections, and we have listed them below. We've also included some of the better general guidebooks, because they're worth reading. The guidebooks have annotated bibliographies or sections on recommended books and maps.

Allen, Charles. *Plain Tales from the Raj.* London: Futura Publications, 1975.

Blank, Jonah. *Arrow of the Blue-Skinned God: Retracing the Ramayana through India.* New York: Houghton Mifflin Company, 1992.

Brata, Sasthi. *India: Labyrinths in the Lotus Land.* New York: William Morrow and Company, Inc., 1985.

Chaudhuri, Nirad C. *The Continent of Circe: An Essay on the Peoples of India.* New York: Oxford University Press, 1965.

Coll, Steve. *On the Grand Trunk Road: A Journey into South Asia.* New York: Random House, Inc., 1994.

Coomaraswamy, Ananda K. and The Sister Nivedita. *Myths of the Hindus & Buddhists.* New York: Dover Publications Inc., 1967.

Crossette, Barbara. *India: Facing the Twenty-First Century.* Indianapolis: Indiana University Press, 1993.

Dalrymple, William. *City of Djinns: A Year in Delhi.* London: HarperCollins Publishers Ltd., UK, 1993.

Darian, Steven. *A Ganges of the Mind: A Journey on the River of Dreams.* Delhi: Ratna Sagar P. Ltd., 1988.

Dew, Josie. *The Wind in My Wheels: Travel Tales from the Saddle.* London: Little, Brown & Company, UK, 1992.

THE NEXT STEP

Eck, Diana L. Banaras: *City of Light*. New York: Alfred A. Knopf, Inc., 1982.

Finlay, Hugh, Geoff Crowther, Bryn Thomas, Tony Wheeler. *India – a travel survival kit*. Hawthorne, Victoria, Australia: Lonely Planet Publications, 1993.

Frater, Alexander. *Chasing the Monsoon*. New York: Alfred A. Knopf, Inc., 1990.

Goodwin, Jason. *A Time for Tea: Travels Through China and India in Search of Tea*. New York: Alfred A. Knopf, Inc., 1990; *The Gunpowder Gardens*. London: Chatto & Windus, Ltd.

Greenwald, Jeff. *Shopping for Buddhas*. New York: HarperCollins Publishers, Inc. 1990.

Harris, Marvin. *The Sacred Cow and the Abominable Pig*. New York: Simon & Schuster, Inc., 1985.

Harvey, Andrew. *A Journey in Ladakh*. London: Jonathan Cape Ltd., 1983.

Harvey, Andrew. *Hidden Journey: A Spiritual Awakening*. New York: Henry Holt & Company, Inc., 1991.

Holt, Peter. *In Clive's Footsteps*. London: Hutchinson, Random Century Ltd., 1990.

Jaffrey, Madhur. *A Taste of India*. New York: Atheneum, 1985.

Kirchner, Bharti. *The Healthy Cuisine of India: Recipes from the Bengal Region*. Los Angeles: Lowell House, 1994.

Kolanad, Gitanjali. *Culture Shock! India*. Singapore: Times Editions Pte Ltd., 1994.

Kripalani, Krishna. *All Men Are Brothers: Autobiographical Reflections*. New York: Continuum Publishing Company, 1990.

Kusy, Frank. *Cadogan Guides: India*. London: Cadogan Books Ltd., Connecticut: The Globe Pequot Press, 1993.

Lewis, Norman. *A Goddess in the Stones: Travels in India*. New York: Henry Holt and Company, London: Jonathan Cape Ltd., 1991.

Mehta, Gita. *Karma Cola: Marketing the Mystic East*. New York: Simon & Schuster, Inc., 1979.

Mehta, Ved. *Rajiv Gandhi and Rama's Kingdom*. Connecticut: Yale University Press, 1995.

Moorhouse, Geoffrey. *OM: An Indian Pilgrimage*. London: Hodder and Stoughton, 1993.

Morris, Mary, and Larry O'Connor. *Maiden Voyages: Writings of Women Travelers*. New York: Vintage Departures, 1993.

Naipaul, Shiva. *An Unfinished Journey*. New York: Viking Penguin, 1986.

Naipaul, V. S. *An Area of Darkness*. New York: Macmillan Publishing Company, 1964.

Naipaul, V. S. *India: A Million Mutinies Now*. New York: Penguin Books USA, Inc., 1990.

Newby, Eric. *Slowly Down the Ganges*. London: Pan Books, Ltd., 1983.

Newby, Eric. *What the Traveller Saw*. New York: HarperCollins Publishers, Inc., 1990.

Norberg-Hodge, Helena. *Ancient Futures: Learning from Ladakh*. San Francisco: Sierra Club Books, 1991.

Nugent, Rory. *The Search for the Pink-Headed Duck: A Journey into the Himalayas and Down the Brahmaputra*. New York: Houghton Mifflin Company, 1991.

Palling, Bruce. *India: A Literary Companion*. London: John Murray Publishers, Ltd., 1992.

Patnaik, Naveen. *The Garden of Life: An Introduction to India's Healing Plants*. New York: Doubleday, 1993.

Rowell, Galen. *Galen Rowell's Vision: The Art of Adventure Photography*. Albany, California: Mountain Light Press, 1993.

Rushdie, Salman. *Imaginary Homelands: Essays & Criticism, 1981–1991*. London: Granta Books, New York: Viking Penguin Books, USA, 1992.

Satprem. *Sri Aurobindo or The Adventure of Consciousness*. Pondicherry, India: Institute for Evolutionary Research, Ltd., 1984.

Sen, Mala. *India's Bandit Queen: The True Story of Phoolan Devi*. London, San Francisco: Pandora, HarperCollins Publishers (UK) Ltd., 1993.

Shand, Mark. *Travels on My Elephant*. London: Jonathan Cape Ltd., Woodstock, New York: The Overlook Press, 1991.

Snyder, Gary. *Passage through India*. San Francisco: Grey Fox Press, 1972, 1983.

THE NEXT STEP

Tully, Mark. *The Defeat of a Congressman and Other Parables of Modern India*. New York: Alfred A. Knopf, Inc. *No Full Stops in India*. London: Penguin Books Ltd., 1991.

Ward, Geoffrey C., and Diane Ward. *Tiger-Wallahs: Encounters with the Men Who Tried to Save the Greatest of the Great Cats*. New York: HarperCollins Publishers, Inc., 1993.

Yapp, Peter. *The Travellers' Dictionary of Quotations: Who Said What, About Where?* London: Routledge & Keagan Paul plc., 1983.

Yeadon, David. *The Back of Beyond: Travels to the Wild Places of the Earth*. New York: HarperCollins Publishers, Inc., 1991.

Zepatos, Thalia. *A Journey of One's Own: Uncommon Advice for the Independent Woman Traveler*. Oregon: The Eighth Mountain Press, 1992.

"THE NEXT STEP" WAS COMPILED BY RAJENDRA S. KHADKA AND THE STAFF OF TRAVELERS' TALES.

Glossary

ayah	nanny
baksheesh	a tip, offering, or bribe
bidi	cheap Indian cigarette, made of rolled tobacco leaf and held togther with thread
burfi	sweet dessert or snack food, made from milk
chaat	hot, spicy snack food, usually served with afternoon tea
chador	Muslim women's veil, head covering
chai	tea
chapati	unleavened bread, disc-shaped
charpoy	rope-strung bed
dacoit	bandit
dahi	yogurt
dak	government guest house
dal/dhal	lentils, cooked in a variety of ways
dhaba	roadside restaurant or snack bar
dhoti	male garment; traditional loin wrap
dosa	crepe-like South Indian dish stuffed with vegetables
firang/farang	foreigner
ghat	flight of steps leading to a river; landing place
ghee	clarified butter
gunda	hired thug
howdah	seat carried by an elephant, usually canopied

jullay	greeting
lakh	one hundred thousand
lassi	creamy yoghurt drink
ludoo	sticky Indian treat
lungi	male garment; cloth that is wrapped around the hips, sarong-style, to form an ankle-length skirt
mahout	elephant trainer and keeper
masala	spicy
mela	festival, fair
muezzin	Muslim prayer leader
mullah	greeting, usually said with palms pressed together
naan/nan	type of bread
namaaz	Muslim prayers, traditionally offered five times per day
pakora	Indian savory fritter
papadums	wafers generally made out of split peas and seasoned
puja	Hindu prayers, or festival
purna	religious merit, earned after visiting a sacred Hindu place
raga	classical Indian musical piece
rimpoche/rinpoche	title given to spiritual masters, literally meaning "precious one"
rishi	Hindu holy person, ascetic
roti	unleavened bread
sadhu	Hindu holy man
samosa	curried puff pastry triangle
sanyasin	Hindu mendicant or ascetic
satyagraha	"truth force," nonviolence
stupa	Buddhist shrine

tika/tikka	caste mark worn by Hindu women on their forehead
vindaloo	spicy Goan meat dish, usually cooked in vinegar
wallah	word affixed to a noun to denote a doer, worker, agent (occupational connection)
zamindar	landlord/warlord

Index

Index of Contributors

Acknowledgements

Special thanks to Raj Khadka, who did the basic research for this book. Heartfelt thanks also to Wenda Brewster O'Reilly, Andrea, Noelle, and Mariele O'Reilly, Paula McCabe, Timothy, Christina and Arwen O'Reilly, Susan and Jeffrey Brady, Cindy Collins, Edie Freedman, Jennifer Niederst, Linda Sirola, Allen Noren, and Maureen and Kerry Kravitz. Thanks also to Katrina Morris, Joel Simon, Robbie Barnett, Pallava Bagla, Ullas Karanth, Paul O'Leary, Scott Doggett, Sean O'Reilly, David White, Deborah Perugi, Michelle McSweeney, Marcia Ciro, Trisha Schwartz, Jennifer Leo, George Hart and Robert Goldman at the University of California, Berkeley, Gautam Vajracharya at the University of Wisconsin, Madison, and to the families of those who must endure our company throughout the book process. Finally, a special thank you to all the story-tellers whose words are this book. May Ganesh and Vishnu protect you in your travels.

"Predator" by Pallava Bagla originally appeared in the March 1994 issue of *BBC Wildlife*. Reprinted by permission of the author. Copyright © 1994 by Pallava Bagla.

"The Calcutta Fowl Market" and "Down the Brahmaputra" by Rory Nugent excerpted from *The Search for the Pink-Headed Duck: A Journey into the Himalayas and Down the Brahmaputra* by Rory Nugent. Copyright © 1991 by Rory Nugent. Reprinted by permission of Houghton Mifflin Company. All rights reserved.

"Food for Body and Spirit" by Madhur Jaffrey excerpted from *A Taste of India* by Madhur Jaffrey (Atheneum, 1985). Reprinted by permission of Elaine Markson Literary Agency, Inc. and the author. Copyright © 1985 by Madhur Jaffrey.

"The Boxer from Calcutta" by Peter Aiken reprinted by permission of the author. Copyright © 1994 by Peter Aiken.

"A Wedding in Mahabaleshwar," "A Vision of Vijayanagar," and "Sick under the Bo Tree" by Jan Haag reprinted by permission of the author. Copyright © 1994 by Jan Haag.

"God and Chocolate" by Andrew Harvey excerpted from *Hidden Journey: A Spiritual Awakening* by Andrew Harvey. Copyright © 1991 by Andrew Harvey. Reprinted by permission of Henry Holt & Company, Inc.

"*Hobson-Jobson*" by Salman Rushdie reprinted from *Imaginary Homelands: Essays and Criticism 1981–1991* by Salman Rushdie (Granta Books, 1991). Reprinted by permission of Penguin Books Ltd. Copyright © 1985 by Salman Rushdie.

"My Delhi Home" by Cheryl Bentley reprinted by permission of the author. Copyright © 1994 by Cheryl Bentley.

"Merle Haggard and the Ambassador" by James O'Reilly and Larry Habegger reprinted by permission of the authors. Copyright © 1994 by James O'Reilly and Larry Habegger.

"The *Dharma* of Heli-Skiing" by Peter Shelton excerpted from the February 1993 issue of *Outside* magazine. Reprinted by permission from *Outside* magazine. Copyright © 1993, Mariah Publications Corporation.

"Greeting the Monsoon" by Alexander Frater excerpted from *Chasing the Monsoon* by Alexander Frater. Copyright © 1990 by Alexander Frater. Reprinted by permission of Alfred A. Knopf, Inc. and Penguin Books Ltd.

"The Other Raj" by William Dalrymple reprinted from the September 1993 issue of *Condé Nast Traveler.* Courtesy of *Condé Nast Traveler* and the author. Copyright © 1993 by William Hamilton-Dalrymple.

"Through Rajasthan by Rail" by G. Bruce Knecht reprinted from the July 1994 issue of *The Atlantic Monthly.* Reprinted by permission of the author. Copyright © 1994 by G. Bruce Knecht.

"Stairway to Heaven" by Madhur Jaffrey reprinted from the July 1989 issue of *Travel & Leisure.* Reprinted by permission of Elaine Markson Literary Agency, Inc. and the author. Copyright © 1989 by Madhur Jaffrey.

"Worshipping the Wicket" by John Ward Anderson reprinted by permission of *The Washington Post.* Copyright © 1994 by *The Washington Post.*

"The Boys' School" by Bridget McCoy reprinted by permission of the author. Copyright © 1994 by Bridget McCoy.

"The Die Is Caste" and "Shifting Gears on the Grand Trunk Road" by Steve Coll excerpted from *On the Grand Trunk Road: A Journey into South Asia* by Steve Coll. Copyright © 1994 by Steve Coll. Reprinted by permission of Times Books, a division of Random House, Inc. and Melanie Jackson Agency.

"The Suffering of Eve" by Jim Landers reprinted from the March 7, 1993 issue of *The Dallas Morning News.* Reprinted with permission of *The Dallas Morning News.* Copyright © 1993 by *The Dallas Morning News.*

Additional Credits (arranged alphabetically by title)

Selections from *All Men Are Brothers: Autobiographical Reflections* by M. Gandhi. Copyright © 1990 by Columbia University Press. Reprinted by permission of the publisher.

Selections from *An Area of Darkness* by V. S. Naipaul reprinted by permission of Aitken, Stone & Wylie. Copyright © 1964 by V. S. Naipaul.

Selection from *Ancient Futures: Learning from Ladakh* by Helena Norberg-Hodge reprinted by permission of Sierra Club Books. Copyright © 1991 by Helena Norberg-Hodge.

Selections from *Arrow of the Blue-Skinned God: Retracing the Ramayana through India* by Jonah Blank. Copyright © 1992 by Jonah Blank. Reprinted by permission of Houghton Mifflin Company. All rights reserved.

Selections from *The Back of Beyond: Travels to the Wild Places of the Earth* by David Yeadon. Copyright © 1991 by David Yeadon. Reprinted by permission of HarperCollins Publishers, Inc.

Selection from "A Back Seat to Nobody in Fight against Sexism" by Edward A. Gargan reprinted from *The New York Times.* Copyright © 1991 by The New York Times Company. Reprinted by permission.

Selection from *Banaras: City of Light* by Diana L. Eck reprinted by permission of Alfred A. Knopf, Inc. Copyright © 1982 by Diana L. Eck.

Selection from "Benares: Holy City" by Karen Eberhardt reprinted by permission of the author. Copyright © 1994 by Karen Eberhardt.

Selection from page 72 of *Cadogan Guides: India* by Frank Kusy, copyright © Frank Kusy 1987, 1989, 1993 by permission of Cadogan Books, London House, Parkgate Road, London, SW11 4NO and Globe Pequot Press.

Selection from "Chasing the Rainbow: A Western Sadhu in India" by Mark Antrobus reprinted by permission of the author. Copyright © 1994 by Mark Antrobus.

Selections from *City of Djinns: A Year in Delhi* by William Dalrymple. Copyright © 1993 by William Hamilton-Dalrymple. Used with permission of HarperCollins Publishers (UK) Ltd.

Selections from "The Confounding Allure of India" by Peter Jon Lindberg reprinted from the May 8, 1994 issue of *The New York Times.* Copyright © 1994 by The New York Times Company. Reprinted by permission.

About the Editors

James O'Reilly and Larry Habegger first worked together as late night disc jockeys at Dartmouth College in New Hampshire. They wrote mystery serials for the *San Francisco Examiner* in the early 1980s before turning to travel writing. Since 1983, their travel features and self-syndicated column, "World Travel Watch," have appeared in magazines and newspapers in the United States and other countries. James was born in Oxford, England, raised in San Francisco, and lives with his family in Leavenworth, Washington and France; Larry was born and raised in Minnesota and lives on Telegraph Hill in San Francisco.

TRAVELERS' TALES GUIDES

*W*OMEN'S TRAVEL

SAFETY AND SECURITY FOR WOMEN WHO TRAVEL
By Sheila Swan & Peter Laufer
ISBN 1-885211-29-5, 159 pages, $12.95

WOMEN IN THE WILD:
True Stories of Adventure and Connection
Edited by Lucy McCauley
ISBN 1-885211-21-X, 307 pages, $17.95

A MOTHER'S WORLD:
Journeys of the Heart
Edited by Marybeth Bond & Pamela Michael
234 pages, ISBN 1-885211-26-0, $14.95

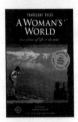

A WOMAN'S WORLD:
True Stories of Life on the Road
Edited by Marybeth Bond
ISBN 1-885211-06-6
475 pages, $17.95

Winner of the Lowell Thomas Award for Best Travel Book – Society of American Travel Writers

GUTSY WOMEN:
Travel Tips and Wisdom for the Road
By Marybeth Bond
ISBN 1-885211-15-5, 124 pages, $7.95

$\mathcal{W}$OMEN'S TRAVEL

GUTSY MAMAS:
Travel Tips and Wisdom for Mothers on the Road
By Marybeth Bond
ISBN 1-885211-20-1, 148 pages, $7.95

$\mathcal{B}$ODY & SOUL

———★ ★ ★———
Small Press Book Award Winner and Benjamin Franklin Award Finalist

THE ROAD WITHIN:
True Stories of Transformation and the Soul
Edited by Sean O'Reilly, James O'Reilly & Tim O'Reilly
ISBN 1-885211-19-8, 464 pages, $17.95

LOVE & ROMANCE:
True Stories of Passion on the Road
Edited by Judith Babcock Wylie
ISBN 1-885211-18-X, 318 pages, $17.95

———★ ★ ★———
Silver Medal Winner of the Lowell Thomas Award for Best Travel Book – Society of American Travel Writers

FOOD:
A Taste of the Road
Edited by Richard Sterling
Introduction by Margo True
ISBN 1-885211-09-0
444 pages, $17.95

THE FEARLESS DINER:
Travel Tips and Wisdom for Eating around the World
By Richard Sterling
ISBN 1-885211-22-8, 139 pages, $7.95

$\mathscr{C}$OUNTRY GUIDES

JAPAN
Edited by Donald W. George
& Amy Greimann Carlson
ISBN 1-885211-04-X, 436 pages, $17.95

ITALY
Edited by Anne Calcagno
Introduction by Jan Morris
ISBN 1-885211-16-3, 463 pages, $17.95

FRANCE
Edited by James O'Reilly, Larry Habegger
& Sean O'Reilly
ISBN 1-885211-02-3, 432 pages, $17.95

MEXICO
Edited by James O'Reilly & Larry Habegger
ISBN 1-885211-00-7, 426 pages, $17.95

COUNTRY GUIDES

THAILAND

*Edited by James O'Reilly
& Larry Habegger*
ISBN 1-885211-05-8
483 pages, $17.95

SPAIN

Edited by Lucy McCauley
ISBN 1-885211-07-4, *495 pages, $17.95*

NEPAL

Edited by Rajendra S. Khadka
ISBN 1-885211-14-7, *423 pages, $17.95*

BRAZIL

*Edited by Annette Haddad & Scott Doggett
Introduction by Alex Shoumatoff*
ISBN 1-885211-11-2
433 pages, $17.95

CITY GUIDES

HONG KONG
Edited by James O'Reilly, Larry Habegger & Sean O'Reilly
ISBN 1-885211-03-1, 438 pages, $17.95

PARIS
Edited by James O'Reilly, Larry Habegger & Sean O'Reilly
ISBN 1-885211-10-4, 424 pages, $17.95

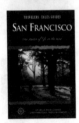

SAN FRANCISCO
Edited by James O'Reilly, Larry Habegger & Sean O'Reilly
ISBN 1-885211-08-2, 432 pages, $17.95

....

SUBMIT YOUR OWN TRAVEL TALE

Do you have a tale of your own that you would like to submit to Travelers' Tales? We highly recommend that you first read one or more of our books to get a feel for the kind of story we're looking for. For submission guidelines and a list of titles in the works, send a SASE to:

Travelers' Tales Submission Guidelines
P.O. Box 610160, Redwood City, CA 94061

or send email to *ttguidelines@online.oreilly.com*
or visit our Web site at **www.oreilly.com/ttales**

You can send your story to the address above or via email to ***ttsubmit@oreilly.com***. On the outside of the envelope, ***please indicate what country/topic your story is about***. If your story is selected for one of our titles, we will contact you about rights and payment.

We hope to hear from you. In the meantime, enjoy the stories!